WOMEN
CONFRONTING
RETIREMENT

WOMEN
CONFRONTING
RETIREMENT

A
Nontraditional
Guide

Edited by

Nan Bauer-Maglin
and Alice Radosh

Rutgers University Press
New Brunswick, New Jersey,
and London

Library of Congress Cataloging-in-Publication Data

Women confronting retirement : a nontraditional guide / edited by Nan Bauer-Maglin and
Alice Radosh.

   p.   cm.

  Includes bibliographical references.

  ISBN 0-8135-3125-X (cloth: alk. paper) — ISBN 0-8135-3126-8 (pbk. : alk. paper)

  1. Women — Retirement — United States.   2. Retirement — United States — Planning.
3. Baby boom generation — Retirement — United States.   4. Women in the professions —
United States. I. Maglin, Nan Bauer. II. Radosh, Alice, 1941–

HQ1063.2.U6 W658 2003
646.7′9′082 — dc21

                                       2002068046

British Cataloging-in-Publication information is available from the British Library.

Excerpts from "Poet on Residence" and "Old Lovers at the Ballet," copyright © 1980 by May
Sarton, from Collected Poems 1930–1993 by May Sarton. Copyright © 1993, 1984, 1980, 1974
by May Sarton. Used by permission of W. W. Norton & Company, Inc.
Excerpt from "Coming into Eighty," from Coming into Eighty by May Sarton. Copyright © 1994
by May Sarton. Used by permission of W. W. Norton & Company, Inc.

This collection copyright © 2003 by Nan Bauer-Maglin and Alice Radosh
Individual chapters copyright © 2003 in the names of their authors

Manufactured in the United States of America

Contents

Preface

We started talking about this book in August 2000, but its origins go back further than that. Maybe the first seeds were the vague feelings in our late fifties that we, like so many of our women friends, wanted to consider changing the balance in our lives by spending more time with family and friends and focusing more attention on our nonwork passions. If we were not ready to think in terms of nonwork, we wanted to rejuvenate our paid job lives, to think in new ways about the work we do or could do. Neither of us had the courage to say the word *retirement* out loud, and we are still not sure it is the right word. We were, however, both beginning to question the central role of work in our lives and were tentatively thinking about what it would mean to loosen the connections that had sustained us and defined us all of our adult lives. The process was all the more confusing because we have both enjoyed the work we have done and understand that it has provided us with an institutional base for our political/social commitment.

Separately, and at different speeds, we began to explore these ideas and to share them with others. One of our first conversations was with our women's study group, a group that has met monthly for over twenty years and which brings a feminist perspective, humor, and love to all the issues we have studied together. We thank them all for assisting us in the early phase of this book and encouraging us throughout the entire process: Dorothy Fennell, Merle Froschl, Betsey McGee, Susan O'Malley, Liz Phillips, Nancy Romer, Florence Tager, and Sandy Weinbaum.

Also separately and at different speeds, we have been making concrete changes in our lives. Alice is now officially retired and has moved from New York City to a small town in upstate New York with her husband, Bart Meyers, who has also recently retired. Any fear or hope of a "rocking-chair retirement" has been dispelled by a life that includes studying the piano, volunteering as a firefighter for the local fire department, serving as an active member of the social action committee of the local synagogue, writing poetry, and climbing mountains.

After twenty-seven years as an English professor at a community college, Nan gave up her tenure to become the academic director of a nontraditional student-centered baccalaureate program for the City University of New York. She loves the work, which is both all consuming and very empowering, but she is faced with the necessity of considering a different life after her contract with the university expires. This tension (loving her job and seeing an end to it) has led her to rehearse various and previously unimagined scenarios, including the Peace Corps, as well as retirement. Editing this book is one of her ways to think her way forward.

Moving from talking about our personal feelings about retirement to producing a book is a long and ragged process. Many friends and walking partners had to put up with us as we obsessed first about our own feelings about retirement and then about the progress of the book. We thank them for their wisdom and patience. Alice particularly wants to thank Jane Hirschmann-Levy, Naomi and Meyer Rothberg, Susan Carey, Carol Fox Prescott, Lolly McIver, and Jim Perlstein. And Nan particularly wants to thank Vicki Breitbart, Kathy Chamberlain, Pat Forman, Daphne Joslin, Linda McKay, Susanne Paul, Benay Rubenstein, and Naomi Woronov.

The "snowball" technique used in gathering essays for this collection relied on friends and acquaintances and friends and acquaintances of friends and acquaintances to spread the word about our search for authors. There is no way we can thank, or even know, all of the people who passed along our original request for contributors. Of course, not every contact led to an essay being submitted or accepted, but we would like to acknowledge some of the people who helped us get out the word. In addition to the women in our study group, we would like to thank: Wini Breines, Anne Wyatt Brown, Gina Duclayan, Linda Edwards, Susan Farkas, Liza Fiol-Matta, Marlene G. Fried, Bonnie Gitlin, Betsy Gitter, Carole Groneman, Yosette Jones-Johnson, Augusta Kappner, Joan Korenman, Avis Lang, Jane Levitt, Karen Page, Donna Perry, Ros Petchesky, Laura Radosh, Pam Trotman Reid, Barbara Rubin, Marcie Setlow, and Molly Shanley.

So many people have assisted us in big and small ways. We wish we could thank them all by name. Among them are Leslie Mitchner, associate director/ editor in chief of Rutgers University Press, and the entire staff there; Susannah Driver-Barstow, our copy editor; Ellen Geiger, our agent at Curtis Brown, and her assistant, Anna Abreu; Beth Kneller for editing assistance; Linda Kovener and Grace Williams for secretarial help; Daniel Radosh for research and computer assistance and for all-round support; Joan Mack, Anthony Marino, and Quintana B. Maglin for our photographs, and Joan for assistance in the presentation of the contributors' photographs; Carole Zimmer for thinking, talking, and writing with us; Christine Ann Price for sharing her manuscript; Toni Calasanti for her extended dialogue via E-mail; Meg Cox and Jenny Onyx for their articles; and Bart Meyers and Jon-Christian Suggs for editing assistance and unstinting intellectual and emotional comradeship.

The women in this book represent only about a third of the people who contacted us and expressed an interest in writing about their lives. Because we had to limit the size of the book, we were unable to include many interesting stories, but we would like to thank all of the women who approached us and who are part of the conversation about retirement occurring all over the country. And, of course, we thank the thirty-eight hardworking and good-humored women in this collection for their thoughtful and probing contributions, which we expect will invigorate this conversation.

Nan Bauer-Maglin and Alice Radosh

February 2002

WOMEN

CONFRONTING

RETIREMENT

Introduction

Nan Bauer-Maglin
and Alice Radosh

A New Conversation and New Definitions

When one thinks of retirement, what images come to mind? A gray-haired man in a polo shirt on the golf links? Early-bird specials and glitzy cruises? Or a woman in the Peace Corps? A woman raising race horses? A woman running a political campaign? A woman renovating houses for profit? When one reads how-to articles about retirement are they about social security, pension plans, and health benefits? Or are they about how to design the next chapter of a life that is committed, complex, and engaged?

Retirement is still pictured in very traditional terms in our society and, for many, it is a troubling, even frightening topic—one that conjures up disengagement from the world, being sent out to pasture, no longer seen as useful to society. In the thirty-two pieces in *Women Confronting Retirement*, the contributors examine, challenge, cringe at, and laugh at the traditional definitions of retirement. And they do what women of our generation have always done at times of major changes in their lives: they share their worries and their hopes.

For instance, Shirley Lim worries that traditional retirement resembles the domestic activities of a housewife. The prevalent images in Ellen Rose's head are those of old women in bridge clubs gardening, traveling, volunteering, and being grandmotherly. For Sylvia Henneberg, retirement looms as no-woman's land: dangerous and forbidding. Barbara Rubin at first tried to keep her retirement secret because of its negative connotations: "I don't want to wear the big black R, an all-consuming label . . . of rest and resignation."

In these stories, women who have challenged traditional models at every stage of their lives are now being challenged by their own negative stereotypes about retirement. For some, it is associated with death. For many, like Carol Burdick, it brings up a fear almost as powerful as the fear of death—a fear of ir-relevancy. Her anxieties are echoed by Phillipa Kafka, who writes, "It still meant to me the step prior to death, the loss of functioning in the world, the loss of service to the world, being out of it." These associations can give one pause as retirement age approaches for the largest group of men and women in history.[1]

There is a need for a new conversation about aging and retirement. In January 2001, Laura L. Carstensen, director of research on women and gender at Stanford University, wrote in the *New York Times:* "In only a decade or so, mil-lions of baby boomers are going to give America a greatly increased popula-tion over 65. . . . It's disturbing that the scope of our discussion about dealing with what's coming is truncated, as though we need only nibble around the edges—say, by deciding whether retirement should occur at sixty-five or sixty-seven or how prescription drugs should be provided. There is another conver-sation to be had: one concerning the optimal design of a new stage of life."[2]

Women Confronting Retirement is about that other conversation. It is a con-versation that can be heard by listening to the stories of the women in this book. They are women who made strong commitments to their careers and who are either starting to think about retirement, or are moving through the process, or have been retired for many years. We also hear from women who have decided that retirement is not for them. Their stories help us approach retirement thoughtfully, instead of the way Rubin describes entering it: "Nothing has prepared me for retirement: not the model of a father who vege-tated in it for thirty years and not a society that really does not appreciate those of us who are 'modernly mature.'"

The process of retirement does not separate neatly into orderly, indepen-dent components. Despite this, we have divided *Women Confronting Retire-ment* into three sections: Thinking about Retirement, Stages of Retirement, and Never Retire. This introduction, however, does not discuss the writers ex-clusively within the sections to which they were assigned. We have taken this liberty because many of the themes in these women's writings cut across all three sections. These are individual stories, but taken together they create a lively discussion, debate, and meditation on retirement.

The central theme of our book is that there is a population of women retiring now in the United States who have had a different relationship to paid work than women have had traditionally, and that this difference is reflected in their attitudes, feelings, and questions about retirement. Paid labor is not a new phenomenon for women. As Shirley Lim points out, women have always labored "in the fields, in kitchens, bedrooms, and other parts of the home" and later in offices. Prior to the women's movement, however, paid work rarely defined a woman's sense of who she was. Women were defined primarily as wives and mothers. If a woman worked for pay, it was generally out of financial necessity rather than a commitment to a career, or it was work that could be done in a way that would not interfere with her primary roles. But since the women's movement began, there has been a transformation both in the kinds of work open to women and in the meaning of work for women. "By 1980, 60 percent of women of working age had paid employment in most developed countries and large numbers of women have held professional positions for twenty years or more."[3]

Almost forty years ago Betty Friedan's *Feminine Mystique* played a major part in encouraging women to question their attitudes about work.[4] The book went from best-seller to cultural icon not simply because of its thesis, but because it spoke to women about a reality that described their own lives. Many of the women who read Friedan in the 1960s and 1970s radically changed their attitude toward their work. Their careers have defined who they are, both for themselves and for others. It is these women who are now retiring or thinking about retirement.

In 1977, the book *Working It Out: Twenty-three Women Writers, Artists, Scientists, and Scholars Talk about Their Lives and Work* by Sara Ruddick and Pamela Daniels explored the place of work in women's lives. The autobiographical accounts by these women described their desire to have their work "make a mark in the world by producing with dignity something of use to others."[5] Like Friedan's book, *Working It Out* spoke to women who were part of the emerging second wave of feminism. The women who wrote for that book are the same women, figuratively speaking, who are writing for our book. Although some of the women included here came of age before the second wave of the women's movement and some after, they are all women whose work was chosen, whose work defined them, and who are now choosing to define their retirement.

Before we even begin to look at their stories, we need to reexamine the definition of retirement. In *Women and Retirement: The Unexplored Transition*, Christine Ann Price indicates that social scientists use various definitions of retirement. These include "complete cessation from the labor force, depending on a pension or Social Security for income, reaching a certain chronological age, self-identification as a retiree, or working less than full-time." For her own study, rather than rely on age, income, or number of hours worked in a year, Price chose to define retirement as "termination of one's employment in a career or occupation in which one had engaged in for ten years of continuous service."[6]

The contributors to *Women Confronting Retirement* agree that the definition of retirement needs to be reexamined. Carole Ganim offers the classic definition: "Retirement for me implies separation of industry and money." Kafka wonders why the term is so scary and why it is not defined simply as a career change: "Had I been in my thirties, forties, fifties, I would not describe leaving teaching as retirement, but as a career change." Lim and Merle Rubine play with the word *retiring*, as in "retiring, little woman." Rubine archly declares: "One retires for the night, the Navy retires battleships, economists talk about retiring the debt. . . . I think we should retire the word *retire*." Although she is collecting her NBC News pension and getting social security, Rubine says the R word definitely does not apply to her; she is simply using these benefits to support herself as she "reinvents her life."

Some of the writers interrogate the word *retirement*. Lanie Melamed, for example, wonders if she is really retired since she is doing so much: "At seventy-three, once again, I ask myself, am I retired? Retired from what? There is delight in knowing that this period of one's life is the final gift of time to be used authentically and with good intent." Joy Dryfoos, who has decided not to retire, asks a similar question: "How can you retire from your beliefs? . . . You can't retire from caring about what happens to other people." Mary Stuart echoes this sentiment: "I am 'retired' from many jobs and careers, but it is difficult to retire from life." Lim agrees: "There can be no retirement from feminist consciousness and work." Juanita Baker writes that she intends to always work for social change: "So even if I retire, it would not really be retirement." At one time such a statement might have been mystifying. But many women retiring today immediately understand what Baker means. Obviously, the search for an acceptable definition is not going to be an easy one.

Just as it is difficult to pin down a definition of retirement, it is sometimes difficult to determine the moment retirement begins. Is Carol Burdick or Esther Ratner retired? Burdick left her position as a half-time professor, reveled in her retirement party, but then, after a brief break, returned to her university as an adjunct. Is she retired? Ratner left her librarian post at fifty-nine but is working more hours than ever at an editing job she created out of her home. Is she retired? The definition becomes blurry—how does working part-time differ from being partially retired? Is there even such a thing as partially retired or is that oxymoronic? While she calls herself retired, Carolyn Goodman at eighty-six is as active as she ever was with major social issues. Certainly retirement is not a static event, fixed in time with a gold watch to mark it. Rather retirement—if that is even the right word—is a multidirectional process that can take many years.

Why Just Women?

Why would a retirement book be devoted just to women since many of these questions are the same ones that men have always confronted when they have retired? In a way that is exactly the point. Unlike men, women have not "always confronted" these issues. Never before have such a significant number of women defined themselves by their work. As Nancy Dailey and Kelly O'Brien put it, "We are . . . the first to work outside the home most of our adult lives. . . . We have changed the landscape of our most important social institutions: the family, marriage, the labor force." Never has there been an extensive population of women who face retirement unsure of their worth without their job.

There is no reason to believe that men and women will go through this transitional period in the same way. The retirement of committed career women is a phenomenon that has not been studied extensively and, except in a small number of academic articles, is one that has not been analyzed from a feminist perspective.[7] It is a phenomenon fueled by the baby boomers who, because of the women's movement, were able to enter into professions that had previously been dominated by men. Women seized these new opportunities and, as they are reaching retirement age, they are discovering what professional men have known for a while: it may be as difficult to leave these jobs as it was to get them. When your identity is intertwined with your work, it is harder to slam the door behind you. For Georgie Gatch and the women in her retirement focus group, a business card can be a symbol of self-worth. The loss of that little card, they remind us, can have a major impact on your self-image.

The issue of self-worth raises another reason for a retirement book focused on women. Still today, older women, more than older men, face the heavy age discrimination that is part of our society. A responsible career provides visibility and respect. For many women, it provides some protection against society's attitudes toward gender and age.

Finally, women's retirement experiences are different because, whether or not they worked at nontraditional careers, women often face the traditional demands of gender roles upon retirement. Many of the women writing here foresee retirement as a time of caring for partners, parents, and grandchildren. Terry Davis watches her grandson Sammy several mornings a week until his school bus arrives; this time is "one of the highlights" of her week. In contrast, Diane Fowlkes, unexpectedly caring for her husband, struggles to come to terms with "how caregiving has restricted the freedom that I struggled to achieve."

Of course, while we have chosen to bring out women's voices in this volume, we understand that women are not alone in facing the conundrums of retirement. Joy Dryfoos declares that retiring is not a feminist problem, and she walks us through the issues her husband has faced regarding work. But the argument in this book is that this is a new moment in retirement, especially for women, and that women can redefine retirement for all of us.

Different Women, Different Retirements

The people who wrote for *Women Confronting Retirement* were never meant to be a representative sample of all women who are considering retirement. Rather, they are a self-selected sample who responded to a request for papers asking to hear from women "who have equated paid work with being taken seriously and with a commitment to issues beyond the personal." Researchers might refer to this method of forming a group as "purposive sampling," and, in fact, we had a specific purpose in mind when we worded the request. We wanted women to focus on the "changing meaning of work for women of our generation and, therefore, on the unique issues raised by retirement." The request was sent to personal contacts and placed on a number of E-mail lists established by professional women's organizations. In addition, we used a "snowball" technique of asking each person who responded to pass the request on to someone they knew who fit the profile described above. We received over one hundred responses from women all over the United States and Canada. The thirty-two pieces we chose for this book remind us that not all women are alike, and that the differences in work histories and retirement stories reflect not only different personal histories, but are also related to race and class and sexual orientation.[8]

In this book we hear mainly from women who have held professional or decision-making positions for twenty years or more. The significant number of women in this category is a new and important development in the United States, but, obviously, it is a small group from a global perspective. Shirley Lim reminds us that the majority of people on this planet "live on less than one U.S. dollar a day," and that "many U.S. women are part of a privileged group whose entitlement to choice over body and profession rests on the material and military superiority of the United States and its Western allies."

The issue of class difference that is imbedded in Terry Davis's observations about retirement comes from her years of trade union work. She points out that both work and retirement differ for white-collar and blue-collar workers: "Blue-collar retirees leave an alienating, exhausting, boring job. It's exhilarating to have free time and newly released energy upon escaping the physical demands of work. Where work is highly structured by others, leisure is simply freedom from that structure. It's being off the clock, getting the boss off your back. It's the opposite of work, not an extension of it." But, says Davis, that very freedom can "bring boredom and depression at suddenly having no purpose." The women in Sylvia Henneberg's family can attest to this. They all worked and they all retired as soon as they could. Henneberg's mother was an office assistant, her maternal grandmother cleaned floors, and her paternal grandmother operated a tuberculosis screening van. "None of these women had fulfilling careers, and . . . they all retired as soon as their financial situation allowed them to. My grandmothers . . . greeted their pensions with all the energy they could muster; my mother took pride in her pre-retirement or, rather, in her ability to benefit from unemployment benefits that seamlessly phased into pension." Henneberg goes on to say, though, "it did not take long for any of these women to feel a sense of exclusion and invalidation that was far from enjoyable."

Unquestionably, the choice to retire or not to retire is available to relatively few people. Unless someone has held a stable job with a good pension plan or has been able to accumulate significant savings, retirement is probably not going to be a comfortable option. Most, but not all, of the women writing here are economically comfortable, although a good many did not begin that way. Except for a few, they have remained at their jobs for many decades and most, but not all, have contributed to pension plans and savings accounts. Most, with careful budgeting, will have the choice to retire.

The contributors have held a variety of positions. These include grant writer/editor, acting teacher, financial consultant and researcher, labor organizer,

family therapist, director of sales and marketing, city government administrator, institutional researcher, psychologist, librarian, reporter, senior fashion
editor, elementary school teacher and paraprofessional trainer, dealer in
African crafts, doctor, writer, youth advocate, and television producer. While
most have worked consistently in the same profession or in closely related
fields, this is not true for all. Mary Stuart, for example, calls herself "a jobhop
at the Restaurant of Vocation" being everything from escrow officer to psychotherapist.

Many of the contributors worked (or still work) in higher education—
mainly as professors, although some were in administration. For example,
Georgie Gatch served as dean of student life at Barnard College, and Marilyn
Katz as dean of studies and student life at Sarah Lawrence College. Lanie
Melamed has been director for programs for women in the Continuing Education Department at McGill University and director of leisure studies at
Concordia University. Carol Burdick has held a variety of positions while at
Alfred University. She has worked in the development office, in public relations, as a secretary, and as a part-time writing and environmental literature
teacher. She made ends meet during these years of part-time teaching by renting apartments in the old Victorian home she had bought cheaply from her
parents and by editing faculty papers, among other odd jobs. Carol Scott has
spent the majority of her working life in academia also, going from a job as
dormitory counselor at Boston University to working as a dean first at a community college in Boston and then at a New York State community college. In
1999, she left academia to serve as the executive vice president of the Urban
League of Greater Cleveland, a nonprofit whose mission is to improve the
lives of people who live in economically and socially marginal neighborhoods.

The contributors to *Women Confronting Retirement* participated in or were
influenced by several of the key movements of the sixties and seventies—civil
rights, antiwar, women's, and lesbian and gay liberation struggles—and most
have maintained a concern and involvement with progressive, social justice
issues. For example, Dorothy Hammer describes herself in the 1950s as a
Superwoman-Mistress-Mom-Cook-Housekeeper-Bottle Washer. Then, when
she was forty-nine, the movements of the sixties and seventies "became a
whole new support system for me . . . to rev up [my] courage to become independent of conventional pressures."[9] Stuart, younger than Hammer and working as an escrow manager during those same years, described how hearing
Gloria Steinem "reinforced my own feminist underpinnings." She was inspired to go back to school and abandon escrow management, an abusive job
staffed mainly by women. In the mid-1960s, at the age of twenty-six, Terry

Davis was a stay-at-home mom with three children. By the end of the decade, she was swept up by "the winds of change" and had joined a women's consciousness raising group. The movement became the core of her life. She began working on an assembly line in Chicago and doing union organizing, her full-time commitment for the next thirty years. Susan Radner, like Davis, tells of union organizing at her workplace—the university. Carolyn Goodman has been an activist all her life. Neither losing her son in the civil rights movement nor her retirement has stopped her activism. Many of the women writing here found a way to integrate their social concerns into their work life so that work represented who they were in profound ways.

Donna DeMuth worked with abused children; Juanita Baker still does. Doris Goldberg served as the medical director of a network of New York City health stations that offered free preventive health care to preschool children. For some of the women who worked in academia, women's studies was the vehicle for a progressive politics. For example, Diane Fowlkes describes how she worked to found the Women's Studies Institute at Georgia State University, which established the Georgia Women's Movement Project that houses the personal and organizational papers of women activists and women's groups. Although the end of work need not herald the end of commitment, many women in this volume find that achieving a balance between self and commitment in retirement is an insistent issue. For example, Shirley Lim is pulled between the desire for luxurious retirement and the consciousness of social justice still unachieved. Terry Davis is happy not to be going to meetings yet she cautiously and a bit reluctantly notices "the activist within me . . . stirring."

Some women are reluctant to give up their institutional base because it provides a sense of satisfaction and social responsibility. Some, like Juanita Baker, state that their institutional base has served as a springboard for their social commitments and they don't want to give that up. "My activism," states Baker, "is stronger when I have the power base of employment." From the psychology department, she reaches out to the community by running a program for sexually abused children. She helps the children and trains students at the same time.

The women in this book range in age from thirty-three to eighty-six and come from a variety of racial, ethnic, religious, and regional backgrounds. While most are European American, there are Lebanese American, Asian American, African American, and Native American women represented. Some state that their present or past religious and cultural orientation will have an important impact on their retirement years. For Juanita Baker, the

Christian work ethic and the focus on love in the teachings of the Presbyterian Church have influenced her choice of work and will influence when and how she chooses to retire. Carol Prescott looks forward to deepening her Jewish spiritual training. Carole Ganim brings her experiences as a former nun to her thoughts about retiring. Laura Weaver's Mennonite background has a strong, and perhaps unexpected, influence on her retirement life, and Terri Baker draws heavily on her tribal beliefs.

These retirement stories are deeply influenced by whether the writer is living alone, with a partner, with her extended family nearby, or in a close community of friends. Here again the book presents a diverse sample. Some of the women have partners of either the same or the opposite sex. Some had partners, but death and divorce took their toll. Some of the women have been single all or most of their adult life. Some of the women have children and grandchildren, but their involvement with family varies greatly. We are reminded by Jennifer Christensen and Holly Crenshaw's piece that we live in a society that restricts the definition of family, a fact that has implications for retirement as it does for every other phase of life. Christensen and Crenshaw explore these implications and document the effect discriminatory practices have on lesbians who are retired: "The challenges heterosexual women face in their retirement years—diminished income, medical concerns, social isolation, and ageism—are the same ones older lesbians confront. But lesbians are also hit with financial, personal, and social barriers in retirement that their heterosexual peers don't have."

The diversity of the writers is also reflected in the various places they live in the United States and Canada and whether or not they will remain there during retirement. Some of the women, like Carolyn Goodman who has strong ties to her New York City neighborhood, plan to stay put. Others have moved great geographical distances upon retirement. And, for some, the great distance is not geographical but rather represented by a significant change in type of environment. Doris Goldberg, for example, left the "bustling and anonymous Big Apple" for the small arts-and-crafts community of Woodstock, New York. Merle Rubine moved from Milwaukee to New York City and then to a small village in Côte d'Ivoire when she joined the Peace Corps. Ellen Rose and Donna DeMuth look forward to returning to beloved settings that their jobs took them away from. Rose will move back to Philadelphia and DeMuth returned to "my pine forest in Florida."

The ease with which the women are able to move from work to retirement varies, and certain careers appear to allow for a relatively smoother transition.

For example, a teacher is probably used to working ten months each year, having more control of her time during the work week, and, at the university level, perhaps even having the option of part-time work after retirement. So for a teacher the change from job to no job may not be as pronounced, although the personal issues can be the same, no matter what profession one retires from. Then again, some professions, like writing, may never demand retirement since they are not necessarily linked to an institutional base, do not require traveling to an office, and can continue for as long as the creative juices flow. In fact, many of the women in this book contemplate using their retirement to write in their field of expertise or to write the short stories, poetry, or novel that they always wanted to.

Looking to Family and Elsewhere for Retirement Models

Positive role models are the exception rather than the rule in these pieces. Some women prepared for their retirement by grappling with examples of their mothers' and fathers' work histories and with the attitudes toward work in their families. For instance, Laura Weaver, whose mother did domestic work until she retired at age sixty-seven, was raised with a strong Mennonite work ethic. Weaver worked from the age of twelve cleaning other people's homes, then waitressing when she attended college, and finally teaching high school and college. Mary Stuart says, "retirement for my parents meant that after thirty or more years in one job you got the gold watch and then lived on your pension and social security." That is not actually what happened to them: her father died at fifty-five and her mother was left in difficult economic circumstances. Elayne Archer's mother worked as a secretary, an office manager, and a script editor, retiring when she was sixty-five on several small pensions. Archer feels she has been fortunate "to work at jobs that were much more rewarding than those my mother worked at for much of her work life" and to "have had some choice about whether to work." Seeing herself working for at least forty years in total until she retires, Archer expects to be busy in retirement like her mother, but not do what her mother did: "buy and sell old houses." Archer suggests that her mother was restless and dissatisfied in retirement.

Race and class joined to make retirement a non-option for Carol Scott's mother, an African American woman who nurtured—in every sense of the word—nine children: "As for millions of women, since she worked in the home, no pension would have been forthcoming. . . . I always think of her as having worked numerous jobs and being paid for none." Scott's father, a coal miner, was forced to "retire" due to failing health from silicosis. Scott learned a lot from her mother about hard work and loving one's children. Her mother's difficult life also taught her some lessons about education, work, self-sufficiency, and, ultimately, retirement.

Barbara Waxman plans to "rehearse my retirement" by looking to older women outside of her family who have managed a creative and nontraditional retirement. Mary Stuart also looks to older women; her model, who has no interest at all in retiring, is an eighty-one-year-old female friend who has become an accomplished artist in later life and is launching a travel business. The book's youngest contributor, Sylvia Henneberg, who does not intend to retire until 2032, is beginning early to search for a counterstory to the dominant one narrated for older women. She, along with several others, finds May Sarton's life (1912–1995) and writing to be such a story: "Aging, for Sarton, did not seem like an exercise in subtraction, but, on the contrary, an experience of enrichment and growth, an opportunity to strengthen her commitment to all that she valued." Sarton never stopped finding intensity by writing, gardening, and engaging in friendships with people of all ages. Henneberg says that reading Sarton's poems and novels gives "me hope that I, too, can define my own peaks in life, that they will recur periodically, and that they need not coincide with what society would acknowledge as my career peak."

Who Am I If I Retire?

A natural confusion occurs about the use of past or present tense when writing about retirement. It comes up in this introduction and in the stories that follow because not all the authors are retired and because we question whether a woman is past tense once she is no longer working. This grammatical dilemma encapsulates the concerns that retirement raises for many of the women writing. How do you create a present tense for yourself that can be recognized and valued by both yourself and others? At a party, Barbara Rubin was introduced to another guest "in the past (im)perfect, as a 'usetabe,' as in 'She used to be, or had been, a chair of women's studies.' And I found myself reinventing myself on the spot so as not to be brushed aside as yesterday's news."

Many of the women address this loss of identity, of being a "usetabe," by describing situations that echo each other: for Rubin and for Dorothy Hammer, it is the proverbial cocktail party where identity is a question mark. It is an image that comes up often: Who will I be without my tags? How do I introduce myself? This is not a superficial question but rather one of profound importance to those who have invested a lifetime in committed, responsible work. For Diane Horwitz, there is dread: "'Retired.' A public declaration! Of aging, a loss of status and identity. . . . What will replace work? How can I fashion a life in retirement that embraces my long-held values?" Shirley Lim asks, "What are some of the contradictions inherent in the narratives of lives dominated by the ambition to emerge from the condition of 'retiring women' but now facing the condition of 'retiring' from the domain of ambition?" Without my work, who am I? And the question is not just one that is difficult in public encounters, but in fact gnaws at women privately. Carole Ganim's long list of fears expresses anxieties felt by many in this book. Here are a few of her concerns:

"I am afraid that I will slide into indolence and purposelessness.
I am afraid that I will no longer want to give to and work with the marginalized.
I am afraid that I will sit down to write and have nothing to say.
I am afraid that the long emptiness ahead of me will tempt me to become a full-time consumer and home beautifier.
I am afraid that anxiety will overtake me because I will worry about not being busy all the time in a structured way and I will fill my time with useless pursuits.
I am worried that I will overdo, that I will become the eternal volunteer or that I will be teaching everywhere every day to prove my worth.
I am afraid that I have no real identity other than the one I have lived with for so long.
I am afraid that I will always feel guilty about something.
I am afraid of becoming too well acquainted with hospitals and funeral homes.
I am afraid that I will never get over feeling rushed and pressured.
I am afraid that I will be making lists on my deathbed."

Terry Davis succinctly captures the "who am I" fears and freedoms in one image: In her first year of retirement, she expresses her feeling of liberation by no longer carrying a pocketbook (read briefcase for some), "but I experience a vague confusion in the blank space the purse has left." In contrast, fear of freedom does not seem to dog Elayne Archer as she approaches retirement. Neither was it among Weaver's repertoire of emotions during her first year of retirement. Perhaps because of their history of work as young girls, moving beyond paid work is not problematic; for them the idea of not having to work is clearly freeing.

Many of the authors use the word *freedom* in their descriptions of retirement. It is a freedom that is sometimes gleefully embraced and sometimes gazed upon with a sense of foreboding. Diane Horwitz writes of a "terrible freedom." For Carole Ganim it is the freedom to make choices and not be bound by some of the constraints of the past. She carefully looks at self, family, community, religion, and profession to create/re-create herself in retirement. Many write about allowing oneself the pleasure of free time. Barbara Rubin writes, "Retirement . . . was a chance to shift from work to the self, from responsibility to freedom, from a set structure to a fluid one. I could turn my attention to the neglected areas of my life where repair and reclamation were still possible." Shirley Lim further spells out "the luxury of rare freedoms available to very few: freedom from want while free from scheduled work, and freedom, empowered by skills, knowledge, and experience, to continue achieving professionally" while retired. In a chapter entitled "Free at Last: Surviving and Thriving in Retirement" in *From Stumbling Blocks to Stepping Stones: The Life Experiences of Fifty Professional African American Women*, Kathleen F. Slevin and C. Ray Wingrove studied retirement attitudes and experience. All but two of the fifty women interviewed expressed satisfaction with their lives in retirement. They view their retirement as "freedom" in a very particular sense that has to do with racism; this freedom allows them to give back to the community.[10]

The Debate: To Retire or Not?

The first section of this book, "Thinking about Retirement," addresses the debate that women go through as they anticipate giving up their work. The section's title is really too tame. It could just have accurately been "Avoiding Thinking about Retirement" or even "Dancing around Retirement." These contributors describe a complex process of investigating retirement, taking steps toward it, and then stepping back. For some the dance of seeking, hiding, and finally confronting retirement can take years. Donna DeMuth's journal of the year before her retirement is a good example of the process. She tried to "unlearn seventy-two years of rushing toward a goal, toward achieving a reward."

Terri Baker calls herself "a kind of Hamletette": "To retire or not to retire. . . . I ponder that question at least once a day." These women are testing the waters. They look for models among family members or literary figures, and speculate about time for pleasure and for new offerings they might give to themselves and to the world. Some are trying to figure out how they will manage on their postretirement budgets, or how and where they will live. They also explore their fears and hesitations and try to come to terms with loss, illness, and death. And a surprising number of women make lists as they start to think about retirement.

Terri Baker's list of responsibilities expands outward from herself to her family, her tribe, her ancestors, Oklahoma, the United States, the world. She sees retirement as a time to strengthen those commitments. Specifically, she wants to speak and write about disability and to do cultural retrieval and maintenance work for the Choctaw Nation. She plans to continue working to create home-based economic structures that support the work of rural and Indian women. As she says, her retirement plan "requires me to keep on working for the good." Carole Ganim lists all the possible contributions she could make: tutoring children, working in a domestic-violence shelter, editing, ushering for concerts and plays, volunteering in museums or libraries, working at a thrift store, teaching English, or doing freelance writing.

A lot of the thinking about retirement seems to be focused more on the future than on what will be missed at work. As Ellen Rose reflects, "My anxieties on the eve of retirement have less to do with what I will be giving up than with what lies ahead." Barbara Waxman is hoping for the intensity of "deep play" as she looks ahead. She has known the intoxication of intensity from her teaching and writing and wants to find it in the daily life of retirement: "I want to be an explorer daily and to follow the bent of my curiosity. . . . Yes to learning to play the flute or returning to the piano. Yes to filling my yard with more day lilies and roses." She also wants to reach out beyond herself by perhaps housing an international student or tutoring newcomers to her community or volunteering at the local Literacy Council. And she plans to fill her grandchildren's ears with family history. The lists go on, unwinding in each story. Elayne Archer thinks she will be "somewhat self-involved" as work and children slip into the background: "I think I will pay some attention to things spiritual and perhaps less to things political. . . . I may join a High Anglican church—especially if it is involved in the community." In addition, Archer says, "I think I will need to do something 'useful'" like volunteering in a youth program. Archer debates doing something radically different than the usual, such as joining the Peace Corps, moving to Europe, or taking up flying, but expects that she will tend her garden literally and spiritually at home instead.

Moving beyond Rituals

The women writing in section two, "Stages of Retirement," are presented chronologically based on how long they have been retired. The first stories are from recently retired women whose offices still sit in just-packed boxes. The middle group is past the initial elation and/or emptiness stage and is searching—sometimes frantically—for the right retirement life for them. The women in the final group in this section describe the lives they have built in retirement. There are similarities and differences among the stories no matter what the stage of retirement, and together they provide us with a map, or perhaps a quilt, of a transition that has many stages.

Most transitions begin with formal or informal rituals. Several people mention their retirement parties, describing them as good and necessary. Others mention unexpected events that provided more closure than a traditional party. Diane Horwitz, for example, movingly describes the twentieth reunion of students in a community college program she founded, at which she received a plaque that says "Your Life's Work Enriched Our Lives." The gathering affirmed the political pedagogy that she had always practiced. In addition, Horwitz invented her own "leaving rituals." She gave a "good-bye-and-thank-you party" to honor the work of all the staff people who had helped her at her community college. Susan Radner's husband helped her mark her retirement in a way that would allow her to continue enriching students' lives after she left her job. He endowed a full-tuition scholarship in her name at her university, something Radner had wanted to do. The first award was given in 2001 to a young Caribbean woman.

Each person talks about who and what she needs to say good-bye to and make peace with. Phillipa Kafka had to make peace with herself and the loss of the class position that she gave up when she left her profession. Donna DeMuth said good-bye to her therapy clients and hello again to the beautiful lake she loves. Several visited their workplaces later and felt welcome or unwelcome or just out of place. And several returned to work at their former workplaces in a part-time or temporary capacity and wondered if this is a smart transition strategy or a clinging to the known.

When to Retire?

The timing of retirement and the reasons for retirement differ. Sometimes the decision is influenced by internal and external signals that it might be necessary to retire. After a year of caring for her mother up until her death, Ida

Henderson felt "physically, mentally, psychologically, and spiritually exhausted." After rumination and spiritual stocktaking, after hearing out the advice of friends, she retired after thirty-one years at the New York City Board of Education. Juanita Baker would retire "this minute if I were incapable, out of date, not able to handle the stress, bored, tired, [or] . . . if I were needed to attend to my devoted spouse or children or grandchildren." She would like to reignite those creative urges left behind when she chose a work path that demanded all her energies. Yet, she tells us that she is not ready to leave the work path. In fact, she says, "I toy with the idea of rejecting retirement altogether." Her thoughts keep her spinning in the one-step-forward, one-step-back retirement dance which can last for months or years.

Most of the women in this book initiated the transition and planned for it in considerable detail. For some, thoughts of retirement arose slowly as work became less and less satisfying. For others, retirement came abruptly because of health problems or other needs of a partner or themselves.

Physical appearance rarely comes up as a major issue for anyone—although looking in the mirror has its surprises. Illness and mortality, however, are a concern and are looked at straight on in this collection. The women talk forthrightly about their health, their bodies, and dying. Breast cancer and a general concern about aging are mentioned most frequently. Terri Baker, who has multiple sclerosis, may retire early rather than "grinding" away at her job, in recognition of her responsibility to her health and the welfare of her family. Diane Fowlkes left her job because of her husband's illness as well as her own breast cancer, but she was more than ready to leave. Susan Radner and Lanie Melamed also were propelled toward retirement by the diagnosis and treatment of breast cancer. In Melamed's case, the stress was increased by the fact that her husband was also ill. "Something had to go," she says. "Since eliminating the two illnesses was impossible, I chose to leave the hallowed halls." Dorothy Hammer retired in part because she wanted to be with her husband during his last days.

Joy Dryfoos, who never wants to retire, was recently struck by a serious back problem. Worse than the pain was that she could not sit at the computer and "grind out my words." Donna DeMuth has a poignant conversation with herself about her body, which is "fading away. . . . The spots on my arms, the fatigue and ache in my legs after I weed . . . So long to Donna the invincible, the ever-youthful woman of a certain age . . . welcome to Donna who just begins to know that she is deteriorating, is dying." DeMuth and her husband come together to talk with her children and their partners about "our dying." They talk of wills, of power of attorney, of the distribution of belongings, of funerals. DeMuth, age seventy-four, wonders how she will swim in the lake she loves when she is unable to climb off or onto the dock. One of her daughters has a solution: "She volunteers to drive me down to the boat ramp, put me into a wheelchair, push me into the water, and pull me out again after my swim."

While not being Pollyannaish, the effort here is to embrace the inevitable changes that come with aging.[11] Carol Prescott looks forward to "the role of the wise old crone, serv[ing] tea and listen[ing] to the struggles of those who are still in the fray." While older women are listening and dispensing wisdom, they are also acting. Melamed, active with the Raging Grannies in Canada, recognizes the "enormous power" of older women. She appreciates that they "are more able to step outside the mainstream, to be outrageous and to commit everyday acts of rebellion. More acutely aware of their strengths and shortcomings, they tend to be less worried about status, fashion, or being obediently submissive." Sylvia Henneberg tells us that May Sarton saw aging as a time of growth and referred to herself as an "old raccoon." In *At Seventy* Sarton declares that she loves being old and that "I am happier, more balanced, and . . . better able to use my powers."[12]

It is not just aging or physical health that can trigger thoughts about retirement. Meeting several times, Georgie Gatch and three other women talked together about retirement. They describe the weariness and intellectual fatigue that came from the dissatisfaction that they experienced prior to retiring. Similarly, Merle Rubine decided to leave her job because "My battery was dead, and I didn't have a jumper cable." Rubine found herself responding to her job dissatisfaction by becoming an "old scold"—not a role she admired. Physical ailments, intellectual fatigue, unwanted personality changes—even strong women who are accustomed to being in control of their work lives do not always have control of the exit scenarios.

But what if you are not given a clear physical or mental signal that it is time to leave? Since there is no longer a mandatory retirement age, how does one know when to go? Shirley Lim takes what for her is an ethical, feminist stance. She believes that somewhere between the ages of sixty and sixty-five one should give way to a new generation of scholars and teachers. Juanita Baker disagrees; she feels she still has a great deal to give and that someone younger does not necessarily have the right to her job. Carol Prescott, after a lot of hard work to establish her career as an acting teacher, now loves her work. She seriously contemplated retirement and listed all the creative things she would do. Despite her list, she realized that "[i]nstead of retiring I seem to be gathering more and more work and touching more and more lives. I love it." It is not always easy to figure out the right time to leave—or whether.

The First Year or So

The early stages of retirement are vividly described. Diane Horwitz experienced a high and then reeled downward; Carole Ganim describes traversing what she calls the necessary desert. Esther Ratner documents the initial anger and breakdown that accompanied a retirement that she neither initiated nor desired. Phillipa Kafka details the anxiety, fears, and loss she experienced. For others there seemed to be little or no trauma. Laura Weaver embraces her free time and the new creative outlets she has developed. Doris Goldberg uses the image of tight clothes to explain her response to her retirement. It "felt freeing," she writes, "like taking off a suit of clothing that constrained, chafed, no longer fit right." Every woman who has ever pulled off a girdle or stepped out of tight pumps knows what Goldberg means when she writes that retirement feels similar to "putting on a looser garment that allows freer movement and lets some of my feelings show—a much better fit for me in my sixties."

Each person writing here about recent retirement has a different rhythm and different solutions and advice for herself and us: Go slow, don't return to previous work/do return; stay in the same place/move; don't work without pay/volunteer; spend more time with your grandchildren/resist becoming a nanny to them. Ida Henderson's "advice to anyone thinking about retirement is to listen to others and then sit with your own inner voice and wait for guidance. You will know when it's your time to retire. To those already retired, I say, 'It's a big world, follow your passion and seize every moment. Come on in, the water's fine. Can't swim? Don't worry; there's always someone willing to coach you.'" Ratner developed an advice list based on her own difficult first years in retirement: "Take chances, have confidence in yourself, and above all, present an agreeable face to the world. . . . Don't be afraid of learning something new. If you have something to offer, a special skill or talent, or enjoy something, tell people about it. Go places where people who may need your services congregate. . . . If it doesn't work out, move on to something else. Appreciate good and generous people. . . . Try to behave in kind." There is no single generalization as each woman carefully narrates her story.

The initial stage of retirement is often exhilarating, if a bit frenetic, for some women. For others, the early phase is a time of reflection, a time to question jumping into things too quickly. A number of people write about wanting to take time to think about both life and death, to enjoy oneself but to face one's mortality. Ganim writes, "Retirement is an acknowledgment that we are in the stages before the end. This is fearsome. . . . The imminent certainty of death does cast a shadow over one. . . . Laughing about our respective frailties and illnesses has become a popular sport with many of my friends. We find ourselves giggling as uncontrollably as we did as adolescents when we talk about sickness and death. . . . I know, upon reflection, that the immanence of death colors the choices and activities of later life, just as surely as does arthritis. What I want to do is to not let it take over. I want to benefit from the shadow by appreciating light and color and beauty and sound and love more. I want my physical senses and my spiritual appetites to be whetted by the approach of death."

Barbara Waxman, who has not yet retired, suspects that retirement will grant "me permission to meditate in the present" and undertake a "life review . . . [that] may give me permission to see the humor of existence, to feel playful, not ponderous and pontifical, as I try to figure out what I've been doing on earth, lo these many years." That is just what many of these writers do pre- and postretirement. Merle Rubine first made an inventory of what she had to offer (a sense of humor and a long career as a producer in radio and television); then she thought about what she did not have (computer skills and connections to the old boys' network); she considered what she was worried about (being old and poor); and she reviewed what she loved to do (ballet and poking around in antiques stores). Following this inventory, she came up with four jobs connected to her favorite activities. Adding up the pluses and the minuses of each, she decided to join the Peace Corps.

What Is Lost and What Is Found

Georgie Gatch, Marilyn Katz, Elizabeth Saunders, and Phyllis Schwartz grouped all the losses they collectively experienced in retirement: income, identity, structure, challenge, appreciation, and community. They "speculate that the loss of community may be felt more by women retirees because we often develop more personal relationships with our younger colleagues than men do." They also list the pleasures and possibilities they have collectively experienced in retirement, such as developing dormant talents, exploring intellectual and cultural areas, traveling more frequently, and being more available to partners, family, and friends. They all enjoy their private lives, and high on their plus list is the opportunity "retirement also gives us . . . to devote ourselves to the causes and organizations in which we believe."

Some people transform themselves in retirement. Others are comfortable continuing in the same groove. Susan Radner does not see retirement as a dramatic transformation: "We will be the people our working, thinking, political, emotional lives prepared us to become." Radner went back to teaching part-time, resented it, and left. Now she enjoys reading the *New York Times* over coffee, rowing on a lake in the Berkshires, and taking in cultural events in New York City. Not unhappily she notes, "I have become a housewife, after fighting it all my life." Others return to a job part-time and are quite satisfied with the arrangement. Some use former work as a transitional aid during the first phase of retirement whereas others enjoy the part-time connection and plan to continue working on that schedule as long as they can. Others have found new occupations, hobbies, or commitments, or they have renewed and deepened old ones. Ida Henderson did both. She gave yoga lessons after training at Kripalu Center for Yoga and Health in Lenox, Massachusetts, volunteered at a nursing home, became a docent at Carnegie Hall, traveled with Elderhostel, and started playing the flute, among many other activities. Noting the absence of people of color at many of the places she volunteered, she worked to change that. Henderson considers "this inclusion of people of color a great accomplishment." Phillipa Kafka devotes herself to what was once a side interest: renovating houses. Laura Weaver, rebelling against her religious background, allows herself "guilt-free play": going out with friends, listening to music, reading, being a student again, and collecting her mother's letters. Doris Goldberg has become an exhibited artist and participates in a group that advocates for breast cancer patients. Diane Fowlkes balances a life of caring for her husband and breeding race horses. Lanie Melamed has thrown herself into two activist groups, Breast Cancer Action and Raging Grannies. Esther Ratner has created a burgeoning business doing fact checking and research for writers and publishers. Dorothy Hammer and Barbara Rubin have both volunteered with the American Association of Retired Persons (AARP) to produce videos for public-access television. Carolyn Goodman produced a film with younger people about activism. The participants in the retirement focus group have found a number of creative outlets. For example, Elizabeth Saunders is working for an off-Broadway theater group that produces plays written and directed by women and Phyllis Schwartz is doing research for the Whitney Museum librarian.

These are only a small sample of the retirement activities of the women in this book. Carole Ganim is open to creating political mischief on a community level. Georgie Gatch and Marilyn Katz have been meeting with other women to strategize about a voice for women in the rebuilding of the World Trade Center site in downtown Manhattan. Dorothy Hammer looks down the road with enthusiasm: "If my energy holds up for the rugged travel I so enjoy I might soon head off to one of the three B's I haven't yet covered: Bhutan, Botswana, and Burma." And while retirement is still in the future for Carol Scott, she dreams about a day when she might pursue two retirement fantasies: opening a bed-and-breakfast in Harlem that would be a center of culture and comfort and working to change public policy so that parents are compensated for the important work of bringing up their children.

Family Become Friends and Friends Become Family

Friends and family are increasingly important for those thinking about retirement and those who are retired. Ellen Rose has a running E-mail dialogue with a friend about retirement. When Rose asks whether it would be okay "just to enjoy" herself, her friend answers: "To hell with the Puritan ethic. . . . Today we get a whole extra lifetime in which to play like the crypto-pagans we are." Rose, uncomfortable with this answer, wants to know how she will be of use. She finally decides to "quit fretting" and "just do it." Looking ahead nine years to age sixty-five, Elayne Archer and a friend are already planning to volunteer in the rose garden at the Brooklyn Botanic Garden. Archer recognizes that "close friendships with women will be as important during this period as they have been throughout my adult life, if not more so." Doris Goldberg describes the friendliness of her Woodstock community. When she was sick, an acquaintance brought over a pot of Chinese matzo ball soup. Carolyn Goodman, age eighty-six, and her ninety-three-year-old friend use each other as supports, literally and figuratively. When they go out to a restaurant, her friend, who walks with a stick, leans on Goodman, who admits to being a bit wobbly herself.

Because she has no children of her own, Carol Prescott fears growing old, but tells herself that "my unusually close-knit family will fill in that very real gap. I pray that will be true." When Carole Ganim retired, she moved in order to be closer to her grandchildren. And Ida Henderson is contemplating moving to North Carolina to be closer to her grandnephew. Terry Davis found that the "allure of my grandkids beckoned me forward" into retirement. Putting family in the forefront was especially important as she felt she had put union organizing and social change in the forefront of her earlier years.

Several people look forward to spending more time with their partners in retirement; others have become their partners' caretakers. Lanie Melamed knew that her retirement would coincide with putting her husband into a long-term care facility. For Diane Fowlkes, however, her husband's descent into a severe anxiety disorder and depression and other illnesses was not expected. She had to revise her retirement priorities to become a full-time caregiver. Juanita Baker's husband would like her to join him in retirement, and while she wants to have a more flexible schedule to be with him, she knows she ought to choose her retirement for herself, not for him.[13]

Nancy Dailey and Kelly O'Brien suggest that interdependence may serve us best in retirement. They are referring mainly to financial interdependence, but they also mean the interdependence women have traditionally and, because of the women's movement, self-consciously built among family (in its widest definition) and friends. For Barbara Rubin, who is single and childless, her "colleagues have been in some ways a substitute family." She lives "without intergenerational anchors or activities," which has significant implications for retirement. Just as she has in the past, Rubin plans to create meaningful family substitutes by enjoying other people's children, tightening friendships, and "'growing' the communities I inhabit and envisioning new ones for the future." Creating alternative living arrangements is one challenge for professional, committed women who do not want to join the stereotypical retirement community of golfers and bridge players. Such a living arrangement is being planned by New York City women writers, artists, and activists. They call it The House of Elder Artists (Thea) and think of it as an "un-retirement home."[14]

Lesbians may be better prepared for aging than their heterosexual counterparts, say Jennifer Christensen and Holly Crenshaw, because, not assuming family as a fallback, many have created a counter culture, a network of friends and others that, hopefully, will stand as a haven in a hostile world as they age and retire. The authors list groups who have formed housing options and retirement communities for lesbians. These include a recreational-vehicle park in Arizona with streets named after lesbian heroes like Barbara Jordan and Helen Keller; Birds of a Feather in New Mexico; The Palms of Manasota in Palmetto, Florida, for gay men and women; and, to be developed, World's Edge Springs Retirement and Longevity Resort in the Appalachian Mountains.

Not Retiring, Out of Choice or Necessity

Section three, "Never Retire," takes its title from Joy Dryfoos's story. Dryfoos loves her work, sees no reason to stop, and definitely does not want to do unpaid volunteer work. While the writers in this section may be rehearsing retirement in their heads, many, like Dryfoos, are fully satisfied with their work. "Although I am now definitely 'over the hill,' why would I want to walk away from continuing to follow my muse? . . . How can you retire from your beliefs? . . . Can one ever really retire from the hunger for recognition?" asks Dryfoos—important questions for professional women. Carol Prescott declares, "I am most alive when I am working. . . . I am funnier and more honest, creative, clearheaded, vulnerable, and strong."

Some of the writers, despite the fact that they had retirement parties and are collecting retirement benefits, do not consider themselves retired. For example, Merle Rubine feels as if she is "starting over" and the Peace Corps is her boot camp for a second career. Carol Burdick, who went through the formal retirement rituals on leaving her half-time position, returned after one semester. Her take-home pay is a small fraction of her preretirement pay. Like Prescott, she realized that she is "addicted" to her students. She loves to teach, she loves being with younger people, and she fears retirement because, she says, "I will become irrelevant." So she asks, "Will I ever retire?" And she declares, "Hell, no."

For Carol Oyster and Carol Scott the "never" in "Never Retire" is not embraced with the lust of Dryfoos, Prescott, or Stuart. It is said ruefully. They worry that they will never be able to retire because they are not sure they will have sufficient financial resources. Twice divorced, Oyster faced serious financial debt. She decided to use her retirement money for a house for herself and her daughter: "I don't look forward eagerly to retirement because I don't know whether I'll have enough money to live—literally." Also divorced, Scott assumed almost all of the cost of postsecondary education for her two children. As an African American parent, she wanted to give them a leg up in a world that does not want to give them a fair share: "It was crucial to me to give them a fine education and to lessen their financial burden upon graduating from college." Scott was, therefore, unable to save much for her retirement. She enumerates the factors that will significantly delay her retirement and the retirement of many other women: "Because of my lack of education regarding retirement, because of divorce laws, because women are often left to care for and educate children alone after divorce, because being black and female can be an extra burden, and because, like most mothers, I wanted more for my children." Oyster's and Scott's experiences are reminders that marriage is often the best way for women to ensure a financially stable retirement, because men generally make more money.[15]

Jennifer Christensen and Holly Crenshaw, however, point out that marriage is not always a legal option. The Defense of Marriage Act prohibits lesbians from marrying, denying them the financial, social, and legal benefits that marriage offers. One of the women described in their piece, for example, cannot collect her partner's social security benefits although they have been together for sixteen years and own a house together. Ironically, she will be able to collect social security on her ex-husband. Oyster advises women, as do Nancy Dailey and Kelly O'Brien, to learn about money at an early age and start packing away as much as you can.

How to and How Not to Retire: Private and Public Lessons

While *Women Confronting Retirement* is not a traditional how-to book, these thirty-two stories offer suggestions about personal retirement choices and public policy. Many of the writers remark that the act of writing about retirement has been helpful for them. The focus group on retirement states that "perhaps our most significant realization was that, as retired women, we need to create new communities for ourselves outside of our social circles, by seeking groups sharing a common interest or cause." Marilyn Katz joined a group of writers; Elizabeth Saunders drew together a group of women directors and playwrights; Phyllis Schwartz works with younger women on the board of the Mount Sinai Sexual Assault and Violence Intervention Program, and Georgie Gatch intends to find a group devoted to the political and social causes that she cares about. The consciousness-raising-group model, developed by the women's movement in the seventies, was very useful. The focus group recommends strongly that women in the process of retiring form such a group to "identify common issues, share experiences, and find creative ways to nurture both themselves and the society in which they live."

As part of the other conversation concerning this stage of life, the writers call for new definitions of both retirement and volunteerism, for new images of the retired woman, and new public policies that support real opportunities for retirement. Retirement is described in this book as another stage of life, not as the closing down of life. Barbara Waxman, quoting Margaret Urban Walker, counters the dominant view of retirement as merely "an unmapped space at the end of the life course—a space . . . by social definition 'empty'."[16] Rather, as Terri Baker says, retirement is "just one more stretch of the road on the journey." That stretch can be a long one, lasting fifteen or twenty years, and the women writing here believe it should be meaningful: creative and active. As Carole Ganim envisions it, "We . . . must create an economy of retirement, an ecology which will sustain us and our progeny as we grow old in an environment of challenge, peace, activity, productivity, freedom, and generosity." To create this economy of retirement, it is necessary to resist society's negative associations with retirement, especially the prevailing notion "that the ideal self [is a] bustling career self, which leads to the notion that the retired individual surrenders not only a job, but eligibility for a centrally valued moral and social identity."

The relationship of work to identity and whether or how to work while in retirement is a question that frequently arises. Those who tried paid part-time work often found it insubstantial, but substantial work makes substantial demands. Horwitz wants "engaged work without the compulsions and restrictions of a full-time job. . . . The sharp disjuncture between worker and retiree, between paid and unpaid labor is too constricting." The same complaint about the inconsequential nature of part-time work is made in relation to doing volunteer work. The women represented here are skilled women who do not want to simply answer phones or file papers. Like the word *retirement*, the word *volunteer* needs reexamination. Phyllis Schwartz suggests another term, "At one time I did pro bono consulting but we called ourselves 'pro bono professionals.' The word *volunteer* is more off-putting." For many, that word is more than off-putting. It conjures up repetitive tasks in organizations that are not prepared for highly skilled volunteers. The women in the retirement support group suggest that "our generation of retirees can be helpful . . . by organizing groups of highly skilled professional women as consultants or mentors who can offer their services for specific projects." Schwartz advocates that we, professional women retirees, "consider ourselves self-employed, freelancers. While freelancers have to seek work and structure their own time, they also have the freedom to refuse work that is neither challenging nor useful."

The book *Prime Time: How Baby Boomers Will Revolutionize Retirement and Transform America* by Marc Freedman constructively advances the other conversation. In the chapters "Reinventing Retirement" and "Leaving a Legacy," Freedman examines the "new beginning" or "new chapter" or "third age," as he calls retirement, that he predicts is about to burst on the American scene. Retired people will design their lives by combining a return to education, a contribution in some form to society, and some degree of work. Freedman suggests various strategies for harnessing this new energy, such as developing an Experience Corps, A Center of Un-Retirement, and an Institute for Learning in Retirement.[17] Shirley Lim sees herself and others like herself as a special kind of retiree: an adaptable, flexible, mobile, experienced, global professional. Several people have proposed something along the lines of a senior Peace Corps, with *senior* signifying higher-level, more experienced input. Feminists, Lim speculates, could organize a "Parachuting Retiree" service through which women could drop into short-term projects to consult, administrate, and teach.

In their study of fifty older professional Australian women, Jenny Onyx and Pam Benton conclude that the traditional dualistic constructions of work and retirement are simply inappropriate and inadequate for professional career women. For these women and for the women confronting retirement in this book,

> Retirement no longer means the withdrawal from active engagement in the workforce, to a life of leisure, but a readjustment, a finer balance of time and energy to allow a more creative and satisfying engagement with the many sides of life and self. This balance is unlikely to be found either in narrowly defined full-time paid work or in the absence of paid employment. Women are looking for a balance of socially useful work, meaningful social relations with friends and family, the opportunity to explore and develop new creative energies, and time for themselves. Such a balance may be found in full-time employment or in retirement, but is more likely to require something in-between. For all the above reasons, older women of this cohort are disinclined to think or talk in terms of retirement, but are seeking new creative forms of living.[18]

Disinclined to think or talk in traditional terms, the contributors to *Women Confronting Retirement* are talking for themselves in ways that should get us all talking.

Notes

1. Americans are turning fifty at the rate of 1 every 7.6 seconds. In 2001, the first group of eighty million baby boomers reached their late fifties. In the next thirty years, the number of people aged sixty-five or older will double to 20 percent of the population, and the United States will, for the first time, become a place where there are more older adults than children and youth.

2. Laura L. Carstensen, "On the Brink of a Brand-New Old Age," *New York Times*, 2 January 2001.

3. Jenny Onyx and Pam Benton, "Retirement: A Problematic Concept for Older Women," *Journal of Women and Aging* 8, no. 2 (1996): 21, referring to J. Martin and C. Roberts, *Women and Employment: A Lifetime Perspective*, Report of the 1980 DE/OPCS women and employment survey, London, 1984.

4. Betty Friedan, *The Feminine Mystique* (New York: W. W. Norton, 1963).

5. Sara Ruddick and Pamela Daniels, eds., *Working It Out: 23 Women Writers, Artists, Scientists, and Scholars Talk about Their Lives and Work* (New York: Pantheon Books, 1977).

6. Christine Ann Price, *Women and Retirement: The Unexplored Transition* (New York: Garland Publishing, 1998), 30. See also Price, "Women and Retirement: Relinquishing Professional Identity," *Journal of Aging Studies* 14, no. 1 (2000): 81–110.

7. Writing in 1982 (*Women's Retirement: Policy Implications of Recent Research*, Beverly Hills, Calif.: Sage Publications), Maximiliane Szinovacz asserted that women's retirement has been widely neglected by social scientists. Since 1982, much more has been written about women and retirement. For a selected list, see the following entries in the bibliography in this volume (not mentioned here are the standard advice books on retirement or books mentioned in previous notes): Dailey; Cort–Van Arsdale and Newman; Freedman; Shavishinsky (the latter two books, while not focusing exclusively on women, are important in helping to advance the conversation about retirement); Cantor (dealing with retirement and other major changes like an unexpected layoff); Calasanti; Cox.

8. Toni M. Calasanti (in "Bringing in Diversity: Toward an Inclusive Theory of Retirement," *Journal of Aging Studies* 7, no. 2 [1993]: 133–150) deconstructs retirement using the categories of gender, class, and race/ethnicity. Her conclusion is that the aging and retirement experience is a diverse one. She points out that "working-class white women and African-American men are similar in that their experiences do not fit the ideology of retirement based on white men's experiences; [retirement for them] does not imply the freedom from labor" (145). For example, "stopping working," she says, is not "relevant for many African-American men, nor is the idea of collecting a pension or Social Security as a way of 'knowing' when you are retired" (143). In "Retirement: Golden Years for Whom?" (in *Gender Mosaics*, ed. Dana Vannoy [Los Angeles: Roxbury Publishing, 2001], 300–310), Calasanti continues this analysis, showing, for example, that retirement is a reduction of work, not a cessation: women's responsibility for domestic labor and for caregiving must be taken into account. In addition to the effect of class, race, and gender on the retirement experience, Maximiliane Szinovacz, David J. Ekerdt, and Barbara H. Vinick, eds., in *Families and Retirement: Conceptual and Methodological Issues* (Newbury Park, Calif.: Sage Publications, 1992) add that "the retirement experience is intricately linked to individuals' past and current experiences in other life spheres and . . . it affects and is also affected by their social networks and relationships, foremost among them their ties to family members" (1). See also note 15 for more discussion of difference in retirement.

9. Similarly, Jane S. Gould in *Juggling: A Memoir of Work, Family, and Feminism* (New York: The Feminist Press at The City University of New York, 1997) describes how in the 1950s she was proud to be "Bernie's wife and Nancy and David's mother" (46), until she had an "epiphany" and realized that she needed

fulfillment outside of the family, becoming part of "a pioneer movement that was to change women's lives" (53). This is a story often repeated.

10. Kathleen F. Slevin and C. Ray Wingrove, *From Stumbling Blocks to Stepping Stones: The Life Experiences of Fifty Professional African American Women* (New York: New York University Press, 1998).

11. For a selected list of books about women and aging, some autobiographical or literary, some more academic, some edited collections, see the following entries in the bibliography in this volume: Minkler and Estes; Alexander et al.; Doress et al.; Martz; Rosenthal; Waxman; Thorne; Wyatt-Brown and Rosen; Friedan, *The Fountain of Age*; Hen Co-op; Steinem, *Moving Beyond Words*; Dowling; Pogrebin; Heilbrun; Gullette; Pearsall; Brown; and Woodward.

12. May Sarton, *At Seventy: A Journal* (New York: W. W. Norton, 1984), 10.

13. In a study of 534 married couples who were either retired or about to retire, Dr. Phyllis Moen found that "retirement itself was a happy time for couples, but . . . the transition to retirement—defined as the first two years after leaving a job—was a period of marital strife for men and women" (Susan Gilbert, "New Portrait of Retiring Is Emerging," *New York Times*, 29 May 2001).

14. Patricia Leigh Brown, "Raising More than Consciousness Now," *New York Times*, 24 August 2000, F1. See also Vivian Gornick, "Alive in NY until the Last Minute," *The Nation*, 24 May 1999, 22–23.

15. Nancy Dailey (*When Baby Boom Women Retire* [Westport, Conn.: Praeger, 1998]) stresses that the social-contextual differences in baby boom women's work-life experiences will negatively affect their retirement. Meg Cox ("Zero Balance: Watch Out! Your Retirement Funds Are in More Trouble than You Think; or, Why Most Women Can't Afford to Retire," *Ms.* [February/March 2001]) quotes Diana Zuckerman, former director of research at the Institute for Women's Policy Research, who says that except for a select group of successful professionals, the generation of boomer women is not going to be as well-off in retirement as we expect. By looking at Social Security rules, pension plans, divorce results, savings, and women's work patterns, among other things, Cox substantiates the statement that most boomer women cannot afford to retire. See also Louis Uchitelle, "More and More, Older Women Unable to Retire," *International Herald Tribune*, 27 June 2001. The trend of not being able to retire at the hoped-for age was reported in the *New York Times* by Mary Williams Walsh, "Reversing Decades-Long Trend, Americans Retiring Later in Life," 26 February 2001 and by Uchitelle, "Workers Find Retirement Is Receding toward 70," 3 February 2002. While this appears true for men and women alike, certain groups of women are disproportionately unable to retire as discussed by Calasanti and Cox and in the selections by Jen Christensen and Holly Crenshaw and Nancy Dailey and Kelly O'Brien in this book. Forty-two percent of all women over seventy-five are living on less than thirteen thousand dollars a year. Quoting a study by the Older Women's League, Cox says, "Older women of color are the poorest in

retirement, [and] the risk of being poor in old age is 70 percent higher for a woman than a man" (59).

16. Margaret Urban Walker, "Getting Out of Line: Alternatives to Life as a Career," in *Mother Time: Women, Aging, and Ethics*, ed. Margaret Urban Walker (Lanham, Md.: Rowman and Littlefield Publishers, 1999), 104, 105.

17. Marc Freedman's *Prime Time: How Baby Boomers Will Revolutionize Retirement and Transform America* (New York: Public Affairs, 1999); see also Jane E. Brody, "Ways to Make Retirement Work for You," *New York Times*, 24 July 2001. For an earlier, rather straightforward study, see *Good Deeds in Old Age: Volunteerism by the New Leisure Class* by Susan Maizel Chambre (Lexington, Mass.: Lexington Books, 1987).

18. Onyx and Benton, "Retirement," 32–33.

One

THINKING ABOUT RETIREMENT

One More Stretch
of the Road

Terri M. Baker

For my ancestors. Especially for Great
Grandmother Lena, Grandmother Maude,
and Mother

To retire or not to retire. A kind of Hamletette in my fifty-third year, I ponder that question at least once a day. On the one hand, I like my job about 80 percent of the time, and I suspect from talking to friends all over the nation that I can't do much better than 80 percent. On the other hand, I have so much work to do on specific projects that I believe I can keep myself happily amused in retirement for the next twenty years or so just setting up structures and creating stability for my notions to grow, develop, and put out new roots.

I know that I will make new friends and see the deepening of associations outside the university where I now teach. Will I miss the students? Of course I will. The students have nurtured me for many years. How will I spend my days? After all, I have devoted my professional life to teaching for almost thirty years—as a public school teacher, as a graduate teaching assistant, as a part-time instructor (oh, those years as a freeway flier), as a full-time instructor. Even as a museum professional I was engaged in teaching. For the last fifteen years I have worked as an English professor at Northeastern State University in Tahlequah, Oklahoma, where I have also served on the Native American studies faculty. They have been good years. However, it is time to move on to a new phase of my life.

I know that in four years or so I will have enough money to live comfortably—oh, not as a jet-setter, you understand. Get a grip, I am a professor in a regional Oklahoma university where the administration believes its job is to keep faculty humble and underpaid. But I will have enough money, what with investments, inheritances, frugality, and consulting work, to get on with what I know my responsibilities to be. Some of the responsibilities are to myself and my family, some to my tribe, some are to Oklahoma and the United States, some are to the world, some are to my ancestors. Gosh, those pesky ancestors just will not let me lounge back, watch reruns of *ER*, and eat chocolates (which I am quite capable of doing with a right good will).

One reason that I need to retire is so that I can spend more time writing and speaking about disability. More and more of late I realize that disability as a condition in the world needs some tender loving care, some press. I realized this last year when a friend of a lifetime spoke of "weaning" me from my walker as though I could walk quite easily if I just put my mind it. To her superficial understanding the walker was akin to a sugartit sucked by an infant. To her, the walker indicated I was just weak in will. Now, this infant holds a Ph.D., has a family, drives a car, dresses herself (okay, except for that *one* time I forgot my skirt and had to wear my raincoat all day, but let's not count that), handles her own investments, reads, and everything. My friend, dear as she is to me, has never experienced disability and so for her it does not exist. While I forgive her, I do find such a view regrettable. So far I have written a play about multiple sclerosis and heard at least one editor gasp when I told her the topic of my most recent essay. The editor implied that writing about disability or even talking about it was in bad taste. I have had an academic supervisor lecture me about how to think about my disability—this after she read a letter of explanation about multiple sclerosis from my neurologist and then apparently decided that the neurologist *had* to be wrong.

Perhaps my work history as a professor points me to speaking to groups and writing articles and essays. After all, teaching and learning surely foster more positive solutions than shooting people. And that is what frustrated people seem to be doing these days. As an Oklahoman who figures that every other person I see is packing a loaded gun, I would rather invite people to a comedy or a discussion than to the Okie Corral. The interludes are so much more fun. And there are refreshments. But writing plays and essays and speeches takes time. That means retirement. Currently I teach four courses each semester, advise students, serve in various capacities for the community, research, and write academically. Multiple sclerosis causes extreme fatigue. My academic responsibilities fill my time from late August until late May. Summer does provide those necessary chunks of time for thinking and writing and then revising after periods of rest so that I make sense to readers, but I have more to put in writing than can be done in one season a year.

In many ways, because I have had arthritis since childhood, this educational project focused on disability is a continuation of what I have been doing for most of my life: coping with disability and helping other people also to cope with its realness. I know, perhaps because multiple sclerosis has complicated my physical situation, that more public conversation is needed because something of a mean spirit has entered the public discourse about disability. I suspect that the able bodied resent our legal right to park conveniently, or perhaps they think that we somehow are receiving more than they. More what?

Something like thirty-eight states do not comply with the Americans with Disabilities Act. I suspect that disabled people make able-bodied people profoundly uncomfortable. We scare people. So, I want to talk with people, educate them, whack ignorance back to its cave. By lighting the path that leads to comprehension of what the disabled offer, I want to invite people to turn away from pity and patronage and instead turn to sympathy and tolerance for difference.

And then there is my responsibility to my health and the welfare of my family. If I keep grinding at the university through rain and sleet and snow to deliver the educational goods, I probably will be carried out on a board, drooling and taking attendance, in about four years anyway.

Would I retire in my late fifties if I were not disabled? I do not know. I am disabled, and I live with that fact. Concerning this question of *if,* I think of a comment by John Lennon that I ran across in *The Little Zen Companion,* "Life is what happens to you while you're busy making other plans."[1] Disability including multiple sclerosis was never in my plans, but there it is.

However, happy thought, if I retire in four years at age fifty-eight, I will know who I am as well as the identities of my husband and son. We can travel out of town, go to bed *after* the late-night news, have hot dinners, enjoy an active social life. Wow! This is sounding better all the time.

This travel thing really perks me up. If I retire I could actually travel to places and stay long enough to carry out research. So many things to research, so little time! I want to poke around in small-town museums, in newspaper offices, and in dusty archives. I want to touch some of those one million letters in the national archives protesting Indian Removal, which put the tribes from the Southeast on what came to be known as the Trail of Tears. Chad Smith, principal chief of the Cherokee Nation, doubts that there are one million letters. Rennard Strickland, Cherokee legal scholar and witty friend, thinks that there *may* be one million. I want to see those letters and write about them. Americans especially need to know about those non-Indians who opposed Indian removal in the early part of the nineteenth century. You know, people like Davy Crockett, who certainly deserves more remembrance than Andrew Jackson, whose very name causes me to pucker up to spit until I recall decorum and my mother. Non-Indian Americans need to know that not all of their ancestors were in favor of a national policy that resulted in the deaths of thousands and the continuing oppression of thousands of this continent's indigenous people. We need to heal as Americans, although the healing will take a *long* time. After all, the wounding began over five hundred years ago. An Anglo friend once asked in response to an American Indian protesting one of those insulting sports team names, "When are they going to get over this?" A Cherokee friend replied, "When the non-Indians go back to where they came from." I suggested ice cream all around. As I enjoy friends from many diverse backgrounds, ice cream is often the only answer in hot moments.

Americans have a lot of hot moments. We have a lot of healing to do, and I know that I must contribute to that healing by using my expertise in exposing the wounds in America to sunlight and air. Constant recourse to ice cream will kill you too, eventually.

I know, as my mother knew, that the wounds will resist healing during my lifetime, and so American Indians today need to find ways to be who they are in security and happiness. This means, in large part, that American Indian tribes need financial independence in order to live as they want to live. Choctaws in Oklahoma are working on this, and on their path they are helping non-Indian Oklahomans by contributing to the general financial health of the state. Knowing this, I am even now laying the groundwork so that after retirement (happy thought) I may consult with my tribe, the Choctaw Nation, in a number of ways. One opportunity occurs during Labor Day weekend when the Choctaw Nation in Oklahoma hosts a festival, and I have begun to contribute to the party, which last year drew over one hundred thousand people into southeastern Oklahoma in just a few days. Boy! That's a "right smart crowd" in Little Dixie, as my old Aunt Evie used to say. A few years ago I wrote a play about three of our Choctaw treaties which eventually resulted in our removing to Oklahoma, and those plays were presented for the third time at the ancestral village during the holiday this year. The Choctaw language classes in southeastern Oklahoma under the auspices of the Choctaw Nation plan to translate them into Choctaw. My goal is to do more of this cultural retrieval and maintenance work after retirement.

I do not want a formal job, you understand, being satisfied to consult to pay my expenses, to earn a modest honorarium from time to time, and to be where the Choctaw action is. Mom made it clear to me some years ago that I need to honor the ancestors by using my talents and skills to support current Choctaw efforts for a better life. So I have set in motion plans to help me contribute in small but real and practical ways.

And what of my longtime concern with women and their lives? The lives of women, especially rural and American Indian women, interest me, since that is what I am—rural and Choctaw—and I am working like a beaver to set up an economic structure in which home-based businesses run by rural women will have markets for their products. The small group to which I belong is conducting a feasibility study and hopes to go forward when the study is finished. The women will be able to work in their homes, and eventually in a central location, creating products for sale locally and, thanks to the Internet, worldwide. These women will then have some control over their own labor and its worth in the marketplace. They will be able to pass on their knowledge and skills to younger women who will be able to maintain traditional American Indian skills as well as traditional rural skills. They will be contributing to the economy of Oklahoma, the nation, and the world.

This project puts me in the lovely company of women with kind hearts, sharp minds, and capable hands. We laugh our frustrations away together as I believe we will continue to do, and we nurture each other when we need nurturing. What more can you ask for?

And the work is necessary. I know. I come from a line of women who exemplify the necessity. My Irish great grandfather (then in his sixties) paid a wagon-load of corn and two mules as a bride price for my Choctaw great-grandmother (then a young girl of sixteen) in a violent time in Oklahoma's history. My mother, abandoned by her Irish/Choctaw father, attended a Presbyterian school for Indian orphans. Mother was always intensely aware of her responsibility to help other women, to join with them in political efforts, and to support the Choctaw tribe. She passed on the bundle of responsibility to me.

Those rural and Indian women need access to financial independence. Oklahoma, after all, moves to the tune of the 1950s in that men still largely control the state. In the rural areas, Bubba is still strong. You know Bubba. He is the stereotype rednecked sheriff you have seen in all those movies—a bully. These days some Oklahoma Bubbas dress better and speak better, having been to a private grammar tutor, and perhaps play golf. But Bubba still lives here and is in control as a banker, real estate broker, dentist, university president, auto mechanic, physician. Sometimes Bubba has hired Bubbette, his insecure sister under the skin. After many years of working with Bubbas and Bubbettes, I have decided that they are just boneheads, and that I would like to work with smart, funny women who want to lend a hand to other women to help in small but real ways.

Perhaps my age simply has resulted in a loss of patience, but a wise Kiowa friend warned me long ago that I should leave academe before the wounds became too damaging to overcome. I know the time is close. I have been on the educational front lines waging a war against ignorance for a professional life of nearly thirty years. I want to leave laughing, before energy is too low to start a fire for my projects.

In some ways, no doubt, all these projects may seem like pretty small potatoes to people living in cities with access to instant world communication and cable TV. But in rural Oklahoma we have computers, satellite dishes, and fairly clear skies and water too at this point. When snow falls I stay home, snug in the Illinois River valley, sipping hot drinks before a warming fire. Unless a tree falls on a power line, we have electricity. There are potatoes and potatoes.

For me, the important thing is that my retirement plan requires me to keep on working for the good. As I have been a minor activist—against the Vietnam War, for civil rights, and in the women's movement—for all of my adult life, working for the good is essential to my well-being. And so I will work to continue to communicate about disability because the world will be better for valuing its disabled people and supporting us as we lead active and productive lives. To work for the good allows me to sleep at night, and I want to help Americans as we work toward constructing an identity that recognizes and so heals painful wounds in our past. The pain from these wounds makes us restless, keeps us awake at night, unable to focus on healing. Americans need sleep. Sleep refreshes and renews. And I want to know that I am using my skills to help women so that they may work their way out of poverty, so that they can know independence of choice and become fully realized as human beings. Fully realized human beings, it seems to me, raise healthy families, make positive political decisions, live responsibly, and recognize the fundamental value of Mother Earth. I am aware, as my mother made me aware, that we do this kind of work for our grandmothers and for our grandchildren and for their great great great grandchildren. I also know that I occupy just a small space in the circle, and not a very important space when compared with something like the Grand Canyon. Just a dust blip.

So after retirement I will continue to work because we all die, return to dust, and blow about to such canyons. I will also play because some play keeps my spirit whole. Choctaws know that. Somewhat like Thoreau, I hope to come to the end of my life knowing that I lived, worked for the good, laughed, walked the balanced road, and shared the road with friends who helped me along the way. Retirement, which is before me, is just one more stretch of the road on the journey. And the journey is the ground of being.

Note

1. David Schiller, *The Little Zen Companion* (New York: Workman Publishing, 1994), 276.

The Old Brown Bag and the Used Tinfoil: Lessons from My Mother about Work and Retirement

Elayne Archer

I think my attitudes to retirement will be shaped by my attitude to work. This was formed, in large part, by the experience of my mother, a working-class widow who worked for almost fifty years, much of the time as a secretary. This taught me that work was work—it wasn't always ideal but you were lucky to have it. My attitude to work was also shaped to some degree by my participation in the early days of the women's movement. This made me less career oriented than I might otherwise have been. As a result of these two forces, I think work was and is less important to me in some ways than for many women of my generation and therefore retirement will be easier.

First My Mother

As a widow, my mother always worked, and my brother and I spent our early years in foster homes and boarding schools because there was no daycare in those days, nor even much in the way of babysitting. My mother was born in 1911, out of wedlock, as they said at the time. Her mother worked as a domestic and had herself been born out of wedlock, her mother also working as a domestic.

However, my mother had neither a typical working-class upbringing nor a typical working-class education. She was raised in a very middle-class neighborhood and went to school with the daughters of the well-to-do. In brief, here's how this happened. When my mother was eight, in 1919, my grandmother got a job as a housekeeper for a man who had lost the fingers of his right hand in World War I. She and my mother moved into a house in Osterley, a respectable middle-class neighborhood to the west of London. My grandmother told the neighbors, as she had told my mother, that her husband had died in a hunting accident in Scotland. (My mother only discovered the truth when she went to Somerset House—the British hall of records—for a birth certificate. When she insisted that the man behind the window put her father's name on the document, he said, "You'd better go home and have a long talk with your mother." But this is a whole other, and very Victorian, story!)

At some point, my grandmother insisted that the father of her child pay for his daughter's education, and my mother was sent off to a very old and respectable girls' school in the west of London called the Green School, where she was educated with the daughters of the upper middle class. And so while my mother did not have a college education, she had a good English secondary education—she studied French and read a lot of poetry and plays and much of Dickens, Thackeray, Eliot, and other such writers. She loved to say how boring much of it had been—all that Tennyson ("Come into the garden, Maud") she was forced to memorize! One of her favorite heroines was Becky Sharpe in *Vanity Fair* by William Makepeace Thackeray. Like my mother Becky was a feisty working-class girl at a rich private school. My mother loved especially the scene of Becky's leaving Miss Pinkerton's Academy (located near the Green School in Chiswick, a fancy section of London), throwing out the dictionary she had received as a graduation prize and declaring, "So much for the dictionary and thank God I'm out of Chiswick!"

After she left school at seventeen, my mother went to work as a secretary in various offices in the City of London and on Fleet Street. She used to say that she worked on Fleet Street. Of course, this did not mean that she was a journalist—although she did not mind if you thought that. She worked basically as a secretary; she knew shorthand and was an excellent typist.

My father was from a much more solidly working-class background. He left school at fifteen to work at various jobs, including as an assistant to the owner of a chain of theaters and cinemas in the West End. At some point he left that and went to work as a journalist for a prominent local paper (his uncle was an accountant for the paper). By the time he was killed in Malta, in 1943, he had worked for about ten years as a journalist on several papers, mostly as a sports reporter.

After my father died, my mother made a complete break and took my brother and me to Canada in 1944. She went with a man whom perhaps she was going to marry—but when she arrived she realized she had made a dreadful mistake and had no intention of marrying him. I do not know a great deal about our family's very early years in Canada—my mother never liked to talk about how much time my brother and I spent in foster homes and boarding schools—but quite quickly she found work by parlaying her Fleet Street experience into a job as a journalist for a prominent left-wing Canadian magazine called *Saturday Night*.

This was a job she loved—for both the writing and the smart people she worked with. After she died my brother and I found a file full of her articles, written to her byline, some of which had involved her traveling to other parts of Canada. My mother often had to work long hours putting the magazine to bed and was late when she came to see us on Saturdays in our foster homes or on visiting evenings in boarding school. I remember her arriving at my school on visiting Tuesdays very harassed, but there was also a sense of excitement—she was clearly energized by the work. While my mother was at this job, I lived with her and my brother for one year before being sent to boarding school. I remember that sometimes, after school, my brother and I would call my mother at work and pretend to be the police or ask for Dagwood Bumstead or Blondie or some such cartoon character. This caused my mother a great deal of trouble—no one else had children calling them at work and it was just not done. There was no understanding that a working woman could have children. Unfortunately, the pay at this job was very poor and finally the magazine went bankrupt.

In retrospect, my mother did feel some guilt about leaving my brother and me in foster homes during this time. In later life, I heard her telling a friend that she had arranged her work to be at home in the late afternoons the year my brother and I both lived with her; she also wrote this in her journal. It was an entire fiction—she was never home until much later—my brother and I made dinner together, did our homework, listened to the radio, and put ourselves to bed (my brother was nine and I was six). We loved it—loved being alone and having the apartment to ourselves. We were the envy of our friends who had their mothers to contend with when they went home. I once gave my mother a story by Tillie Olsen, "I Stand Here Ironing," about a mother thinking about how her daughter has turned out and feeling guilty about her mothering. The story evoked much guilt in my mother but she dealt with it by thinking about how well my brother and I had turned out—both having gone to good universities—despite our early childhood. She also felt tremendously guilty that she had not given us the kind of attention that she saw me lavishing on my children. Of course she had never had that kind of attention either.

At some point during this time my mother met a prominent news broadcaster for the Canadian Broadcasting Corporation. (Later, in the 1960s, he became well-known as an actor in an American Western.) She suggested that he hire her, with her good English accent, to read the news. The man was hysterical at the notion that anyone would listen to a woman read the news. My mother told this story often in later life—as one of the ways she felt that she was too early to benefit from the women's movement.

Fortunately, after the magazine collapsed, my mother got a job as a secretary for a trade organization. She did not love this job but it was a job, and this was a lesson for me: you were lucky to have one. The job gave her some prestige—she was essentially the office manager—but there was a downside. The boss put a lot of pressure on her for sexual favors, especially when we were tenants in the basement of his house after a fire in the rooming house where my mother was living when my brother and I were still in boarding school. (My mother did not talk of this to me but I sometimes heard her talking about it to her girlfriends when she didn't know that I could hear.) At dinner, my mother did not talk about the content of her work—I imagine this was fairly boring. She did talk, usually humorously, about the people she met during the day. She also described the great view of Lake Ontario from her office in a tall building on Front Street. This was another lesson about work: there is always something to enjoy at a job, and one must make the most of it.

To make extra money my mother did the accounts and correspondence for a psychiatrist—a zany Hungarian who had trained with Freud and was in Canada as a refugee after the war. She worked nights and some weekends until she was able to buy a typewriter. How I remember the day my mother brought home a portable Olivetti. It meant she could work at home at nights and on the weekends, and this made a big difference in how much we saw her. Again, even though this second job meant my mother was working five and a half days at her regular job and then another day for the doctor, it put my family in touch with a whole other world—all the rich ladies of Toronto who were the doctor's patients—and that added to my lesson that work could have benefits beyond the pay and despite the hard work. During this time my mother was also trying to write. I remember a screenplay she was working on, a comedy with some real-life characters based on an old Chinese legend about a sacred crane.

After about eight years at the officer manager's job, when she was forty-eight, a big change occurred in my mother's work life and in the life of our family. She had a rather unsuccessful cataract operation. She was young for this operation and was left with almost no sight in one eye. For months after the operation she lay in her bedroom in the dark. I was in my third year of high school. I got up every morning alone; my brother slept late—he was living at home and going to the University of Toronto, nearby. When I left for school, my mother was usually still asleep in the room next to mine, sometimes groaning softly. When I came home in the late afternoon she was still in bed, her face sepulchral against the pillow, the shades drawn, the room almost completely dark. I took her a cup of tea, talked for a while, and left as fast as I could. I sensed how hard a time this was for her and feared she was close to the type of near-breakdown that had sent my brother and me to boarding school when I was seven.

At some point—after six months? a year?—my mother arose from the bed, announced that her "dark night of the soul was over," and went to work as a clerk in a bookstore. I don't know how she experienced the lowered status of her new job. I knew that it was good she was working, but my major image from this period is her going off to work every day, somewhat jauntily with a beret on her head, with a lunch wrapped in much-reused aluminum foil and packed in an old brown paper bag. Every evening she would take the foil and the bag out of her purse to use again the next day. How I longed to see her throw them out! By the end of the week, the foil was dirty and crinkled and the bag rumpled and oily. These days, I would be proud of my mother as a super recycler, but then I just saw it as a sign of how poor we were.

I did recognize, however, that my mother was once again setting a good example and, in her typical the-glass-is-half-full way, being upbeat: she liked her boss, an older woman who had taught at the university for a number of years, it was great to be around books, and perhaps it would lead to something.

And indeed it did. Her boss suggested that she take a script-writing course at a local high school at night and the teacher recommended her for the best job of her life—as a script editor for the Canadian Broadcasting Corporation, where she worked for fifteen years until she retired.

My mother loved this job. She loved reading the scripts—I remember a story about reading an early play by a soon-to-be famous English playwright. My mother started as a script reader and moved up to an editor's job, where she worked with the playwrights. But her boss was a difficult woman and considerably younger than my mother. My mother's lack of college education meant that she could not have a management role in the office.

My mother retired at sixty-five. Considering how poor we had been for so long, she was not badly off. She had an old-age pension from the Canadian government, a modest pension from the Royal Air Force, a CBC pension, and another small pension that she had put money into in the last five years of employment.

After she retired, my mother had a hard time settling down. For a few years before and after retirement, she bought and sold a number of houses—at least four houses in Toronto and two in London. She was restless but also enjoyed the work involved—she had quite an entrepreneurial instinct. (She was also trying I believe to gain back money she had lost when the man she had come to Canada with had refused to repay a considerable sum of money she had given him to take out of England. As a citizen, she could take only a very limited amount "out of the sterling area." I think she felt tremendous guilt about this—that our family would have had quite a different sojourn in the new world had she not lost this money.) She had quite an instinct for house buying, but she could never afford to fix up the places that nicely. In two houses, she rented rooms to students from the university and was a great landlady, charging moderate rents and offering much maternal wisdom.

After two years of retirement in Toronto, my mother returned to London in 1977, where she promptly bought a mid-nineteenth-century house in the north of London. Then, in 1980, with my brother, she bought a house built in 1720 in the newly revived, once Jewish, now Bengali, East End. She lived there, at first without electricity or hot water, until her death in 1988. She loved the neighborhood—Jack the Ripper pub on one corner and a mosque, formerly a synagogue, on the other—and got somewhat involved in neighborhood affairs. She had lunch every weekday at a local café (pronounced "caff") and regaled the regulars with stories of the Blitz, the boat voyage to Canada, and her early years in Toronto. She did not work during this time but she was always busy—puttering around the house, searching out bargains in the various markets, supervising the workmen, playing a minor role in community events, reading, or watching the BBC. I have an image of her sitting in the walled garden of the house, with a cat on her knee, reading a biography of Chekhov. On her deathbed my mother spoke about her work—especially her last job—and about her failure to write fiction.

My Attitudes to Work

With all my mother worked, you would think that I grew up with a healthy attitude to work and convinced that I would always work. But this is not quite how it was. My mother's working was a sign of how hard up our family was, without a father as a major breadwinner. My model was still the woman who didn't work—like the mothers of most of my friends. Growing up, the only other working mother I knew was the mother of a high school friend. She was English like my mother but much more educated and a landscape gardener to the rich families of Toronto. All the other mothers I knew had perhaps worked for a few years before getting married, but, as far as I could see, spent most of their time cleaning and cooking, wearing aprons with their hair pulled back into buns, and playing bridge in their spare time.

In high school my teachers always told me that I would be an English teacher. I resisted this notion—wanting to be something more artistic (a writer) or more "nonfeminine." My ideas were vague, but I thought about studying government or economics and going into politics in some way. My mother sometimes suggested that I might be a journalist like my father but it wasn't much talked of. But it was with my father as a writer I identified, not my mother.

In college I tried majoring in government but it was a very masculine major at the time. I entered my first government class a week late, and the instructor said, "Well, Miss Archer, it's nice to have"—I thought he was going to say "you" or even "a 'girl' in the class"—but he said "a nice pair of legs in the class." After a semester of *Marbury v. Madison*, I switched to English. After graduation, I spent a year in England, worked at various jobs, and applied to graduate school. I still did not have much idea of what I wanted to do, but I received a generous fellowship and that made it easy to decide.

During my last year of graduate school—I was married at this point and had a year-old son—I fell into teaching. A job came up, it paid quite well, and it gave me freedom to be with my son. I was determined to be a more present mother than my mother had been able to be. I needed a job; I was the sole support of my family at this point since my husband was still in law school. However, I worried that I did not set high enough work standards for myself. At a time when many women were talking about the primacy of work, I felt the primacy of family.

And Now the Women's Movement

In one of many discussions about work in one of my various women's liberation groups (before we called ourselves feminists), one group member, from a wealthy family in which women had been college educated but had not worked outside the home, said to me: "Well, it's so much easier for you to work because of your mother." I bristled at first—seeing my mother struggle for years was not easy—but I realized that there was truth in what my friend had said. Quite simply, it was easier for me to work because I did not have such highfalutin ideas about work and did not regard it as a choice (once I got over my fantasy about marrying a rich man and never having to work). In addition, having been left in foster homes and boarding schools, I was not guilt ridden about leaving my son in playgroup while I worked. I did, however, want to arrange my work to be with my children as much as possible, one reason I ended up teaching (and living communally for a dozen years—but that is another story).

For lack of a better phrase, my attitudes to work were more "working class" than those of many women I met in the early days of the women's movement. Work was something you did to earn money. In the various groups I was in—a consciousness-raising group, a mother's group, and a women's health group— many women talked of what work should be. When I heard a woman say that work should be "enjoyable, meaningful, well paid, politically relevant, flexible, and have good vacations," I thought, "This person is from Mars." I felt that if work was rewarding, flexible, well paying, et cetera—or even a few of these—you were very lucky, and you were certainly not "entitled" to it.

Another woman in my consciousness-raising group maintained that she would not work at any job that did not make a "contribution to the revolution." Another decided she was not going to "work for the man"; instead she would do volunteer work. Many women echoed these sentiments. One friend who did not work full-time, or hardly at all, until she was thirty-five, felt guilty because her work in a local hospital was not "political" enough. But like me she did not feel guilty about not using her education as she had originally thought she would. She had a doctorate in chemistry and had always assumed she would be a scientist of some sort. A little work in that area had convinced her she was not going to do hard science; she dedicated herself to women's health and got the hospital job doing obstetrics gynecology research.

I think the women's movement—at least as I experienced it—with its emphasis on sisterhood and not on individual women made it much easier to do the nonindividualist thing than it is today. My involvement in a women's health group—where I taught women's health courses, among other things—made it much easier for me to drop out of graduate school before getting my doctorate and give up my notion of having a career in academia. I see young female colleagues today, working so hard for their careers, having benefited from the greater opportunities for women in the last thirty years. I envy them and I don't. They have much higher expectations for themselves in terms of career but have none of the sisterly supports that we had. They have the rewards but did not go through the struggle—and the struggle was great. This may be putting a positive spin on it—"to make a virtue of necessity," as my mother used to say when one rationalized something one was going to do anyway—but I have never regretted dropping out of graduate school.

My Work History

I have worked for thirty-two years as a teacher, writer, and editor. My first teaching job was for three years at The City University of New York during the heyday of open admissions. I taught three sessions of basic composition to first-year students. I loved them and loved the work, but it was very hard: every week I graded at least seventy-five out-of-class assignments and seventy-five in-class assignments. On the whole, the work was not how I had imagined teaching college-level English when I sat reading Keats under the cherry trees in Radcliffe Yard!

My next teaching job was as a basic skills teacher in the Public Policy Program at St. Peter's College in Jersey City, New Jersey. The program had been set up to help entry-level workers in social services and education gain a college degree and move up in their institutions and assume positions of leadership. It was an urban studies program with a community-organizing slant and was very much a product of the sixties: its philosophy was that if you educate people, they will advocate for change and help bring about the revolution. The students were mostly working-class blacks and Hispanics who worked as teachers' aides, welfare workers, tenant managers, et cetera. They were great but, on the whole, their writing was very poor.

I loved this job and felt that what I was doing was political in the broadest sense of the term, but to some degree I felt alienated from the field; I felt I was not politically correct enough in my approach to teaching the language. There was a lot of talk in those days about standard English as the "dialect of power," casting English teachers as major oppressors of their students. Articles in *Radical Teacher* (a magazine aimed at teachers with a New Left orientation, first published in 1975) exhorted you to respect your students' dialect, not "correct" their "mistakes." I could never understand how helping people write the dialect of power—done respectfully—could be oppressive. I told students that they, like everyone, must learn to operate in several dialects; indeed most of us already did. As one of my students put it, "You mean you talk differently to the preacher in the bar on Saturday night than you do in the church on Sunday morning!" No matter how hard I tried to empower my students, I did have to correct their written, and sometimes their spoken, English. It was certainly a long way from Freire.[1]

At some point, I realized that I was not going to be "blessed" when it came to work. I would work hard and like many things about my job, but I would almost always prefer to be with my family or doing something else. I realized that my students shared my views about work; they would almost always rather not be at their jobs, and certainly not in my class. No matter how much they liked me as a teacher and recognized that I was trying to help them improve their writing, they were always glad when the class was over.

One of my students, an older black woman who had worked for years as a domestic in the South before coming North and getting a job as a teacher's aide, told me of being interviewed about her "job satisfaction" by her granddaughter, a high-school senior at a private school in Montclair, New Jersey. The granddaughter simply refused to believe that the grandmother had not enjoyed her work cleaning homes all those years, and kept asking her to rate the most rewarding aspects of her work. The grandmother kept saying "Honey, the only rewarding thing was the food I put on the table and the rent I paid." I really identified with what the woman was saying about work being work—they paid you for it and you did it because you needed the money.

I left this job after eleven years. I figured out that I had been through the Holland Tunnel between my home in New York City and my job in New Jersey over twenty-seven hundred times and it was time to quit. I had only one requirement for a new job—an easier commute.

For the last fifteen years, I have worked as an editor and writer for many nonprofit organizations, the last eight of which I have been on staff with the Academy for Educational Development, a multinational nonprofit organization with an office in New York City that does mostly educational research and provides technical assistance to schools and districts undertaking reform. At some point I decided that I did not want to take on an area of expertise— for example, pregnancy prevention—but would be a generalist, the writer/editor for the whole department. This is what I currently do. In some ways it is less rewarding than my teaching (to which I have returned as an adjunct from time to time), but it is also less draining. I love my colleagues, the area of the city where I work, the challenge of keeping the language somewhat well written, the connection to a larger organization, the occasional opportunities to travel, and the amusement of dealing with the Gen-X prose of my young colleagues—for whom mention of a pronoun's antecedents conjures up images of genealogy! I love having a work context, meeting people I would not otherwise meet, and having an office. When I look at my plants and out the window across Fifteenth Street, I think of my mother gazing out across Lake Ontario.

At this point, I have worked for over thirty-two years and will work for close to forty before retirement becomes a reality (at age sixty-five). I have been fortunate to work at jobs that were much more rewarding that those my mother worked at for much of her work life, and I have had some choice about whether to work. For my mother, the essential thing was having a job. There was simply no choice about it. I also felt I had to work but was the sole support of my family for only about six of the last thirty years. I could have chosen not to work but above all I loved that feeling of competence that work gives—of being able to make it in the world and of sharing the responsibility of supporting the family. I think my not working would have made for a very unequal relationship with my husband. And work also helps you appreciate nonwork; I really do not envy the few women I know of my generation who have never worked. All of this is to say that the rewards of work are many—and exist whether or not you love the work itself.

Retirement for Me

As I said at the beginning, I look forward to retirement since work, despite its rewards, has never been the only or major source of satisfaction in my life, and I don't dread not having a work focus. Further, I don't see myself stopping work completely. I may continue to have some professional involvement with the English language through occasional editing, teaching a course, volunteering in a literacy program, or maybe writing a column on language for the local newspaper. But I will not want to be doing, for no pay, work similar to what I did for years—I certainly will not be writing proposals or annual reports as a volunteer or even for pay!

One thing is certain: I will not follow my mother's example in retirement. I will not buy and sell old houses. No, I see myself in a small, modern place, surrounded by some books, plants, and perhaps a cat, with a landlord to call on when something goes wrong.

However, like my mother, I am sure I will be very busy in retirement. I do see myself wanting some sort of context to get me outside the house and keep me in contact with people I might not otherwise meet. I could volunteer in Prospect Park if I am still in Brooklyn or become a docent in the Brooklyn Museum. If I am still in New York—or any city—I see myself having more time to do city things. I would also like to travel a little more, at least in early retirement and if my health allows, and be a more active grandmother. I could walk/run most days instead of just a few times a week. I could reread Marcel Proust (not that likely!) or read the second half of *War and Peace*. I could finally learn Spanish, brush up on my French, take up piano, or get a dog.

I think that I will be somewhat self-involved in retirement, as work and children play much less central roles in my life. Specifically, I think I will pay some attention to things spiritual and perhaps less to things political—and more so the older I get. I see myself reading John Donne, George Herbert, Gerard Manley Hopkins, and some of the other English poet-priests. I may join a High Anglican church—especially if it is involved in the community. These activities—reading the Metaphysical poets and returning to High Anglican church—would be to return to my roots in a way.

I do worry that I will not settle down, that I will do a little of everything and not feel good about it—I am enough of a Protestant to believe that one should not be frivolous or waste time, even in retirement. Seriously, I worry that my retirement—as I describe it above—will be a little too self-indulgent—doing all those things that I enjoy doing now but don't have enough time for. I think I will need to be doing something "useful." This could be volunteering in a youth program or an adult literacy program. But I know I will be hesitant about getting too involved and having the pressures—time and emotional—of that involvement. I think this will be a major challenge of retirement, after the first flush of "freedom": how to have some involvement but keep it limited so that I don't find myself as busy as I am now without time for the other things I want to do.

I know it will be very important to share retirement with my close women friends and that close friendships with women will be as important during this period as they have been throughout my adult life, if not more so. My friend Karla and I are already planning to be volunteering in the rose garden at the Brooklyn Botanic Garden in nine years, when she turns sixty-five.

However, even with the support of friends, I think that retirement will be an enormous challenge emotionally. Work has given me a great sense of competence over the years—a feeling that I can make it. I will miss that feeling. Of course the biggest emotional challenge will be facing the reality that retirement means that the final stage of my life is beginning. This will be an end to looking forward. I imagine that more than ever it will be important to follow William Blake's advice about "kissing the joy as it flies"—living in the present.

In some ways, I am tempted to think that one should do something quite different in this final stage—join the Peace Corps, move to Europe, take up flying—what has one got to lose? In my case, if one of my children were living somewhere I wanted to live—like California—I would be tempted to move, although this would mean leaving a neighborhood where I will have lived for thirty-five years and have so many friends. But as I see my retirement in somewhat existential terms—dealing ultimately with the challenge of living and dying well (not to be too morbid about it!), being more on my own might be acceptable, even appropriate.

Perhaps most important, I would like to think that in retirement I could address the biggest unfinished business of my life—writing fiction. Like my mother, I have struggled to write fiction for a number of years; I have parts of two novels on the computer. I would like to think that, like Frank McCourt, I could finally, in retirement, give the time and attention to my writing that I have given to work and family all these years. When I think of regrets that I might have as I look back at my life, this is the one that most comes to mind: how will I feel if I do not finish at least one of my novels?

I have written so far about my retirement plans without mentioning my husband's. This is largely because he is two years younger than I and will retire later, and I will deal with the challenges of retirement, for the first two years at least, without his daily company. When he does retire, we can, I hope, travel more and do more things together around the city. If by chance we move to another city or to the country, I imagine we will spend more time together.

When I read *Macbeth* many years ago, I was charmed by the description of old age as the season of the "sere and yellow leaf." I wonder if I will be as charmed by the autumn of my life when "I'm it," as my mother once said about her amazement at being old—meaning that somehow you never think it will happen to you. In summary, I do look forward to the freedom of retirement—but freedom is always a challenge.

Note

1. Paolo Freire, a Brazilian sociologist, philosopher, and linguist, author of *The Pedagogy of the Oppressed*, published in 1970, a very influential book about the liberating nature of literacy, the oppressive nature of much traditional pedagogy, and the obligation of teachers to teach in a way that empowers students.

Exploring the No-Woman's Land of Old Age; or, How May Sarton's Counterstory Prepares Me for Retirement

SYLVIA HENNEBERG

Whenever it becomes apparent to people that my research interests lie with women and aging, they are perplexed because they feel that as an academic in my mid-thirties at the beginning of my career, I am too young to be worrying about such bleak issues. Their reaction reveals any number of assumptions about aging, the most obvious of which is that aging and its accompanying circumstances are so thoroughly depressing that no woman in her right mind would voluntarily concern herself with them. Retirement, my subject here, is also a delicate topic. Although there are certainly those who idealize it and those who value it, most people I know, retired or not, perceive it negatively. They do so with good reason, for there is very little that tells us that retirement is a valuable period of life. What Betty Friedan calls our society's "categorical imperative of work versus retirement" creates an often unbridgeable chasm between people who are pre- and postretirement.[1] Retiring women are particularly affected; in their mid-sixties, many find, they embark upon a journey into a no-woman's land of old age, an ill-defined, little-known space in the outer margins of society where, perceived to be past beauty, reproductive ability, and productivity, they are unlikely to regain a position of visibility. Rarely can they enjoy the benefit of a tradition that at least sometimes venerates the elder patriarch for his wisdom and that wholeheartedly promotes the careers of older men far beyond retirement age.

Searching for a person who has undertaken that journey successfully, a woman who has resisted negative constructions of retirement and aging and who offers a counterstory to current perceptions of the last stages of life, I found a different model in the contemporary American writer May Sarton. As I compose this piece, I hope to construct a counterstory of my own, conveying that later life and retirement are rich and meaningful, that it is exhilarating to locate and learn about positive models of aging, and that no, it is not at all depressing to deal with these issues head-on in early adulthood.

Trying to understand women's role and stake in retirement, I look at my own roots. The women in my family, all Germans, all worked, though none of them had careers. Having lost her husband during World War II, my maternal grandmother made a living for herself and my mother by cleaning the floors of a private school in the German city of Minden. My divorced paternal grandmother, fleeing East Germany before the Berlin Wall transformed westward movement into a death sentence, and subsequently arranging for the escape of first my father and then my aunt, began a new life in the West by renting part of a family's attic and operating a tuberculosis screening van. It was a hazardous occupation that forced her to leave her children unsupervised and that led to years of paralysis resulting from her daily exposure to radiation. But it did provide a minimal living for the time being. My mother was a secretary for a few years before she quit her job to marry and to raise my sister and me. She took up part-time work as an office assistant when her daughters no longer required her full attention. None of these women had fulfilling careers, and it is not surprising to me that they all retired as soon as their financial situation allowed them to. My grandmothers, physically exhausted from a life of hard and, in one case, debilitating labor, greeted their pensions with all the energy they could muster; my mother took pride in her early retirement or, rather, in her ability to benefit from unemployment benefits that seamlessly phased into pension.

Yet it did not take long for any of these women to feel a sense of exclusion and invalidation that was far from enjoyable. Oma Lina, my maternal grandmother, died a lonely woman whose only reason to be was my mother. Oma Irene, my father's mother, had more people in her life; she remarried, and when Onkel Gustel also died, she "took" a boyfriend, our Polish-German Josef, who was ten years her junior and who faithfully cared for her until she died. Yet even this woman's correspondence with me attested to a certain emptiness; the three-pronged anchor of every letter she sent was the cake she was baking, the backgammon games she played, and her weekly visit to the steakhouse. My mother, who bragged about the freedom to travel her re-tirement would bring, does indeed travel a lot; transatlantic visits to me are only part of a busy itinerary that ranges from hikes in the nearby mountains of the Palatinate to fortnight-long tours through Tunisia and Kenya. Still, Mutti seems discontented, saying more and more often that she needs a hobby for when it's rainy out. She is fortunate to belong to the category of "whoopies" (well-off older people), but despite financial security and globe-trotting habits, she herself admits that her postretirement years have a slight taste of "too much time and no world," to use Carolyn G. Heilbrun's phrase.[2] I cannot know the full emotional impact of retirement on the women in my family, but I do know that the postretirement lives they lead/led fail to provide me with a model for how to go about it myself one day, especially since I do have a career and am much more attached to my work than they ever were to theirs.

What I need is a model who speaks to me in detail about the quotidian of later and late life, a woman who has planned to age and who has dealt with the aging throughout her life. I need to look up to someone who has never ceased to grow and who knows the difference between aging and dying. In other words, I need someone who has sought to transform the no-woman's land of retirement into a charted territory, who provides a counterstory, to bor-row Hilde Lindemann Nelson's term, to prevailing conceptions that equate retirement with disengagement and decline.[3] There is probably no single indi-vidual who can give me all I need, but there is one person who has come close. That person is May Sarton.

This is a bit surprising, even to me, as in many ways I have absolutely noth-ing in common with May Sarton. Born in Belgium in 1912, she was the daughter of an intellectual father and an artistic mother, who both challenged and nurtured her talents rather than preparing her for a traditionally female role.[4] Though she had many intimate friends, mostly women but also men, she never married and never had any children. Granted an allowance by her father and later living on income from her books and lecture tours, there was hardly a time when Sarton was a regular wage earner. She did not assume or withdraw from any societally configured preretirement roles. Writing up to her death in 1995, sometimes by dictating her thoughts to a tape recorder, Sarton never retired from anything.

My profile is radically different. Born many decades later, in 1967, I was told early on that rather than going to college, I should "just marry," and whether or not I was under the influence of that advice, I confess that I spent some years indulging in the luxurious, easy passivity that both accompanied and blinded me to my own sexual objectification. Unlike Sarton, I married, albeit at the belated age of thirty; unlike her, I want to have a child; and unlike her, I am a salaried employee, an assistant professor of English scheduled to retire in 2032. Still, Sarton keys me into how I must approach postretirement life. Paradoxically, it is the woman who never retired and who claimed that "The most fatal thing in American life is the arbitrary retirement age" who teaches me how I must retire.[5] In what follows, I want to single out three of the many ways in which May Sarton has provided me with guidance.

Sarton's Engagement with Aging and Aging Individuals throughout Her Life

As Sarton states in a conversation with Janet Todd, "All my best friends were much older and all the people I was in love with."[6] As an adolescent student at Shady Hill School, she worshipped Katharine Taylor, a woman in her thirties who had just become the school's new principal. Sarton made Taylor her first muse, setting the stage for what Taylor referred to as Sarton's obsession with older women.[7] Further lovers and intimate friends included Juliette Huxley, sister-in-law of Aldous and sixteen years older than Sarton, Judith Matlack, fourteen years older and the only person with whom Sarton ever shared a home, and the poet Jean Dominique (Marie Closset), Sarton's senior by thirty-nine years. Signaling her eager willingness to leap across generations, she writes in a letter to "Jean-Do": "Only the question of age has no place here. The soul does not have age. And my soul is not young, nor yours old— they are fresh and eternal."[8] Sarton remained involved in the lives of many of her close friends and lovers and saw them through to old age and death. Tenderly describing her relationship with Jean Dominique, she notes, "I was twenty-six and Jean Dominique was sixty-five. . . . Yet from the first afternoon when I sat for hours on the small hard sofa by the window in her study and we talked of poetry, of ourselves, of everything under the sun, we found together once and for all what was to be an uninterrupted communion until her death. Time did not exist."[9]

Given her personal life, it is not surprising that Sarton's writings from all periods reflect her interest in aging individuals. Some of her earliest volumes of poetry, *The Lion and the Rose* (1948) and *The Land of Silence* (1953), render various responses to aging, responses that evolved and reached their fullest expression in her last volume of poems, *Coming into Eighty* (1994). Although

Sarton was not free from fear of aging and could be ageist herself, her dominant attitude in these poems, perhaps best represented in "Old Lovers at the Ballet" (1980), is positive.[10] In that poem, Sarton's speaker gradually convinces the reader that dismissing old people is nothing short of a total failure of the imagination. The old lovers who watch the ballet from their balcony seats initially feel dismay; "Watching the ardent bodies leap and freeze," they think "how age has changed them and has mocked." Yet before long, "a vision is unlocked," and "Imagination springs the trap of youth." The "old lovers reach new wonders and new answers," realizing that

> . . . in the flesh those dancers cannot spare
> What the old lovers have had time to learn,
> That the soul is a lithe and serene athlete
> That deepens touch upon the darkening air.
> It is not energy but light they burn,
> The radiant powers of the Paraclete.[11]

The speaker moves through stages of envy and regret before the pivotal moment of reconciliation with her and her companion's aging selves occurs. The lovers who thought themselves mocked by youth recognize their "radiant powers," which allow them to feel and appear just as graceful and dignified as the ballet dancers. Indeed, the lovers, old and frail though they may be, seem almost majestic in their elevated position on the theater balcony and their advanced stage of life. By the end of the poem, being "at" the ballet has become far more important and desirable to them than being "in" the ballet.

Sarton's novels express the same interest in aging. She was only forty-three when she published *Faithful Are the Wounds* (1955), a novel that is revolutionary in its almost exclusive concentration on middle-aged and old characters. Notable among them is the political activist Grace Kimlock who, in her seventies, continues to fight for her radically liberal cause and who, as Sarton writes, "was still a passionate person; the source of whatever evils she knew, neuralgia and that fast-beating heart, came from exasperated nerves which she had never bothered to control."[12]

Published a decade later, *Mrs. Stevens Hears the Mermaids Singing* (1965) is a fictionalized autobiography of Sarton's projected older self. The middle-aged Sarton was so interested in exploring the point of view of the old artist that she contrived the astonishing maneuver of first imagining herself to be twenty years older than she actually was and then looking back at her newly extended life and work. She thus anticipated her life review, a process that is normally prompted by the realization of approaching death, and began to raise and integrate unresolved conflicts three decades before she could begin to argue that she was dying.[13]

In her fifty-eighth year, Sarton presented the public with *Kinds of Love* (1970); hardly old enough to receive a foretaste of her own late life, she was here nevertheless able to imagine a story in which the marriage of Christina and Cornelius Chapman reaches fulfillment only when they are past seventy years old. In *A Reckoning* (1978), the sixty-six-year-old Sarton again used characters older than herself to paint a comparative portrait between "Aunt Minna," a vital octogenarian who has experienced only "the slightest diminution of energy" since her eightieth birthday, and her sister Sybille, a faded, senile beauty condemned to spend the remainder of her years in a nursing home.[14]

I do not mean to imply that I can draw directly on the experience of Sarton or her aging personae/characters to plan my retirement. Her case is different because, as she writes, "Day to day life does not change all that much if one is a professional who cannot retire," and because it is probably true that "Growing old is certainly far easier for people like [her] who have no job from which to retire at a given age."[15] And although some of her protagonists begin brand-new careers in midlife, few of these women experience institutional retirement as I presumably will. What I mean to suggest is that Sarton's lifelong attentiveness to aging in her life and in her writings prompts me to develop a similar attentiveness. To be sure, she occasionally idealized age—*Kinds of Love* is a good example—and she sometimes also cast it in the worst possible light, as in the harrowing nursing home tale *As We Are Now* (1973). But most of all, she carefully observed and recorded the experience of aging and, in so doing, persuades me to break free from the narrow dictates of a culture that may have shed a few "male blinders" thanks to the women's movements but that is still a long way from giving up any of its "youth blinders."[16] Inviting me to embrace the prospect of aging with courage and anticipatory joy, Sarton also urges me to confront my escapism, and I think the awareness she raises in me will help when I retire.

Sarton's Belief in Continued Growth

For Sarton, personal growth was never bound to a particular age. Rather than organizing her life around society's idea of steadily moving toward a climax and then withdrawing from all activity, she grew in spurts throughout her life and often saw her own aging as a source of inspiration rather than an impediment to productivity. Indeed, reading her journals, learning there about her daily routines, her iron self-discipline, and her determination to continue to evolve, one begins to regard Sarton as what Barbara G. Myerhoff has referred to as the "professional elder," an individual bringing to old age "the same consciousness, intensity, hard work, high standards, and demands for growth and success" as before.[17] Significantly, it was at age seventy that Sarton proclaimed: "For the first time in my life I have a sense of achievement."[18]

Sarton was never an uncomplicated person; up to the very end, she was involved in numerous struggles whose resolutions, however incomplete, required a willingness to grow. Ranking high among her challenges were her lifelong quest to receive acknowledgment from the literary establishment, her never-ending need for new lover-muses, and her continuous efforts to begin yet another of her many books, each of which constituted "a pilgrimage, a long long walk where faith in the eventual destination ha[d] to be renewed again and again."[19] She was also plagued by tortured negotiations between solitude and the human interaction, both of which she needed to thrive. Such battles resurfaced constantly for her and called for perpetual self-development and renewal. Her life thus resembled a succession of bumpy ups and downs rather than one big hill whose wrong side, the no-woman's land of postretirement life, would trap her in later life.

That Sarton did not see growth as reserved for the young is evidenced in several of her works. Her main argument in the poem "Poet in Residence" (1948) is that art is "the discipline / That fosters growth within [age] and is ever fertile." While young students must understand that "It takes a long time to live what you learn," that "it cannot happen yet," older generations have had "a long time for words to become thought, / For thought, the slow burner, to burn through / Into life where it can scorch the palm of a hand." Only they can begin to grow and experience "the great freedom . . . that comes with this."[20] Sarton's middle-aged and old fictional characters are similarly entitled to growth. In *Crucial Conversations* (1975), the middle-aged Poppy Whitelaw is perhaps the character Sarton invests with the greatest capacity to grow, for it is Poppy who radically transforms herself from homemaker and mother to artist, leaving her unfulfilling marriage ties behind with conviction. Harriet Hatfield's determination to begin a new life and open a women's bookstore at age sixty in *The Education of Harriet Hatfield* (1989) again bespeaks Sarton's ability to imagine activity, change, education, and growth in characters nearing and moving beyond retirement age. It is with honest bewilderment that she asks in *Plant Dreaming Deep* (1968), "Growing old . . . why, in this civilization, do we treat it as a disaster, valuing as we do the woman who 'stays young'? Why 'stay young' when adventure lies in change and growth?"[21]

In tune with the spirit of these questions, Jane Reid, the retired teacher-protagonist of *The Magnificent Spinster* (1985), becomes more involved with people and politics the older she gets:

> For the first time in her life since college Jane had no job, but for that reason her life seemed fuller than ever. Old friends, former students, family, all felt she was there and would welcome a visit, so hardly a day passed without someone "dropping in" and whatever she had been doing had to be laid aside. . . .
>
> And of course all those threads and interests she had held in her hands still pulled her to the Community Center in Cambridge, to New York for the Refugee Association—extremely active as the Russians took over one country after another in the north, Estonia, Latvia; pulled her to Philadelphia to see Lucy and be sure all was well with Russell; pulled her to the island plans for the summer months, not only juggling the calendar to fit everyone in, but going up at least twice a year to arrange about the summer jobs, the opening of houses, the endless things to be attended to: boats, the vegetable garden, the bedding plants for Muff's garden. Added to this was Jane's passionate interest in what was going on in the world.[22]

As she grows older, Jane Reid becomes more and more involved and, at the same time, more and more evolved. She "[comes] into her own" in her midseventies, when she can provide friends and family with the respite of the family island, assuming the role of the "reigning queen of the kingdom her father had founded and her sister had ruled for so long" (295). While she may have to slow down, Jane perceives such an impediment as useful to her self-development: "She didn't walk quite as fast as she used to, but that meant she noticed a lot of things she used to miss" (363). Firmly grounded in the sensual pleasures of the present—the smells, tastes, touches, and sounds of the island—she thrives more than ever before because she can practice "the art of life" (296). Her last years are not a rapid descent down the hill, but "a long, radiant sunset," during which intensive growth is possible (384).

Unlike Poppy Whitelaw, I may not transform into an artist in midlife, and unlike Harriet Hatfield, I am not likely to open a bookstore as I near retirement age. I am also fairly certain I will not own several chalets on an island that I can use to welcome my friends and family, a scenario that, incidentally, does not entirely correspond to the late life of Anne Longfellow Thorp, the person after whom Sarton modeled Jane Reid.[23] Nevertheless, Sarton's ideas give me hope that I, too, can define my own peaks in life, that they will recur periodically, and that they need not coincide with what society would acknowledge as my career peak. Reading Sarton's poems and novels, I get a sense that if the bureaucratically ordained rules of the U.S. economy tell me I cannot be an elder professional, then I can, like Jane Reid and Sarton herself, perhaps become a professional elder.

Sarton's Ability to Distinguish between Aging and Dying

Because Sarton was able to see aging as a time of growth, she could recognize a very clear distinction between aging and dying. In her journal *At Seventy* (1984), she observes, "I suppose I have always believed that one must live as though one were dying—and we all are, of course—because then the priorities become clear" (45). Yet it was precisely this insight that led her to write hundreds of pages about "good" and "safe" aging that have little, if anything, to do with death and much to do with becoming one's true self. As Sarton's journal recorded an overscheduled life in which readings and avalanches of mail begging for replies constantly interfered with her writing, she overcame her feelings of frustration by thinking that "it is only when one is dying . . . that one is allowed to shut life out and concentrate on 'the real connections'" (48). Clearly, she did not, at seventy and many years thereafter, consider herself among the dying, for she bravely responded to as many people's needs as she could, whether or not these individuals constituted "real connections," whether or not she even knew them.

In *At Seventy*, Sarton exclaims that "I love being old" because "I am more myself than I have ever been. There is less conflict. I am happier, more balanced, and . . . better able to use my powers" (10). "Thinking of old age at its most splendid" (62), she feels that "Life is so rich and full these days" (161) and that "It cannot be denied that it is these days a very good life for an old raccoon of seventy" (210). Although she occasionally complained of being tired, Sarton filled her later life with such vitality, intensity, and energy that the difference between aging and dying is thrown into sharp relief. In one of the rare instances that she paid attention to her physical appearance, her ruminations led her to conclude that "one mourns one's young face sometimes," but "A face without lines that shows no mark of what has been lived through in a long life suggests something unlived, empty, behind it" (61). As she contemplated some older photographs of herself, she found that "my face is better now, and I like it better. That is because I am a far more complete and richer person than I was at twenty-five, when ambition and personal conflicts were paramount and there was a surface of sophistication that was not true of the person inside. Now I wear the inside person outside and am more comfortable with my self." What she saw was not the face of a dying woman but the face of a woman who had aged, evolved, and matured.

Having entered "real old age," as she phrased it in her journal *At Eighty-two* (1996),[24] Sarton opened her final collection of poetry *Coming into Eighty* (1994) with a poem, also titled "Coming into Eighty," that realistically traces the loss and fear she experienced in old age. Dealing with breast cancer, a weak heart, the aftermath of a stroke, and severe diverticulitis, Sarton here does seem to see a clear connection between aging and dying. In an extended metaphor that casts her body as a battered ship, "One sail torn, the rudder / Sometimes wobbly," the speaker's physical vulnerability is closely associated with her impending death:

> But we can't stay anchored.
> Soon we must set sail
> On the last mysterious voyage
> Everybody takes
> Toward death.
> Without my ship there,
> Wish me well.[25]

In a journal entry from *At Eighty-two*, Sarton makes even fewer attempts to veil the harsh reality of her advanced age:

> Nancy has MS and George has cancer, in remission now, but last year it was very bad. . . .
> Susan Kenney lost her beloved husband, Ed, eight months ago. For two years her life was given over to taking him back and forth from hospitals and the doctors hoping to find a cure or even at one time a diagnosis. It was a long hell.
> We were all walking wounded. . . .

Nevertheless, her use of the past tense, "We *were* all walking wounded," is indicative of her affirmation of life in old age; however tangible the setbacks and losses became, she never concluded that her life was essentially over, and there was no age at which she accepted that happiness and satisfaction were bygone pleasures. In the same journal entry, she describes herself as "fulfilled" thanks to "life-giving" encounters that give rise to feelings of "bliss."

Sarton attributed much of her late-life happiness to her writing. As she states in *At Seventy*, "If you are a writer or an artist, it is work that fulfills and makes you come into wholeness, and that goes on through a lifetime" (106). Although I plan to remain as committed to literature and literary analysis as I am now, I simply cannot know if I will feel as Sarton did. Yet I do know with some certainty that her careful distinction between aging and its implications on the one hand, and dying and its implications on the other, will be crucial to my happiness. Sarton's differentiation between aging and dying—something she obviously sought to make crystal clear in *A Reckoning*, in which the death of the terminally ill cancer victim, Laura, is portrayed alongside the aging of various family members—challenges me to concentrate on living rather than dying once the cessation of officially recognized and compensated activity is upon me. Her work does not seem to give in until I offer in response a firm postretirement commitment to resist perceiving myself as withering into passivity, insignificance, and death.

It is important to understand that Sarton did not trivialize the disempowerment old age can bring. In a journal entry from *At Eighty-two*, she shows clearly that her late life is about balancing advantages and disadvantages: "A good thing about being eighty-one is that I can say that I do not want to do something and simply not do it instead of feeling I must show I can do it. It no longer matters" (63). Her sense of late-life power is tempered by the resignation in the words "It no longer matters." Her self-admonishment to "Act now to wrest some positive thing out of the chaos" sends a similarly mixed message (23). Indeed, Sarton could get so depressed about her physical decline and her sense that she had somehow missed her professional boat that she sometimes felt the need to express that "the death wish is rather strong" (146). In moments of frustration, she could also be guilty of ageism in the extreme, as when she exclaims in her mid-forties: "I am in a bad low which makes me believe that I am utterly mediocre and might as well settle for lecturing to elderly ladies and children on poetry."[26]

Yet there are countless ways in which I find May Sarton's approach to postretirement age inspiring. Rehearsing late life from the start, embracing and identifying with it long before she entered it, and recognizing its potential and diversity, Sarton cast and recast her own late-life roles and saw no reason for resistance or escape. Aging, for Sarton, did not seem like an exercise in subtraction but, on the contrary, an experience of enrichment and growth, an opportunity to strengthen her commitment to all that she valued. Late in life she writes, "Preparing to die we shed our leaves, without regret, so that the essential person may be alive and well at the end," elaborating, "What I am getting at is that in old age we have greater freedom than ever before to be our true selves. Everything is opening out inside and around us. The walls are dissolving between being and essence, and when they dissolve altogether, when our *selves*, as we have known them, dissolve into death, it will be that we have grown into another dimension."[27] Sarton spent a lifetime invading the no-woman's land of postretirement age, charting its territory, and creating a counterstory that defies the dismissal of postretirement age as well as the very categories of pre- and postretirement. Reflecting on her life, she comments in *At Seventy*, "I have always longed to be old, and that is because all my life I have had such great exemplars of old age" (11). Far from depressed about having studied this writer of later and late life, I am glad to have found my own exemplar in her.

Notes

1. Betty Friedan, *The Fountain of Age* (New York: Simon and Schuster, 1993), 222.

2. Carolyn G. Heilbrun, *The Last Gift of Time: Life beyond Sixty* (New York: Ballantine Books, 1997), 45.

3. Hilde Lindemann Nelson, "Stories of My Old Age," in *Mother Time: Women, Aging, and Ethics*, ed. Margaret Urban Walker (Lanham, Md.: Rowan and Littlefield, 1999), 77.

4. That this was not consistently the case is evidenced by the following description Sarton gives: "my father's criticism was erratic, irrational, came from my disappointing *him* in some way. ('Why don't you marry?' he shouted at me when I was twenty-seven or twenty-eight and in the middle of a devastating love for a woman. . . .)" See Sarton, *House by the Sea: A Journal* (New York: W. W. Norton, 1977), 272.

5. Sarton, interview by Barbara Bannon, in *Conversations with May Sarton*, ed. Earl G. Ingersoll (Jackson: University Press of Mississippi, 1991), 17.

6. Janet Todd, "May Sarton," in *Women Writers Talking*, ed. Janet Todd (New York: Holmes and Meier, 1983), 13.

7. Margot Peters, *May Sarton: A Biography* (New York: Ballantine Books, 1997), 49.

8. Quoted in ibid., 99.

9. May Sarton, *A World of Light: Portraits and Celebrations* (New York: W. W. Norton, 1976), 241.

10. All dates of individual poems refer to the publication dates of the volumes in which they were originally collected.

11. May Sarton, *Collected Poems: 1930–1993* (New York: W. W. Norton, 1993), 447.

12. Ibid., *Faithful Are the Wounds* (New York: W. W. Norton, 1955), 44.

13. The term *life review* was coined by Robert Butler in his seminal essay "The Life Review: An Interpretation of Reminiscence in the Aged," *Psychiatry* 26 (February 1963): 65–76.

14. May Sarton, *A Reckoning* (New York: W. W. Norton, 1978), 17.

15. May Sarton, "Toward Another Dimension . . . ," in *The Other Within Us: Feminist Explorations of Women and Aging*, ed. Marilyn Pearsall (Boulder, Colo.: Westview Press, 1997), 230; *House by the Sea*, 27.

16. Friedan's terms, *The Fountain of Age*, 154.

17. Barbara G. Myerhoff, "A Symbol Perfected in Death: Continuity and Ritual in the Life and Death of an Elderly Jew," in *Life's Career—Aging: Cultural Variations on Growing Old*, ed. Barbara G. Myerhoff and Andrei Simic (Beverly Hills, Calif.: Sage Publications, 1978), 171. Myerhoff discusses the case of Jacob Kovitz, but many of her observations can be applied to Sarton.

18. May Sarton, "The Art of Poetry XXXII: May Sarton," interview by Karen Saum, in Ingersoll, *Conversations with May Sarton*, 123.

19. May Sarton, *At Seventy: A Journal* (New York: W. W. Norton, 1984), 226. All subsequent page references to this journal appear in the text.

20. Sarton, *Collected Poems*, 69–70. It is worth noting that Sarton was only in her early thirties when she took the position of poet in residence at Southern Illinois State University, and she no doubt projected some of her own insecurities about her age onto her students. Nevertheless, the poem clearly testifies to the correlation between aging and creativity she insists on throughout her career.

21. May Sarton, *Plant Dreaming Deep* (New York: W. W. Norton, 1968), 179–180.

22. May Sarton, *The Magnificent Spinster* (New York: W. W. Norton, 1985), 260–261. All subsequent page references to this novel appear in the text.

23. In *House by the Sea* (254–255), Sarton gives a more balanced account of the old age of the real Anne Thorp. There, Sarton still sees reasons to celebrate old age, but she is more careful to account for the vulnerability and disabilities of the elderly.

24. May Sarton, *At Eighty-two: A Journal* (New York: W. W. Norton, 1996), 15. All subsequent page references to this journal appear in the text.

25. May Sarton, *Coming into Eighty: New Poems* (New York: W. W. Norton, 1994), 15–16.

26. Quoted in Peters, *May Sarton: A Biography*, 216.

27. Sarton, "Toward Another Dimension . . . ," 230, 231.

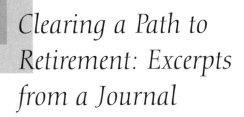

Clearing a Path to Retirement: Excerpts from a Journal

DONNA HILLEBOE DEMUTH

*T*he new millennium had just begun. My husband and I were settled in a condo on the west coast of Florida, as I took a three-month leave of absence from my clinical work. I was beginning to think about ending my thirty-four-year career as a family therapist, teacher, and consultant.

I was seventy-two years old and still felt like a young woman. In the past year, my husband and I had celebrated our fiftieth wedding anniversary, and there had been many losses: several of our longtime friends, my sister-in-law, and our beloved golden retriever. Our kids and grandkids seemed well settled into their lives. I had become weary of the long commute to my office and of the constrictions of the clinical hour. I was fed up with the arduous winters in Maine, where we lived, and my physical limitations in dealing with them. It was clearly time for me to move on.

For some time I had been itching with ideas that had spilled over from my work. Unedited papers crammed my files, luring me at the same time as they pushed me away. For almost five years, I had been absolutely unable to move any of my thoughts onto the white, fine-lined paper that I use for first drafts. Still, I had a vague notion of leaving some kind of a legacy of my life and work and a faint hope that writing might bring a sense of direction for my new life after retirement.

I needed a fresh start. So, I changed my audience. No longer would I write for a Reader, but simply for myself. I created a daily (well, almost daily) routine, putting down whatever words came to me at that moment, not censoring for grammar or organization. How wonderful it was to be free from the constrictions of academic/professional disciplines! I became an addict. The pen developed a life of its own. Ideas and feelings poured out, and I found, to my surprise, that writing freely, without structure, could bring clarity.

As it turned out, the work is not a journal, nor a traditional memoir, and not a professional paper, although it certainly has elements of each. Over time, I began to see a pattern emerging in the seemingly random musings, as if I had been making a scrap-bag quilt with a free-form design.

As in a quilt, some patterns, some colors kept reappearing. Unsettled themes from my life and work emerged, especially those of failures with clients and of relationships between the psychological world and its social context. I needed to face, yet again, the images of darkness that I had been working with as a therapist and nuclear activist, in order to lay them to rest. At the same time, I needed to reconnect with the feelings of strength and hope I had gained from this work, as well as from the legacy of my family. I needed to draw from the beautiful settings in which I lived, constantly reminding me of the resilience of the natural world. I needed all this in order to move on.

No wonder I had been frozen! My work had been arduous; I had been too drained to look at the meaning of the long affair. Until I started writing, I didn't know that my task was to look for meaning. I didn't know how painful . . . and ultimately how freeing . . . it would be to let the unresolved feelings surface.

As I wrote, I drew from my courses at a senior learning center and from my knowledge of systems theory. I drew from my therapeutic discipline and from my practice of Yoga and learned to stay quiet with my thoughts. The New Age cliché "live in the moment" became my mantra. I had to unlearn seventy-two years of rushing toward a goal, toward achieving a reward.

I trivialize as I sum up. I have returned to my stuffy, more distant, academic style.

A rigid frame no longer fits. Let me try again.

Simply, I recorded the story of my reflections during the year before I retired. I came up with no formula for an effortless journey. Indeed, the effort, the struggle itself became the way for me to make the transition. I found no firm answers, only a few precious moments of clarity, which, themselves, came effortlessly.

In essence, I was, without conscious intent, writing my way into letting go of my life as a professional woman and embarking on whatever was to happen next.

01–15–00

So I begin. I commit to writing for a short time each morning after breakfast. No agenda, no goal, just seeing what emerges. Keeping my soul alive, nourishing myself . . . mmmmmmm.

The writing itself is only one part of the experience, but very symbolic and very concrete. I will close the door to the study; I will not answer the phone, I will negotiate silence with my husband.

01–22–00

Writing is becoming the stuff of my life.

I am happy in Florida: weather, family, friends, leisure, and my husband's cheerfulness. I will have to face letting go of my practice at the end of this year, but I feel no angst, at least for now. I have a new life.

At a time when my body shows more obvious signs of fading away, when the Threat looms right up in front of me since my friend Carol's death, it is a miracle to feel my mind flexing and stretching and growing, to feel agile and young. My path now is to be a learner.

I am aware of how short and precious is a life, how quickly it can end. . . . I am truly ready to "be here now" whatever "now" may bring.

That's enough. I can now return to the mundane, which also brings me great pleasure.

02–02–00

I fight the nagging push to make this writing more purposeful, more "valuable." There is too much pain in this world. Could my professional voice be of some use? Writing in itself is a self-centered luxury. In time might it soothe my social conscience if something of value comes out of this luscious self-indulgence? I will give it time. Even at this stage of my life, there's no point in forcing the blooms.

In my younger days, I was always falling in love with a project—either professional or political. So, what stops me from starting a new project now? I am suddenly aware of leftover feelings; the weak responses to the nuclear psychology work, the negative responses to the work in divorce "prevention"; my old role as a maverick, an outsider. I may not be brave enough to take on more apathy and/or opposition.

More to the point, I am not brave enough to work on my own. Aha! Here comes the pain. I have lost the groups that supported me in the other work I have done. I have no energy to start again, to invent, to connect, and then to lose.

I really didn't know until this moment how deep the loss has been.

I guess I need to keep my heart open for a place to attach to this new life, minus kids, mortgage, and job. And, of course, I need to keep writing.

02–04–00

I am preoccupied with the presence of evil, with Günter Grass's Black Witch, as I study *The Tin Drum* for a course at a senior learning center.[1] How can I face the darkness left over from my work without either running away or being drowned in it? How do I avoid becoming so overwhelmed that I lose the capacity for action?

I am haunted by memories of the deep rage felt by some of my former clients—a man who had beaten his wife, one who had sexually abused his daughter, a 300-pound woman diagnosed as a paranoid schizophrenic who threatened me with a butcher knife, a four-year-old "dropout" from Head Start. I see these faces, feel their presence and our eternal connection. And I remember my feelings of impotence to help them change their lives. I need to write about them, as a way of cleansing my soul. I need to face my "failures" with them, my terror of their rage, my struggle to keep contact with them anyway.

And I need to write about how they were influenced by their social environments and by the influence of cultural values—violence, gender, power—upon them. And about how tiny my compassion and skill seemed in comparison.

I have always been geared to "Doing Something" about evil: child protective work, early childhood intervention, work with troubled teenagers, divorce, adults coming to terms with childhood abuse. My work has taught me how to stay still and centered and to use all my resources and, especially in the nuclear work, to live through the terror and not become numb. My work has also taught me, a hard lesson, not to rely on outcome.

When I give up my role as therapist, will I also give up the most powerful weapon I have against the Black Witch? I fear the loss of power and credibility. If I find a way to take action, will I have to learn how to base it in myself, not just in my professional armor? Another women's issue! Who am I if I am "only a housewife" (with a condo in Florida and a lake house in Maine)?

3–23–00

I have again made my life too complicated. I need to eject visitors so that I can pack to return home, I need to cancel plans to go to San Francisco as a side trip from Los Angeles and Phoenix. My lifelong habit of crowding too much into a short frame dies very hard.

Interesting words . . . the metaphor, part of the puzzle . . . time is running out.

The body; hearing aids, aching arms and back, weight that doesn't come off despite my higher activity level and my feeble attempts at controlling my intake of food. (God, I love butter!)

It's still hard for me to get in and out of a boat, despite nine months of training with weights. (Intermittent to be sure.) I keep trying . . . and don't get anywhere. Not trying hard enough? Trying the wrong things, the wrong way. And then there is my troubled breathing; I'm pumping myself full of expensive steroids, which wreck my skin, so that I can no longer enjoy the sun. . . .

What would happen if I just gave up? How tempting! And let my lungs clog up, my muscles get flabby, become grossly fat. It takes so much hard work now just to stay alive and moving! And I don't even have a major illness.

Oh, how nice it would be just to lie around eating and drinking and rotting away.

Ugh. This part of the struggle oddly becomes harder when I have so much leisure time.

05–28–00

I have returned to my "real" life in Maine. Here I sit, another glorious morning. I am delighting in the moment, soaking up the sun, the feel of the slightly cool air.

I notice that the branch cut off by last winter's ice storm still hangs suspended from the huge oak tree in front of our house. The severed branch is so hidden by the life around it that I must strain to notice it. I am constantly aware of both the fragility and the resilience of the natural world.

Suddenly I remember, with a rush of feeling, the destruction we created in 1987, when we remodeled our cottage into a year-round home . . . and the miracle of its restoration. In April, when the bulldozers excavated a new foundation, they dumped tons of fill onto the once-green forest floor. I was knee deep in mud from the melting snow and the continual rain, mud that could easily slide down the unprotected hill into our pristine lake.

So miracles happened. The rain stopped, the sun shone. The sturdy Maine granite underneath the mud held the hill. The house began to take shape, and it was beautiful.

But best of all, I found a nineteen-year-old magician and artist, almost illiterate, and the father of two babies, to help me rebuild the hill. It did not slide into the lake and, by now, is beautiful again.

I need to remember, as I start to rebuild my personal life, that nature IS dependable and resilient IF we have enough love and enough energy to do the hard work. We also need vision . . . and faith . . . and community . . . and a bit of luck.

06–08–00

And, of course, it slips out again . . . awareness of mortality. The spots on my arms, the fatigue and ache in my legs after I weed, my hearing loss, my struggle to grasp the computer.

So long to Donna the invincible, the ever-youthful woman of a certain age . . . welcome to Donna who just begins to know that she is deteriorating, is dying. It is scary to write that. Also confusing and depressing.

All of the ideal media images of successful older women show them living life as they did when they were younger . . . never needing naps, not getting fat or lazy, triumphing by sheer grit over the failings of their bodies. Bullshit! I can't do that.

I must go into the murk of this, over and over again. I can't abide becoming an incompetent old woman! There, I said it. No one but me knows how tempting it can be just to be a slug. Tempting, even as I fear it.

I feel a pull to address the enormous suffering of the world . . . at the same time, I am drawn to the quiet pleasures of my house and garden. I feel real passion about the sound of the lake lapping against the metal boat . . . the sound and texture of the breeze. I could simply stay here, and not move.

Even though I know that not moving means, for me, paralysis and death.

Will I have enough time to read all my books, travel to Rome, Japan, Greece, Czechoslovakia, and Ireland, and return to Scotland, Norway, Tuscany? Will I have time to make my quilts and knit my sweaters? And (oh, God, what a pang this brings), will there be enough time for me to write whatever it is I need to say to the world?

If I believed in praying for specific events, I would pray . . . to *want* to write seriously again, to have enough energy for the tedium, enough passion to get going, enough commitment to finish. The spiritual teachers can help.

They say . . . just stay there in the longing and then let go. So I will do just that.

07–20–00

I HAVE to write this, interrupt my attempt at a nap, ignore my bulging bladder, and put off the swim that will cool me. . . .

I AM LEARNING TO LOVE THE LIFE OF A DILETTANTE! Actually, I ADORE IT!

I am sitting on the deck. It is the first definitively sunny day in weeks. I am reading a lovely book sent by a lovely friend . . . *I Know Just What You Mean* by Ellen Goodman and Patricia O'Brien.[2]

I am remembering stories of my own friendships and feeling the delight in being connected to my sister and to my women friends.

And I love the beautiful place where I live, and I love Maine in the summer. I love how my day has gone, eating breakfast on the porch, interviewing another young magician to help me in the garden, having coffee with my nephew and his bride.

What else goes in my litany of thanks? I loved my clients of yesterday, making adventurous leaps into new territory. . . . I loved shopping at the Italian grocery, making careful plans for tomorrow's dinner; shopping quickly at TJ Maxx and finding the perfect Tencel skirt for our Greek trip for only $12.98. . . . I loved finding out that the man at the old-fashioned dry cleaners remembered my name and promised to clean up my ancient Mexican tunic as best he could. . . . I love the fact that the trunk in which that tunic was hidden for ten years is beginning to smell okay again after a dowsing with Clorox and sunshine. I love having a few good housekeeping skills, many of them inherited from my mother.

And I love reconnecting with my husband, both of us shaken by the sudden death of yet another lifelong friend.

I am doing it! Actually savoring every moment. Yummmmmm . . .

7–29–00

It is finally time for me to take the chance of writing about the work that consumed me for fifteen years, exploring the ways in which families cope with the threat of global annihilation. It is time for me to let go of unfinished business from that work.

So why am I haunted on this perfect summer day? Because the work is unfinished. Oh yes, for those years I gave it all of my heart and my mind and my younger energy. Oh yes, with a team of dedicated volunteers, I studied Maine families' responses to nuclear threats and ultimately published the results.[3] Indeed, I wrote chapters and co-edited a book, *The Global Family Therapist*, looking at the perils for families in this perilous age.[4] And yes, I did give endless talks, to parents in churches and schools, and to professionals in stuffy conference rooms, helping them look at ways to use family strengths to counter children's fears of global disaster.

I did all those things, and more, but . . .

I NEVER FOLLOWED UP ON OUR STUDIES. I never wrote the popular version which could have further reassured parents that talking with children about their fears might not be harmful after all. I never brought the work up to date with recent findings on children's responses to environmental threats.

And . . . I am troubled by the possibility that all that hard work was to no avail. Our results were not strong, our study was too small, our instruments imprecise. The world is still under major threat of self-destruction. Families still do not talk about their fears.

Stop!!! There is really no point in measuring results. I am happy that we did the work. If nothing else, it eased some of my helpless feelings. And, as it is with this journal, the gain came from the doing. A few brave and creative souls learned that we could face the Black Witch head on, and we were stronger for that.

Of course, it is now clear that we were a small part of a much bigger movement that brought the realities of the nuclear world to its other frightened, paralyzed citizens . . . and may have helped to slow down, at least temporarily, the rush to nuclear disaster.

Maybe.

08–11–00

A report.

My husband and I have come together to talk with our son, our daughters, and their partners about our dying.

Very matter-of-factly, I begin by telling the specifics of our wills. I say that I would not want to live unless I could be conscious and mentally competent, at least as much as ever. Laughter. Don is not quite so clear, leaving it up to the kids to decide what to do as he deteriorates.

We agree that they could work out the distribution of our belongings as they wish; we know them to be responsible. A classic response; "Oh, Mother! Don't worry about THAT."

Jodi asks for Don's blue Polartec shirt, Barb has already put in a bid for the red Fiestaware pitcher we use for making iced tea. Some debate follows, but, as the eldest, she is practiced in getting her siblings to give in. Mike thinks it is ugly, anyway.

Next, we talk about funerals. Don and I agree. We each want a memorial service open to the community. We will each be cremated. Family and close friends will scatter our ashes next to those of our beloved dogs, Jake, Sugar, and Casey, on the hill between the big house and the lake.

Jodi presses on, so like her! She asks what we have thought about the time between now, when we are relatively vigorous and healthy, and when we begin to fail.

"You'll have a hard time with me when I have to give up driving," says my husband.

I add, the first tears coming, "I hope you could find a way to bring me out here in the summer, even if I am too weak to be here on my own."

Barb has already thought this one out. She volunteers to drive me down to the boat ramp, put me into a wheelchair, push me into the water, and pull me out again after my swim.

The thought of a ski tow, however, is not altogether ruled out.

Everyone realizes that Don will be an ideal candidate for a nursing home. On the other hand, it is clear to all that I will be a disaster in congregate living.

So we move into a noisy group discussion about the choices for my care if I refuse to go into "The Home." The three non-nurses choose the two nurses as the most suitable candidates, of course. Point by point they debate. But the workings of the system are reliable. The sisters join in coalition against their younger brother. They work on details . . . changing diapers, mushing up the food, handling dementia. . . . It is arranged.

The grandchildren, quiet for so long, race from their sanctuary. We are finished. For now.

Sixteen years ago I wrote of my fear of dying alone. Last month I wrote that I would never be alone in the universe.

Today I know that the imperfect love we have for one another will last, in whatever form it will take, as long as I need it.

11–07–00

By 9 A.M. the sun is already behind the trees. A time for depression, illness, retreat. I like December when it gets *really* dark, solstice time . . . but the in-between sucks.

So many losses: the election, my friends, my young body. I am facing these;

I am grieving them. But believe it or not, I do NOT grieve for the ending of my practice, soon to come. It is time to let go of that part of my life, just a matter of slogging away, one step at a time, hoping I have enough energy to sustain me until the end.

(Now the sun is streaming into the living room. How corny!)

11–11–00

I am not temperamentally suited for old age.

All my life I've hurried, eagerly pushing on, disregarding the moment in order to reach a goal. Some of this came from excitement and passion, some from anxiety, but most of it from my very own temperament. I could serve a dinner for my family of six after coming in from work at 5 P.M., talk on the phone for an hour, listen to my husband and children, never missing a beat.

Sure, I took naps and slept late sometimes on weekends when Don made breakfast. . . . We always took vacations, both short and long.

But I was busy, busy, busy; moving fast, fast, fast.

Now I find, of course, that such a pace not only leaves me worn out, but also leaves a trail of big and small mistakes in its wake. I lose my glasses and my Visa card, forget to call a client, and literally fall on my face, stumbling over some unnoticed object.

I hate it. I miss that boundless energy. I feel stupid at the end of a day when I have accomplished "so little." I struggle to maintain my focus on enjoying the moment, on being quiet and observant, on simply noticing.

Yet, there are a few times when I can actually enjoy slowing down! Yes, I admit it. There was always a dreamer, an indolent soul waiting to emerge from behind all that energy. Welcome, old slob! You have been long awaited, even as you have been feared and resisted.

So, the year comes to an end. I am packing for Florida as I take out the Christmas decorations for our family celebration. Still busy, busy, busy—my daughters have offered me full-time work as a mother's helper, but I have refused. The slowing down, though strange, is welcome.

12-14-00

And, I am free! The last struggles with clients are over. I think I am breaking away from them, but my ambivalence shows up in my mistakes. I try too hard to resolve issues that I know to be intractable. I "forget" to mention that my January retreat to the south will be permanent. I change my mind about the actual dates of my leaving. I back away before I need to.

I have made many other mistakes. (This is not self-deprecating, Donna, it is honest.) And I have had to pick myself up and redo. Like living. Like dying. In hopes of tempering my errors, I do leave my clients with great tenderness and appreciation. I even suspect that some of our work together will prove to have been valuable. (I have learned painfully that it is wise to be humble on that topic.) I feel incredibly blessed to have had work which I have loved, most of the time . . . and for which, some of the time, I have been gifted. I am blessed that my clients, once they learned to trust me, have been infinitely loveable.

I am blessed to have had work that has enlarged *me*, forced me to grow, which has tapped the healthiest part of me. I pray now that it will have some lessons for the rest of my life . . . the real laboratory.

And my clients are letting go. Sam and Sandra (the intractable ones) give me a gorgeous piece of jewelry, the Tree of Life, out of their modest incomes. Susan, almost at the last moment, conquers her terror of being without therapy for the first time in twenty years. She will walk out the door of my office, ahead of me, into her new life as an independent and confident woman, and into our new relationship as colleagues. Mary, who doesn't cry easily, tears up and touches my hand as I tell her, finally, that I too have struggled with the life-threatening illness of a daughter. Larry asks *me* to say the prayer at our ritual of ending . . . actually, he seems a bit embarrassed by my New Age meditation . . . and then takes me for a symbolic ride in his new Jeep, the macho man. Fourteen-year-old Caterina tells her younger sister about the causes of her depression and talks about what helped her to get over it. Then she looks at me with deep, dark eyes and says, "I will never forget you." (Nor I you, dear young friend.) Hugs from Harold and Stephen, awkward, testosterone-driven guys who let me help them talk to their loving but uncertain parents as they wiggle and move around and burp and tease one another. . . .

Tears fill my eyes. How lucky I am!

And, even luckier to be free! Not really free of the clients, of course, they are all inside my heart, but free of the logistics, sitting in an office meant to be used by dear lawyer friend, looking out at an ugly parking lot, keeping track of each hour, driving fifty miles in the early morning or late afternoon, in the cold and dark, schlepping my multitudinous bags and papers, hurrying, hurrying, hurrying.

And there is so much which lies ahead . . . more courses, more writing, and Florida sunshine, lazy summers at the lake, Colorado, France, Ireland, Japan, long visits with my friends and family. So much joy, so much ease.

Whatever happens.

01–04–01

Charlottesville, Virginia.

I *am* beginning a new life, sitting here during this time between journeys, overlooking the brown fields and the truly blue mountains, safe in my decompression tank as I come up to a different level of pressure. Like the divers, my body must get used to it slowly. Here I am protected by dear friends, nurtured, not needing even to clear the table. It feels a bit odd, but right.

Today was a joyful rite of transition . . . I scoured the used-book stores for paperbacks for the courses I will take in Florida . . . How freeing not to be *teaching*, to be learning *literature* instead of social science and psychotherapy! I picked up novels and mysteries, of course, to ease my journey . . . and I had time to sip a cappuccino, to sit in a café with other students, taking in the scene, as they say.

My friend Doris asks, "What will you do with the sadness?"

I actually don't feel it at the moment. I am too full of cappuccino and good books and good company. I am energized by a walk in these lovely, wintry open spaces, warmed from a bath. I felt a little sadness on the bus yesterday, and I expect it to reappear. After all, I have felt the loss, not only of my cherished way of being in the world, but of four longtime friends.

The tears come now, naturally. They are soft on my cheeks, they belong to me. And today they coexist with the quiet joy of my refuge. It's okay. The sadness is simply there, tears and joy together, and some kind of peace. I do notice. I am alive.

And tomorrow I will get on a plane and be able to greet my pine forest in Florida. (And my husband.)

So it ends, so it begins.

Afterward
08–08–01

Seven months later. The Reader may be curious to know—did it work? Did the writing really help to prepare me for retirement?

Well, of course it did—primarily by pulling together some themes from my life, which needed either to be put to rest or to be affirmed. I also gained from venting some of my worst fears and complaints, putting them in perspective.

But, like the rest of my life's work, the writing did not solve everything. (Surprise!) I am still (and forever) learning how to live in the moment, and to keep focusing on what I can realistically accomplish. I have learned to slow down, but I have not yet found a way to contribute to the painfully troubled world without resuming my old habits of over-functioning. I have not taken the job as nanny, though I have loved having more time to spend with my children and grandchildren.

Reworking our marriage on these new terms is still a challenge — but our marriage has always been a challenge, a long-enduring one. I wrote a great deal about our relationship in the journals, but omitted those sections for the Reader, in honor of a proud and very private man. I hope to find a way to write more about my professional work with marriage and divorce so that it reflects my personal experiences, as well.

In fact, those unedited papers resting in my files begin to call me again, as does the cool, clear water of the lake and my shady corner of the deck, a perfect place to read and reflect. As do my friends and family, and hanging out the wash, and making jam from my raspberries, and tending the garden, and reading murder mysteries.

I think these pulls will not change with retirement. But they don't press on me now; I have time, no matter how much is left to me, to make the choices.

Acknowledgments

This chapter will not be complete unless I express my gratitude to my longtime friend Carol Burdick for her support, inspiration, and ruthless editing.

Notes

1. Günter Grass, *The Tin Drum*, in *The Danzig Trilogy*, trans. R. Manheim, (New York: Harcourt, 1987).

2. Ellen Goodman and Patricia O'Brien, *I Know Just What You Mean: The Power of Friendships in Women's Lives* (New York: Simon and Schuster, 2000).

3. Donna Hilleboe DeMuth and Joseph Melnick, "What Happens When They Talk about It? Family Reactions to Nuclear War," *Peace and Conflict: Journal of Peace Psychology* 4, no. 1 (1998): 23–34; Donna Hilleboe DeMuth, "The Family Interviewing Project: A Group of Clinicians Looks at Family Reactions to the Threat of Nuclear War," in Berger-Gould and DeMuth.

4. Benina Berger-Gould and Donna Hilleboe DeMuth, eds., *The Global Family Therapist: Integrating the Personal, Professional, and Political* (Boston: Allyn and Bacon, 1994); Donna Hilleboe DeMuth, "Some Implications of the Threat of Nuclear War for Families and Family Therapists," in *The Social and Political Contexts of Family Therapy*, ed. M. P. Mirkin (Boston: Allyn and Bacon, 1990).

Retiring into Intensity, Experiencing "Deep Play"

BARBARA FREY WAXMAN

I want to live in the instant, the very center of the moment." These words are by poet and novelist May Sarton, from her journal *After the Stroke*, written when the author was over seventy. An entry in another of her journals, *At Seventy*, asserts that to live intensely in the moment is to transcend time, to bathe in "eternity's light."[1] Sarton's words have become my shibboleth since I first came upon them in the 1980s. They express an attitude and a goal I want to pursue when I retire from professing English at the University of North Carolina–Wilmington. I am fifty-four years old and I see this next decade of my life as a rehearsal for retirement, a time to cultivate the habit of living more in the present, with intentionality and passion. Rejecting our culture's widespread assumption that later life is a stage of passivity, decline, and increasing isolation, Sarton's words awaken in me the desire to intensify or spiritualize time and experience, to energize interactions between me and others and between me and nature. They also urge me to observe and reflect more when in solitude. The further along I journey into later life, the more time becomes a precious commodity and the more ways I seek to number my days, to make each one count.

Sarton's journals and other writings have led me into an intensive study of what in her novel *As We Are Now* she calls "the foreign country of old age," as depicted in a host of fiction and nonfiction published during the last quarter of the twentieth century.[2] I have joined such literary gerontologists as Kathleen Woodward, Anne M. Wyatt-Brown, and Margaret Morganroth Gullette in developing the scholarly field of literary gerontology, where we analyze literary works about old age and the elderly and consider how these works prompt readers to reimagine and live out old age with intensity. This scholarly work has shaped the course of my professional life, to be sure, but what have Sarton's words come to mean to me personally? What have the works of others writing about later life taught me about how I want to "perform" my retirement or narrate its "plot"? What have older friends and relatives shown me about the search for intensity? Indeed, must I constantly seek impassioned moments? Perhaps I will tire of so much intensity—if I am fortunate enough to live much beyond age sixty-five, my target retirement age. Maybe I will prefer to assume a Golden Pond detachment from life in old age (not likely). Or to seek some middle ground between intensity and dissociation.

Lately I have been trying to imagine this middle ground in my future. Perhaps for retirement it is to be found if I reflect upon what my life's work has meant to me, especially the intoxication I often feel when I teach a class of animated students or write an essay that prompts others to think about my ideas; from both kinds of work come an effervescent and wonderful "I-Thou" relationship. If I can pursue similar activities in retirement that foster these relationships and continue to produce intoxication, I think that I will be content. In this respect I subscribe to the gerontological concept of continuity theory, that is, that later life is simply a continuation of one's life course, not distinct from midlife. My life's work has not, to me, been mundane, but has offered many moments—crystalline, transcendent ones—of intellectual and emotional stimulation, intense contact with others, accompanied at times by the sense of causing a breakthrough in people's lives or of prompting in them an important epiphany. Hence, I don't have a yearning to retire in any abrupt sense from this work. And because my field involves teaching and scholarly writing, I have the luxury of being able to pursue these activities, even after I relinquish formal ties to a university. There are many volunteer settings in which I could offer my teaching skills. And the possibilities for more writing projects seem to be expanding as retirement nears. Several academic colleagues have shared with me their plans to continue writing after retirement from the university; they confide that they think there is still "another scholarly book in them," or that they wish to try their hand at other, less scholarly, forms of writing, such as personal essays or memoirs. I don't imagine myself writing the great American novel, but I would like to experiment with essays, poetry, and autobiography. It would be wonderful to contribute to these literary forms, which I have read, taught, analyzed, and admired over the past thirty years.

Yet having a satisfying later life may involve other things besides simply continuing my work in new venues. Work can go hand in hand with play. I want to seize the opportunity to get more fun out of life through play, play of a particularly absorbing and satisfying kind that elders may be peculiarly qualified to pursue. Sara Ruddick in her essay "Virtues and Age" examines what she considers typical elders' outstanding virtues, including curiosity, a capacity for joy in living, and the ability "to resist regret."[3] These virtues open them up to the intensity that Diane Ackerman has called "deep play," a concept developed in her recent book of the same name.[4] Deep play may be even more salutary and promising for retirees than ordinary play.

As Johan Huizinga observes in his seminal work on play in culture, *Homo Ludens*, play serves important biological and cultural purposes in human society. It is a completely absorbing behavior that allows us to step "out of 'real' life into a temporary sphere of activity . . . [located] outside the immediate satisfaction of wants and appetites" and that creates a temporary but perfect space of order.[5] For example, even though I am no Serena Williams, I am a tennis player. I love the unambiguous, perfect structure of a tennis court, the clear rules of play and fast motion of the ball; I am challenged to perform backhand strokes or overheads, to get my serves in the right place in my opponent's service box, to meet my opponent's challenging returns, and to make the right choices from the overall menu of winning strategies. When I am immersed in the flow of a match, my mental and physical skills are honed and keenly focused. Win or lose, I emerge from this play a rejuvenated person. At any age, play may be a significant pathway to good health and happiness. But I don't think I could spend my retirement just playing tennis. Being a tennis bum may not be the kind of play that enables me to move "out of common reality into a higher order."[6] I wish to seek that exalted form of play, deep play, in which one's perspective widens and becomes more complex, where trivial distractions are exchanged for a fuller and more spiritual experiencing of life.

Deep play, according to Ackerman, is an ecstatic state of intense meditation and absorption either in one's surroundings or in a space that transcends time and self, a state of higher consciousness where the individual encounters some risks, physical and emotional challenges, as he or she travels "into a zone of ambiguity" (73). The deep player can make contact with the sacred or transcendent hidden in the ordinary things of daily life, particularly in the world of nature. Such contact can cleanse or heal us, perhaps by triggering endorphins in us as we listen to the quietness of a starlit night or inhale the fragrance of salt air at the ocean's edge: "We drink briefly from [nature's] miracle waters. We inoculate ourselves against the aridity of a routine, workaday life" (156). And there are other resources for deep play besides nature. I have a friend Paul, a writer, teacher, and family man, who periodically takes up residence in a monastery to move beyond mundane, familiar existence, to slow down and expand his existence. I like his way of breaking the monotony of life's routines. And I want to discover my own ways, perhaps through yoga, bird watching, or the creation of my own retreat for solitude.

Such options seem more appealing and more available to me as I travel toward retirement. Purified and inoculated, shielded in retirement from the harassment of work's relentless demands, the older deep player can let slip the self and contemplate the universe, perhaps more freely than the person fully enmeshed in the work world. With nature or solitude (or both) as catalyst, the deep player's creative imagination is freed, fed, and intensified. While a natural setting or a monastery may trigger deep play, the mentally absorbed player normally moves beyond the initiatory setting. Detachment from self and surroundings is a typical effect of deep play. This detachment may be a pathway to a wider perspective and greater wisdom in elders.

Although she does not reflect much on deep play in relation to later life, Ackerman does observe that as people grow older, deep play often shifts from the physical to the mental, to "the high plateau . . . where one feels the rapture of witnessing and appreciating" (207). While exotic, intense experiences such as mountain climbing or trekking in Antarctica may energize the imagination of the more physically fit and extend the edges of the known and knowable, they do not appeal to this warmth-loving acrophobe. I have undertaken some exhilarating physical activities, such as whitewater rafting in Colorado—but I was a youthful forty then and I do not wish to repeat the experience now or in my sixties! I worry about brittle bones and a less reliable sense of balance. Other mental activities are readily available to the less fit and to older deep players, in the world of nature, the arena of religious meditation, and the realm of poetry and wordplay. Ackerman observes, "To reach deep play sometimes means tackling activities more complex than one encounters in everyday life (such as chess), or simpler than one usually encounters (such as sitting still and watching every movement of a deer)" (118). I have found deep play in the complex activity of writing; playing with words and with ideas as they intersect with other ideas is a focused, all-absorbing intellectual and emotional challenge. The simple activities of examining patterns of shells in a small space at the shore or observing the movements of birds in a mountain forest are other kinds of deep play for me. And I think about my friend Sylvia, a retired sociologist, who is often mentally absorbed in the simple activity of nurturing the flowers in her garden: planting, arranging, watering, weeding—and witnessing signs of growth. Such simple mental play is a spiritually nourishing gift, for the retiree's asking. So is complex mental play: my role models are Ethel and Irv, a retired pediatrician and a retired surgeon, who study Jewish history and Talmudic commentaries on the Torah, the Five Books of Moses.

Older deep players are more often able to give full attention to these complex or simple activities. A less crammed life in retirement allows time for study, close observation of nature, more leisurely and playful reading or writing of poetry, or uninterrupted reflection upon friendships, love, and death. Elders' deep play, simple or complex, may lessen the cynicism, despair, or boredom that sometimes occurs as a person ages and becomes more limited in physical capacity, conventional productivity, or social contacts.

Deep play also encourages elders to take more mental or emotional risks because a deep player learns to put death in its place vis-à-vis life: "Given something like death, what does it matter if one looks foolish now and then, or tries too hard, or cares too deeply? A shallow life creates a world flat as a shadow."[7] As many of us age and begin to face the larger issue of mortality, other people's opinions of us seem to matter less, and we feel freer to take on new activities in which we are less than competent. As I age, the possibility of looking foolish, failing at new undertakings, or caring too deeply fazes me less and less. These things are not the enemy, indifference is; and deep play is the antidote to indifference. Courageously plunging into new experiences, elderly deep players often gain new insights and attain self-acceptance for their bravery—as well as simply having more fun. Deep play tempers the psychological demand for self-perfection and at the same time fosters a sense of personal integrity. A profound life and a multi-dimensional world await the deep player: both seem well worth the risk. I want to claim for my retirement this playfulness and the wholeness and self-acceptance that it can bring.

To what other arenas will I turn for deep play? Some of these arenas may not be distant, exotic, or wholly new to me. The psychoanalyst Samuel Atkin, in an essay he wrote with his son Adam when he, Samuel, was eighty-eight, suggests that normal daily life offers new opportunities for elders to experience intensity: "Paradoxically, ordinary moments of life, the prosaic flow of experiences, have become newly interesting. I see things in a fresh way. . . . Existence has become adventurous. . . . I feel a little like . . . [a] ten-year-old immigrant boy, entering a strange, fascinating world. An Alice-in-Wonderland quality colors my existence. I feel the excitement of an explorer."[8] Like Atkin, I want to be an explorer daily and to follow the bent of my curiosity—which I have often had to curtail in midlife in order to prepare for classes or meet a deadline for an article. When I retire, I can explore new books, surf the net for myriad topics that interest me already and also for some as-yet-untapped subjects of interest, and will follow up net surfing with related activities: Yes to Victorian literature, and multicultural memoirs, novels, and women's studies, but also yes to medicine, ethics, dogs, tai chi, Hispanic cultures, cooking, herbs, container gardening, dance, and art. Yes to learning to play the flute or returning to the piano. Yes to filling my yard with more day lilies and roses. And yes to the deep acquisition of a second language, delving into Spanish with a passion, instead of just rushing through four semesters of Spanish classes in my "spare time" during the middle years. So what if I stumble in my elementary Spanish, sound like a gringa, and lack the fluency and precision I display in my native tongue? I will be more comfortable taking that risk of sounding foolish as I continue to learn in retirement. At least I will be absorbed in the play of the Spanish language and will be making progress toward fluency.

In general, I want to converse more often with more people who are different from me, people that I don't necessarily have to go abroad to meet, perhaps by housing an international student (my family had the honor of hosting a high school student from Russia for a year, but my schedule did not permit me to experience her presence as much as I could have), by tutoring Hispanic newcomers to my community, or by volunteering at the local Literacy Council. Activities that attract people from the community—beyond the university crowd—may also open up new conversations for me: why not through learning to salsa dance or through volunteering at the Humane Society? New people, other ways of speaking and thinking, will continue to educate me. I want to indulge my curiosity and keep my mind questing—at home or on the road.

In Frances Weaver's cheerful little book, *The Girls with the Grandmother Faces,* she touts the marvels of international cruises for seniors, the excitement of new acquaintances, and the wonders of hostels for seniors to foster this curiosity and joie de vivre in later life. These activities serve an important purpose, Weaver claims: "The best way to enjoy the freedom and independence of these older years is to keep our heads working, our imagination and curiosity alive . . . when we understand more of the world around us— . . . when our awareness is working—we are more interesting to our family and to ourselves. This is one of the keys to successful aging."[9] Weaver's advice is pragmatic and sensible, not concerned with finding the transcendence that deep play can bring; yet she does show me some pathways to deep play. I see hostels for seniors in my future, as learner and as teacher perhaps, offering more of those heady, breakthrough moments in the classroom that I've cherished in my professional life. My Aunt Rita, a woman in her seventies, is an advocate of hostels for seniors, and has enthusiastically signed on for several, usually with art themes, one of her passions. Hers is a mind continually growing and responding to new specimens of art and ideas about art in other cultures. The richness of her retirement pursuits inspires me to follow her lead. Besides hostels for seniors, travel beckons to me, especially where I can immerse myself in a culture and language not my own, see other customs in practice, experience new ways of thinking, observation, and interaction. I long to explore lands where Spanish is spoken and where the landscape is exotic: rain forests of Costa Rica, the Amazon, the Andes, the Galápagos Islands, and the Yucatán Peninsula. And I imagine meeting *los indigenes* of these lands, eating their foods, discovering the beauty of their crafts.

Yet I also see in my future some intellectual and psychological adventures of discovery close to home. For example, as I rehearse my retirement, I anticipate, one day, the pleasure of unpacking, at a leisurely pace, formerly unnoticed meanings of one of my favorite poems, Tennyson's *In Memoriam.* Then I'll try writing a piece about this poem as a guide to mourning the death of my parents—without needing to stop in order to attend to teaching duties or to rush to meet a publication deadline. I imagine taking breaks from these activities to watch my day lilies opening throughout the day. Such varied activities close to home offer the promise of many wonderful days in retirement.

Like Sylvia, I want to tend my garden regularly, tracking my plants' signs of growth, and closely watch indigenous creatures of the insect and bird world that people my yard. And infected with the enthusiasm of my university colleagues Eric and Mark, I might join the Audubon Society and go birding in my home county of New Hanover. I once wistfully voiced this desire to my students after we read an Emily Dickinson poem about a bird. They thought I was just an eccentric English professor. But in retirement, I can become a birder. And I can return to the writings of Wordsworth, Thoreau, Annie Dillard, and Diane Ackerman, which can help reawaken my senses to the complexities and machinations of the natural world.

I once wrote an article, published in *The Gerontologist,* in which I argued that much contemporary literature about elders, often penned by older authors, depicts them as latter-day Romantics because they are intimate with nature and can contact the transcendent spirit that threads through the natural world and all living beings. This is the spirit that poets like Wordsworth and Coleridge wrote about in the nineteenth century, the spirit that Thoreau captured in *Walden.* In a recent novel by Terry Kay, for example, octogenarian Sam Peek chews a leaf and communes with a white dog (*To Dance with the*

White Dog). Sarton depicts seventy-six-year-old Caro Spencer luxuriating in the fragrance and simple, elegant shape of a rose (*As We Are Now*). Doris Lessing places Maudie Fowler, who is over ninety, in a garden at a restaurant where she contentedly drinks in the beauty of her surroundings (*The Diaries of Jane Somers*). I want to claim for myself the status of a latter-day Romantic, placing myself in such surroundings more often and experiencing them more fully. Like Wordsworth in his autobiographical poem, *The Prelude*, I see and hear in nature the "Wisdom and Spirit of the Universe / Thou Soul that art the eternity of thought, / That giv'st to forms and images a breath / And everlasting Motion!" (Book First, ll. 401–404). I live near the ocean, where, surely, the wise eternal Soul of the universe dwells; I will take the time to hear the ocean's roar and smell the salt breezes, to collect shells, to sit and watch the waves and other sea-goers. I also live near some exquisite southern plantation gardens; tourists are more familiar with Orton Plantation than I, a twenty-year resident of southeastern North Carolina. I plan to remedy this when retirement permits.

All around me are these natural toys of deep play, a pantheist's delight, a transcendentalist's paradise, which I wish to take up wholeheartedly in retirement. And the meditative framework available in my own religious tradition of Judaism may help me to play with these natural toys more deeply. I can "play" in the synagogue, chanting with other congregants the oneness of God's existence, or I can pray alone at the ocean's edge, in a forest, or at the birth of a child for our extended family.

I imagine retirement as granting me all sorts of permissions, especially permission to slow down and stop planning for the next day, the next week, the next year. Retirement grants me permission to meditate in the present, in the center of the moment, as Sarton counsels me, and to pursue deep play, as Ackerman urges me.

As I catch my breath, I will claim more moments for contemplation, trained on the natural world and also directed internally. After a professional life of full-time teaching and scholarship, and a personal life of parenting two children, I want to reflect more before writing about my ideas and experiences. Then I will undertake what gerontologist Robert Butler has called the life review, a survey, recollection, and analysis of what I have done and been, the important people in my life, the meaning(s) of my life, my place in the universe. The life review is for me, my husband and children, my siblings and siblings-in-law, and my close friends. Reviewing my life may give me permission to see the humor of existence, to feel playful, not ponderous and pontifical, as I try to figure out what I've been doing on earth, lo these many years.

This life review is not just a nostalgic revisiting of the past, but a potentially transformative experience in the present, as Sara Ruddick has pointed out: "There is a sense in which the past is not unalterable but can be remade through focused remembering. Without denying facts or pain, a person may actually remember more compassionately, with a sharper sense of context and complexity. . . . [R]emembering may shift the balance from denial to acceptance, from vengeful obsession to letting go and letting be. . . . One of the great boons of this transformation is that remembering itself can be turned from obsessive reenactment of all that 'you have done and been,' transforming itself into a pleasurable experience of undirected, forgiving reminiscence."[10] Such reminiscence seems to me to be a very productive form of deep play because it fosters self-transcendence. My friend Aida is very good at this transformative, self-transcendent, forgiving reminiscence of the past; the retelling and fresh interpreting of events and experiences with her parents, her daughters, and their father weave through most conversations she has with family and with friends, reinforcing her familial ties and spinning threads of connection between her family and her friends. Ruddick notes that friends and loved ones can participate in revising these memories for the improvement of long-standing relationships, seeking deeper understandings and wider reconciliations.

My own children love to hear bits and pieces of family history from before their births and also to hear about ways in which I, my husband, or other relatives, living and dead, resemble them. These tales connect them more to the whole idea of family. With the time afforded by retirement, I would extend these historical narratives a bit, helping to nurture in my son and daughter a respect for family and a context for their own belonging. I can, in a sense, take on the role of "culture-tender," which anthropologists and sociologists observe in the elderly of many cultures. I would also benefit from this pursuit, which will probably intensify my reflections about what being a mother has meant to me.

Replenishing relationships in this way takes time, and thankfully there is more of it in retirement. A shared life review is like family members undertaking the project of expanding old photo albums with the addition of new photos, all rearranged and mounted into a psychological narrative that reinterprets family history and articulates the family mythology. I want to participate in such a group project, become more aware both of my individual existence and also of what Margaret Urban Walker describes as "connections that enrich but transcend individuals . . . a lateral integration of life . . . [that] supplies not only the pleasures of individual memory but the satisfactions of loyalties and meanings that transcend one's individuality."[11] Placing the individual within the group context, revisiting past events and experiences to figure out the *ousia* or

essence of oneself vis-à-vis other "characters" in the family saga, this is absorbing, deep play. It is such interesting stuff, the stuff of the family and how it has
shaped us all. I could spend years on this shared life review.

And so I resist my society's negative associations with retirement, especially
the prevailing notion challenged by Walker: that life is a career and the ideal
self is the bustling career self, which leads to the notion that the retired individual "surrenders not only a job, but eligibility for a centrally valued moral and social identity." Retirement is not merely "an unmapped space at the end of the
life course—a space . . . by social definition 'empty.'"[12] I look forward to it as a
place of growth, discovery, intensity, here-and-nowness, and deep playfulness.
And I anticipate in it a myriad of opportunities to reconnoiter: to figure out who
I've become; to strengthen my ties with other people; to place myself more
firmly within intersecting, and even expanding, communities; and to situate myself comfortably within the natural world, in sync with its energizing forces. In
retirement, therefore, I'll choose life, and live more fully, for the fun of it.

Notes

1. May Sarton, *After the Stroke: A Journal* (New York: W. W. Norton, 1988);
May Sarton, *At Seventy: A Journal* (New York: W. W. Norton, 1984), 190.

2. May Sarton, *As We Are Now* (New York: W. W. Norton, 1973).

3. Sara Ruddick, "Virtues and Age," in *Mother Time: Women, Aging, and
Ethics*, ed. Margaret Urban Walker (Lanham, Md.: Rowman and Littlefield Publishers, 1999), 54.

4. Diane Ackerman, *Deep Play* (New York: Random House, 1999). All subsequent quotations of Ackerman are from this volume; page numbers appear in the
text.

5. Johan Huizinga, *Homo Ludens: A Study of the Play-Element in Culture*
(Boston: Beacon Press, 1950), 8–9, 10–11, 13.

6. Ibid., 13.

7. Ackerman, *Deep Play*, 196.

8. Samuel Atkin and Adam Atkin, "On Being Old (A Psychoanalyst's New
World)," in *How Psychiatrists Look at Aging*, ed. George H. Pollock (Madison,
Conn.: International Universities Press, 1992), 10.

9. Frances Weaver, *The Girls with the Grandmother Faces: A Celebration of
Life's Potential for Those over 55* (New York: Hyperion, 1996), 182.

10. Ruddick, "Virtues and Age," 56.

11. Margaret Urban Walker, "Getting Out of Line: Alternatives to Life as a
Career," in *Mother Time*, ed. Walker, 107–108.

12. Ibid., 104, 105.

On My Own Terms

CAROL FOX PRESCOTT

I can remember seriously mocking my newly acquired brother-in-law way back in the early sixties, when we were both barely in our twenties, because he was making decisions about his future lifestyle based on retirement benefits. I was a free spirit, an artist, a singer, an actress, and I was not going to live with the fear of money running out or the stock market rising and falling or of the unknown itself. My life was going to be about embracing the unknown. I fully expected to make a lot of money, but not because it was about the money itself. I was going to have a successful career in the theater. Everyone said I was taking a chance, but I didn't really believe it.

After college, I concentrated on working and building my career. Most of those years I did work as an actress, much of the time on the road, often severing the tenuous relationships I had made in my previous jobs or the last city where I worked. Friendships are difficult to maintain when you rarely find yourself in the same town at the same time with the people who were important last year. I collected enough unemployment payments to see me through the lean times so I didn't have to wait tables or do telephone marketing or some other unpleasant day job that I knew I would hate. Once I worked in an off-Broadway theater box office, once on a synagogue switchboard, but for relatively short periods of time. Some of those years I was married or living with an equally struggling artist, some of the time I was on my own, but I was always financially responsible for myself. I still didn't worry about retirement or old age.

Then in 1976, in my mid-thirties, I hit a deep bottom. My marriage broke up, I had a fire in my apartment, I gained weight, and I couldn't get an acting job to save my life. I lived in a building that was a former hotel, a collection of studio apartments, where many of the residents were elderly and alone. I would help when I saw them struggling with their shopping carts and smile at them in the elevator when we were trapped there together, but they frightened me. I saw myself in their lonely eyes. For the first time I began to worry that I would be alone and without resources in that ever uncompromising, less and less distant future. "There's always the old actors' home," I'd strangely comfort myself.

Just as my unemployment was about to run out, I talked myself into a job teaching acting at the American Academy of Dramatic Arts. I had been looking through the phone book one day and had seen a listing of drama schools. I sat down, wrote out a résumé, and sent it out to every school on the list.

Two responded, a modeling agency and the academy. The very week my unemployment ran out I reported to work for a six-week summer term that grew into a nine-year stint, learning about teaching, directing student plays, and totally changing the direction of my life.

I remember walking into the Sanford White building on Madison Avenue, where the academy held its classes. In the middle of the fading beauty of the lobby there was a marble staircase with a gracefully carved, polished maple banister leading up to the theater on the second floor. I put my hand on the smooth, warm wood and felt the energy of the ghosts of all of the actors who had passed through the hundred-year history of the academy and knew that I was home. From the very beginning I knew what to do in my classroom and how to do it.

Slowly, through the years, my identity changed from that of an actress to that of a teacher. Although it was a long time before I could let go of the childhood fantasy of being a famous Broadway star and actually call myself a teacher, now I sometimes wonder if I didn't have to be an actress so that I would eventually have something to teach.

I fell in love with teaching. It offered me a security I had never known, one that was more than a paycheck every week. The results were immediate. I was living in a space where, once again, all things were possible. Young actors, some with dreams of fame and fortune and some with true artistic souls, who were ready to work like crazy to get what they wanted, filled my classes. It was assumed that I knew what I was talking about until and unless I proved otherwise. And I did know. That was the best part. I was organizing my thoughts, pulling out everything I had ever learned about acting from my own experience, from my teachers, from the productions I had seen, the books I had read, and a life devoted to theater. I loved it when people asked questions so that I could hear what I would answer, sometimes thinking, "How did I know that? Where did it come from?" To this day I am most alive when I am teaching. My undivided self is demanded every moment. Sometimes this means my own physical involvement as I demonstrate an exercise, actively creating a safe space in which my students can maneuver the sometimes dangerous emotional territory of a playwright's world. Most often it is the wholehearted concentration that is required as I observe and comment on their work that energizes me and brings me peace.

My classroom is where I trust myself the most. I don't second-guess my decisions. I am not afraid to be wrong and change direction when something is not working. I am funnier and more honest, creative, clearheaded, vulnerable, and strong there than I am anyplace else.

Most people think of acting as a craft of pretense or manipulation of feelings. It isn't. Acting is an art in which, with the use of oneself as the instrument, the goal is to reach the clearest truth of each experience, moment by moment, in the presence of others. Because it is usually done within the context of someone else's story, there is the freedom to walk away from the imagined situation, the actual risk is lessened, and it becomes possible to be more deeply involved in the game.

Unexpected dividends exploded out of my newfound profession. I became a better actress as a result of teaching. I made new friends among my colleagues, who taught me almost as much about the process of acting as did my students.

Living in this world where all things were possible brought a sense of the spiritual back in my life. Day after day, year after year, as I was privileged to witness the depth of the work, the clear commitment, the candor, and the pure, honest communication between actors, between classmates, I began to think, "This must be what God is." People fully living their own emotional, intellectual, physical, and spiritual truths, in the presence of others. God, I decided, is what passes between them.

Teaching saw me through the rest of my thirties, forties, fifties, and into my sixties. At fifty-two another life crisis brought about by the failure of another marriage led me back to the community of Judaism, my early religious tradition. I began to see my study of theater and my study of Judaism as mirror images of one another. Both disciplines asked for a searing search for truth in the presence of others. I rejoined my childhood synagogue. I became an active member going to services every Friday night and Saturday morning, celebrating the holidays with an intensity and joy I had previously only known in my work. I joined a community outside of my professional life and my primary relationships. I realized I had been living without a social network, without a life partner, without children, and although my work was more and more fulfilling all the time, it was not a whole life. I feared a time when I might not be able to work. Who would I be then? The picture of the old folks in my former apartment building had been haunting me. I couldn't think of retirement until I had a life and now I had begun to gather one together.

Then I read *Journal of a Solitude* by May Sarton and began to conceive my first fantasy of life after work.[1] She wrote about living in a rose-covered cottage on the New Hampshire coast, where she spent her days gardening and writing. I had never grown more than a stringy avocado plant and had not written more than a short, personal letter since the time I graduated from college, but I was captivated by the idea that one could live a self-sustaining, solitary life with satisfaction and comfort.

I started thinking about leaving the city. This was a surprise to me as I had always loved living in New York and through the years watched everyone in my family move away, one by one, swearing I would always remain. Now, I wanted to live where I could look out the window and see something beautiful. My apartment window on the Upper West Side of Manhattan overlooked the gourmet food store Zabar's. It wasn't enough.

Then, on a teaching gig in Boulder, Colorado, I had a vision. Looking out of the window at my view of the Rocky Mountains I decided I would sell my apartment (where, by that time, I had torn down the wall between the living and dining rooms, created an acting studio, and was in business for myself), find a new acting studio space on the Upper West Side where I could spend a night or two in the city and move to Woodstock, New York. I knew no one there except a young rabbi I had studied with three years before at Elat Chayyim, a Jewish retreat center in the Catskills, and who spoke to my heart. Wherever he had a congregation, I knew there would be a community for me. Amazingly, I was right. It seemed an impossible dream and made no sense, but month by month it began to fall into place. When I found my studio, it was being used as a storeroom in the basement of an old Columbus Avenue tenement building experiencing life anew as an Upper West Side co-op. Walls had to be taken down there, too, and the wood floors which had become gray with age and grime had to be savagely scraped and sanded, revealing good, old, sturdy, shining hardwood floors. But now I knew that it could be done. Miraculously (with the help of a synagogue friend, a high-powered real estate attorney who took me on as a favor), the landlord agreed to do most of the work, and with an advance in the monthly equitable distribution payments from my ex-husband, I opened my own doors to my own acting studio, Carol

Fox Prescott: Acting Classes at the Basement Space. I had no idea how I would pay the rent from month to month but the miracle went on and from the day I opened I was able to rent space, when I wasn't using it, to other teachers doing their own classes. I put my apartment on the market, met my present husband (a total surprise to me as I hadn't even dared to dream that love would enter my life again), and moved to Woodstock. I had just celebrated my fifty-fifth birthday.

Although happy and partnered again, I remained the primary breadwinner as my husband is fifteen years my senior, retired, and living on a fixed income. As a result of my marriage, the move, and a growing change in the market for my work in places outside of New York, the idea of my retirement shifted to a new way of life, not an end to work. In Woodstock, I made friends with people my age who were facing the same kinds of questions and fears about the future. From the beginning, I felt at home. I arranged my work schedule so that I would only be in the city two days a week. I added periodic weekend workshops and some week-long acting retreats, in beautiful places, to augment my income and reach more people. I began to self-publish a book about my work which I sell to my students. I included myself in a group of colleagues I am proud to know and honored to work with. I bought a house. I planted daffodils, tulips, and peonies. The deer ate the tulips, but left the rest for me.

Of course, there is the work I do at home to run my business, but it takes nothing like nine to five and leaves me time for long walks and lunches with friends, synagogue services and activities, yoga classes, writing, and learning how to garden. Still, I would love to have more time at home to take frequent day trips through the Hudson Valley with my husband, explore country roads with my dog, sprawl out on the couch with good books, or watch the occasional old movie on cable TV.

But I am not done. Now that I am sixty-one, I know that I may be entering my last fully active years and I want to take advantage of my energy and drive. I want to expand my student base. I am planning a teacher-training course to be offered in the fall of 2001. Last summer I taught deaf actors from Deaf West Theater in Los Angeles and hope to do more of this work. I want to finish my book and have it published by someone else.

And how can I replace the relationships that I have with my students? Where else can I openly fall in love with every person who walks through the door simply because we have a similar desire to express and lose ourselves through the amazing art form of acting? Instead of retiring I seem to be gathering more and more work and touching more and more lives. I love it and I pray every day that I remain healthy enough to continue as long as possible.

On the other hand . . . the lease on my acting studio in New York City is up the month before my sixty-fifth birthday. My fantasy is to give up the space to one of my present tenants and then rent from him or her. I think about closing down my ongoing classes and continuing to teach one or two weekends a month, five or six week-long retreats a year, in wonderful places around the world, and perhaps do some private coaching on roles for students doing plays or movies.

With a wistful look back at my long-term-planning brother-in-law, I will live simply on a mixture of workshop fees, investments, and social security. I will take a larger part in the activities of my synagogue and my town. I will look for reasons to sing. Much of my work in my acting days was in musical theater and a singer was just who I was. In the third grade, every day at milk time I got up in front of my class and sang "Wonderful Guy" from *South Pacific*. It was something I shared with my mother, who had been a professional singer before my older sister was born and who, I felt, had the most beautiful voice in the world. Although I took advantage of every opportunity at family parties, in the intervening years, to sing for a captive audience, I forgot to sing in my teaching years and only in the last five or six years (through the perseverance of some dedicated and gifted students) even thought to teach musical theater.

When my mother was dying in October of 1999 I sang to her every day I could get to the hospital and our last conscious communication was singing together the special Jewish prayer, the "watchword of our people," known as the Shema. I hold this moment as dear as any in my life. In February 2000 a tumor the size of a grapefruit was discovered on the back wall of my left lung. My first thought when the doctor told me about it was that I had somehow collected all the music in all the songs I had not sung in all the years since I had stopped acting right there on the back wall of my left lung. So when I recovered from surgery, in which it was discovered that the tumor was nonmalignant, and with my sixtieth birthday approaching, I planned a concert for my family and friends. I sang my heart out and, oh, boy, it felt good. Since then I have invented other occasions to sing. Few things me give me more pleasure. Perhaps when I'm sixty-five I'll put together a cabaret act and develop a following at the small clubs and restaurants in the area that feature live entertainment.

Maybe I'll direct a play or act in one. Maybe my Lee Strasberg fantasy will come true and one of my students will give me a part in a major motion picture that will lead to a whole new career for me as an aging movie star (as when Strasberg's student Al Pacino cast him in *The Godfather, Part II*, which led to a revived career as an actor in the movies).

I look forward to more time for family. As a woman without children, I have concentrated on developing close relationships with nieces and nephews (now some great-nieces and great-nephews) and the children of my cousins, my students, and my friends by playing the role of "the cool aunt from New York" as one of them put it. These relationships are vital to me, and as more children are born into this younger generation, I hope to have an active part in their lives as well. My travels to Los Angeles have allowed me to create very special bonds with my West Coast family, and I will hold on to that piece of my working life for as long as I can in order to continue to have an excuse to go there.

I fear growing old without children of my own, but I tell myself that my unusually close-knit family will fill in that very real gap. I pray that will be true.

I used to think I'd want to travel a lot. Now, with all the traveling I have been doing for my work, I am happy not to have to get on an airplane more of-ten than necessary. However, my husband and I had a lovely short vacation in Tuscany last spring and I have begun a whole new fantasy life about spending more peaceful days exploring the many medieval villages and the countryside of this extraordinarily beautiful piece of earth. So maybe some longer vaca-tions—three months in Tuscany, or the south of France, or the fjords of Nor-way—would be just the thing to soothe any ruffled nerves. But not someplace difficult, where poverty and scarcity are the first thing to greet the eye and the sensibility of the traveler. Not now.

I treasure the days I have at home with my husband (who has recently grown tired of his own retirement and taken a full-time job) and living the life of a couple among other couples. This phenomenon, that many people take for granted, is a new and wondrous toy that I play with. Simple dinners and movies with other couples who are good friends give me access to a world I had only dreamed of in my acting days.

My friends in Woodstock are the people I will grow old with. We have al-ready shared the mixed pleasures of momentous birthdays, the accomplish-ments of children, the loss of parents. We will take care of one another when we are sick and mourn with one another as our spouses die before us. Because of the difference in my husband's age and my own, it is likely that I will have some time of life as a widow. Although I fear that time to come, at least now I feel more prepared to negotiate life on my own again.

Recently, I have become interested in perusing the study of Jewish Spiritual Direction. This work, counseling people in their concerns about living a life based on a relationship with God, could be a natural outgrowth of the work I already do, simply shifting from a theatrical context into a Jewish one. The job of helping people feel their feelings, live in the moment, and share their truths is a familiar one to me.

I like the idea that if the time comes that I can't get around very well, people will come to me and I can share my life's wisdom from a comfortable chair, sitting by the warmth of a fire in the woodstove surrounded by snow-covered trees outside. After all, I have spent the last thirty years in acting classes, which I have always considered to be a state-of-the-art human laboratory, and where I have gained valuable insights into the workings of human relationships. It would be fun to put myself in the role of wise old crone, serve tea, and listen to the struggles of those who are still in the fray.

If the time comes when all I can do is sit in my rocking chair and look out on the world around me, I can think back to all the people who have come through my classes and into my life. People whose lives have been touched by my teachings. People who have changed me forever. I can remember (if I can remember anything) that for the most part, I stayed true to myself and pursued my dreams. I have been blessed in ways I didn't plan for or think possible. I have maintained my passion for living and my wonder at creation. I pray now for health, for the stock market to keep my pension plans afloat (with a nod of recognition to my brother-in-law), to live each day in appreciation, and to keep my heart open to love.

Note

1. May Sarton, *Journal of a Solitude* (New York: W. W. Norton, 1992).

Cut Me Some Slack: Reflections on the Eve of Retirement

ELLEN CRONAN ROSE

Seated at the computer this Saturday morning in April 2001, surrounded by all the usual inducements to composition—an empty campus, sun streaming through the window, Renée Fleming singing an aria from Carlisle Floyd's *Susannah* (on a CD brought from home, since the broadcast season of the Metropolitan Opera ended last Saturday)—I discover that I do not want to write this essay. This surprises me, since I responded immediately and eagerly to the editors' call for papers, when it was posted on WMST-L, the women's studies listserv, in January. "You bet I'm interested in contributing to your book," I fired back immediately:

> At sixty-two, I am planning that the twenty-fifth anniversary NWSA [National Women's Studies Association] conference—which we at UNLV [the University of Nevada, Las Vegas] are hosting in June 2002—will be my last hurrah, after which I plan to move back to my beloved and much missed Philadelphia and do whatever it is I will do in my retirement. I've been thinking a lot about what retiring means to me and it would help me find out what I think—as it always has—to write about it.

It is as true today as it was three months ago and has been for the last thirty-five years that I find out what I think by writing. So my reluctance to write this essay must mean there is something I don't want to know. Perhaps I am more ambivalent about the prospect of retiring than I thought I was.

I am certainly not ambivalent about wanting to move back to Philadelphia. Despite the fact that Las Vegas is the fastest growing metropolitan area in the United States (it is said that six thousand people move here every month), it is not and probably never will be a city. I discovered when I first lived in a city (London), in 1968 and 1969, that I enjoyed the "structural" rather than "personal" attachments one forms with one's fellow city dwellers. In London I had daily—and increasingly meaningful and valuable, though never personal— contact with the greengrocer. We exchanged formulaic pleasantries ("How are you today, love? Nice sprouts these—will you have a pound?" Even my "Oh, I think I'll have some Coxes today rather than grapes; I'd rather not buy South African fruit just now" wasn't prologue to a discussion of international politics, just a way of passing time at the greengrocer's) that paradoxically—since they never led to an exchange of intimate information—established us as neighbors. In Philadelphia, where I shopped every day at the Reading Terminal Market, a vast farmers' market housed in the old Reading Railroad train shed at Twelfth and Market Streets, I had exactly the same kind of—can we call them conversations?—with the woman who sold me bluefish and the man I bought vegetables from. I can recall my mother having similar "conversations" with tradespeople when I was a child in Middletown, Pennsylvania, population ten thousand, and I have frequently heard it said that a real city like Philadelphia or New York or Boston is in fact a collection of small towns called neighborhoods. I've lived in both a genuine small town and in several real cities (London, Boston, Philadelphia), and I believe cities reproduce the best of small-town living (the ritual, formalized pleasantries that make living in close proximity to other people bearable) without duplicating their oppressiveness, the knowledge that everyone knows almost everything about you, from how well you're doing at school to what flavor ice cream you order at the corner drugstore, and everyone probably knew your mother when she was a little girl, too. In a suburb like Las Vegas, however (and Las Vegas will never be more than a suburb with elephantiasis—one gated community after one strip mall after another, with no city center), I have never experienced the sense of neighborliness-without-intrusiveness I felt in London or Philadelphia, only a mild sense of anomie. So I am unreservedly eager to return to Philly.

I am just as unequivocally eager to free myself from aspects of my work that have lost their former zest. This ennui has crept up on me gradually, almost imperceptibly. As recently as ten years ago, for instance, when my copy of *Signs* arrived in the mail, I ripped off the plastic cover and immediately read the journal cover to cover, eager to keep abreast of the latest feminist scholarship not only in my own discipline (English) but in areas as remote from my expertise as international relations and health care policy. So it was with anticipatory relish that I settled down a month ago to read Robyn Wiegman's lead article in the winter 2001 issue. Wiegman is, by general agreement, one of the rising luminaries in women's studies/feminist scholarship. She gave one of the plenary addresses at last October's conference "The Future of Women's Studies" at the University of Arizona and has recently been appointed to a named directorship of women's studies at Duke University. Even so, I discovered, seven pages into a thirty-three page article (which I may never finish), that I could sustain interest in it only by reading as if I were Jenny X, one of our brightest new women's studies majors, whom I taught with considerable pleasure last fall in a required course in feminist theory. Jenny must be all of twenty-eight, and everything she read in Linda Nicholson's *The Second Wave: A Reader in Feminist Theory*, from the introduction to Simone de Beauvoir's *The Second Sex* to Uma Narayan's "Contesting Cultures," was so exciting to her, so fresh and illuminating, that it almost rekindled my interest in what were to me, for the most part, well-roasted old chestnuts. To borrow a trope from Judith Butler, one of the theorists we predictably (and, for me, boringly) read last semester: it seems that I can sustain an interest in the scholarly aspects of my chosen profession only if I perform the identity of the neophyte I once was, in the person—for now—of Jenny X.

Twenty-seven years ago I earned my Ph.D. from the University of Massachusetts with a dissertation on Doris Lessing. It was, I believe, the fifth U.S. doctoral dissertation on Lessing. In addition to reviews in the *New York Times* and the *New York Review of Books*, my secondary sources included only two books and a handful of scholarly articles. By 1985, fifty-two American academics had entered the profession with a dissertation on Doris Lessing in hand. By that year, five more books on Lessing had been published by major university presses and more than three hundred articles had appeared in a gamut of journals from *Critique* to *PMLA* (including special issues of *Contemporary Literature* and *Modern Fiction Studies*).

The decade between 1974, when I graduated from the University of Massachusetts, and 1985 was a heady time for Lessing scholars. We were working on a writer who spoke personally to us, as we learned when we exchanged stories at special sessions on Doris Lessing at the annual Modern Language Association (MLA) conference. I had scrapped the dissertation I had been writing on time in the works of James Joyce and begged my advisor to let me substitute a study of Lessing's Children of Violence series. I was in the process of getting a divorce and struggling with the question of who should have custody of the children, had been in therapy for four years, and was active in the movement against the war in Vietnam. I read the novels in that series as if they were what Margaret Drabble later called all of Lessing's fiction, borrowing a metaphor from *The Golden Notebook*, a "blueprint" for living.[1] Although the first dissertations on Lessing were written by men—John Carey and Paul Schlueter—it was especially women readers who were drawn to Lessing's fiction. She seemed to know us better than we knew ourselves, "naming" us—as *The Golden Notebook*'s Anna Wulf would say—and the welter of ambiguities in which we floundered: disenchanted with politics-as-usual, confused by the sexual revolution, struggling to reconcile the conflicts we felt between public responsibility and private need. At the same time, to our surprise and delight, we were able to parlay our personal investment in the novels of Doris Lessing into professional advancement. We formed a Doris Lessing Society in 1979 that shortly thereafter became an allied organization of the MLA; began publishing the *Doris Lessing Newsletter*; submitted articles on Lessing to respectable journals (which accepted them!); and in the course of a decade, transformed a "mere" popular novelist into a canonical author, a process Carey Kaplan and I documented at some length in *The Canon and the Common Reader*.

Even as we celebrated it, however, Carey and I wondered whether this was an unqualifiedly positive accomplishment. Could a prophetic book like *The Golden Notebook* have the same life-transformative effect on a student who had been assigned it in a course as it had had on our generation of readers, who had stumbled on it haphazardly and, as it came to seem, fortuitously? But it didn't occur to us to ask what might be the consequences to *us* of Lessing's having been admitted to the canon of twentieth-century British literature.

When one works on a canonical author, one is obliged to consider her or his entire oeuvre. Take D. H. Lawrence, an author with whom Lessing has frequently been compared. If you are a Lawrence scholar, you can't ignore second-rate books like *Aaron's Rod* or *Apocalypse* to write only about such uncontested works of genius as *The Rainbow* and *Women in Love*, which may affect you very personally. Similarly, if you are a Lessing scholar, despite the fact that she has published nothing since *The Fifth Child* with the emotional richness and moral ambiguity of that 1988 novel, which is by no means Lessing at her best, you write about it all—including *Mara and Dann*; *Love, Again*; and *Ben in the World*—as contributors to the *Doris Lessing Newsletter* and panelists at Doris Lessing sessions at the annual MLA convention continue to do.

You take all the works of a canonical author equally seriously (even if you personally like some better than others), because you are working on an *author*, an academic abstraction whose dimensions and characteristics bear no necessary or even, sometimes, discernible relation to the living, breathing human being who held the pen or tapped the computer's keys. This is most clearly evident in the case of pseudonymous authors: one studies George Eliot, not Mary Anne Evans.

But even as I was working with my friends and colleagues to gain canonical status for Lessing, I never thought of her as an "author" in that sense. I devoted the first twenty years of my professional life to studying and writing about Doris Lessing because she wrote intelligently about what it was like to be a woman, seeming to speak to me directly as one woman to another. I no longer write on Doris Lessing. I have lost interest in her, in part because she has grown cantankerous and crotchety. Worse, she has ceased writing intelligently about what it is like to be a woman: *Love, Again* is an embarrassing, senile romantic fantasy. I still believe that *The Golden Notebook* may be the greatest novel in the English language of the second half of the twentieth century and am glad I belong to a generation of scholars who devoted the greater part of their professional lives to securing the woman who wrote it a place in the canon. But I no longer consider myself a Lessing scholar.

In 1993, my career took a new turn when I accepted a job at the University of Nevada, Las Vegas as UNLV's first director of women's studies. Like the early scholarship on Lessing, women's studies at its inception, in the late 1960s, was a grassroots, amateur enterprise—literally an effort of love on the part of (mostly junior) women faculty and community activists determined to challenge the epistemological foundations of the educational establishment. Like the child who dared to proclaim that the emperor had no clothes, these pioneers insisted that what had been held to be absolute verities in disciplines ranging from biology to sociology were, like the canon of English literature, the constructions of white, economically privileged men. So they set out to construct alternative knowledge—about, for the most part by, and, very importantly, *for* women. "From the beginning," Marilyn Boxer writes, in her definitive history of women's studies in the United States, "the goal of women's studies was not merely to study women's position in the world but to change it."[2] It may be true, as Boxer claims, that women's studies was conceived as "the academic arm of women's liberation."[3] But in a 1996 special issue of *Signs* on feminist theory and practice, in a collective interview with other scholars and activists, Charlotte Bunch accused today's women's studies programs of having strayed "far from the origins of women's studies, which was to use the academic arena to deepen our understanding of the problems women face and to encourage women to be activists."[4]

By the last decade of the twentieth century, women's studies had become institutionalized. From a handful of courses in the 1960s, often taught at the free universities that proliferated then, women's studies has burgeoned in the last quarter century: the September 1999 issue of *PMLA* lists 625 women's studies programs or departments in U.S. colleges and universities, and in 8 of them it is now possible to earn a Ph.D.

But it was relatively new to me in 1993—and to UNLV where, although a resolute group of faculty in a few disciplines had succeeded in getting a major in women's studies approved by the administration, the curriculum consisted of a smattering of courses in English, history, psychology, and sociology, and there was no infrastructure or budget to support the major. Studying all the available models—we read publications of the National Women's Studies Association, and I attended the daylong exchanges of information by women's studies program administrators that preceded the annual NWSA conferences and joined a regional consortium of women's studies program administrators—over the next seven years we created a democratic governance structure, developed a genuinely interdisciplinary curriculum, dramatically increased enrollments, and graduated more and more majors. In January 2001, the UNLV Board of Regents upgraded women's studies' status from program to department and the president approved a graduate certificate in women's studies.

Although there are a few challenges in the offing—we are as yet a department without faculty, and we have a national NWSA conference to host—the institutionalization of women's studies at UNLV has pretty much been accomplished. Have we, here, managed even so to remain true to the original vision of women's studies as "the academic arm of women's liberation?" I like to think that we have. The first of our stated program objectives is to insure that students graduating with a B.A. in women's studies "will connect women's studies scholarship and social activism and will be able to become agents of social change," and our capstone course is not a research seminar but a course in feminist praxis.[5]

But teaching the same required upper-division courses year after year to women's studies majors has become for me a rote exercise. I no longer need either to deploy the arts of seduction required to interest the average undergraduate in the arcane delights of one's chosen academic specialty or to exercise consciously and creatively the principles of feminist pedagogy about which I am supposed to be something of an authority.[6] Similarly, chairing the department has become merely a matter of making sure the trains run on time.

If in its every aspect—scholarship, teaching, and administration—my work has lost its zest, what possible reservations can I have about leaving it? I have examined my conscience rigorously, and I do not believe that I will regret relinquishing the modicum of power and authority my position here has afforded me. Another perquisite of seniority is serving as mentor to the next generation. But even if I choose no longer to attend the program administrators' "pre-conference" at the annual NWSA conference after 2002, I can still be of use to younger colleagues, sharing what I have learned about building a women's studies program with anyone who seeks me out by way of the old girls' network that has by now become well developed.

No, my anxieties on the eve of retirement have less to do with what I will be giving up than with what lies ahead. At least one of my worries is probably shared by many people approaching retirement: will I be able to live comfortably, if not opulently (I have never aspired to opulence), on my retirement income, a combination of social security, the retirement fund my employers and I have regularly contributed to throughout my working life, and personal savings, invested (wisely, I hope) on the advice of a financial advisor? If I need to supplement my retirement income, what kind of work can I find? For some years, I have served as an unpaid editor for friends and colleagues, suggesting new organizational strategies and cleaning up their grammar and spelling before they submit articles to the critical scrutiny of journal editors. Is it reasonable to hope that in Philadelphia, which abounds in institutions of higher education, I can find graduate students and junior faculty members willing to pay for these services? Or even that I might do some freelance copyediting for one or more of the university presses and trade publishers based in Philly? Surely, if worse came to worst, I could get a part-time job in retail sales. (Me selling ladies' undies? Hardly. But maybe books.)

But these concerns, though real, are as nothing compared to the question of what to do with the rest of my life. The women in my family are long lived: at ninety, though she uses a walker to get around, my mother has all her wits about her, and I had a great-aunt who was still—as they say in my part of the country—"full of piss and vinegar" when she died at one hundred. As I am in good health, then, I can reasonably anticipate living twenty-five or even thirty years after I retire at sixty-four.

For the first sixty-two years, my life unfolded along the lines of a *Bildungsroman*, or novel of development. First I was a good little girl, then a model student, then a wife and mother, and finally—as of this writing—a scholar/teacher/academic administrator. The first two of these roles were constructed by my parents, of course, but also by the culture in which I was nurtured—middle-class, small town, Protestant, mid-twentieth-century America—and it was very clear what behavior, attitudes, and values were required of me. It was equally clear how I should behave as a wife and mother, even though that behavior was at odds with, indeed required the demolition of, the identity of model student some of the mentors who were urging me to marry had earlier praised. Reared in a different environment, my women's studies students today recoil in shock as well as horror when I tell them that after the birth of my first child I dropped out of graduate school. What did I need a Ph.D. for? I reasoned: I have a professor husband and a beautiful baby. My students read Betty Friedan's *Feminine Mystique* as a historical document; many women of my generation lived it.

Originally a male genre (the prototype is Goethe's *Wilhelm Meister* and the most familiar English avatars are Dickens's *David Copperfield* and *Great Expectations*, Joyce's *Portrait of the Artist as a Young Man*, and Lawrence's *Sons and Lovers*), the *Bildungsroman* does occasionally tell the story of a woman's life (e.g., in Brontë's *Jane Eyre*, Eliot's *Mill on the Floss*, Alcott's *Little Women*, Cather's *Song of the Lark*, Lessing's Children of Violence volumes). But whether the development charted is a man's or a woman's, the *Bildungsroman* ends with the protagonist's attainment of adult identity (Doris Lessing and Sigrid Undset are the only authors in this tradition I know who follow their female protagonist through middle age into old age). The twentieth-century variation on the nineteenth-century female *Bildungsroman*, which marked a woman's attainment of adulthood by either her marriage (Jane Eyre) or her death (Maggie Tulliver in *The Mill on the Floss*), allows women as well as men to define themselves through work (Thea Kronborg in *The Song of the Lark*).

But what defines a woman and renders her life meaningful after she retires? We have neither literary nor cultural narratives to answer that question. My friend Carey says moving from full-time employment to retirement must be "kind of like moving from childhood to adolescence, with the same transitional horrors, only not documented at all."[7] If she's right, and I think she is, that retirement is just another developmental stage, she is equally right to observe that it is a stage that has not been documented. Research on women's retirement is sparse.[8] Whatever notion we have of a life cycle that includes a retirement phase is based on the premise that the retiree is a white, middle-class male.[9]

If there are no narratives of women retirees, there are some culturally prevalent images of old women. A number of the retired professional women Christine Price interviewed for her book on women and retirement report belonging to clubs of various sorts (from bridge to bowling), gardening, traveling in the United States or abroad, volunteering at local libraries or food banks, reading for pleasure.[10] My older daughter hopes that when I return to Philadelphia, a mere two hours by train from her suburban home outside Baltimore, I will devote a significant amount of time to my grandchildren.

The vision of retirement as one long bridge game is utterly alien to someone raised, as I was, according to the Puritan ethic. One of my greatest fears is that, without a job to go to, I may spend my days as I now do many of my weekends, virtually inhaling mystery novels by P. D. James, Ruth Rendell, Minette Walters, Sue Grafton, Sara Paretsky, and Lisa Scottoline. And while I certainly look forward to guiding my grandchildren through Philadelphia's Please Touch Museum and Franklin Institute, taking them on picnics in Fairmount Park, and introducing them to the pleasures of classical music at the new Kimmel Center for the Performing Arts, I cannot live my life through my grandchildren. When I asked Carey whether it was okay just to enjoy myself, to be primarily a consumer (of free student concerts at the Curtis Institute of Music and Philadelphia's wonderful street life as well as of mystery novels) rather than a producer when I retired, she assured me it was "just fine to do whatever the hell you want to do":

> To hell with the Puritan ethic; you have done enough work in the past 40 years to satisfy a whole bunch of Puritans, led by Cotton Mather. Puritans didn't have to be lively and productive in their sixties; they died. Today we get a whole extra lifetime in which to play like the crypto-pagans we are.[11]

But it doesn't feel right to me. I must not be even a *crypto* pagan. Maybe if I had spent my working life as a coal miner or in some other form of alienated labor, I might feel justified in going on a really extended vacation. But I loved my work as a feminist scholar and women's studies administrator and believed it had what we used to call in the 1960s "socially redeeming" qualities. What can I find to do in retirement that will equally engage my energies and satisfy my apparent need to be of use?

Carey says I sound increasingly like an adolescent because, like an eighteen-year-old, I seem to need to have an answer to the question, "What are you going to do with [the rest of] your life?" Because I am the kind of person I have become over the last sixty-two years, I want to answer that question in terms of the *use* I intend to make of (the rest of) my life. On line, I scour the

Philadelphia section of the *Philadelphia Inquirer* every day and the alternative *City Paper* every week, looking for stories that will give me some clue. Today's *Inquirer* featured a story about a ceremony honoring this year's participants in Temple University's Center for Intergenerational Learning, a program that "matches Philadelphia School District students with senior citizens from nursing homes and community centers in their neighborhoods."[12] I don't know if I'll ever be as old or as wise as the old people in that story, and I suspect that I will choose to impart whatever life wisdom (as contrasted with job-related expertise) I do have to my own children and grandchildren. But the cover story in this week's *City Paper*, about the upcoming Democratic primary in which incumbent District Attorney Lynne Abraham is being challenged by black attorney and former city commissioner Alex Talmadge,[13] reminded me of how thoroughly I enjoyed working seven days a week as an unpaid volunteer at Clinton/Gore headquarters in Philly in 1992 and of how profoundly political both the city of Philadelphia and I are.

So maybe I should cut myself some slack, quit fretting about what I'm going to do when I retire, and just do it: move back to Philly; settle into an apartment in Center City; resume my daily walks to the Reading Terminal; call my old friends at Drexel and Temple Universities and Haverford College; check out the free concert schedule at the Curtis Institute; read the *Inquirer* and the *City Paper*; and wait for the next chapter of my life to write itself.

Acknowledgments

For the title and any wisdom that may have found its way into this essay, I thank Carey Kaplan. I also had helpful conversations with Katy Steinkamp and Lynn Walterick.

Notes

1. Margaret Drabble, "Doris Lessing: Cassandra in a World Under Siege," *Ramparts*, February 1972, 52.
2. Marilyn Boxer, *When Women Ask the Questions: Creating Women's Studies in America* (Baltimore: The Johns Hopkins University Press, 1998), 13.
3. Marilyn Boxer, "For and about Women: The Theory and Practice of Women's Studies in the United States," *Signs: Journal of Women in Culture and Society* 7, no. 3 (spring 1982): 678.
4. Heidi Hartmann, Ellen Bravo, Charlotte Bunch, Nancy Hartsock, Roberta Spalter-Roth, Linda Williams, and Maria Blanco, "Bringing Together Feminist

Theory and Practice: A Collective Interview," *Signs: Journal of Women in Culture and Society* 21, no. 4 (summer 1996): 936.

5. Women's Studies Program, University of Nevada, Las Vegas, "Assessment Plan for Women's Studies" (November 1997, photocopy).

6. Based on a collection of essays on feminist pedagogy I coedited with my colleague Maralee Mayberry, *Meeting the Challenge: Innovative Feminist Pedagogies in Action* (New York: Routledge, 1999).

7. Carey Kaplan, "Re: Stuck," personal E-mail, 24 April 2001. The French call old age *le troisième âge* and French Canadians refer to senior citizens as *les adolescents recyclés*, or recycled teenagers. Robert C. Williamson, Alice Duffy Rinehart, and Thomas O. Blank, *Early Retirement: Promises and Pitfalls* (New York: Plenum Press, 1992), 12.

8. For exceptions, see Christine Ann Price, *Women and Retirement: The Unexplored Transition* (New York: Garland Publishing, 1998), and Nancy Dailey, *When Baby Boom Women Retire* (Westport, Conn.: Praeger, 1998), as well as studies cited in Christine Ann Price, "Women and Retirement: Relinquishing Professional Identity," *Journal of Aging Studies* 14, no. 1 (2000): 81–101. Price notes that the most popular adult developmental models (e.g., Erikson, Kohlberg, and Levinson) "simply do not represent the experiences of aging women" (*Women and Retirement*, 11).

9. He may, of course, have a wife, in which case, if she doesn't join him on the golf course at their Del Webb Corporation–built "active adult community" outside of Phoenix or Las Vegas or Orlando, she will be depicted playing bridge or doing arts and crafts with the other wives in the recreation center.

10. Price, *Women and Retirement*, 134–135.

11. Carey Kaplan, letter to the author, 20 March 2001.

12. Monica Rohr, "Students, Seniors Find Opposites Attract," *Philadelphia Inquirer*, 11 May 2001.

13. Daryl Gale, "Ready to Rumble," *Philadelphia City Paper*, 10–17 May 2001; available at www.citypaper.net.

Making a Difference

Juanita N. Baker

What amazing times we live in. Women in our society have many more choices today than in previous generations, and many more than other women around the world. There is unprecedented wealth in the upper and upper-middle classes, allowing men as well as women to take greater risks in choosing careers they love. I'm not a typical American working woman; I'm one of the advantaged ones in our society—I never *had* to work. I see it as a privilege to work, not a necessity for economic reasons. The great majority of women do not have a choice as whether or not to work or what kind of job to work at. Few of us are allowed or allow ourselves to have a passion and to follow our unique talents and desires. Now at age sixty-one, I have the opportunity and fortune to have a choice about retirement. Many of my friends my age can't wait to retire; they, however, have not had the same choices and opportunities I have had. I can afford to retire and could have chosen not to work at all.

Thinking back, I realize that the bases for decisions I made at the beginning of my work life continue to be the factors shaping my career decision as to whether or not to retire toward the end of my life. The same pulls I felt then hold true today: my valuing science and its utilization to aid others, my valuing education to further the human enterprise, my work ethic, my sensitivity to the world's pain, and my interest in people, nature, and art. I see overpopulation, people not living up to their potential, children being hurt and other kinds of violence, injustice, discrimination, poverty, lack of education, our environment being destroyed, and I want to change these things. In the sixties I led a study group in which we debated whether individuals can make a difference and bring about change. I am still very idealistic and optimistic that we can bring about change, especially if we work together.

The Origins of My Notions of Equality and Sense of Confidence

In my youth I had grandiose ideas of what I would do about changing the world. Although I had few role models of women changing the world, my parents purposely tried to keep their biases and prejudices from their children and did an excellent job of raising me to think that women could do anything that men can do. *Annie Get Your Gun* came out in 1946 and I remember well my high school friend belting out the line in the song, "Anything you can do I can do better!" I believed it—or at least that we women could do it as well.

When I moved to Champaign, Illinois, in third grade, in 1947, we could not wear boys' clothes (blue jeans) to elementary school; but I lived in blue jeans the minute I got home from school. With a friend I built forts, climbed trees, explored construction sites, whittled pretend Indian knives out of sticks, and in the winter trudged purposefully through snow drifts in the "arctic wilderness" at the country club, imitating the male heroes in the comics and radio stories. My next-door neighbor and I built a tree house on top of a twelve-foot-high stump. It was only a very small platform with room enough for two and had boards nailed into the trunk to get up to it, but, oh, the sense of power, control, and choice atop that tree!

My girlfriend and I were very competitive with each other. She was older and bigger, and I perceived her as stronger, brighter, and more verbal and much more daring than I, though I did my best to surpass her. We competed in swimming, and it is amusing that in our adulthood she remembers that I won all the blue ribbons (not true, and I never remember swimming faster than she did). The neighborhood boys and we girls would play baseball and football in the street in front of our house and basketball in our driveway. Another activity was jumping off of garages—that took daring. While we had girls' baseball as a competitive sport in grade school and I won the sixth-grade marble championship, in public junior high and high school there were no sports for girls except in PE. In the neighborhood sports, though, I still felt equal to the boys.

My older brother (who was four years older) and I alternated in washing and rinsing the dishes together (he always finished first whether he washed or rinsed!); we both had to wash windows; I helped my dad paint, lay a tile floor, and put in insulation in the addition we (he) built onto our house. When my brother went off to college, I was assigned the lawn-mowing chore, although physically that hand mower challenged me when the grass was let go too long. Still, I did it and was shown I could do anything a man could do—except push-ups and pull-ups! However, I did observe that boys and girls had different roles and tried to figure out the reasons why we did things differently. Most notable was the fact that my older brother worked at jobs to earn money to buy a car and take girls out on dates. In high school (1953–1957), I did get a job at a department store and worked for a summer at a camp; in contrast to my brother, I seemed to work mostly to gain "life" experience.

My mother took care of us at home although she had worked at two jobs before she married: taking taste samples of Crisco house to house and, for the telephone company, teaching others how to use a dial telephone. She had been trained in fine arts and gave me an appreciation of the beauty of the world. She was an avid reader, contributed to the community (e.g., she volunteered to hold babies at the hospital), and pursued weaving. My father, having been wounded at Fort Bragg, North Carolina, in 1941, resulting in a stiff hip, was a thinker and brilliant, an electrical engineering professor. Perhaps due to traditional male-role pressures, one of my brothers became an engineer and the other went into business. My parents did not pressure me to pursue any career, allowing me to consider a variety of choices. I considered many fields, from astronomy and chemistry to philosophy, art, and the social sciences. The fact that I was considering a career, when most of my friends were solely interested in getting jobs, marrying, and having families, was unusual.

Most middle-class women in previous generations were not expected to work for pay after they married. If they did work, it was in a limited capacity. Many women had to quit teaching when they married. An exception was my grandmother (after whom I am named), whose husband died of a heart attack just three months after the birth of my mother, in 1907. Although her parents supported her living with them in a hotel with full service, she started an art-and-antiques shop in Cincinnati. Her home was full of interesting treasures to explore and she provided me a different role model, though when I was growing up I was not conscious of how unusual and brave she was.

I went to graduate school from 1961 to 1965. Gender differences were just beginning to be identified, emphasized, and researched. Studying achievement motivation, I read about Maslow's hierarchy of needs,[1] leadership, early learning, and intelligence, and I identified myself in all of these concepts. Behavior theory conceptualization simplified the world of psychological processes for me. Sexual urges did not seem the organizing principle of the world and I dismissed the Oedipus complex and penis envy (along with

Freud's other concepts) as farfetched explanations couched in language that just did not express what life was really about. My study of psychology showed me that there was no difference between men and women, although different roles were traditionally designated for men and women. I remember one male supervisor during my internship at the University of Maryland School of Medicine reacting with surprise when I said that there were really no differences between men and women. I measured the world in terms of my own experience, not according to gender stereotypes of the time.

The Origins of My Value System and Career Choice

Although my religious beliefs have since evolved, as a youth I followed the teachings of the Presbyterian Church. I was dedicated to being a loving, caring person. I was aware of racism and children less fortunate, splitting my church donation fifty-fifty to help others both at home and abroad. The Christian work ethic and focus on love has continued to guide me.

My family's time in Hawaii (1945–1947)—my father remained in the army just before returning to graduate school in the Midwest after the war—our summer trips in the United States and Canada, and the magazines *Life* and *National Geographic* initially widened my vistas. Thinking I would settle down in the Midwest as the wife of a high school teacher, I readily agreed to my mother's suggestion to go abroad for my junior year in college (1959–1960) and have an adventure while I was still single. Having been a lifelong subscriber to *Vogue* magazine, having sent me on Saturdays during high school to finishing school in Chicago, and knowing I would thrive on the art in France, my mother, I'm sure, pictured me going there for "culture and refinement" and hoped I would really learn French. But that was not to be. I went to India, sponsored by the Presbyterian Church, and began to fully realize the pain of the world. I met dedicated missionaries devoting their lives to the education of Indian women. I saw the sick, extreme poverty, and the lavish richness of the culture. I was most influenced by reading Gandhi's autobiography, which showed me a revolutionary method to bring about change, the effectiveness of nonviolence, and the necessity of getting people together to work toward change.

A guiding principle for me has been that what we do makes a difference and can make ripples around the world. These altruistic feelings, the curiosity I had for studying human actions, and the desire to have a flexible career led me to choose clinical psychology. I could have been an engineer like my father, an artist like my mother (who did art for her own enjoyment and a few things for the family), a lawyer like my grandfather, a shop owner like my grandmother, a druggist like my other grandfather . . . or a housewife or elementary or high school teacher like most women role models I had when I went to college. But my choice depended upon my philosophy and encouragement from my significant other, who said, "I'm going to graduate school, and of course you will too."

As one of two women in a class of sixty-plus in the psychology department at the University of Illinois, I was striking out into new ground. I did not realize it at the time, although I thought that in order to get in I had to say to the faculty admissions advisor, "You don't discriminate against women, do you?" I can recollect no female professors at the university in undergraduate or graduate school except one practicum supervisor. I also looked at the practical side. I could be a clinical psychologist and follow a husband anywhere. I didn't imagine it would be around the world!

Thirteen Years in Pakistan

Shortly after we finished graduate school and had our first child, in 1965, my husband had the opportunity to work in Pakistan to do mosquito research. Living thirteen years (1966–1979) in Lahore allowed us to have a new perspective on U.S. culture and permitted us to separate our beliefs from our parents' beliefs. In Pakistan, I accepted that I was not on the usual career track, although I did part-time counseling at the American school, had a clinical psychology private practice, consulted on a few research projects, started a psychological clinic in the heart of the old city, ran psycho-educational courses and consciousness-raising groups, and taught psychology at a small all-male college. Monetary remuneration was minimal, but the work was very satisfying and allowed me to practice my skills and keep up in psychology. Bringing about change on the individual, small-group, community, and world levels was always at the forefront of my thinking. I followed up on art interests and issues of the time, focused on stimulating and educating my children, spread my early-learning ideas to others by teaching kindergarten for a year, was involved in local cultural activities, taught high school art, enjoyed a variety of friendships, and read widely. Focusing on changing the world through encouraging education, one of my last and most gratifying projects in Pakistan was to get the community behind establishing a children's library in an area where there were twelve thousand children with no access to books.

Returning to the U.S. Career Path

When we returned to Baltimore, in 1979, I thought I could get full-time work in my field, continuing my career. To my shock, even though I had taught, published one paper in a Pakistani journal, completed other research, experienced another culture in depth, provided psychological services, and (I thought) achieved a lot considering the circumstances and raising two children, a prospective employer said that "based on the last thirteen years since your graduation you are not a good risk." Employers I applied to were looking for a more traditional career person (male, full-time employed since graduation, no time out living abroad or having children), so I was back at part-time work. I worked at a mental health clinic, volunteered at a domestic violence shelter, taught a variety of courses as an adjunct professor, supervised practicum students at the clinic, obtained a license, and started a private practice again, all the time helping my family adjust to the United States and enjoy the culture of the Baltimore and Washington, D.C., area. Again, I went in many directions and my remuneration was not commensurate with my skills. After three years, we as a family decided to move to Florida to support my husband's career, and I found my way to my current position at a small, private engineering university. The salary was outrageously low in comparison to the salaries of males in similar positions (my students in their first year after graduation earned more than I did), but I allowed myself to be taken advantage of because I had few options as a female wanting to stay with my spouse and because I loved the job and the opportunities. It was gratifying to be doing important and meaningful work again and validating to be paid a regular, full-time salary for the first time in my life. I have worked at this position for the last seventeen years.

My activism, as I see it, is stronger when I have the power base of employment, the status and resources of an academic appointment. I think I can have more influence and make more of a difference in this role than I could if I retire. I run a program for children who have been sexually abused. From my academic position I can help these children directly as well as teach students the skills and understanding needed to work with them. Research indicates that 20 to 25 percent of children are sexually abused, and they are more likely than the average population to have mental health problems as a result, even as adults. It is essential that clinicians be trained well to work with them. I have a passion to teach students to have a research-based practice and to emphasize high standards of excellence and ethics. It is challenging and stimulating to work with young people as well as in a community where my presence can make a difference.

Reasons to Retire

I would retire this minute if I were incapable, out of date, not able to handle the stress, bored, tired, or beginning Alzheimer's (this is a worry as my mother had Alzheimer's and the probability of my having it is high,[2] especially now that I am sixty-one—though I am trying to reduce that possibility by taking vitamin E and, until recently, hormone replacement therapy, and keeping my cholesterol low; I should exercise but don't enough). If working compromised my health, I would retire. But all research indicates that being intellectually stimulated and active prolongs life, so work is one of the best ways to stay active as long as one is happy with the work and work conditions. I would certainly want to retire before my abilities lessen and I hope to do so before I get to the point at which I don't know I've deteriorated. In addition, I am recognizing that science is rapidly changing my field and my paradigm of how I conceive the world may not speak to the new generation or may not include some new findings, though of course I try to fit new research into my conceptualization. Am I indispensable? No. There are better teachers, better researchers, greater thinkers that might be hired. But, I still have my unique contribution to make.

An argument one hears about retiring is that one should do it in order to make room for the young. I think it is presumptuous for the young to think I take up space where someone younger should have the opportunity. All young people must find opportunities and build on them, using their skills and ingenuity to create their career work. It has taken me time to build what I have and at my age I could not readily switch to another paid position, but I can do a great deal where I am.

If someone in my family would benefit from my retiring, if I were needed to attend to my devoted spouse or children or grandchildren—these are reasons I would retire immediately. I was able to be with my children when they were young, and I appreciated sharing those times. I seriously have considered retiring for those I love on a number of occasions. My father was very ill with cancer, and after he died I looked after my mother for six years, but made arrangements to allow myself to continue to work. I try to be available when people do need me, and my work schedule in academia is, fortunately, flexible.

Another draw toward retirement is the thought of being able to fully use my creative, artistic talents. I have really enjoyed painting, pottery making, sculpting, making murals, doing collage, printmaking, and drawing. I have had visions of making masterpieces and building artistic playgrounds and designing any number of everyday objects, including clothing and cars. I think I would love to work in glass and wood, do computer graphics, make films, and pursue architecture. It would be fun to take courses in any of these or work with a mentor to learn some technical skills and mass marketing. (Oh, oh, there I go again with the goal of making a difference. My art would be gratifying because, I think, if it spread widely it would beautify our environment!) These urges get left behind when teaching full time.

Certainly there are frustrations that I could leave behind if I retired. My frustrations at work are primarily my failures: the failure to be an outstanding, dynamic teacher all the students adulate; the failure I own when even one student is disgruntled or not working up to her or his potential, or quits a project; the failure to teach the students enough skills in the right combination, to utilize or perhaps motivate them to utilize the techniques that would make their work the state of the art; the failure to convince colleagues, the dean, the university to do things the way I think would make a positive difference; the failure to design research that would lead to fruitful results and to more sharing of my wisdom with colleagues, through publication; the failure illustrated by my messy desk and disorganized office—the accumulation of many incomplete projects, paper files, boxes of someday-to-be-useful notes, books that could be sorted through; the failure to complete articles and submit them for publication. However, I know me. Escape from these failures would not happen if I were retired. I would not be without projects. The next projects would cause these same frustrations and pull in too many directions. So I get back to deciding to continue the job, which helps me focus on accomplishing things I value.

One of the most important reasons to retire is for one's life partner. My husband and I have shared so much. We love and care about each other deeply; we have worked at loving and examined how to maximize our love. My spouse at sixty-five is semiretired and wishes me to retire to have the flexibility to do what we have done on our vacations in years past. It is probable that we have only some ten to fifteen years more, if that, and we are lucky to be healthy enough to do things now. He is quite busy with his own projects: he is on the boards of several local groups (the Audubon Society, Land Acquisition, and the Environmental Health Board), oversees a nature preserve, monitors manatees, is concerned about development and the destruction of wildlife habitats, volunteers to take people birding and canoeing once a month, and is active in supporting the Envirothon competition for high school students. Though he is involved in many projects, he has more time at home, and he is not used to spending his time at home alone. I know what it is like to wait for him to come home, nights and weekends, since I had that experience during the years of raising children and not working full-time away from home. He would like me to have the time to get into our van and go traveling, to go canoeing, or to events held during the school year (e.g., spring birding), or to take courses together. We are working together on a book of photography and poetry, historical description, and interesting true stories about happenings at a lovely lake area nearby. We enjoy doing anything together, but especially having new adventures. This probably will be the main reason that I'll retire; however, at the moment it would be for him, not for me. For now I find fulfillment in my current work and don't see retiring any time soon.

Rejecting Retirement for Now or Altogether

Although I have seriously thought about retirement, I am not ready. I still enjoy my work; I am still heady over the freedom of being able to work at a job I think is so important and the satisfaction in finally achieving some degree of respect as a working woman. I guess this means I do not feel I gain as much respect in other roles. I believe I have the power to make a difference, to do what I can for the causes I support. I'm still energized by and find meaning being out in the stimulating career world. I have exposure to the exciting scientific advances and controversies in my field and the opportunity to discuss these with colleagues, learn new skills, and keep up with current technology (computers and the Internet can do so much to facilitate teaching and therapy). I still have much health and vigor. In fact, I toy with the idea of rejecting retirement altogether. Even if I retired from this paid job, I would do unpaid work just as I did many years ago (even though I sometimes resented not getting paid); it would really not be retirement. Knowing my values and what brings me happiness, I do not think I would get far away from my basic aim of leaving this world a better place, every day.

Notes

1. A. H. Maslow, *Toward a Psychology of Being* (Princeton, N.J.: Van Nostrand, 1962).

2. D. Kuhn, A. Ortigara, and D. Lindeman, "The Growing Challenge of Alzheimer's Disease in Residential Settings" (Chicago: Rush Alzheimer's Disease Center, Rush Presbyterian-St. Luke's Medical Center, 1999); retrieved 20 February 2002 from www.alzheimers.org/slides/Mod1/sld016.htm.

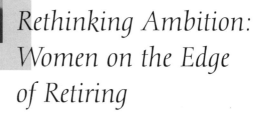

Rethinking Ambition: Women on the Edge of Retiring

SHIRLEY GEOK-LIN LIM

*R*etiring, as a term used to describe women, functioned as an adjective rather than a verb in an earlier century. It was frequently applied in approving ways to women seen as reserved, shy, unobtrusive, and contented with private lives of domestic seclusion. As one component of the larger civil rights movement or as a catalyst to feminist ideals, beginning in the 1960s many U.S. women, participating in the criticism of the mystique of the household, entered the public sphere of paid work. Academic achievements, careers, and professions fill the life stories of twentieth-century women who are constructed as role models for a younger generation.[1] While *competition* and its corollary *ambition* have not been closely theorized in feminist dialogue, *profession* and *success* appear in many studies of contemporary U.S. women.

But what happens when ambitious women, who have spent their lives breaking the mould and acting as pioneers in the world of work, reach the so-called age of retirement? What are some of the contradictions inherent in the narratives of lives dominated by the ambition to emerge from the condition of "retiring women" but now facing the condition of retiring from the domain of ambition? How do professional women give up what they have fought so hard to achieve? Why would someone like me, a few years away from sixty, consider stepping down from a position I have struggled so hard to achieve, and what does my ambivalence over the world of acknowledged success have to say about feminist ideology?

Retirement is not an entirely new question in women's studies. Earlier social research defined retirement for men and women in similar terms.[2] Many did not attempt to distinguish between the experiences of gendered subjects from different ethnic and class backgrounds.[3] In the late 1980s, a number of sociologists looked specifically at the psychosocial and economic factors women faced when considering retirement from the work force.[4] Many of these studies confirmed that retirement can and should be a fulfilling stage in women's life trajectories. Activities, hobbies, relationships, issues postponed or never considered may now be developed and enjoyed.

Such research has been criticized for its focus on white and middle-class retirees and for its assumption that "retirement itself is a gender neutral concept, and consequently the characteristics of male retirement are assumed to be normative for women professionals as well."[5] Kathleen Perkins's 1993 study, for example, demonstrated that, for working-class and black women, retirement is an anxious and difficult experience combining involuntary retirement, poverty, and the absence of preretirement planning that would offer a financial safety net.[6] Even many women professionals, especially those who have worked outside or on the margins of institutions, are looking at retirement with trepidation after years of irregular, low-paying, or nonpaid work.[7]

Because I wish to examine some of the choices facing women professionals looking at retirement at or near the top of their careers, I am aware that the options mapped here are privileged and not available to all older women. But, while my approach to retirement here is chiefly unraced and middle class, I hope it is grounded in some consciousness of feminist ideology, in the concept of remaining embedded in the world of the struggle for social justice, because that is the only world we share.

Reading the available popular literature on retirement that fills much of the AARP's (formerly the American Association of Retired Persons) Web pages and its magazine, *Modern Maturity* (reportedly the largest circulating magazine in the United States), I am struck by the peculiar resemblance of examples of retirement activities to the domestic activities associated with the traditional non-career-bound housewife. Retirement thus viewed appears much like the condition of "stay-at-home" women whose husbands' salaries traditionally have secured for them a leisurely distance from the eight–to-five routine of the working world. Betty Friedan's 1963 *Feminine Mystique* decisively overthrew the notion that "stay-at-home" wives in the United States were happy, healthy, or fulfilled.[8] In the late twentieth century, however, dissenting voices were never far from public hearing. Some contemporary Western women, more skeptical of feminism's promise of fulfillment through paid work, have sought to redress the unremitting focus on profession and career with a balance of personal satisfactions through self-chosen domestic duties. And there are still examples of U.S. women whose career is that of being a wife. Women's magazines continue to address them in respectful terms, as equal partners to their working husbands; and the phenomenon of "trophy wives," younger women married to older executives and professionals and testimony to male success, is so common as to pass without comment everywhere in the United States.

Such elite wives are commonly known as "*tai-tai*" (literally "supreme of the supreme") in Hong Kong. The term's original meaning is "wife," but it has come to signify the state of luxury enjoyed by women who are maintained by rich men, not necessarily their husbands. Working women, whether CEOs listed among the Fortune 500 or academics, are usually not considered tai-tais, for they lack the luxury of free expendable time, an item paradoxically so expensive that their income, no matter how munificent, can never purchase it. It is not clear to me whether retired women CEOs can achieve a tai-tai condition, as tai-tais are also associated with a certain youthfulness, even in the midst of middle age, and with social gatherings and practices permitted only if they are admitted into the exclusive circle of tai-tais. Hong Kong tai-tais employ maids from third-world countries, whose services 24/6 keep the tai-tai's home, clothes, meals, and schedules shining and smooth.

The proper feminist will find this domestic arrangement obscene, structured as it is on the exploitation of globalization's inequities.[9] In the United States, where there is less cheap third-world domestic help, technology has replaced human labor. With contraception, women now have choices about how to use their ensuing leisure, leisure limited to a minority of the world's six billion people and only in the late twentieth century imaginable without the institution of domestic enslavement or its equivalent. Women in technologically advanced societies, of course, have used the leisure offered by machines and their release from childbearing to be "productive," to do useful work or at least work that is paid.

Feminist ideology is not premised on the right to work. After all, women have always labored: in the fields, in kitchens, bedrooms, and other parts of the home. Much of this labor was and is involuntary, enforced by economic necessity or patriarchal law. This work was and is seldom valued as productive, and even less often remunerated so as to afford women independence from male control. In many societies, humans gendered as female have had to struggle for the right to choose their paths to productive work that would be socially valued and recognized through equitable pay that permits them economic means for a life with dignity. Activists and academics have only been able to theorize feminist ideology on the premise of choice, over bodies and the workplace. This goal appears modest: the right to what many Western men take for granted. However, in a world where the majority live on less than one U.S. dollar a day and have no access to clean water, shelter, sufficient nutrition, education, and security, many U.S. women are part of a privileged group whose entitlement to choice over body and profession rests on the material and military superiority of the United States and its Western allies. In order to complicate and sharpen our decisions, middle-class and upper-class women may wish to juxtapose the factors underlying the choices ahead of us that permit us to view retirement through the lens of entitlement and plenty, with those affecting the majority of the world's women. That is, retirement for U.S. women professionals may be approached not as just a personal decision but as another of the politically oriented actions that constitute feminism as a set of practices in the world.

After two years as chair professor and head of the English Department at the University of Hong Kong, I have recently returned to my home institution, the university in which I am tenured, to mull over my Asian venture and to ponder on my choices for the future. Retirement from the University of California, Santa Barbara, in a few years, between sixty and sixty-five, appears forcefully to me to be an ethical act. It will open a position for a junior colleague whose contribution to the university and to the profession will be no less than mine has been and possibly will be much greater. Although there is no mandatory retirement age for university faculty, I believe that as teachers whose lives have been dedicated to the transmission of knowledge to a younger generation, we are beholden to observe natural law and so to give way to a new generation of scholars and teachers. Retirement is therefore, for me, a political act, particularly in light of the crisis of academic unemployment for English Ph.D.s. Joulain, Mullett, Lecomte, and Prévost's discussion of perceptions concerning appropriate ages for retirement shows us the range of social expectations on this sensitive issue that will become more pressing as demographic pressures change with different stresses for different occupations, some pushing for professionals to retire to open up positions for younger colleagues, and others compelling later retirement ages as the numbers of available workers decrease.[10]

It is one thing to step aside from a tenured position; it is another to consider what one should step into. The wife of a colleague well past retirement, a man who appears determined never to retire, remarked that my desire to retire early was understandable considering how very hard I have had to work all my life. She concluded that retirement would be a cessation from work, a well-earned rest. She could not know that I read cessation from work as an abhorrent privilege. From my childhood of hunger and poverty I have associated not working with the undeserving rich and perhaps more stringently with deathly boredom, the aimlessness of the unproductive. I hurried to clarify that giving up a tenured position would permit me instead a larger range of choices of productive work. I could continue to teach part-time at the university or for short full-time appointments elsewhere. I would be working on writing more novels, short fiction, poetry, and creative nonfiction, the plethora of genres that fill me with greedy pleasure. Official retirement, I explained, would make possible fuller entry into those positions that I had been eyeing for much of my adult life: writer-in-residencies, fellowships at campuses with a diverse set of colleagues and library holdings, and yes, gardener, chef, and homemaker. The last three would not keep me sufficiently busy as to merit the category of occupation, but writer and teacher (rather than tenured faculty member) would.

Still, after this encounter, a nagging voice tells me that none of these postretirement choices bears the colors of feminism. The contradiction between desire for luxurious retirement which some older Americans believe is owed them—golf courses, early bird specials, expensive retirement communities, indulgence in pampered travel, unlimited health care, and so forth—and the consciousness of social justice still unachieved may be the most pressing ethical issue looming ahead for me and for many baby-boom women professionals facing retirement. The former is eminently achievable for those of us with pension plans and social security benefits. But I would like to believe that in unretiring ambition, the desire to remain ideologically close to the present self burns as brightly, and that there can be no retirement from feminist consciousness and work. However, even as an early stage had primed us for struggle and a middle stage for ambitious and activist striving in academe, so we are looking at this late stage and finding few models for late-age activist women. Excepting those who have never chosen to retire or who have partially retired.

Partial retirement. Unlike the many agencies that counsel young Americans, few agencies counsel older workers on their psychological, emotional, and professional options. Most universities offer emeritus professor status that may or may not permit the retiree office space, photocopy, E-mail, and telephone privileges, and the right to teach a course or more each year. According to a new report by the American Association of University Professors (AAUP), "Nearly half of all colleges have offered financial incentives to encourage faculty members to retire early at some point since 1994."[11] The *Chronicle of Higher Education* noted that of the "608 public and private colleges and universities with 75 or more full-time faculty members" covered in the "Survey of Changes in Faculty Retirement Policies" conducted in 2000 by the AAUP's Committee on Retirement, "[a] common financial incentive, offered at more than a third of the institutions, was a negotiated buyout or other special arrangements on a college-by-college or case-by-case basis. . . . One option for institutions is a phased-out-retirement program, in which an older faculty member could continue to teach on a part-time basis and at a reduced salary." According to Ernest Benjamin, the AAUP's director of research, "In general, institutions ought to think of plans that are highly flexible and can adjust to changes in the market so they can retain those they want to retain, and help others leave."

For feminist and activist faculty, this form of partial institutional retirement—doing the same as, only less of it—may be one productive approach to their retirement years. The desire to see their gains on campus ensured and even advanced will encourage them to maintain a relationship with the university. Even where they may discover teaching one course annually unsatisfactory, they can always cut away to volunteer for committees that may assert influence on the institution. As Benjamin noted in a larger context, universities will do well to make use of these desires, for women academics have usually proven themselves resourceful, flexible, articulate, passionate, and public spirited, qualities that are invaluable to recruiting students, junior faculty, alumni and alumnae, and donors. Arguably, instead of having retired feminists do more of the same teaching and committee work, universities might begin seriously to deploy them for what they do so well as public intellectuals.

This course, however, assumes that we will retire geographically where we have our final appointment. But I wonder whether such fixity is altogether a positive good, albeit it permits the deepening of community bonds and institutional memory. If retirement is not to be a retiring from the field of active service but a redeployment of changing rather than diminishing energies, then perhaps the field of engagement itself may have to be rethought and revised. Few local communities will not be enriched by the expertise of retired women professionals, but many impoverished communities elsewhere in the developing and underdeveloped world urgently need such expertise. Freedom from scheduled work in our daily community, from paid routine, should free us for voluntary work in projects that take us out of our normal community: teaching in less developed locations; consulting and practicing in nonprofit, non-governmental organizations, for example.

Perhaps not so ironically, U.S. business has been quick to do something about the present cohorts of healthy retired executives wishing to put their still salient talents and skills to a greater service in the world. The International Executive Service Corps (IESC) was formed to "ship retired U.S. business-man to poor countries to help businesses grow into large ones." The seventy-two-year-old president of IESC, Hobart Gardiner, has recently joined forces with Geekcorps, a group of young technologists, "pairing 'geezers and geeks' to try to stem the growing gap in technology between rich and poor countries."[12] These kinds of international consultant/advisory services form a model for what I imagine retired women could be organizing to do. Parachuting retirees into volunteer, short-term projects may ensure that fields will not be dominated by older professionals but can still benefit from their experience and energy. I would like to see national and international bodies develop structures that match retired women professionals to costly tasks—consulting, advising, administering, and teaching—achievable on a temporary and short-term basis.

Retired professionals like myself, should I still be healthy at that age, possess the luxury of rare freedoms available to very few: freedom from want while free from scheduled work, and freedom, empowered by skills, knowledge, and experience, to continue achieving professionally. That is, we can achieve while free from the need to earn. This privilege of class, which I owe to my good fortune of being a citizen of the United States, will make me a special kind of retiree: an adaptable, flexible, mobile, experienced, global professional, unencumbered by children or employer, and unfettered by the need for a high income.

This brief disquisition on retirement brings me back to the crossroads that opened the essay, leading to two different models for my future. The tai-tai with access to free time and ready money, who stereotypically uses these resources for consumption and social show; and the older woman who uses similar resources to engage with the world as a voluntary professional. Retirement, it seems to me, need not signify cessation from public work, a move to unsalaried, voluntary domestic work (gardening and culinary endeavors, for example). Rather, I imagine retirement may well be approached as a move from long-term, scheduled, salaried, and regular labor, tied to one institution, to more flexibly scheduled, nonregularized, volunteer, perhaps remunerated, projects that are geographically mobile. Onyx and Benton, in research with Australian professional women, note that a dominant motivation in [the women's] professional career involved personal development . . . of new skills, pushing the personal boundaries of understanding, learning new ways of being effective. Indeed, once the challenge had been met, interest in the job waned, and this was usually a signal to start looking for new directions. . . . These dimensions of professional employment continue to be important to the women as they consider future retirement options. That is, whether they are paid or not, these women continue to seek work that is personally challenging, socially useful, and produces a sense of personal achievement and recognition.[13]

Moving from regulated work to free work, ambition need not take a back seat but will instead finally move into the forefront, where it will prompt us to ask not what the institution wants but what we want out of our lives and the work we can and wish to do. Approaching sixty and wishing for time for "my own work," I am comforted to learn that "Nearly all the women interviewed expressed a desire to have more time to develop some sort of creative interest. . . . The desire for creative self-expression often appeared to be linked to the desire to have more time for oneself."[14] Personal decisions regarding retirement that women academics arrive at possess broader policy implications for the professions that may be losing their contributions, and further studies of their processes of decision making could lead to continuity rather than abrupt breaks, both for the individual and the institution.[15] Writing, after all, is both a private and a public creative act. I am in the process of inventing a retirement that will shift continuously between private and public societies, when my ambition to write will converge with my desire for continuity in community work. Looking toward a retirement when I can continue to teach creative writing in postcolonial places where English and creativity form part of a necessary global cultural confluence, I am also looking toward foregrounding ambition, to making time and space for that young girl who so desperately wanted to write her self into the world.

Notes

1. Rachel Blau DuPlessis and Ann Snitow, eds., *The Feminist Memoir Project: Voices from Women's Liberation* (New York: Three Rivers Press, 1998).

2. R. Atchley, *Social Forces and Aging* (Belmont, Calif.: Wadsworth Publishing [1977], 1990).

3. Helen Dennis, ed., *Retirement Preparation: What Retirement Specialists Need to Know* (Lexington, Mass.: Lexington Books, 1984); and Diana Cort-Van Arsdale and Phyllis Newman, "Women's Transitions in Retirement: The Role of

the Retirement Planner," in *Women in Mid-Life: Planning for Tomorrow*, ed. Christopher L. Hayes (Binghamton, N.Y.: Haworth Press, 1993).

4. For example, Harvey Catchen, "Generational Equity: Issues of Gender and Race," in *Women in the Later Years: Health, Social, and Cultural Perspectives*, ed. Lois Grau and Ida Susser (Binghamton, N.Y.: Harrington Park Press, 1989); Mark D. Hayward, William R. Grady, and Steven D. McLaughlin, "The Retirement Process among Older Women in the United States," *Research on Aging* 10, no. 3 (1988): 358–382; Lois B. Shaw and Rachel Shaw, "From Midlife to Retirement: The Middle-Aged Woman Worker," in *Working Women: Past, Present, Future*, ed. Karen Shallcross Koziara, Michael H. Moskow, and Lucretia Dewey Tanner (Washington, D.C.: Bureau of National Affairs, 1987); and Ruth Ann Erdner and Rebecca F. Guy, "Career Identification and Women's Attitudes toward Retirement," *International Journal of Aging and Human Development* 30, no. 2 (1990): 129–139.

5. Jenny Onyx and Pam Benton, "Retirement: A Problematic Concept for Older Women," *Journal of Women and Aging* 8, no. 2 (1996): 21.

6. Kathleen Perkins, "Working Class Women and Retirement," *Journal of Gerontological Social Work* 20, nos. 3/4 (1993): 129–132.

7. See Virginia E. Richardson's excellent critique of economic inequities facing retired women in her "Women and Retirement," in *Fundamentals of Feminist Gerontology*, ed. J. Dianne Garner (Binghamton, N.Y.: Haworth Press, 1999), as well as the examination of social strategies that help empower aging women workers in Paula Rayman, Kimberley Allshouse, and Jessie Allen, "Resiliency amidst Inequity: Older Women Workers in an Aging United States," in *Women on the Front Lines: Meeting the Challenge of an Aging America*, ed. Jessie Allen and Alan Pifer (Washington, D.C.: Urban Institute Press, 1993).

8. Betty Friedan, *The Feminine Mystique* (New York: W. W. Norton, 1963).

9. L. Ling and K. Chang, "Globalization and Its Intimate Other: Filipina Domestics in Hong Kong," in *Gender and Global Restructurings: Sightings, Sites and Resistances*, ed. M. Marchand and A. Sisson Runyan (London: Routledge, 2000).

10. Michèle Joulain, Etienne Mullet, Christèle Lecomte, and Rebecca Prévost, "Perception of 'Appropriate' Age for Retirement among Young Adults, Middle-Aged Adults, and Elderly People," *International Journal of Aging and Human Development* 50, no. 1 (2000): 73–84.

11. Cited in Piper Fogg, "Early-Retirement Offers to Faculty Members Are Common, a Study Finds," *The Chronicle of Higher Education*, 10 August 2001, A10. The two citations following in text are also from this article.

12. "Older Execs Join Techie Youths," *Los Angeles Times*, 16 August 2001, T2.

13. Onyx and Benton, "Retirement," 25.

14. Ibid., 27.

15. Patricia J. Villani and Karen A. Roberto, "Retirement Decision-Making: Gender Issues and Policy Implications," *Journal of Women and Aging* 9, nos. 1–2 (1997): 151–163.

Circling the Wagons: A Guide to Lesbian Retirement

Jen Christensen and Holly Crenshaw

On a scruffy plot of land in Arizona, away from prying eyes, a few old lesbians have carved out their own version of utopia in a recreational-vehicle park. They have circled their metal wagons, thrown up a protective shield, and established close bonds with the other women who have come to enjoy their retirement years in a safe and supportive environment. For some who have spent years hiding their true identity from their family, their friends, and their co-workers, there is a sense that they can finally be who they really are. And the community members look out for each others' physical needs. "Any time anyone gets ill here, immediately a notice goes on the 'We Care' board we put up in the public area of our community," said Vera Martin, a seventy-eight-year-old resident of the Arizona park, in a phone interview. "It lists the needs of the person who is sick or the needs of their family, and then we sign up for whatever needs to be done. We go to the market for them. We prepare meals for them. We take them to doctors' appointments. We see to it that no one struggles through illness alone. We make sure we take care of each other."

But this strong web of support could not stop an ugly dose of reality from crashing into their world. When a resident suffered a stroke that left her unable to speak, her daughter came rushing over to the park within hours—

almost as if she had been waiting for that day to come. She cleaned out her mother's things, took the RV—a beautiful, new pullout rig the mother and her life partner had made their home—and issued an edict to her mother's companion: she was never to see her partner again. "The only thing that saved the partner was that her name was on the papers for the rig," Martin said. "So the family at least had to give that back. There were no other laws to protect her."

The story Martin tells is sad but not uncommon. It points out both the vulnerabilities that older lesbians face under our current legal system and some of the savvy strategies they have devised to get around them. The challenges heterosexual women face in their retirement years—diminished income, medical concerns, social isolation, and ageism—are the same ones older lesbians confront. But lesbians are also hit with financial, personal, and social barriers in retirement that their heterosexual peers do not have.

On average, lesbians are not as economically well off as married women. Because lesbians cannot legally marry, they miss out on the financial benefits that come with those vows: they are ineligible to collect their partner's Social Security benefits, cannot collect their partner's pension without being highly taxed, if they can collect it at all, and shoulder a heavier tax burden for their shared property. Lesbian couples typically must maintain separate health insurance policies. They may lose their joint-owned property under Medicaid. They may suffer from unfair treatment from homophobic health care providers, be denied access to their partner's financial information in the event of an emergency or refused a role in their partner's health care, and be prevented from visiting their sick partners in the hospital. Lesbians must maintain a complicated set of legal papers in order to protect their partners from potential financial trouble. They must keep a living will, sign over power of attorney, and set up a proper will or a trust so their partner will be able to inherit; married couples automatically have these benefits. When seeking social services, lesbians may be subject to homophobic treatment from nursing-home workers, may not be welcome at senior centers, may not be able to live with their partners in senior housing, and may even be denied visitation if their partner is moved into a nursing home.

Some right-to-marry groups say a marriage license comes with about 1,049 rights, responsibilities, benefits, and protections under federal law.[1] Lesbian relationships come with no automatic legal protections. And without this right to marry, advocates estimate, the lesbian and gay community loses about $124 million in social security benefits alone each year.[2] Without these spousal perks, more and more elderly lesbians—both single and coupled—are relying on gay-friendly attorneys, grassroots groups, networks of friends, and histories of activism to build as many safeguards as possible for their retirement years.

As they are members of three much-studied groups—women, the elderly, and gays and lesbians—each with a legacy of civil rights success, it is surprising that lesbians face so many challenges in retirement and that they do so without much notice. The government does not study retired lesbians, and critics within the gay community say it has a hard time dealing with issues involving people over thirty. Here we hope to give lesbians—both those of retirement age and those years from it—their due. Drawing from personal interviews with lesbians across the country, we will look at the barriers lesbians face in retirement and examine some of the creative approaches they have devised to overcome them.

The Poverty Problem

One popular myth about the gay community is that its members are rich. If this were the case, lesbians would be better prepared for retirement than most women, since wealth is one of the biggest determining factors in how well someone lives in retirement. But in reality, the few existing studies show lesbians are worse off financially in retirement than their straight counterparts.[3] As they approach retirement, lesbians will need to be better prepared if they are to survive the financial challenges specific to this community.

"I don't ever really like to think about retirement," Melanie Otis, a forty-two-year-old lesbian who works at the University of Kentucky at Lexington as an associate professor in the School of Social Work, told us. "At one point, I was given the information on how much I would get when I started collecting social security and I thought if I had to live on just that . . . well, that's really no way to go." Until two years ago, social security was all Otis would have had to live on in retirement. Hanging next to her Ph.D. in her book-filled university office is the certificate she received for completing her general equivalency diploma (GED). Otis quit high school to get married at the age of sixteen. She had two children before she turned twenty. Eventually, while living in the isolation of eastern Kentucky, she realized she was a lesbian and left her husband. On her own, she raised her children, held a variety of full-time jobs, went back to school, and became a tireless civil rights activist fighting on behalf of women and Kentucky's gays and lesbians.

Now, pictures of her grandkids sit on top of her television, but this grandmother still has a long way to go before she can retire. In fact, it wasn't until she turned forty that she was able to find a full-time job that could help her prepare for her retirement years. Saddled with student loans, a mortgage, and significant debt from raising two children and supporting a couple of her partners, Otis said she was actually grateful when the University of Kentucky told her it would take money out of her paycheck to put toward her retirement. Without the university's retirement savings plan, Otis knew there would be no comfortable retirement for her.

Countless women in the lesbian community face Otis's earlier uncertain future; many others have not been lucky enough to find a job with any kind of retirement plan at all. Talking about her neighbors in her RV community, Vera Martin told us, "They don't stand a chance working in the mainstream." She added, "They just work in survival jobs, and the result of having to move around and change jobs just to make ends meet is that they are the ones who have very limited funds in their retirement. About half the people here don't have any medical coverage, and many of them have to take on part-time jobs long after they've 'retired.'"

Women still earn 21 percent less than men do.[4] Studies show Americans are more likely to be poor in retirement if they are female or if they are single.[5] Many lesbians of retirement age are single. A 1999 study conducted by Senior Action in a Gay Environment (SAGE) found that fewer than one in five seniors who are lesbian, gay, bisexual, or transgendered (LGBT) live with a partner, while about half of the elderly heterosexual population is married. And even if the lesbian has a partner, because the government does not recognize that relationship legally, it would classify the couple as two single women who happen to live together. Studies show the best way for a woman to ensure a financially stable retirement is to marry, because a husband—by virtue of being a man—generally makes more money.[6] With the passage of the Defense of Marriage Act (DOMA), federal law prohibits lesbian couples from marrying, even if they have been in an intimate partnership for decades. Lesbians earn salaries on average that are comparable to those of heterosexual women, but their paychecks—even when combined with a partner's—cannot compare to the monetary advantage of being a man, or being married to one.

Social Insecurity

Nancy Edwards is a fifty-nine-year-old lesbian who works part-time as a social policy professor at St. Cloud University in Minnesota and as a potter. Her partner, Barbara, who asked that we not use her last name, said their eyes met across a crowded room when she was conducting a social work seminar dealing with the local homeless population in Duluth. Barbara walked up to

Edwards and introduced herself. "She says she knew right then that she was going to spend the rest of her life with me," Edwards said. While they say their relationship is the most significant either one has had in her life, the government considers their shared life inconsequential. Nowhere is this more apparent than in the way the Social Security system regards the two.

While it isn't all that Edwards and her partner will have to rely on, social security will constitute a significant part of their retirement income. Sixty-two percent of Americans say that social security accounts for half or more of their annual retirement income. But 50 percent of unmarried women—which, under the current system, includes lesbians—rely on Social Security for their sole support.[7]

Lesbians in couples, like Nancy and Barbara, can only collect their own personal social security checks. No matter if they remain together for decades; partnered lesbians are denied both the spousal and survivor benefits that their heterosexual peers automatically receive from Social Security if they are married for a minimum of twelve years. "I will actually be able to collect social security on my ex-husband because we were married long enough," Edwards told us. "But isn't that just amazing? That relationship with my ex-husband has been over for a long time. I'll have been with my current partner for sixteen years by the time I collect social security. We own a house together, a summer home, we share our life together—but because she's a woman, the way the Social Security system is set up, we don't have access to each other's social security benefits."

In the current Social Security system, legally married people who reach the age of sixty-five and have earned less in their lifetimes than their spouse are entitled to additional partner benefits. That means they can collect a check for whatever benefits they have earned, plus half of the value of their spouse's social security checks. The combined income can be significant. But without a legal marriage, lesbians are not eligible to collect.[8]

The current system also denies survivor benefits to couples like Nancy and Barbara. In a legal marriage, when one spouse dies, the remaining spouse receives the deceased's social security check. In 1998, $4.1 billion went to survivors collecting social security, but not a dollar went to the surviving partner of a lesbian couple.[9] Survivor benefit checks average about $442 a month, an amount that could significantly help the remaining spouse who can no longer rely on her or his partner's income to help pay the bills.[10]

Without these benefits, the surviving partner of a lesbian couple could stand to lose everything she and her partner had owned together if they had not planned ahead. "My only ace in the hole for retirement is my partner. She is fourteen years younger than I am and she'll still be working when I retire," said Edwards, who—although a well-educated professional—has a self-described "checkered employment history" that has left her without significant personal retirement money. "If I were on my own, without Barbara, I would really only have social security and just a small savings to survive on. If Barbara and I hadn't put all our paperwork in order in case she dies before me, I doubt I would be able to maintain my house, or live the rest of my life how I'm now accustomed."

Pension Tension

Vera Martin, who is the feisty national coordinator for Old Lesbians Organizing for Change (OLOC), said she's glad she's not like her many peers who have to rely so much on social security. "Every day I count my blessings that I worked for the county of Los Angeles, which was in the forefront of retirement pensions," she said. Prior to her life as an activist, Martin spent thirty-nine years working as a systems analyst in a department that bought everything from "an elephant to a paper clip" for Los Angeles County. When she started working there, in 1946, one of the strongest attractions to the job was the county's pension plan. Its formula was based on length of service and a worker's salary. For Martin, that now translates into a regular pension check that equals about 98 percent of her last salary; plus she still has medical, dental, and vision insurance. "I believe I am doing well now, in part, because I had a good retirement plan set up for me," she told us. The kind of pension that is so essential to Martin's financial survival is not something her partner, if she were to have one, would ever be able to directly benefit from. Martin was married to a man, but he died several years ago. If they had remained married and she had died before he did, he would have automatically collected her pension. Under a joint survivor and annuity option of the Retirement Equity Act of 1984, the surviving partner automatically receives the spouse's pension without being taxed. If Martin died while in retirement and left her pension, or even a 401(k), to a lesbian partner, the partner would be able to collect the pension money, but there would be less of it. Pensions and 401(k)s left to people who are not one's spouse are taxed automatically at 20 percent.[11]

Lesbians who die before they are fully vested in their pensions leave their partners even worse off financially. If a married man dies before he is fully vested, his widow gets his pension at the time he would have received it. The same is not true for lesbian couples. If an unmarried lesbian dies prior to collecting her pension, the money she paid into the plan disappears. Studies estimate lesbian couples lose hundreds of millions of dollars through this un-equal system.[12] At one time, Martin had a partner who could have been helped significantly by her pension plan. Martin said one of the reasons they broke up in 1997, after twenty years together, was that she couldn't bear to watch her partner, who was severely diabetic, fail to take care of her health. Had Martin's pension benefits been extended to her partner, as they would have been to a traditional spouse, perhaps this health concern would not have been such a big issue.

Financial Planning

Without the protections that come with a legal marriage, financial plan-ning is more complex and more costly for lesbians than it is for married het-erosexuals, as it often involves an attorney. Not long ago, most workers like Vera Martin would typically put in forty years or more at a municipal or cor-porate job, become fully vested in their employer's pension plans, and then re-tire on fixed income. But retirement is rarely so simple today.

Knowing they are not entitled to a partner's social security benefits, pension income, and other financial resources after death, lesbians must plan ahead to create as much financial security as possible. "If you have a partner, you need to have these kinds of conversations," Nancy Edwards told us. Lesbians are ad-vised to follow many of the basics of financial planning that apply to women in general: start early, determine how much money you need to continue liv-ing in the manner you want to, and choose 401(k) and IRA plans wisely.[13] "I think there is a real generational difference between lesbians who haven't re-tired yet and lesbians who have," said Melanie Otis. "Regardless of what kind of work they do, women my age now are potentially better off because they can get a little more creative about figuring out how to build a retirement plan, especially with help from attorneys."

Typically, experts recommend that clients plan to replace 60 to 80 percent of their preretirement income. But since they are not entitled to traditional spousal benefits, lesbians' postretirement financial needs could be even greater. Financial advisers often remind their gay and lesbian clients that they must plan differently for retirement than their nongay counterparts.[14] "Of course, I think people should save," Sandy Warshaw, SAGE's director of pol-icy and education, said in a phone interview. "I did it through a city pension, but you could do it through IRAs and 401(k)s. But if you have the opportunity to do it, do it." Reverend Ken South, director of elder policy for the National Gay and Lesbian Task Force (NGLTF), told us, "Economically, it's more difficult for lesbians because women earn less than men. And there are more women than men who have children, so they have that extra responsibility when they retire. People make a big mistake when they assume gay men and lesbians experience aging in the same way, because they experience it very, very differently."

Lesbians: The Great Under-Cared-For and Underinsured

Americans' biggest expense in retirement is health care.[15] As we age, our health declines and the price of our medical bills climbs. For lesbians, health insurance carries its own problems. Unlike married couples, lesbian partners are not guaranteed access to their partner's health benefits. In fact, just 15 percent of municipalities or companies with more than 3,500 employees offer domestic partnership benefits.[16] That number has grown significantly in the last decade, but until there is a uniform federal law that mandates companies must insure their same-sex employees' partners, many lesbians will remain like Nancy Edwards, who does not qualify for Barbara's employee health insurance policy.

"My plan is to keep working just so I can have health insurance—that is, until I am eligible for Medicare, when I'm sixty-five," Edwards said. "The big worry for me about retirement has always been health care. Of course, if we had domestic partnership benefits in Minnesota, my working wouldn't even be an issue. My partner works for the county, which—if we were legally married—would give me excellent coverage. But of course we don't have domestic partnership benefits in Minnesota. At least, not yet." Edwards said her relationship could provide the kind of case study that Minnesota needs to understand why state and county employees should have domestic partner benefits. She and her partner hope to become a test case if anyone takes the state to court over this kind of discrimination.

Lesbians are uninsured at a much higher rate than their straight counterparts, and this lack of domestic partnership benefits may be one of the main reasons. Being uninsured can create a financial and emotional crisis for lesbians, particularly those of retirement age. "I'm a good example of what it means to be living on the edge," said sixty-five-year-old Patricia Nell Warren, best-selling author of *The Frontrunner* (1974), the landmark first novel to meet with popular success with a gay central character.

Warren is a success in many senses of the word, but she is not as well covered in retirement as she would like to be. She had health insurance when she worked as an editor with *Reader's Digest,* but now that she runs her own

business, Wildcat Press, she doesn't have access to traditional healthcare benefits. "Now, fortunately, I have Medicare, but it's kind of scary to think of the
catastrophic things and not being under any other kind of coverage," she told
us. Warren says she has been healthy most of her life but has suffered from
Lyme disease. This autoimmune disease is so serious it makes her ineligible
for life insurance. And chances are—if she is like most Americans—as she
ages, she can plan on making even more trips to the doctor. While only 9 percent of all Americans report they are in fair or poor health, people of retirement age are three times as likely to report that they are not in good health.
Some studies show lesbians may be even more vulnerable to illness than their
aging heterosexual peers. Poor eating habits, obesity, smoking, and infrequent
doctor visits—all problems in the lesbian community—may be contributing
factors to their higher risk for cancers, especially breast cancer, and other
deadly diseases.[17] Being nulliparous, or not having children, also increases
their breast cancer risk.[18]

There are ongoing national efforts to educate minority groups such as
African Americans and Latinos about health, and there are even nutrition programs specifically for the elderly, but there are no government-funded programs targeting older lesbians. Cancers, which strike millions of Americans
each year, may be more deadly in the lesbian community. For example, according to the 2001 Gay and Lesbian Healthy People Survey, lesbians get pap
smears and visit their gynecologist every twenty-one months, as compared to
the general population of women, who get a pap smear every eight months.[19]
Survivable cancers become deadlier if they go undetected and are not treated
early.

Lesbians are not necessarily cavalier about their health. Many lesbians do
not like to visit their physicians; a significant number of doctors disapprove of
their sexual orientation. The Gay and Lesbian Medical Association—then
known as the American Association of Physicians for Human Rights—
surveyed 711 of its physician and medical-student members to assess the
prevalence of antigay discrimination in the medical field. They found that homophobia was rampant. According to the 1994 survey, more than two thirds of
lesbian patients reported receiving poor care—or were actually denied care—
because of their sexual orientation. Two thirds of doctors and medical students reported biased caregiving by their professional peers, half reported
witnessing poor care, and a whopping 90 percent had heard disparaging remarks about their lesbian, gay, bisexual, or transgender (LGBT) patients.[20]
With such blatant homophobia in the medical system, lesbians like Patricia
Nell Warren—who relies solely on Medicare for her health coverage—may

be even more disappointed with the quality of the care they receive. Medicare uses an HMO-type system, which pays only designated physicians. That means there is a good chance a lesbian's trusted physician will not be covered under Medicare. Without that personal physician as an option, lesbians may not get the kind of care they need to survive well into their old age.

The only other fully federally funded health care program available to lesbians, Medicaid, also shortchanges them. Medicaid pays for extended health care, but only after a person's assets and funds are depleted. This system—one that was designed to protect women who were dependent on their husband's income—actually hurts women in couples who cannot marry. For instance, if Nancy Edwards's partner, Barbara, were to get sick and neither one carried extended heath insurance to pay for the nursing home, Barbara would have to go on Medicaid. And if Barbara's name appeared on the mortgage, they would have to sell their house, no matter if both she and Nancy had been contributing jointly to the house payments. If, however, the two were legally married, Barbara could go on Medicaid and into the nursing home and Nancy could continue living in the house. The government would recoup its losses from the married couple's estate only after both were gone. This means that Medicaid is another senior health service that directly discriminates against lesbians. Essentially a program that was designed to help those who cannot afford to pay for nursing home care, it ends up bankrupting a lesbian couple.[21]

Getting Paperwork in Order: "Legalizing" Lesbian Relationships

It is essential for lesbians to take the proper legal precautions to protect themselves from Medicaid and other systems that can bankrupt them. Couples should also take a number of legal steps to ensure they can remain involved should their partner fall sick. Legal documents are needed to give lesbians everything from the ability to make decisions about their partner's care to the ability to visit them in the hospital.

"You know there's a lot of apathy when it comes to looking toward the future in the lesbian community," Candice Stimson, who manages Sam and Hawle Enterprises, a prepay legal services company in Asheville, North Carolina, told us. "But we definitely have to plan for it, particularly as lesbians. You have to have the right paperwork in place, because your blood relatives legally have more right to your things, and to make decisions, than your life partner does if you were to get sick."

Stimson met her partner, Barbara Hladick, at Herwords, a writing group for women in Asheville. "Over watermelon on a warm day, we fell in love,"

Hladick told us. Partners in life, they also became partners in business, together running Sam and Hawle Enterprises. They help women in Asheville's growing lesbian community prepare for the legal difficulties they may face as a couple. Some of those preparations would become very important in their own lives. The two had been living together for a year when Hladick was diagnosed with endometrial cancer. "I wanted to make sure that my partner could make choices for me in the hospital," Hladick said. "If I didn't make a trip to the lawyer right before I went in for surgery, there was no guarantee that Candice would've been able to make those medical and financial decisions for me if I weren't able."

The proper paperwork, such as a living will and power of attorney, among other documents, allows a partner to make financial and medical decisions and gives a partner the same visitation rights that are automatically given to a spouse. Lesbians must plan carefully if they are to remain a part of each other's lives. All too often this does not happen. "I know of a person who was dying and had been taken care of by the community and by her partner for years," Edwards said. "But when it got really bad her family came in, and the community and partner that had cared so much for this woman were not allowed to be around this person anymore. Can you imagine being denied the right to see someone you care so deeply about?"

Visitation would only be a small part of a lesbian couple's problem if the proper legal papers were not in place and the partners owned shared property. If one partner gets sick, or dies without a will, and the mortgage on their house is not set up jointly, blood relatives—even a distant cousin—have more claim to their property than the surviving life partner does. Stories like the one from the Arizona RV park, where a partner almost lost her home are all too common. Many lesbians refer to *If These Walls Could Talk 2*, an HBO movie for which Vanessa Redgrave won an Emmy Award, when discussing this issue. The broadcast was one of the first popular programs to look at the issues facing older lesbians. The story is set in 1961, when an aging Redgrave loses her longtime companion and finds no compassion from her partner's relatives, who fail to grasp the nature of their relationship. The family comes in and has every legal right to take home and shared possessions away from Redgrave's character. While the story is set more than forty years ago, lesbians have no more rights now to prevent this scenario than they did in 1961.

It is not that lesbians are ignorant of the law. In part, it may be that the current crop of retired lesbians does not make it to the attorney's office to talk about their partnership either because they cannot afford it or because they fear the legal system itself. "This lack of doing the necessary legal papers to protect the one you love comes from a personal homophobia," Vera Martin said. "There is a fear of losing their family and friends, or a fear of a society that for much of their life has been punitive when it comes to our issues. I mean, we lived through the McCarthy era. As lesbians, we're not necessarily going to trust the system to protect us." For years, activists have been urging lesbians and gay men in committed relationships to make sure they lock in as many legal protections as possible. Bookstores now offer how-to publications for gay couples in search of legal advice, and gay-friendly lawyers can help their clients plan ahead.

The most crucial aspect of estate planning for all gay couples is a will. No state's intestacy laws provide for the surviving lesbian partner. A will can ensure that property passes on according to the intentions of the deceased.[22] Without one, the estate goes to her legal relatives. Edwards, who has been with her partner ten years, said, "If you make legal wills and draw up legal documents leaving each other all of the property, then you're less likely to have a homophobic kid or homophobic parent come in and think they deserve it and take it all away from your partner. But of course, if someone really contests it and they are blood relatives, they'll probably win. It is scary." Even knowing how essential a will is, Edwards admitted it took her a while to get around to signing one. "We'd been trying to get it done for a good many years," she said. "I went to Nepal with my son and I made sure we had it done before I went," she added, laughing.

Most lawyers advise their lesbian clients that they need to draw up more legal papers than just a will. Among the other legal precautions lesbians should explore are:

- Life estate: When the home-owning partner dies, this allows the remaining partner to live in the house they shared for the rest of his or her life. The surviving partner is obligated to maintain the property and continue to pay taxes on it.[23]
- Personal trust: This is a legal relationship that softens the blow of probate taxes and allows the person who dies to maintain some control over her assets. Trust beneficiaries must spend the money as the deceased intended.[24]
- Financial power of attorney: If one partner becomes disabled or incapacitated, this gives the other partner the ability to manage the other's finances. Experts say failing to do this is the biggest mistake that LGBT couples typically make.[25]
- Guardianship of minors: If there are children involved in a relationship, usually only one partner is the legal guardian or parent. Lesbian couples need a number of legal documents—possibly including a court order— to ensure the other's right to raise the kids.[26]

- Life insurance: For legally married couples, life insurance automatically goes to a surviving spouse, but lesbians must specifically designate each other as beneficiaries, or else life insurance may revert to another family member.

Homophobic Social Services

In addition to having to legally circumvent their lack of marriage rights, lesbians have been forced to find creative ways of dealing with an unwelcoming social service system, which plays an essential role in the lives of retired heterosexuals. "One thing we've learned in studying why lesbians don't use social services—it's not just a real homophobia that keeps people away from using senior services," said Nancy Edwards, who is working with a board in Minneapolis to make a local nursing home accessible to gay men and lesbians. "It's that lesbian seniors don't always know how they'll be accepted. Lesbians like myself really do want lesbian-specific or gay-friendly services."

In a 1994 study by the New York State Area Agencies on Aging—a regional group that decides how to spend federal dollars on senior services in the state—nearly half of the agencies interviewed reported that gay men and lesbians would not be welcome at the senior centers in their areas if their sexual orientation were known.[27] The National Gay and Lesbian Task Force's 2000 study, Outing Age, found many lesbians who worried they would not be accepted at senior service centers, just like Edwards does. Three fourths of these polled lesbians felt they would not be welcome or would not be treated well in these programs.[28] Only 19 percent of lesbians said they actually participated in senior center activities.[29] A poll of senior centers found that while they generally offer programs to welcome minority groups—including outreach to African Americans and the Spanish-speaking elderly—96 percent of the facilities reported they had no outreach to lesbians or gay men.[30] A poll of Americans between the ages of sixty-five and seventy-two showed that 52 percent of those surveyed expressed homophobic opinions.[31]

Gay activists frequently suggest that as the baby boom population ages, and lesbians are naturally included in that growing demographic group, more social services will become available to address their needs. But to ensure those services are fully accessible to lesbians, social agencies should be encouraged to include questions about sexual orientation in their initial client assessments; offer service training provided by LGBT elders to their staff; develop outreach strategies for reaching the gay community; collaborate with LGBT service organizations; and make an effort to market themselves in an inclusive way.[32] "I certainly recognize it's important for us to have our own supportive services for people that are gay friendly," Patricia Nell Warren told us. "But I also think it's really important to get AARP [American Association of Retired Persons] turned around on the subject of gay people—that's just something that's got to happen. I've written them and told them I used to belong, but didn't renew my membership. And I told them I won't belong until they change."

But unless their local community has been unusually active in this area, most lesbians don't have any lesbian-specific senior services available to them. Since 1965, the Older Americans Act has been giving hundreds of millions of federal dollars to home- and community-based senior services. For the fiscal year 2000 alone, the government spent $933 million on this program.[33] Some of the recipient programs target minority populations, but not a penny of this money went to lesbian-specific programs.[34]

Lesbians are generally invisible in the national discussion about how Americans should take care of their aging population. It was not until 1994 that the White House Council on Aging included lesbians and gays in its conference agenda. Even when they were included, they were not successful in persuading the group to add sexual orientation as a protected category in White House policy.[35] Without that protection, many lesbians in retirement feel betwixt and between about the services that are available to their peers—they use these services, but keep quiet about their sexual orientation, or skip these services all together.

The White House Council on Aging finally included lesbian and gay issues on its agenda in part because of the efforts of Del Martin and Phyllis Lyon, cofounders of the Daughters of Bilitis, and Nancy Moldenhauer, who was serving as the vice president of the Older Women's League. Other groups, including Lesbian and Gay Aging Issues Network (LGAIN), were instrumental in the conference, which resulted in a list of priorities for older gay men and lesbians. The conference's far-reaching goals called for federal leadership in providing equal access to senior services, nondiscriminatory funding for senior programming, inclusive federal housing, and sensitivity training for senior service providers and health care professionals.

Seeking Shelter

Senior housing programs, essential to many elderly, are not meeting the needs of retirement-age lesbians. With limited income and little in the way of a retirement plan, lesbians such as Patricia Nell Warren, for example, may want access to senior housing when they reach retirement age. Nationwide, there are nearly three million senior housing units funded under the Department of Housing and Urban Development (HUD) that, technically, would have been available to Warren last year. But as lesbians apply for that housing, they may wonder if they would really be welcome. HUD is on record as saying it does not discriminate against lesbians. But while the program's own policy prevents the agency from discriminating against people of a racial, ethnic, or religious minority, or because of physical disability, there is nothing in writing that stops discrimination based on sexual orientation.[36] Even if lesbians were to move into a particular housing project, they might not feel comfortable being honest about their sexuality while living in such close quarters with a population that might not be friendly to them.

While married couples can apply for joint housing, it is commonly known among senior housing providers that the lifelong relationships of lesbians are not recognized. A couple like Candice Stimson and Barbara Hladick, who will have been living together for at least twenty years by the time they may consider senior housing, could be split apart; managers are under no legal obligation to house them together.

Stimson and Hladick may have an even harder time living together if they need to move into an assisted-living facility or a nursing home. While only 6 percent of all seniors end up needing nursing home care, the prospect of such a move is terrifying to most lesbians.[37] "I actually worked for a long time in a nursing home," Stimson said. "I would come across lesbian couples who were not treated as such, and these couples would actually either be forced to live separately in the facility or the nursing home would not allow them to visit each other, and their partner would not be allowed to take an active role in their care."

There is nothing legally stopping a retirement home from splitting couples up, or from writing into its policies that same-sex couples cannot visit each other. Such a ban may sound too terrible to be true, but a random survey of social workers in twenty-nine New York nursing homes found that 52 percent said their co-workers were either intolerant or condemning of homosexuality. The same survey revealed that staff members refused to bathe a resident because they did not want to "touch a lesbian." A home care assistant threatened to "out" a gay male client if he reported her negligent care. Only 17 percent of surveyed New York nursing homes had any kind of sensitivity training for dealing with elderly gays and lesbians; these disheartening results come from a state with an active and visible gay and lesbian elderly population.[38] Would a nationwide survey of nursing homes—the majority of which are in small towns—find even that many staff members sensitive to gay and lesbian issues?

It is no wonder that the majority of lesbians surveyed said they want to "age in place," to continue living in their familiar home surrounded by their family of friends.[39] Studies show that friends typically share the burden of care for many aging lesbians, and yet there is no funding to support people who take on such expensive care. Insurance does not cover someone's drive to the doctor or trip to the store for their elderly friend.

A New Wave of Activism

Two positive trends have started to emerge. Many older lesbians have reached a point in their lives where they feel liberated from the social confines of their past and are ready to come out more visibly, more vocally, and more politically. And younger lesbians are priming themselves to tackle ageism and retirement issues with the same fervor they have demonstrated as out lesbians all along. The coming together of those two groups may create a new wave of activism for lesbian aging issues. "There seems to be a reconnection that's starting between the generations that's still pretty fragile, but I think that's happening," said Patricia Nell Warren. Ken South agrees a change for the better is underway, though in smaller increments than he would like to see: "When you look at the whole aging LGBT movement—actually, I'm not sure that it's even a movement yet—we're probably where the whole gay movement was in 1968. This is very new stuff. There are probably three million LGBT people out there, and there are basically two social services programs for older gay people in the country, only two housing programs that are open, and maybe a dozen social programs. So there's a growing consciousness, but it's very small and very new and very slow."

Coping Skills

The good news is that most recent studies indicate that gays and lesbians are happy and well adjusted and report high satisfaction with their current life situation. And, ironically, the discrimination that has harmed the gay community for years has created positive aftereffects: in some cases, it has equipped gays and lesbians with a stronger sense of self, strong support systems, and better coping skills to draw on in times of hardship, experts say.[40]

According to *Outing Age*, "The history of GLBT people is the story of transformation. It's the story of a people whose experience, communities, histories and even moral worthiness have been stigmatized, but who have emerged with courage and creativity to secure respect and create cultural and institutional change."[41] Some cite its reaction to AIDS as an indicator of the gay community's inner strength, a strength that can now be applied to a new set of concerns. "When AIDS came along, the gay and lesbian community was able to respond better than the general public and federal and state agencies to try and reduce the number of AIDS cases, to try and take care of each other as a community," said Melanie Otis. "We did this without anyone's help. That means we have the skills already. I think those same skills will kick in and the old dykes and old queens will raise hell if no one is helping to take care of all of us."

Linda Woolf's 1982 study delineates four reasons why gay men and lesbians may actually be better prepared for aging than their heterosexual counterparts:

- They are not wedded to specific gender roles, which makes them more competent in all areas of life;
- They do not assume their families will take care of them in old age and therefore they make alternative plans;
- They do not fully invest themselves in the role of a spouse and thus suffer less role loss when a partner dies, and having dealt with the crisis of being homosexual and the reaction of their friends, they are better prepared for the crisis of old age;
- After retirement, some gays and lesbians may come out publicly for the first time in their lives, no longer worried about losing their jobs if their sexual orientation is discovered. Freed from those fears, they then may become more politically active, knowing their financial livelihood is no longer at risk.[42]

The Support of Friends

Since work relations usually do not make up the majority of personal contacts outside the home for gays and lesbians, their networks of friends remain generally unchanged when they retire—making them less likely to become isolated. And overall, according to Woolf's study, they are more likely than their heterosexual counterparts to have a close network of friends.[43] In this, many believe that lesbians hold a distinct advantage over gay men. Woolf described the lesbian community as a "haven in a hostile world,"[44] an advantage that may serve them well throughout the aging process.

"When you go to these co-gendered aging conferences, you find out from the men they don't have a community that takes care of them," said Vera Martin. "Hell, they can't even name a good friend. And from there comes the resentment of the women in the community. The older women, many of them, we have it going on." Melanie Otis said the quality of her life would be greatly diminished without her close network of friends. "The lesbians in my community are still very much a part of me," she told us. "I think I would lose something if I wasn't active as a part of the community. We are all so very much an important part of each other's lives."

In 1989, Sarah Raphael and Mary Robinson argued that the assumed decline of social relationships and the withdrawal associated with old age is not inevitable with lesbians.[45] In fact, this is only a "response to restrictive and discriminatory social circumstances and attitudes."[46] Lesbians in particular have a complex set of close relationships, which are the key to successful aging. Even older lesbians who don't go out to bars and clubs—the main social outlet for some segments of the gay community—still maintain close relationships with their friends and gather in each other's homes. Remaining well integrated in the community, in turn, leads to greater self-esteem and a stronger sense of self-worth.[47]

When it comes to how they hope to live out their retirement years, lesbians are not much different from most seniors: they choose to "age in place," to grow older and die in a familiar, heterogeneous environment where they have spent most of their years. "I want to say here—forever and ever, amen—in my own apartment," Sandy Warshaw told us. "I have a pension and more than enough to cover my expenses. And I've made it clear that I do not want to go into a nursing home, and do not want to be resuscitated."

And while there is an increasing awareness of older lesbians and their particular housing needs, the few options that are available are only affordable to a small, affluent part of the community. Like many lesbians, Melanie Otis has talked with her friends about retirement housing and wondered if they might be able to band together. "I have had conversations about this over the years, talking to friends about starting retirement communities for lesbians, but I haven't done anything about it. Folks are already taking care of each other informally, so it would be natural for us to start up a place here."

One of the biggest trends for retired lesbians is RV living. Many such projects are in the works. The *Arizona Republic* reported that more than a million people (who the Internal Revenue Service refers to as the "semi-affluent homeless") have sold their homes to live and travel full-time in recreational vehicles.[48] Arizona leads the nation in lesbian mobile home retirement communities, including the one where Vera Martin has set up home with other lesbians from diverse social and professional backgrounds. "When I look around me and I see all these retired women, there is a wide variety of professionals—doctors, teachers, military—and they all seem to be doing well because they had good retirement plans that were set up for them," she said. There is also a number of women who held "survivor jobs," forced to take on subsistence-level employment because of the complications that came from being open about their sexual orientation. Those are the women without the pensions, who must still take part-time jobs to be able to afford to live in the community.

Not named for security reasons and still debating how lesbian-identified it should be, the RV park where Martin lives has sold all of its 225 lots with prices ranging from $23,000 to $60,000. A board of directors oversees the community, which includes a locked gate, a large clubhouse, a library with lesbian classics, a pool, spa, outdoor tennis courts, recycling center, and patio. Its street names honor lesbian heroes such as Barbara Jordan and Helen Keller, and its residents—a mix of women including hippies and ex-military women—number approximately four hundred in the winter. Sixty women stay year round, even when temperatures reach 120 degrees.

Other notable housing options include:

- World's Edge Springs Retirement and Longevity Resort: a cluster of cabins in the Appalachian Mountains, which is mostly in the planning stages;
- Birds of a Feather: a new residential community in New Mexico, just twenty-five miles southeast of Santa Fe;
- The Palms of Manasota: a residential retirement community with an assisted-living facility in the planning stages which is just outside of Palmetto, Florida.

Politics Are Personal

Despite positive factors in their private lives—from the sense of liberation that comes from leaving an antigay workplace, to the support offered by a strong network of friends—older lesbians should remember that their struggle for equal rights involves more than facing down a single opponent, Nancy Edwards cautioned. "It's really a two-pronged battle," she said. "It's ageism in the gay community and it's heterosexism in the straight community."

NGLTF's Ken South believes one action carries more weight than anything else when it comes to making lasting political and social change in the lives of older lesbians. "It is absolutely important for old lesbians to come out," he said. "For one thing, it's a self-fulfilling prophecy: if you don't see anybody old, you think nobody is old—because they don't come out. It's very, very important for the gay community and the straight community to see old lesbians and to realize there's life after forty." Gay activists and their supporters must continue to combat discrimination in housing policies and other single-focus issues that oppress lesbians and gay men.

But in terms of its potential to usher in sweeping, comprehensive reform, no issue may be more important to gay people of all ages than the right to marry.[49] The legalization of same-sex marriages could foster a new era of equal rights for gay and lesbian couples—revising tax and inheritance laws and Social Security regulations and delivering to gay people the hundreds of other rights, benefits, and protections that come with a marriage license.

Even if same-sex marriage isn't legalized in the near future, the presence of a long-term partner is believed to provide older lesbians with significantly higher levels of life satisfaction than their single counterparts have.[50] In the 1990s, about 45 to 50 percent of lesbians were estimated to be in committed relationships, and those with partners were viewed as having a greater sense of well being, fewer sexual problems, fewer regrets about their sexual orientation, and less likelihood of being depressed.[51] And as they age, Patricia Nell Warren said, "Someone in a good relationship has a better chance of having someone in their world during those final stages who will help them to have a decent life, keeping a roof over their head, not having to go into a retirement home."

Conclusion

Leaders in the aging movement believe that the resolve of a united gay community could lead to more visibility for its older members. And that show of numbers would increase the odds for improving the lives and equalizing the rights of retired lesbians. Patricia Nell Warren said she hopes to see the entire gay community working together to address ageism and the specific needs of its older members. "The separatist thing can be very damaging," she said. "There's so much in gay life that tends to splinter into ever-smaller entities and you can't ever have power that way. Your odds for success are greater the bigger you are and the more you ally with people and create coalitions. That's the only way you will really be powerful. The odds against your success rise the smaller you become."

Two organizations have taken the lead in providing social and educational support for older lesbians. Old Lesbians Organizing for Change first met in Los Angeles in April 1987, when 160 lesbians age sixty and over came together to discuss ageist attitudes. Since then, OLOC has held conferences, developed a network of chapters, and in 1992 created the first edition of a facilitators' handbook, *Confronting Ageism for Lesbians 60 and Over: A How-to Guide on Educating about Ageism.* "OLOC has been around quite a while," said Ken South. "OLOC organizes. They teach, they advocate, they harass," he said, laughing. "They do all kinds of things. They're kind of the ACT UP of aging and it's been great because they've done lots of education around aging."

Another major force in the movement is SAGE. With about seven thousand members and still growing, SAGE reaches out to seniors who are isolated, educates the public about gay and lesbian aging issues, and organizes social events that draw up to 150 people in New York, with chapter membership rising throughout the country. Its meetings allow older lesbians to meet new friends, discuss common problems, share their grief and bereavement issues, and even occasionally find a new life partner. "Growing old is the greatest adventure I've had," said SAGE's Sandy Warshaw, who proudly wears a pin which says "Aging to perfection." "I've been an activist all my life," she added. "As you get older, you care less and so you can do more. So I think my advice is don't be afraid of getting older. I think some of what happens is that we get held back by our own fear. I say, 'Come join us and help crack through this internalized ageism. Come join us and speak up and make yourself heard.'"

Among the other groups fighting for the rights of older lesbians are:

- Griot Circle: a gathering of LGBT elders in Brooklyn;
- RAAP: the Rainbow Aging Awareness Project in New York, which consists of Griot Circle, Pride Senior Network, SAGE/Queens and SAGE/New York;
- Lesbian and Gay Network of the American Society on Aging: a clearinghouse organization;
- GLARP: Gay-Lesbian Association of Retired Persons, an international nonprofit group that helps elderly gays and lesbians with chapters in forty-three states (AARP does nothing to help the different needs of LGBT people, according to this group);
- Veterans of Stonewall: a New York organization for people who were present at this landmark event in gay history;
- Golden Threads: a social network for women over fifty;

- Lambda Legal Defense and Education Fund: In 1998, this national organization made elderly issues a priority. Among its efforts are fighting for the right to marry; working to change discrimination laws in housing so nursing homes can no longer refuse to admit an openly gay person and forcing nursing homes to take action against homophobia; working to make senior centers available to all people; and educating judges about gay issues.

Ken South joked that, to lesbians' advantage, the stereotypical way in which they differ from gay men continues to play out in old age. "Women organize and guys want to party," he said. "And that doesn't change when we get older. Take, for example, a group like the Red Dot Girls in Seattle. They came together as a mutual helping organization, pitching in with chores and shopping and visits and delivering food when they are sick. There's no comparable organization like that for gay men." He added, "Lesbians already have a different view of aging than gay men, with more respect for older women, more mentoring, more intergenerational contacts. So to lesbians I say, 'Please come out and let people know there's a whole new life after forty, fifty, sixty, and even seventy.' And for many people, that life is a wonderful one."

Sandy Warshaw believes a more accurate portrayal of older lesbians could go a long way toward bringing about constructive change. "I think there has to be effort on the part of those of us who are old to really pressure the media—and especially the LGBT media—to present us as we are," she said. "Yes, we have some hardships, and some physical hardships like hearing loss and sight loss. But we also have a tremendous, vibrant culture, and people have to begin writing about it not as if we're an anomaly or exception, because we're not." Added Vera Martin, "My number-one priority with lesbians is to get them to understand that being old is not a punishment. If you live, you get old, and you still have worth, and you still have something to say, and don't let anyone take that away from you. Don't let anyone make you invisible. You are all worthwhile."

Notes

1. "Retirement Planning Strategies for Gay Men and Lesbians," *Seattle Gay News On-line* (October 1998), www.sgn.org/Archives/sgn.10.23.98/retirement.htm.

2. Sean Cahill, Ken South, and Jane Spade, *Outing Age: Public Policy Issues Affecting Gay, Lesbian, Bisexual, and Transgender Elders* (The Policy Institute of the National Gay and Lesbian Task Force Foundation, 2000), 52.

3. Ibid.

4. Lisa Lee Freeman, "The 2001 Annual Salary Survey: A Report on Gender-based Salary Gaps by Industry," *Working Woman* (August 2001), 38–42.

5. Cahill, South, and Spade, *Outing Age*, 5.

6. Monika Kehoe, "A Portrait of the Older Lesbian," *Journal of Homosexuality* 12 (1986): 157–161.

7. Cahill, South, and Spade, *Outing Age*, 5.

8. William Mann, "Gray Gays: Aging Gay Men and Lesbians Face Unique Challenges," www.bostonphoenix.com/archives/1997/documents/00451890.htm.

9. Cahill, South, and Spade, *Outing Age*, 5.

10. Mann, "Gray Gays."

11. American Association of Retired Persons, *Your 401(k) Plan: Building toward Your Retirement Security* (Washington, D.C., 1992), 18.

12. Ibid., *A Woman's Guide to Pension Rights* (1992), 11.

13. "Retirement Planning Strategies for Gay Men and Lesbians."

14. Ibid.

15. Gay and Lesbian Medical Association, *Healthy People 2010: Lesbian, Gay, Bisexual and Transgender Health—Access to Quality Health Service* (2001), 2.

16. Ibid., 56.

17. Ibid., 108.

18. Cahill, South, and Spade, *Outing Age*, 22.

19. Gay and Lesbian Medical Association, *Healthy People 2010*, 121.

20. L. Bowen, J. M. Marrazo, K. Stine, H. H. Handsfield, N. B. Kiviat, and L. A. Koutsky, "Epidemiology of Sexually Transmitted Diseases and Cervical Neoplasia in Lesbian and Bisexual Women" (paper presented at the eighth conference of the National Lesbian and Gay Health Association, Seattle, Wash., 13–16 July 1996), cited in *Lesbian Health: Current Assessment and Directions for the Future*, ed. Andrea Solarz (Washington, D.C.: National Academy Press, 1999), 67.

21. Cahill, South, and Spade, *Outing Age*, 47.

22. "Retirement Planning Strategies for Gay Men and Lesbians."

23. Ibid.

24. John Ryan, "A Personal Trust Protects Assets," www.gfn.com (24 July 2000).

25. "Retirement Planning Strategies for Gay Men and Lesbians."

26. Ibid.

27. Peter Lundberg, "Retirement Homes for Lesbian, Gay, Bisexual and Transgender Elders," *The Business and Aging Networker* (winter 2001), http://www.asaging.org/networks/bfa/networker-103.html.

28. Cahill, South, and Spade, *Outing Age*, 50.

29. Robert Behney, "The Aging Network's Response to Gay and Lesbian Issues," *OutWord Online: Newsletter of the Lesbian and Gay Aging Issues Networks of the American Society on Aging* (winter 1994), www.asaging.org/networks/lgain/outword-082.html.

30. Cahill, South, and Spade, *Outing Age*, 49.

31. W. W. Hudson and W. A. Ricketts, "A Strategy for the Measurement of Homophobia," *Journal of Homosexuality* 5, no. 4 (1980): 357–372.

32. Behney, "Aging Network's Response."

33. Administration on Aging, Older Americans Act Appropriation Information: www.aoa.gov/oaa/oaapp.html.

34. Cahill, South, and Spade, *Outing Age*, 23.

35. Ibid., 60.

36. Gerard Koskovich, *OutWord Online: Newsletter of the Lesbian and Gay Aging Issues Networks of the American Society on Aging* (summer 1999), www.asaging.org/networks/lgain/outword-082.html.

37. Cahill, South, and Spade, *Outing Age*, 41.

38. Marcia Freedman and Carlos Martinez, *OutWord: Newsletter of the Lesbian and Gay Aging Issues Networks of the American Society on Aging* 1, no. 2 (winter 1994): 2.

39. M. Wasow and M. Loeb, "Sexuality in Nursing Homes," *Journal of the American Geriatric Society* 27 (1979): 74.

40. Gay and Lesbian Medical Association, 73.

41. Cahill, South, and Spade, *Outing Age*, iv.

42. Linda Woolf, "Gay and Lesbian Aging," www.webster.edu/~woolflm/oldergay.html (1998).

43. Ibid.

44. Ibid.

45. Sarah Raphael and Mary Robinson, "The Older Lesbian: Love Relationships and Friendship Patterns," *Alternative Lifestyles* 3: 207–229.

46. Ibid., 210.

47. Ibid., passim.

48. Koskovich, *OutWord Online*.

49. "Retirement Planning Strategies for Gay Men and Lesbians."

50. Andrea Taylor Rumpf, "Support Networks and Life Satisfaction Among Older Women: A Comparison of Lesbians and Heterosexual Women," *The Discourse of Sociological Practice* 1, no. 2, http://omega.cc.umb.edu/~sociolgy[*sic*]/Journal/issue2.2.htm.

51. Ibid.

Baby Boom Women: The Generation of Firsts

NANCY DAILEY AND
KELLY O'BRIEN

We are a generation of firsts. The first to work outside the home most of our adult lives. The first to have the choice to marry, divorce, or neither. The first to choose motherhood or not. The first to be single mothers by choice. We have changed the landscape of our most important social institutions: the family, marriage, the labor force. "What a long strange trip it's been," to quote the Grateful Dead. As a generation, we will now turn our size and influence to changing retirement. We hope to be the first group of women to define our own retirement. We will be the first to join our parents in retirement.

Baby boom women (born between 1946 and 1964) have traversed the stages of working girl, working mother, and working woman. We will now make the transition to working old woman. We will not replicate the retirement experience of our mothers. In addition, our life in retirement will be fundamentally different from that of our male counterparts—spouses, brothers, bosses. The reasons are found in our work history, our demographic profiles, and in the basic fact that we continue to be society's caregivers. These factors are intersecting with existing retirement mechanisms, which have not accommodated women's long-term security needs, yet are now shaping our future.

We, Nancy and Kelly, are quintessential baby boom women, especially since we represent the chronological spread of this cohort; "early" boomers were born between 1946 and 1954, "later" boomers were born between 1955 and 1964. Nancy is an early boomer (born 1953, married, three kids, two dogs) and Kelly is a later boomer (born 1963, divorced, no kids, one cat). Our life choices cross a range of social and economic institutions: marriage, divorce, singleness, full-time work, self-employment, college, graduate school, corporate life, entrepreneurship, parenthood, no parenthood.

We are business partners, the ultimate job-sharing role for women. We are two of the hordes of women small-business owners, another social trend created by baby boom women. We met in 1989 in corporate America. Discouraged by the glass ceiling and the lack of real opportunity, the small-business venue looked like a path to financial and intellectual control and, as important, time flexibility. In the late 1980s and early 1990s, both of us were employed by corporations that were building and operating nursing homes and assisted-living facilities. In that business, the clients are almost all women — both the residents themselves and the guarantors or family members (daughters, daughters-in-law, sisters, nieces) who admit them. Observing the emotional and financial anguish of dealing with old age heightened our sensitivity to the impact of aging on the individual, the family, and society.

Our research and personal journeys as working women and long-time business partners, which we share here, shed light on the major issues baby boom women need to consider. If baby boom women want to thrive or just survive in retirement, we must be purposeful, conscious learners about our old age and retirement. As members of a generation of women who have been at the vanguard of every major social change over the past fifty years, we believe there is still time to take control of our retirement destiny if we act now.

What We Know about Baby Boom Women

For a generation that has had so much influence on society's structures, little attention has been given to predicting what retirement life will be for baby boom women. Explanations for this can be attributed primarily to the fact that women's retirement has been treated as a subset of men's retirement.[1] The history of retirement really only documents the experience of white men in old age. The retirement literature is far behind our work and life experiences. Research models that expose the unique aspects of women's work and life histories have yet to be utilized in studies that can predict the retirement future of this cohort. As the generation of firsts, we once again are a work in progress.

Baby boom women will chart new territory as we carve out new meanings for retirement, just as we did for marriage, work, and motherhood. Looking to the past (our grandmothers' experiences) or even the present (our mothers' experiences) gives few clues as to what we can expect. Looking at our own work and life experience may shed the strongest light on what we can expect in our old age.

We are working girls:

- We are the best-educated female cohort in American history—87 percent of us have earned a high school diploma or equivalent and almost 25 percent of us are college graduates.
- Two-thirds of us will work or have worked part-time at some point in our careers.
- On average, we will work ten years less than baby boom men will.
- Ninety percent of us who work outside the home work in the service sector of our economy; 43 percent of us are in technical, sales, and administrative support jobs—nurses, cashiers, secretaries, receptionists, bookkeepers, teacher aides.[2]

We are working women and working mothers:

- Most (83 percent) of us are or have been married, but we never left the labor force because of marriage; about one-third of us are single or divorced.
- Most (85 percent) of us are mothers.[3]
- By 2008, 80 percent of us will work outside the home.[4]
- We created dual-income marriages, and in 22.7 percent of dual-earner couples, wives earn more than their spouses do.[5]
- In 2000, we made 71.9 percent of what baby boom men earned; our younger sisters are doing better with 81.9 percent.[6]

We will be working old women:

- If we live to be sixty-five, we can expect to live until eighty-five.
- By 2030, when all baby boomers will be sixty-five-plus, they will represent more than 20 percent of the U.S. population, about seventy million strong (and frail!); two-thirds of this group will be baby boom women.
- Most of us will be widows by age sixty-seven; fewer than one in ten of us will remarry.[7]

- By 2050, there will be twenty-eight people over the age of eighty-five for every three preretirement adults (ages 55–64).[8] Given this ratio, most of us will become adult caregivers for the elderly either just before our retirement years or right when we are ready to retire ourselves.

Our Prospects for Retirement

We rejected dependence and sought independence—through education, paid work and pursuits outside of the home, within our marriages, or through divorce. Ironically, what may serve us best in retirement is *inter*dependence. Our economic progress through entry into the paid labor force has not guaranteed us financial independence by any means. Rather, what has been created is financial interdependence—with our spouses, our extended families, our children, and, for many women, with a close social network of friends. The husband of a baby boom woman may be just as likely to need her retirement income as she is to need his retirement income. A childless widow may turn to friends for alternative living arrangements when the activities of daily living in old age become a challenge. The notion of interdependence will be a dominant theme for baby boom women in retirement for every significant aspect of her life: economic, relational, physical, and psychological.

The real risk for baby boom women is not in making bad investment decisions. Rather, our retirement prospects hinge on our ability to "age successfully" by gracefully embracing interdependence and building relationships that will stand the test of growing old.[9] Interdependence will mean different things for different women, ranging from the emotional support found through a strong social network and companionship to the more practical needs of daily life such as sharing expenses, housekeeping, doctor visits, errands, and personal care. Baby boom women have been caring for others for a long time. We have learned to accommodate caregiving to paid work, dual careers, and divorce. The journey into the next phase of our life will require that we be comfortable with asking for and accepting help from others—our children, our siblings, our friends. For baby boom women who have worked hard for financial freedom and independence, this may be an uncomfortable transition. But if we wait until our old age, it may be too late to get the help we need on our terms, or at least on terms in which we have a voice. It is never too early for us to ask ourselves and our loved ones things like:

- Financially, who will care for me when I grow old if I have inadequate resources?

- Does my family expect me to be the family's elder-caregiver? And will that mean I'll be asked to leave paid work at a time when I need to be saving for my own retirement?
- When or if I am a widow, how will I care for myself?

By starting now to negotiate what interdependence will look like, we lay the groundwork for our retirement future.

Two Issues We Must Confront: Caregiving and Financial Literacy

Baby boom women are the country's caregivers. No amount of career advancement or financial independence can obfuscate this social fact. Population aging has guaranteed the continuation of women as society's caregivers. We only have to shift from changing Pampers to changing Depends.

As we move closer to and into our retirement years, it will become clear that we will shoulder the caregiving burden of our aging society. Many baby boom women will be swallowed into the caregiving role, regardless of a lifetime of labor force participation, offering little or no resistance. Today fewer than 5 percent of our elderly are institutionalized; 95 percent are cared for by their families.[10] In other words, by women, since 80 percent of caregivers to the elderly are women.[11] Caregiving costs an individual upwards of $659,000 over a lifetime in lost wages, lost social security, and pension contributions. These costs are due to time off from work, having to leave jobs entirely, or lost opportunities for training, promotions, and plum assignments.[12] The reality for most of us is that unless we can pay someone else, we will be a caregiver for several frail elderly relatives. We need to learn how to say no to caregiving, or at least to ask for help, when it jeopardizes our economic security.

Over the recent past, researchers, policy makers, and the media have focused on the question, "Will boomers be financially prepared for retirement?" With proposals like the privatization of Social Security, this discussion is now expanding to address whether boomers possess the financial know-how and discipline required to ensure adequate retirement savings. The new economic reality has made individual responsibility for retirement savings a baby boom social fact. The wild card, therefore, is whether or not boomers can be educated and motivated to develop investment, insurance, savings, and spending strategies which will help them achieve financial well-being in retirement.[13] Financial literacy—needed to make choices to secure financial health—requires both the knowledge and the confidence to sort financial myth from fact.[14] Various studies show that there is a growing collective consciousness among baby boomers of the individual's responsibility for retirement security. Out of necessity, baby boomers will wake up and embark on a conscious path towards retirement. But can boomers become financially literate in time to secure their retirement? And can they use this literacy to make good choices and act on their own behalf? The answers are a function of this cohort's ability to learn and change. Given that, on the whole, women earn less, save less, and live longer, these questions are even more pressing and time sensitive for women than for men.

The fear of being a bag lady is alive and well. For many women, it could become a reality. At this point in the life cycle of baby boom women, the cost of errors is tremendously high for those who do not prepare or who make the wrong life and financial choices.

Retirement Advice

When asked what advice we give women about the future of retirement, we share four basic tenets we have learned from our research on women and retirement:

1. The shortest distance between poverty and retirement security is learning. If you are worried about being a bag lady, then start learning about what it will take to secure your retirement. Confront any vestiges of the Prince Charming myth or any Scarlett O'Hara habits of "I'll think about it tomorrow."

2. It's about much more than money.
   It's about negotiating elder care. It's about building solid relationships with significant others who will be there for you in old age (spouse, children, siblings, nieces, nephews, friends). It's about realizing that the investments you make in important relationships today will dramatically impact your long-term future.

3. As with your physical health, you cannot delegate your financial health. Develop a strong sense of personal responsibility for your finances, seek sound advice, but don't relinquish control. We must not delegate responsibility for our personal finances, no matter how challenging (or boring) learning about money and finances can be. Regardless of how busy or tired we are, we must stay actively involved in all aspects of our financial health—saving, spending, investing, and protecting our future.

4. It's about choice, not chance.

Retirement is an earned benefit. It is an entitlement based on the concept that hard work during the early and middle adult years will produce a comfortable life upon retirement from work.[15] However, this entitlement may not apply to many, many baby boom women because of our implicit social contract as caregivers. If you leave it to chance, you are almost certain to retire in a manner in which you are unaccustomed to living. Committing to learning about your retirement and making thoughtful and purposeful decisions now will give you a retirement of your choice, not one of chance.

We still have time to make a big difference in the quality of our life in retirement. The retirement age to receive full social security benefits is inching higher. Early boomers have twelve to twenty years before collecting social security checks at age sixty-seven. Later boomers have more time to learn from the mistakes of our older sisters. But remember that those mistakes are very costly at this time in our life. This includes even basic mistakes of omission, like not participating in an employer-sponsored retirement plan. Better to make the decision now about whether or not you will be a working old woman, and do something about it.

Two Boomers, Two Perspectives

As to forecasting our own retirement experiences, we both approach old age with trepidation and anticipation. Typical of entrepreneurs, we have invested heavily in our human capital and in building our business. Investing in long-term savings has not been as consistent as we would like. The jury is still out on whether or not we will pay too high a price for being small-business owners. We have been willing to take that risk to date. As we grow older, the notion of compound interest in an employer-sponsored retirement plan looks more appealing—but the quality of life offered by a traditional employer is not an attractive alternative (yet).

Armed with knowledge and experience about elder care and no illusions about what our retirement *could* look like, we nonetheless approach the prospect of continued caregiving from different perspectives. Nancy will work to minimize her caregiving role. Sustaining a long-term marriage and parenting three boys is enough caregiving for one lifetime. She looks forward to freedom from caregiving, but expects it to continue to some degree within her immediate family. Kelly looks forward to the companionship that caring for others will offer her daily living into old age. Having lived a life free from significant caregiving responsibilities except to help with aging or ill family members, she welcomes the opportunity to provide care for loved ones, family and friends alike. Likewise, she anticipates that continued engagement in close relationships through caregiving will be an important part of her own successful aging process.

Even though we research, write, and speak on the topic, personally we are no closer to shaping an ideal retirement for ourselves than most baby boom women. Life choices made in our twenties (whether to marry, have children, or invest in education, career choices, and the like) have been shaping our retirement, but we were middle aged when we discovered this fact. To a certain degree, we are now playing catch-up by accelerating our efforts to earn and save for future financial security, as well as reinforce relationships with family and friends whom we will likely call on some day in our old age to care for us. In the meantime, we hope to let younger women know that there is a direct correlation between decisions you make or do not make in your twenties and thirties and the retirement you can expect in your old age. Rest assured we will let our nieces and granddaughters know about it.

Notes

1. N. Dailey, *When Baby Boom Women Retire* (Westport, Conn.: Praeger, 1998).

2. Ibid., 118–119.

3. Ibid., 31.

4. H. Fullerton, "Labor Force 2008," *Monthly Labor Review* (November 1999): 19–32.

5. A. E. Winkler, "Earnings of Husbands and Wives in Dual-Earner Families," *Monthly Labor Review* (April 1998): 42–48.

6. U.S. Department of Labor, Bureau of Labor Statistics, *Report 952* (August 2001), 1.

7. Dailey, *When Baby Boom Women Retire*, p. 39; and U.S. Department of Commerce, Bureau of the Census, "Marital Status and Living Arrangements: March 1990," in *Current Population Report* no. 450 (1991), 20.

8. Cynthia Tauber and Jessie Allen, "Women in Our Aging Society: The Demographic Outlook," in *Women on the Front Lines: Meeting the Challenge of an Aging America*, ed. Jessie Allen and Alan Pifer (Washington, D.C.: Urban Institute Press, 1993), 11–45.

9. J. W. Rowe and R. L. Kahn, "Human Aging: Usual and Successful," *Science* 237 (1987): 143–149.

10. Dailey, *When Baby Boom Women Retire*, 41.

11. Center for Aging Research and Education (CARE), General Electric Center for Financial Learning, *STAT: Secure Tomorrow's Autonomy Today*, 2001.

12. MetLife Mature Market Institute, MetLife Juggling Act Study, 1999.

13. Neal E. Cutler and Steven J. Devlin, "A Report Card on the Baby Boom's Retirement Planning Efforts," *Journal of the American Society of CLU and ChFC* 50, no. 1 (January 1996): 30–32.

14. Fannie Mae Foundation and the Institute for Socio-Financial Studies, *Personal Finance and the Rush to Competence: Financial Literacy Education in the United States*, 2001.

15. Dailey, *When Baby Boom Women Retire*, 16.

Two

STAGES OF
RETIREMENT

Notes from the First Year

DIANE HORWITZ

I'm an inveterate saver. Faded bits of long-ago prom corsages vie for closet space with my son's preschool potato prints. Pants, size ten, huddle next to old miniskirts, waiting to be taken to a local thrift shop, but saved just in case. And during three decades of teaching, I amassed hundreds of students' papers, letters, and fragments of journals. They sit, piled high, in my basement office, next to the contents of my old file cabinets from school. When I cleaned the file drawers out just before I retired in the summer of 2000, I discovered an original *Our Bodies, Ourselves* (cost: just forty cents), a copy of *The Birth Control Handbook* from 1975, *Ramparts* clippings, and pamphlets from the New England Free Press all tucked in next to student evaluations and old exams.[1] I brought home a carload of syllabi, course handouts, and journal articles. Along with my students' papers and boxes containing mementos from earlier jobs, these documents are a veritable archive, papers from a life of work, remembrances of things past. I could create a little museum of teaching: a syllabus under glass, an exam carefully matted and framed, a bound collection of student evaluations, maybe a multimedia exhibit. Instead, I decide to spend the second month of my retirement cleaning up, throwing out, letting go, moving on. After all, it's the end of my teaching career and my working life.

I find a letter dated 16 May 1970, from a group of teachers' aides whom I taught. It was written to the president of Columbia University, bitterly protesting the end of a promised degree program. In a worn folder I discover a pamphlet on tracking in elementary school—translated into Spanish and Chinese—from my days at Two Bridges, a community organization on New York's Lower East Side. And a 1985 collection of poems and essays from adult women students, whose cover features a middle-aged woman, book bag in hand, about to board a yellow school bus as her children wave good-bye, shares a carton with numerous issues of *Speak Out and Be Heard!*, a student broadside circa 1973. A shoe box holds photos: scenes from *The Sound of Music* performed by seventh graders in a Mobilization for Youth program, faded images from the radical New York newspaper *The Guardian*, of me teaching at the Freedom School in Meridian, Mississippi.[2]

In the dim basement light, I sift through my teaching souvenirs, examining memorabilia from my life's work, arranging and rearranging them like a china collector sorting delicate cups on kitchen shelves. It's hard to give them up, these aids to memory, reminders of decades of meaningful work.

Then I get caught up in reading: a Vietnam veteran's nightmare of time in the jungle, a tale from a woman reinventing her life after divorce, a story chronicling years of work at a factory that had just shut down. I'm wrapped up in narratives collected from some of the hundreds, even thousands of my former sociology students. So many students passed through my life, so much work. And each story evokes a memory: the Bridgeview, Illinois, Fourth of July parade, where the announcer blares, "Let's hear it for the southwest side Vets Against the War"; a class held one day in the nearby forest preserve; a policeman who sat quietly in a back seat, only to disclose that last day of class, "I'm leaving the force to devote more time to my church."

I always thought that one day I'd write about these students, telling their complex and powerful stories, and so I begin a few pages, but my writing friends tell me, "This is really your story, your journey." I slowly realize that I'm reviewing my life of work, searching for purpose and validation. My students' papers tell me, "Your work was useful, you've made a difference in my life," or so it seems to me. Perhaps I'm grieving, trying to stave off loss by clinging to the memories that resurrect my youthful, teaching self.

I spent weeks in my basement mired in the past, apprehensive about what would come next. One night, I remembered a first visit to a doctor's office the year before I retired. When I started to fill out the customary forms and reached the lines asking for occupation and place of work, I unexpectedly panicked, encircled by a sense of dread. At that very moment, I knew I had an identity, a place, and a purpose. I could comfortably record "teacher," "Moraine Valley Community College"—badges of identification that I had carried around with me for three decades. But what of next year, I worried—at another office, applying for a new credit card, or confronting any of the innumerable times when my identity would be checked. Filled with dread, I realized I'd have to write "retired." A public declaration! Of aging, of a loss of status and identity, work and teaching, central to my life for so many years. Who am I without these markers? What will replace work? How can I fashion a life in retirement that embraces my long-held values?[3]

I've worked since I was fifteen, growing up with a fierce sense of making my own way. I had models: my parents, hard-working, first generation Russian Jewish immigrants, my father a cutter in a factory that made flannel shirts and jackets, and my mother a bookkeeper. My dad had quit school at sixteen to help support his family. My mother had worked part-time, staying home one day a week to go to the beauty shop and prepare Friday night dinners. I don't recall any family conversations about work, but by the time I began working, as a teen, I had absorbed their work ethic into my being: diligence, productivity, industry, self-sufficiency. For me, these were pathways to dignity, to efficacy. Work well done brings satisfaction, a sense of accomplishment, and pleasure.

I remember my first job, at Goldblatt's, a department store in Chicago's Uptown neighborhood. To get the position, I lied about my age, and soon spent Saturday afternoons selling sometimes ladies lingerie and now and then automotive supplies. My next sales job was at a nut store down the street, in the shadow of the El. To compensate for the low wages, employees could eat all the nuts we desired—cashews, walnuts, peanuts. I ate heartily the first day, but later the oily smell and the stickiness made me long for the more genteel atmosphere of Goldblatt's.

My mother counseled me to take typing and shorthand, as "something to fall back on." Soon clerical work at downtown offices replaced neighborhood sales jobs. I can still see myself at Bauer and Black or Commerce Clearing House, hunched over filing cabinets, my steno pad with little Pittman characters lined up neatly, and on my desk, a Dictaphone transcribing machine that I used to translate the boss's spoken words into perfectly typed letters.

I dug through my treasure box of old photos to uncover signs of other work, other passions. A Jewish Community Center (JCC) summer day-camp group proudly displays an American flag they had patiently stitched together (latter-day Betsy Rosses) with me in the back, scrubbed and smiling brightly, arms around the two tallest girls. The following summer I traveled with a JCC co-worker to the World Festival of Youth in Vienna, Austria.[3] Drawn to this event by her life in a left-wing family, she had invited me to join her and off I went, eager, naive, idealistic, and impatient for expanded horizons. Events in

Vienna shocked me. I met communists for the first time, listened to anti–United States critiques, and was stunned to see accounts in U.S. newspapers about the festival that contradicted my own experiences. I reread the faded articles, and relive my first brush with political doubt.

I had brief encounters with politics before then. In college, I joined National Association for the Advancement of Colored People (NAACP) picket lines to integrate barbershops in Champaign, Illinois, rehabbed old houses with the American Friends Service Committee, flirted with joining the Unitarian Church, more for its political discussions and social concerns than any theology. Pete Seeger and Guy Carawan sang on campus, and I absorbed the radical values of social justice, peace, and friendship around the world along with the folk revival scene. What drew me to such things? Maybe it was reading Albert Camus or Alan Paton's *Cry, the Beloved Country,* a boyfriend who taught me to play the guitar, a quirky professor, an inchoate indignation at injustice. Somehow I breathed in the winds of change blowing through late 1950s America.

In the early sixties, I moved to Greenwich Village, joined Ban the Bomb demonstrations, Marxist study circles, and a support group for the Cuban Revolution. I worked with children at settlement houses and walked the precinct with the Village Independent Democrats. And in the summer of 1964, I traveled to Meridian, Mississippi, to teach in a freedom school.

In one *Guardian* photo, a teenager sits at an old typewriter as I hover over his shoulder teaching the touch method I had learned because of my mom's admonitions; in another, small children perch on cots as I read a story. I remember learning how to ask questions that could get at the heart of things: "Why do the white schools have new books and the black schools don't? Why can't black people register to vote?" Simple questions that looked segregation, oppression, and power right in the face, questions that invited alternatives and summoned change. After school I walked the fields and streets with my students to encourage people to "freedom register"—to sign on to the Mississippi Freedom Democratic Party, the organization challenging the official party for seats at the 1964 Democratic Convention. It was the first time I discovered up close the powerful connections between education and political change. The civil rights movement embodied for me the essence of morality, purposeful action, and the power of ordinary people to change their lives. The lessons I learned that summer inspired my work for years.

Antiwar protests and women's liberation groups soon captured my energies along with my paid work in community education projects. I saw myself as a movement activist, and by then work was important to me not only to satisfy my old work ethic, but also because it was a place to put my convictions into practice, a way to impact people's lives and shape a new world. By the close of the decade, my life seemed all of a piece—organizer, educator, radical, activist, feminist, working person.

In the fall of 1970, I came back to Chicago, drawn by an unpaid organizing position with the New University Conference (NUC), a group of radical educators working in colleges throughout the country. I took a job teaching sociology at a community college just outside of Chicago. Revolution was in the air, and I was going to bring it to the southwest suburbs! I never imagined that I would stay for thirty years.

During those early years at Moraine, I organized "Our Bodies" classes with the Liberation School of the Chicago Women's Liberation Union, brought the antiwar movement to the college together with students who were veterans of the war, went on strike to gain recognition for our local union, and called on every activist I knew to share their work and ideas in my classes.[4] I took students to demonstrations, to rallies, to meetings and meetings and more meetings, all of them lasting until very late at night. I had my "collective" that helped me strategize about work, and organizations (the Women's Liberation Union, NUC, the Indochina Peace Campaign) that made my teaching seem more than it was, part of a larger project for change.[5]

But by the 1980s, all of these groups were gone. As I was absorbed by child rearing and adrift as the movement withered, my teaching (now disconnected from larger social movements) increasingly became the center of my political work. I remember that when my son learned to read I introduced him to *Coleen, the Question Girl*, whose title character asks innocently, "Why do some children live in such big houses, and other children such tiny ones? Why don't some children have playgrounds?"[6] Questions just like the ones I had asked at the Freedom School. I wanted my students to be older versions of Coleen: inquisitive and critical. While I never lost sight of that goal, my objectives narrowed. I spent more time counseling students and less recruiting for the revolution. As the years progressed, if students read assignments, worked on their writing skills, or added a thought or two to class discussion, I was content; delighted when they developed a bit of empathy, or took themselves and their studies seriously; exhilarated when some willingly questioned long-held assumptions and made leaps of understanding.

I cared about my jobs, sometimes passionately. Of course I encountered those frustrations, irritations, and annoyances that come along with any job, but teaching and other education projects were, for me, a calling, a political endeavor.

Yet, I chose to retire, from a school where I influenced hundreds of students every year. I decided to abandon a life of useful work. Why? I turned sixty. I spent two hours of each work day driving, often through snowy Chicago winters. Five, sometimes six classes each semester produced hundreds of papers to grade; after the first ten, I would grow weary. The college offered just two or three different sociology courses, so I often repeated Introduction to Sociology four times a day. While each class presented new challenges, I ached for variety. My union negotiated a buyout plan and a good pension. Unlike most women workers in this country, I could retire with financial security. My office mate of almost thirty years decided to retire. "Let's evacuate our side of the office together," she urged. I wanted to spend more time in the city, have new adventures, test myself. What else, I wondered, could I do besides teach? Are there other skills I could develop? Yet I had no plan. And longtime immersion in an institution, all those years in one workplace, conferred hard-to-replace ties. I worried about lacking the structure that daily work provides and about isolation. I had no interest in solitude. I enjoyed being connected to people, groups, and political currents. But like others moving into their sixties, I knew I'd have to face aging and the challenge of fashioning a new life sooner or later. Desires and misgivings—up and back I went, but the impulse to move forward prevailed over doubt.

My first struggle was how to deal with my imminent departure. As my retirement loomed closer, I took note of the "lasts": the last syllabus preparation ("Put it on pink paper, adorned with flowers," one of the secretaries advised), the last set of papers to grade, the last student conference. I worried even more about the really last lasts to come: a final glimpse of my classroom, cleaning out my office, good-byes all around, my voice out of phone mail, my E-mail account in the trash. It was then that I developed a heightened appreciation for the reassuring ordinariness of everyday routine, of my taken-for-granted surroundings.

I never thought about my office until I considered leaving it. Small, just one-fourth of a room shared with three other teachers, the centerpiece a nondescript metal desk, my worn blue book bag tucked underneath, two bookcases on either side overflowing with magazines and sociology books, a pair of large file cabinets just off to the left, a shared table right in back. Two chairs (one that I used for over twenty-five years, another for a student or occasional visitor) faced each other. It was a small space, but functional, cozy, messy.

I'd sit at my desk first thing in the morning, look out my large picture window at the passing scene (students scurrying to class, ducks visiting from a nearby pond), coffee cup in hand, and prepare to meet students in my first class. My desk served as a lunch and dinner table, a surface for grading papers, a spot to lay my head down, write notes, sort mail. I came back to that desk many times in the course of a day, catching my breath in between classes, sitting with a student worried about continuing in school because of too many outside responsibilities, another wondering what to do with her life, one more challenging his last exam grade. The red plastic chair: a home for hundreds of students over the years.

In the last few months of teaching, I realized that my office was my second home for three decades. What I had taken for granted, and often complained about (too small, no privacy, noisy!), became a sanctuary of sorts. I relished being in it, setting up my coffee, riffling through my mail, checking the last set of student quizzes. The familiarity of it all, the security, the sense of place. Now my computer shares a room with the TV and a sofa bed for guests; my basement houses files and books. A place to work, but not a public space.

Last summer, in the very last week of my teaching career, the new faculty member assigned to occupy my office asked to move in his books, plants, and desk supplies while I was still moving my possessions out. About to go on vacation, he didn't want to wait until the week before school to set things up. Not wanting to seem too proprietary or too sentimental, I said, "Sure." Why couldn't he wait until I had left? He didn't notice or perhaps he didn't understand attachments and endings.

I knew I wanted to invent leaving rituals for myself, closing ceremonies to mark the end. I dreaded the official ones: a "thank you for your years of service" plaque and picture with the dean, the requisite watch from the smiling college president at a board meeting, formalities that had little to do with the meaning of my life as a teacher, with what mattered.

I had a strong desire to sum up, to mark my accomplishments, to be acknowledged. All those years at one workplace; still, who would ever remember me? Why not leave a historical document, I thought. So I made videos for Moraine's archive and my basement collections. One featured me, the retiree, with a new young teacher, sharing lessons learned from decades of teaching, passing down teacher tips and philosophy. Another captured my very last class discussing the merits of voting; others were rambling discussions with small groups of students on subjects ranging from why some chose to come to college in midlife to the merits of grades. Why hadn't I thought to do this before? Suddenly the details of daily work took on grand dimensions for me.

I had a good-bye-and-thank-you party to honor the work of those people who had helped me throughout the years: secretaries who typed my syllabi and exams, aides who delivered audiovisual equipment to my classroom, library workers who put my books on reserve, the woman who handed me my biweekly paycheck for years, another who photocopied articles. About twenty people came. We gossiped and took pictures. I promised to send postcards from an upcoming trip, to visit in the fall, to stay in touch. And just before I left, I sent a letter announcing my retirement to friends around the country, a proclamation to mark and celebrate my big transition. Up in the right-hand corner of the letter, I placed a picture taken about 1972. I'm in class, listening intently, chin in hand, dark hair cascading down my back. I remember that the students in the photo are Vietnam vets; the guy with the long hair and beard is Manuel, another is Paul. It's my youthful teaching self, my passionate political self I sometimes long to recapture. Below the photo, the letter read, "I look forward to this next phase of life, hoping to find new means of affecting people's lives, to be of use." I had no idea what shape this search would take.

As it turned out, the most meaningful endings came unexpectedly. A reunion and celebration to mark twenty-five years of Moraine's Returning Women's Program took place in the spring of the year I retired. It was early April and a snow-and-ice storm hit Chicago with a vengeance, but almost two hundred women ventured out to see old friends and teachers, reminisce, and, as our invitation put it, to "celebrate the power of women's education!" I began this program in 1975, energized by the women's liberation movement, inspired by the power of women's groups to change our lives. Over the years, more than one thousand women found in this program a way to enter college with support, nurturance, and intellectual exhilaration. Women joined the program at pivotal points in their lives—the last of their children off at school; a marriage dissolving; a layoff at work—wanting better jobs and sharper minds.

At one table, bedecked with shimmering candles, sparkling confetti, and violets in colorful cloth-covered pots, sat seven middle-aged women, members of the very first class, the class of 1975. One student was Rose, one of twenty children. Her parents had not been able to afford to send her to college, but when Rose's daughters were teenagers, she saw an article about the program and realized this was her big chance. "I was ready for a big change, and I got it," she told me. As we munched on student-made pastries and drank raspberry tea, another student, Kathy, announced, "I have all my old work in the trunk of the car." Another saver! She pulled on her coat, ran through the slush to her car, and moments later proudly showed us her carefully outlined notes on "Oil Spill in Santa Barbara," an article from *Ramparts* I had used to show how the corporate power structure worked. Then she pulled out and read a poem composed by class members about women's lib. It was dated, silly, and impassioned, and I was stunned. All these years she had saved this radical stuff, meaningful reminders to her and to me of our time together.

The following Wednesday, a headline in the Woman News section of the *Chicago Tribune* read: "The Semester that Changed 1,000 Lives." Such a huge part of my teaching work encapsulated in a simple phrase. Here was the story of the reunion and the program, along with interviews with former students: Dorothy, a onetime dropout from Gage Park High School and now a graduate from the University of California, Berkeley, and Mary, once a welfare recipient, then a GED (general equivalency diploma) graduate, now a social worker at a women's shelter. The writer had created a tribute to my students' perseverance and diligence, a recognition of women's work—theirs and mine. At the reunion, I received a plaque that read: "Your Life's Work Enriched Our Lives." I cried, mumbled an incoherent thank-you speech, and at home that weekend celebrated the power of the political vision that helped to shape this work.

A letter, handwritten on lined yellow paper, arrived in my faculty mailbox shortly after. Another returning woman student had learned of my retirement and wanted, before I left, to catch me up on her life. I had last seen her fourteen years ago. Her letter told me that it had taken her four years to get her associate's degree, and how proud her kids and the rest of her family were. She went on to say, "I didn't know exactly where to go from there but life took over and my path changed. My husband was stricken with a work-related asbestos form of cancer which took his life when I still had two teenagers to educate. I worked with my daughter on medical records for a law firm and was able to handle the finances that way. However, when saddled with huge medical bills, I decided to take on the company that made the product that had infiltrated every organ in my husband's body." When I talked to her later, Ellen told me that her husband had begun to work at that company when he was just fourteen, following his father and uncles. His doctors said that he was as healthy as could be except for the asbestos scarring his lungs and finally taking his life.

In the letter she wrote that the "corporation had a huge staff of lawyers representing them, but I remembered some of the lessons from your class and I was adamant about taking them to court. The months after my husband's death, I was testifying in a courtroom so full of lawyers they had to flow out into the hallway." The jury had voted in her favor and she and her family set the record for the greatest amount ever determined against a company in Illinois at that time. The company immediately appealed but three years later lost the appeal. "The union and the law firm informed me that my case changed the course of payments to injured asbestos workers in the state of

Illinois, and the company is now willing to negotiate instead of ignoring workers who are terminal," Ellen wrote.

And then these words jumped out at me: "I could never have gone through this experience if I hadn't met you. You gave me confidence to fight for what I believed in and to not be intimidated by wealth and power." There it was—right in print—almost the whole point of my teaching! Like many teachers, I always found it difficult to measure the impact a class had on students. I carried conflicting emotions, going from grandiose expectations (I would change students' consciousness and lives in five short months; they would become activists ready to march out to the barricades) to gloom (whatever interest they had in social problems and political change surely would soon be forgotten like so many algebraic equations or Spanish verb conjugations).

Ellen's letter went on to say, "Diane, I'm sure you had no idea the lives you have influenced over the years, but I never forgot you, our classes, and projects and the opportunity you presented to those of us who went to high school, started a job the next day, married and had kids. Without your program I would not have had the courage or confidence to see to it that a corporation owes its workers fairness."

I cried in the hallway at school as I read this, cried for Ellen and her husband and her family, for her generosity in sharing this with me, cried because it all felt so worth it—all those years of work, hundreds of classes, thousands and thousands of students. To me, these endings were a validation of teaching, making a difference, one student at a time.

All teachers get affirmations, endorsements that come along with crocheted potholders and body lotion at Christmas. We treasure our notes. "This was the best class I ever had." "It changed my life." Yet as I tell these stories, I feel as if I'm flaunting my work. I'm uneasy. I wonder if my sense of self is so fragile that I need these visible reminders, tangible proof of work well done, something to hold on to as I begin to fashion another way.

As far back as I can remember, my year began in September: a student for sixteen years, a teacher for thirty, time in between immersed in educational projects of one kind or another. Septembers promised a fresh start, renewal, a second chance. That first September of retirement, I wanted to be somewhere else, to miss the opening of the new semester. I decided to travel, a transition from one life to the next and a typical retirement ritual, I have since learned. A just-retired old friend and I took a meandering road trip through the Southwest where I toyed with new possibilities. Perhaps I could teach at a school on the Hopi Reservation, maybe volunteer at Mesa Verde with the National Park Service.

In October, I retreated to the basement, but I have to confess: my initial portrait of cellar withdrawal—poring over remembrances from my past and reading through life fragments, filled with uncertainty and longing—is an incomplete rendering of my chronicle of retirement beginnings. Delights also entered: lingering over a second cup of morning coffee, reading two newspapers leisurely, taking daily walks, indulging in longer phone conversations. But then, what to do after breakfast and the walk? Practically everyone I knew worked. I had to fashion the shape of my day from scratch, no recipe, no map. Not an easy task for someone defined by the rhythms of work.

Wild ambivalence ensued. I often yearned for the familiarity of Sunday night paper grading, preparing a take-along lunch, predictable routines, habits of a lifetime. My old work ethic came calling. It was difficult to have nothing to show, no evidence of productivity. Too much choice, gobs of freedom stretching out endlessly. "You can do anything you want, everything you always wanted to do," nonretirees pointed out enviously. But what is that "anything," that "everything?" I smiled, nodding assent, secretly alarmed by my lack of imagination, my narrow interests, my need to have a structure in place to function.

By November, I had signed up for everything: senior yoga, a writing class, a book club, volunteer work at the Old Town School of Folk Music, ushering for dance recitals and theater. I got my piano tuned and sat down to try playing melodies I hadn't attempted for years. And wondered, "Am I doing these things merely to fill up time, or are these misplaced pieces of myself, activities I didn't have time for before, long-buried interests?" Then I took a job. Just part-time, I rationalized, only a three-month commitment, postponing the "who-am-I-if-I'm-not-working" question. I breathed a sigh of relief as my days slowly filled up.

I made a lot of lists those first months: rosters of people who knew about education work, inventories of political projects I might check out, catalogues of possibilities. I flailed about, this way and that, lurching between loss and opportunity, unsettled, no permission to give myself time and space to "do nothing," unsteady, vacillating, ruminating, completely self-absorbed. Searching for definition, for meaningful work, for political expression. Yet I made no decisions, found no candidates to seize my attention.

Spring has finally arrived in Chicago. It's almost the end of the school year, and my retirement enters month nine. My basement is a mess: scattered papers and artifacts, a huge plastic bag filled with stuff to be tossed. I realize that I haven't been down there for weeks.

My desk and computer are making the guest room take on the feel of an office. It's the nicest room in the house. Three large windows give me a view of a school-yard park. I bring morning coffee in while I check E-mail, read the *New York Times*, and think about the day to come. I'm no longer yearning for the public space.

I start to write a bit, slowly, tentatively. First, I begin to get down some of my students' stories. Hesitantly, I write about my childhood neighborhood. Then an homage to my mother, dead seven years—a reflection about her piano and music that flew off my fingers. I send off scathing letters to the editor about privatization of community colleges. None are published.

I've come to understand that revisiting the past through writing may be a bridge between my working life and my life to come. Perhaps being mired in the past isn't totally self-indulgent, purely sentimental, or a substitute for action; it may signify an active engagement with the present. Now and then I feel that I'm trying on a new identity, searching for a writing voice and the confidence to bring ideas and stories dancing in my mind to light. I want to learn the craft, write boldly, engage readers. When a few sentences click, when a friend is moved after reading the piece about my mother, I'm pleased.

But writing is a struggle. I proceed cautiously. Mostly I read books about writing, or become immersed in other people's essays, anything to avoid writing myself. But I find I'm reading with a new eye. Toni Morrison said, around the time of her Nobel Peace Prize acceptance in December 1993, "It is words that empower meditation and enable us to make some sense of our existence by allowing us to stand aside to narrate it." I can feel what she means. I know that taking a step back to examine my working life through writing helps me think more clearly about it, sorting out the past while I gingerly dip my toes into the future. I'm more reflective, not such a bad trait for someone who's trying to handle this immense life change.

I think at times of my mementos. They represent the cumulative work experiences that defined my life. I carry them with me. I'm still the girl with the flag, the student reading Camus, the antiwar demonstrator, the teacher. I wonder what my memories have to offer me in retirement. Do they give me clues, a guide to the present? Often they declare, "continue on."

Writing about my students is one way of carrying on my education work, to share experiences with new teachers and activists. Ellen's letter and the returning women at the reunion are two of the stories I want to tell, but I have many more—tales of everyday transformations, examples of how students developed fresh ways of seeing their lives and the world. Yet, while writing pleases both my work ethic dictates and my desire for meaning, it's a solitary activity. What I miss about teaching is the immediate, direct, intense connection with people, the chance to engage in daily conversation about issues that matter to me: social class, race, the economy, work, politics. I often consider immersing myself in education projects again: tutoring a child, teaching a literacy class, going back to Moraine Valley as an emeritus professor, being an adjunct somewhere else. But my inner voice cautions, "You've done all that. Move on."

As I consider what to move on to, I bump up against the inadequacy of part-time work. While the three-month job I recently completed gave me an opportunity to interview public school reform activists, I was peripheral to the project and the organization. I don't like the consultant role, essentially that of a temp worker. I find the part-time work possibilities I've discovered wanting. They don't really make full use of my knowledge and skills; I feel dispatched to the margins. In one of my favorite books, *Working*, Studs Terkel talks about his job as a radio broadcaster: "I'm able to set my own pace, my own standards, and determine for myself the substance of each program. I like to believe I'm the old-time cobbler, making the whole shoe."[7] That just captures my feelings about my previous work. Unlike most workers, I had autonomy, self-direction. Work was, as Terkel says, "in my hands." I don't know if I can accept less than that, if I can handle being on the border, not central to the work of a group. I don't mind this role as just another gray-haired senior ushering at the Steppenwolf Theater, or an old folkie volunteering at the Old Town, but political organizations or educational settings are different. I know more, care more, I'm more invested.

On the other hand, I fear being totally swallowed up in an intense, demanding full-time project. I delight in my free mornings, yoga twice a week, walks, music and theater, a new dance class, time to write, swim, read. I crave a work replacement that satisfies my need to be competent, a place to use my knowledge and skills carefully honed over forty years in the labor force. Still, I recognize that for now I need a substitute that's not as totally absorbing as teaching or the movement. I want engaged work without the compulsions and restrictions of a full-time job, perhaps a contradiction impossible to resolve.

Though I'm figuring out this first year of retirement by myself, larger factors circumscribe my choices. The personal is political after all! My sense of dislocation in the beginning months, the ambivalence and dilemmas I'm experiencing suggest a critique of the very way that work is organized. It's hard to imagine what different institutional arrangements could look like, but the sharp disjuncture between worker and retiree, between paid and unpaid labor is too constricting. We need a blurring of boundaries. Building meaningful outlets for skills fashioned over a lifetime of work must be on our agenda, as well as finding a way for us to become more central as we age, rather than marginal, even though our work is part-time or volunteer.

And if I can't find a way—in the absence of education work on my terms, work that's important, meaningful, that makes a difference—what of other political routes? Choosing an issue or an organization to work with is new for me. In an earlier time, it seemed as if issues and groups chose me; events reached out and pulled me in. I was so much younger then; the path seemed so much clearer. Politics was a way of life, all consuming. But issues I care about passionately stare me in the face daily: the Middle East conflagration, child poverty, environmental peril. I'm perched on the edge, surveying the devastation, almost ready to jump in, return to my activist days, wondering what I can commit to wholeheartedly, and how to find a political group to embrace.

From time to time, I think that my mementos aren't enough of a guide. Perhaps I should open a different door, strike out in a different direction. I've had three decades of carefully planned-out years, organized by semesters, circumscribed by the confines of my weekly lesson plans. I've lived by schedules, regularity, routine; traveled down one path. I carry my old habits into retirement: planning, list making. Possibly, new qualities are called for: being adventuresome, spontaneous, improvisational, daring. Attributes I possessed when I sailed off to the youth festival, moved to New York as a young woman, leapt into the movement. What are the equivalent adventures for a woman in her sixties? In a different time? I heed Carolyn Heilbrun's warning: "The major danger in one's sixties is to be trapped in one's body and one's habits, not to recognize those supposedly sedate years as the time to discover new choices and act upon them."[8] New choices, different dreams? My imagination can't quite fathom these just yet.

The absence of daily imperatives heightens my struggle to find a place. There are no boundaries or limits. It's a terrible freedom. Yet there's also an urgency, alongside the freedom. Once in a while, I feel like this is the last chance, what Heilbrun calls "the last gift of time." Aging and mortality hover over my quest, sometimes translating into an urge to pause, to delay choices, to wait until just the right thing to do comes along, the perfect project presents itself. But I know this won't happen.

In the meantime, I dabble, try on, explore, noticing what feels true. One day I'm a judge at the citywide high school history fair, the next day I'm at a meeting discussing strategy to protest the Israeli government's violations of human rights. Monday night I'm the oldest by at least thirty years dancing at a YMCA cardio-funk class. "Give me an attitude," the instructor shouts. "Be sexy. Roll those hips. Your parents aren't here to watch." On Tuesday afternoon, I'm in the park district field house for senior yoga, the baby by far. "Would you like a towel to put under your knees?" my solicitous teacher asks. And amidst all the doubts, I'm polishing up a resume. I plan to teach one class in the fall.

Lately I notice just how different each day is from the other. I suppose I could see my life as fragmented, even dilettantish, but then again, I now taste, absorb, observe what went unseen before. I've come to accept that I haven't quite figured anything out yet in the definitive way that I thought I would just a year ago. Rather than planning the future, I guess I'm living it: hopeful writer, slightly arthritic but intent dancer, educator still, would-be activist, music listener, occasional pianist, reader, agonizer, question raiser, list maker.

Notes

Almost as soon as I thought of my title, "Notes from the First Year," I realized another first-year journey had been similarly named. So credit and thanks to the New York Radical Women, who published their *Notes from the First Year*, an important collection of early women's liberation articles, in June 1968. See: http://scriptorium.lib.duke.edu/wlm/notes/.

1. *Ramparts* was a monthly journal of opinion published out of Berkeley and San Francisco, California, from 1962 to 1975.

2. Mobilization for Youth was a set of innovative, experimental programs for low-income and minority youth and a precursor to the War on Poverty. *The Guardian* was an independent newspaper published weekly in New York City from 1948. It covered national and international news from a radical perspective. The Freedom School was a project of Freedom Summer in Mississippi (1964) and was sponsored by the Council of Federated Organizations (COFO) which included the Congress on Racial Equality (CORE) and the Student Nonviolent Coordinating Committee (SNCC).

3. The World Festival of Youth and Students for Peace and Friendship, an international gathering of young people, was held from July 26 to August 4, 1959. The festival was sponsored by Communist parties from around the world. Seventeen thousand youths from eighty-two countries participated in lectures, discussions, pageants, social events, music, sports, and international solidarity.

4. Chicago Women's Liberation Union (1968–1976) was a citywide socialist-feminist organization, with a wide array of projects including workplace organizing, the Liberation School, a rock band, a graphics collective, community organizing, work on health, abortion rights, and law, and work with women in prison. For an on-line historical archive see: http://www.cwluherstory.org.

5. The Indochina Peace Campaign, a grassroots national antiwar organization, was active from 1972 through 1975. It focused on community education and intensive congressional lobbying to end the war in Vietnam.

6. Arlie Russell Hochschild, *Coleen, the Question Girl: A Children's Story*, designed and illustrated by Gail Ashby (Old Westbury, N.Y.: The Feminist Press, 1974).

7. Studs Terkel, *Working: People Talk about What They Do All Day and How They Feel about What They Do* (New York: New Press, 1974), xix.

8. Carolyn G. Heilbrun, *The Last Gift of Time: Life beyond Sixty* (New York: Ballantine Books, 1997), 35.

Time to Look Back: My Family and the Movement

TERRY DAVIS

Activists, especially in the labor movement, make intense and painful personal choices. Fighting corporate America can easily become more than a full-time job, leaving very little energy and time for loved ones. Some of the best organizers I know have left behind them wrecked families, bitterness, and pain. I have tried to reconcile my family time and my movement work and keep them both in focus, being unwilling to give up either. Sometimes my efforts have been clumsy, or painful, or disastrous. But stubbornly I persist in thinking that eventually I'll get it right. Retirement is my chance to figure out some of that, without the pressures of a job. I can go back along the road and see what went wrong, what fell off the train, what might still remain to pick back up. I can search for lost pieces.

For the last thirty of my sixty years, I've been in the labor movement. For most of that time, I worked for a union, organizing the unorganized. It was what I wanted to do, and a job I am suited for. I made good use of an argumentative, combative personality—fighting union busters and negotiating contracts. I'm restless sitting at a desk, but I never had to stay at one too long. My obsession with details helped in planning campaigns or working out contract proposals. My propensity to talk a lot even was a good thing since that is what I had to do most of all. I love talking to people and figuring out what makes them tick. I love seeing people learning how to take power into their own hands. I love fighting against unfair, greedy bosses. I was lucky in finding just the right job for me. But it's a burn-out occupation. And I was at it a long time.

When I decided to retire last year, I felt spent. Though only sixty years old and healthy, I was desperately tired and couldn't find the inspiration that had always kept me going. I saw my grandchildren growing up before my eyes, and I longed to spend more time with them. When I found I could retire with a modest income, I went for it, even before figuring out the next phase of my life.

My retirement came as a shock to my co-workers. "She'll never retire," they said. "You couldn't imagine Terry not working for the union. Why, she's a workaholic!" "How could she possibly retire? She'll be back in six weeks. She won't know what to do with herself." But here I am, nine months later, and retirement feels natural and delicious to me. In these first few months, my main activity has been catching up with my children and grandchildren. And, freed from the daily necessities of work, I've thought about the past as I contemplate the future.

My parents, a pair of Marxist intellectuals, saw no conflict between political commitment and raising a family. They had five children, and they raised us in the left movement. We learned while still small about capitalism, socialism, and the fight for racial equality. We listened to Paul Robeson, Woody Guthrie, the songs of the Spanish Civil War. Although my father grew up in a family with money, we were always broke — my father lost just about every job he ever had as the result of sticking up for what he thought was right, regardless of the controversy that inevitably followed. We were proud of him.

My mother inspired me to be like her. She had a warm, embracing aura that made me, and many of my friends as well, feel nurtured and included. She taught me to do the right thing, hate racism, love peace, and respect ordinary working-class people. Now, forty years after her death, I wonder if she felt confined as a woman: she abandoned her promising scholarly career and devoted herself to family and the movement. I think she must have felt conflicted, but I never heard her complain about it.

As a young child I read books like *We Charge Genocide*, an indictment of American racism, and they were emblazoned on my consciousness. I listened to the grown-ups debate about politics far into the night. I wanted to grow up and fight the good fight. A loyal red diaper baby, I fantasized that when the fascists captured me and pulled out my fingernails one by one, I'd never tell them where my comrades were hidden.

When I reached my teens in the early fifties, McCarthyism changed our lives. Against the sinister backdrop of the Rosenberg trial and execution, I felt isolated and exposed when my parents, like so many others, were fired and blacklisted for their politics. I retreated into conformity. I decided my parents must be naive about communism and socialism; I wanted to look cautiously at both sides of everything before making a commitment. I was apolitical. Youthful rebellion for me meant retreat from radicalism, not acceptance of it.

I went to an elite college that reinforced my quietism, although I detested its snobbishness. Yearning for security, I married very young. I had no clear life plan or involvement with politics. The only thing I was sure about was wanting kids. By the time I was twenty-six, we had three—Adam, Josh, and Leah. My husband's scientific research dominated the household—I stayed home with the children while he pursued an academic career. I changed and washed diapers, wheeled my kids in strollers to the park, read them stories, drove them to nursery school. In my spare time I read books, baked bread, cooked ambitious dinners out of gourmet cookbooks, got involved in musical groups. I was busy, and ambivalent about leaving the kids with baby-sitters; I postponed thoughts of work or further schooling.

In the early sixties, the winds of change blew hard at me and my complacency. My bubble of neutrality burst. I thrilled to news of the sit-ins in the South, I campaigned for nuclear disarmament, and as the war in Vietnam grew, so did my rage at the killing. Looking at a poignant photograph of a young Vietnamese woman carefully nursing a baby covered with napalm burns, I could only think of my own babies. Soon I was collecting signatures against the war while wheeling my stroller, or dragging the kids to a march against race discrimination. I went to meetings, made phone calls, handed out leaflets, and got a whole new set of friends, all activists. It felt natural to me to wade deeper and deeper into the left movement.

By the late sixties, the movement was at the core of my life. In 1968, I joined a women's consciousness raising group, which gave me—suddenly, dramatically—permission to take myself seriously. Tending kids and housework didn't seem like enough any more. The very idea of cooking began to nauseate me. In search of an identity and a teaching career, I went to graduate school, but it seemed boring and stilted compared with the immediacy of organizing. It was around this time that my son Josh, just barely in grade school, organized a "Children's Liberation" group with a 10-point program, demanding equality with the grown-ups and the right to use the living room. Well, I thought, if I am ignoring them, at least they are picking up tools to defend themselves.

My husband, Lenny, didn't have a left-wing background and was grounded in academic life. Although he waded deeper and deeper into the movement too, he didn't wade as fast or as far as I did. A desire to get closer to "real" people was pulling me beyond where Lenny wanted to go. As a faculty wife living in the shadow of the University of Chicago, I felt stifled, frustrated, privileged, hemmed in. I wondered how that radical Huey Newton poster on our wall looked to the middle-aged black woman who baby-sat while I went to classes or ran around doing political work. I didn't want to be a hothouse radical in a university environment; I wanted to be on the front lines.

With a nice home, no financial worries, a good husband, and smart, adorable children, I maybe should have been satisfied with my life. But all of a sudden, except for the children, it didn't feel like the life I wanted. In those days I was humorless, thin, frowning, driven. Lenny thought I had taken leave of my senses.

By the early seventies, I had developed a set of political ideas that I wanted to live by. Put simply, it went something like this: A broad movement, like that of the thirties, would be needed to bring fundamental change. This movement would have to be based in the working class. And the main obstacle to a working-class progressive movement was white racism. So the big task was to find ways to bring white workers into unity with people of color, thereby advancing their common interests and attacking racial divisions and white supremacy.

At that time, the black freedom movement was challenging white progressives to organize in our own communities, yet many of us felt organizing whites apart from people of color was risky. In Chicago our neighborhoods were (and still are) segregated by race; organizing white people separately could easily turn into an antiblack movement. So where would one find the opportunity to organize white workers to unite with black and Latin workers? On the job, at the point of production, where workers have power and experience a common exploitation, I believed, there would be potential and reason for unity. I longed to get out there into that multiracial working class and organize.

When I look back, I see that those ideas have stood the test of time. Naive as I was in some ways, my basic plan made sense. What I didn't anticipate, and couldn't always cope with, was how changing my own life would also change life for my kids. By 1973, Lenny and I were divorced. Leaving the groves of academe, the kids and I had relocated in a working-class neighborhood. I was working on the assembly line in a huge Chicago factory and had teamed up with a man (whom I would soon marry) who shared my desire to plunge into working-class organizing.

The kids were plunged into a whirlwind of change. From their stable, middle-class university community they were suddenly transplanted to a West Side neighborhood which, it turned out, was turning almost overnight from all white to mostly African American. Their new public school was in chaos from the drastic changes caused by "white flight." But home offered no haven either. Gone was their father, gone the nuclear family—instead a changing cast of characters in the semi-commune we lived in now. When I look at snapshots of the kids during this time, I see that betrayed, lost look that kids' eyes get during a divorce, and it is enough to tear my heart out. But at the time, I kept telling myself that things would work out (although at times I wasn't so sure) because they just had to. There was no turning back.

My new partner, Bob, and I devoted ourselves completely to organizing at Stewart-Warner. It was a huge, decrepit plant with a workforce of 2,500—white, black, Latino, a little of every ethnic group in Chicago—and had a company union. We were up at dawn to go to work, and by the time we had made our last phone calls in the evening it was time to fall exhausted into bed. Everything else fell by the wayside. No more gourmet cooking. No more music groups. Sometimes the tooth fairy even forgot to show up for the kids. Adam wrote her a letter that started "Dear Fucking Tooth Fairy." We became immersed in the lives of our new friends from the plant, whether they were black workers from the West Side, Appalachians from Tennessee, Mexican Americans, Puerto Ricans, Filipinos, or the Chicago-born, white, skilled-trades guys who had moved out to the suburbs. Men, women, young, old, here they were under one roof—overworked, underpaid, segregated by sex, divided by racism, surrounded by dirt and noise, held down by a union that represented management more than it did the workers. These were our co-workers, who we set about to organize. Absorbed in our new life, we didn't even notice as the movements of the sixties began to wither and shrink. We had entered another world that absorbed us completely.

Nothing before or since has felt so compelling to me as our seven-year campaign for justice at Stewart-Warner. Old friendships lapsed, there was no time for reading, everything and everybody that didn't fit somehow into the project was set aside. Stewart-Warner even dominated our family life. In the mornings my kids made their own school lunches as Bob and I raced off to the plant to work. In the afternoons, we often lingered there to talk to people or to hold a meeting. This meant late dinners on the table. When we cranked out our monthly newsletter at home on our own mimeo machine, the kids helped us collate and fold. When we took the kids camping, it was with Stewart-Warner families. When we socialized, it was with Stewart-Warner people.

Bob and I and our Stewart-Warner friends learned about each other and about racism, struggle, unity, and unions. Out of the small multiracial group we founded, Concerned Workers, step by step we built a plantwide movement that finally led to victory: the ousting of the company union and the formation of a new, democratic union that affiliated with the United Electrical, Radio, and Machine Workers of America (UE).

By 1979, I'd become a trade union activist through and through. At Stewart-Warner, I had weathered some storms, managed not to get fired, and learned new confidence in my skills. But Bob, ever the vagabond, itched to move on from Stewart-Warner. I went with him—even though the kids were still in high school and our Stewart-Warner project hadn't really come to closure. Leaving behind the dirt and noise of plant work, the bosses breathing down our backs, and all our friends in Chicago, we went to work for the UE, a progressive union we had come to respect, and moved lock, stock, and barrel to the South. My experiences in the plant helped me to understand organizing in a new context. While Ronald Reagan was declaring war on unions, we were bucking the tide.

I dragged my kids along as we wound up moving from place to place in Virginia and North Carolina, according to UE's organizing agenda. My two younger kids, Josh and Leah, each went to three different high schools. Going from Chicago's West Side to the South was culture shock. Leah came home from ninth grade wide-eyed with shock to recount the racist comments of the other kids; I suddenly realized that living in the black community had meant not learning about white racism!

Meanwhile, my marriage to Bob had moved beyond the closeness of early Stewart-Warner days to increasing problems. After a stormy period of tension and conflict, which took a heavy toll on the kids, we divorced in the early eighties. Bob left the UE and went on to other things; but I continued on, working for the union around the country. As my kids one by one left for college, the union work became my life more than ever.

Believing in the UE, I worked enthusiastically—whether it was to organize rural white workers in southwestern Virginia, Mexican immigrants in low-paying plants in Chicago, African Americans in Milwaukee, or hospital workers in California. There was always a set of important negotiations, a crucial rally, bosses and union busters to fight, an election to win, a leaflet to write, some kind of crisis. There were victories and defeats, tears and laughter, conflict and solidarity, new members organized into the union and old factories (eventually including Stewart-Warner) closed forever. There were bitter conflicts and many warm, lasting friendships born in struggle (which I've found are the deepest kind). My fellow organizers and the UE members we worked with were like a family in many ways.

My twenty-one years with the UE were a rich, rewarding, maddening, exhausting, exciting, depressing, thrilling ride. I was lucky to work for an organization I trust. I never felt that my commitment to the workers' struggle was compromised in the UE—just the opposite—and talking to lefties who work for other unions makes me think this is unique and wonderful. But as a lifestyle, being an organizer wreaks havoc on your personal life.

Union organizing culture is like the system of triage in an emergency room. When you can't possibly do everything that's absolutely necessary, you have to rank tasks in order of importance. You need to be hard-hearted about the things you can't get to. If the leader of the Organizing Committee suddenly gets fired from the plant on Friday afternoon, you just forget about heading home for that fun weekend you had planned. You trudge back to the office and take statements from witnesses, and maybe write a leaflet for Monday morning as well. And translate it into Spanish. You might even wind up talking to the union's lawyer, or the distraught family of the person who was fired, or half the Organizing Committee members, before the evening is over. Whoever you had plans with—your family, friends, or significant other—will have to be told, and they may or may not understand. That's just an example of a Friday afternoon triage. But over the years, this kind of triage multiplied over and over caused repeated strain in my relationships with the kids. If there was a way to avoid this dilemma, I didn't find it.

Somewhere along the line, moving from place to place, I lost the box in which I had stored the pictures and projects my children had made over the years. Thinking of that is like a wound that doesn't heal. And there were countless ways, while I was preoccupied with union matters, that I lost focus on my children—failed to pay attention, to listen, to have time, to let them know how much I loved them. I wasn't unaware of the problem, nor was I callous to it. I didn't know what to do about it. Like my own mother, I felt somehow the kids would make it through any adversity and understand the sacrifices required by the struggle.

My kids didn't buy into the notion that sacrifice—at least, that imposed by your parents—is good for you. As they reached adulthood, they all three, together and separately, gathered their forces and confronted me with searing criticisms of my life choices and the ways they affected them. Some of the criticism was so painful to hear, I've just blanked it out, although the pain remains. And they will never talk to me about the union at all. (This has forced me to think of something else to talk about, which may have been just as well.) I know our family didn't invent parent-child conflict, and that there's always more to it than political choices; but my absorption with the union and the movement surely took away some of the energy I might have used to face problems sooner.

My kids have all turned into strong, capable, socially conscious adults. Their work is worthwhile, and they do it well: a consumer protection attorney, a creator of curricula for urban classrooms, and a bilingual teacher, they carry as part of their core personal identities a respect for people and a consciousness about racism and class. One could say their exposure to struggle and diversity in their childhood helped them to become who they are, and that is surely true. But they tend to avoid political commitment and activism. Now they all have beautiful children of their own. The arrival of the grandchildren brought a softening of the conflicts between me and my kids, who often say they never realized how much work it was to raise children until they had their own. I admire the way my kids approach child-rearing—with endless patience and energy. They (and, interestingly, others in their generation) believe in protecting their children far more than we did, putting them at the center of the parents' lives. Our cohort didn't—on purpose. We dragged the kids from one demonstration to another, we pushed them aside as we talked politics, or union, or whatever. It's not that we didn't love them, but we were more concerned with making the world a better place for their future than with making life comfortable right then. We had a revolution to make. We may have accomplished even more than we realized at the time, but our kids paid a price. They didn't feel safe, protected, important. Now as adults, they are making sure that their kids do.

As I began to think about retiring, the allure of my grandkids beckoned me forward. The only thing I knew for sure was that I wanted more time with them. And I figured I could be helpful as well, especially to the three (now four) that live in Chicago. My three-year-old grandson, Sam, has Down's syndrome and needs special schooling. Getting him to school meant a transportation nightmare for his working parents. By watching him several mornings a week until his school bus comes, I'm filling a gap. But those mornings are also fun! Sammy and I laugh and sing and read and laugh some more, then tromp around outside. These mornings are among the highlights of my week.

The two oldest grandkids, Sofia and Benjy, also have special times with me. I'm not in a hurry and I can enjoy those times calmly, without worrying about the work that is piling up meanwhile, because it isn't. We play in the park, start a project, go on an adventure, and we all three look forward to it. My two-year-old grandson, Jack, lives far away, but now I'll have time for extended visits with him too. Grandkids are an unqualified joy for me. And I love being able to help their parents.

But the truth is, the grandkids go to day care and school, their parents go to work, and these relationships don't occupy my whole life now, even though they are a big part of it. What is this new life? When I retired, I walked through the door to the future without really knowing what would be on the other side.

Most of the retirees I have known have fallen into two categories: industrial workers and academics. Blue-collar retirees leave an alienating, exhausting, boring job. It's exhilarating to have free time and newly released energy upon escaping the physical demands of work. Where work is highly structured by others, leisure is simply freedom from that structure. It's being off the clock, getting the boss off your back. It's the opposite of work, not an extension of it. But that very freedom can bring boredom and depression at suddenly having no purpose.

For academics (especially at elite schools), work is more self-directed, a seamless part of life. Retirement may just be a gentle continuation of what went before: reading, research, writing, teaching. Work is less alienating, leisure less distant from work. Cultural and intellectual pursuits and travel are an expected part of one's career. One is expected to just keep going in retirement.

I don't fit either category. Although I mostly didn't work on the clock, and I identified with my job deep down inside, I was engaged in work that absorbed almost all my energy and left me little time for leisure. I was occupied in fighting bosses, but they were other peoples' bosses. I approached retirement without clear expectations and decided to play it by ear.

I spent the whole year before my retirement day out of town on a big campaign. It provided closure of the best kind in two ways—a rousing victory for the UE and for the workers, and working with young organizers, who make me feel better about the future. When I got home, I returned to my private life like Odysseus returning from the sea. My apartment in Chicago seemed like the home of someone else. I didn't know where things were, I didn't even feel responsible for making changes in it. Gradually I noticed that the phone cord was too short, the lamp by my bed was bad for reading, I needed something in the kitchen to hang things on, the living room couch was musty and dilapidated.

I began to settle in. I bought a new couch, a longer phone cord. I rearranged my lamps, my kitchen shelves. I painted the hall, the kitchen. I reclaimed my private space. It took months. How alienated I'd become from my own little personal necessities! I lived for several months like a hermit, only seeing family and a few friends. This process healed me inside.

Now my phone rings less than before. No emergency in this plant or that, no organizing missions to pack my suitcase for. I do a lot of reading, play the banjo. I got a puppy, who goes with me on walks. And I hang out with my kids and grandkids.

I know this solitude is a phase; everyone tells me so. Already the activist within me is stirring. I've noticed that when you're not politically engaged, it's even more painful to read about the world—whether it's the attacks on trade unions worldwide, the ascendance of the ultraright with Bush in the White House, the huge growth of poverty and suffering on one hand and of unbelievable wealth on the other. I need to be involved in the struggle. But there are some things I am not likely to do any time soon. I don't want to persuade anybody of anything. No persuading! If you want to learn something I know, I'd love to explain it to you. But I'm not going to persuade you. I'm not going to round people up. I don't want to do anything that involves endlessly contacting people and urging them to do things. When I get E-mails marked "urgent," I find I just have to delete them. Somewhere along the road, I simply overdosed on persuasion and urgency.

I've started going to a few demonstrations, a few Jobs with Justice committee meetings. It's good to see old friends again. And there are a new crop of young people who want to change the world. It's fun to stick my nose out the door, cheer at a rally, sit in on a meeting. I feel at home, and itch to do more work.

So far, I don't think that terrible pull between family and politics will rear its ugly head again, not with my luxurious supply of free time. I can even anticipate mixing them creatively. My nine-year-old granddaughter, Sofia, the eldest, has started taking a real interest in social justice and she comes to me with probing questions about the civil rights movement. When I took her and Benjy to a march recently, she asked her mom (my daughter): "Did she use to take you to marches too? Isn't it fun?" Leah circumspectly answered, "Sometimes." Sofia wants to go to more of them. God knows, if she and the other grandchildren ever want to be activists, their work is waiting for them.

If they don't, that's okay too. I know how wonderful I find my kids as adults, and the grandkids are on their way to being wonderful adults too. I do know I want them to learn about what I have cared about and worked for. I don't wish them to have less passion or commitment than I did, even though I can wish them to avoid mistakes I made.

I have renounced carrying a purse. That big purse now seems a burden: a weight on my shoulders, a collection of things I have to carry with me, a responsibility not to lose it, something to guard, something that keeps my arms from swinging free. It's very liberating, no purse. But the problem is, what takes its place? I have no use for the purse; it's history. But I can't ever find my keys or my wallet. My arms swing free, there's no load on my shoulder, but I experience a vague confusion in the blank space the purse has left. Just as with the rest of life, there is no going back. But it will take a while to decide what treasures to put in the blank spaces.

Every Day a Sunday?
Reflections on a First
Year of Retirement

BARBARA RUBIN

I am one year into retirement—a frequent flyer now—sitting in a meeting room at the President Hotel in Istanbul about to meet my co-travelers on a "mad dash" tour through Turkey. We are asked by the guide to introduce ourselves which, of course, means telling each other what we "do," once our nationalities have been established. The go-around reveals that there are four doctors, one pharmacist, a sculptor, and many educators and business people in the group. When my turn comes, I tell them that I've been a professor of women's studies for many years, never mentioning that I no longer do it. Retirement is my secret, I decide on the spot. I want to be seen as in the world—and I don't mean just on the road. I do not want the vitality my work suggests or the youth my blessedly young face feigns to be taken away in one moment of admission. I do not want to wear the big, black R, an all-consuming label to others, I think, of rest and resignation. No, not just yet.

Several days into the trip, however, I spill the beans. Being evasive has become too uncomfortable, and I need the practice of moving around in this new state of retirement that still, after a year, is alien and troubling even as it is deliciously self-indulgent and freeing. Nothing has prepared me for retirement: not the model of a father who vegetated in it for thirty years nor a society that really does not appreciate those of us who are "modernly mature," to borrow a phrase from AARP. But here I am in May, about to sail the Bosporus as my former colleagues read final exams. When I return home, I will write that essay on retirement I've promised my editors and make some sense of all this ambivalence. Yes, I am so happy to have something to write, something to tell others I am doing, as though I were still working.

The End of the Run

Retirement would sneak up and announce itself, I believed, not like some unexpected visitor hiding behind a door, but rather as an expected one with a loose arrival time. I had always known I would stop working eventually, earlier than my artist and therapist friends, given my institutional location; I just hadn't set a specific age for doing it, like a rounded-out sixty, for example. I would simply reach a point when my grand passion for teaching feminist studies would burn itself out. The responsibility of repeatedly chairing a still-marginalized program would become too burdensome, if not martyrlike. In short, I would feel the exhaustion of being too long at these academic acts of labor, even as my commitment to the existence of the women's studies program I cofounded would live on. Probably hazy still in a certain uncertainty, I would come to the end of the run. And last year, at age sixty-three, I did.

Other circumstances propelled me toward retirement as well. My mother died at fifty-six of ovarian cancer, and for me, genetics was a crapshoot. I wanted to grab any good years left to shape a less stressful, more artistically expressive life. Every health magazine I subscribed to "encouraged" me in this direction; so, too, a huge retirement industry whose mostly unappealing ads reminded me that I was of a "certain age." There were institutional signals as well: the increasing support of grants and other professional goodies going to younger faculty; in-passing, subtle inquiries by administrator friends who really admired my work, about my plans for my future; generational, though collegial, disagreements among women's studies faculty about new theoretical directions for the program; and the increasing numbers of colleagues my age who had already retired. You got the message that your remaining days at the place were being counted, if not by you, then by somebody else. At every institution, retirement has its insidious ways of insinuating itself. I would not have left, however, had I not really been ready to—no innuendos, no market-driven imperatives on campus, no proliferating youth culture would have edged me out.

But taking leave has not been easy. I left a good salary, a top rank and its concomitant respect, and a university that had been my community for more than three decades. As I am a single, childless woman, my colleagues have been in some ways a substitute family. I can walk across the small campus and greet any number of them, exchanging pleasantries or confidences, even with a few with whom I have publicly tussled. I've made good friendships, mentored junior faculty, created political alliances, and endlessly received the professional generosity of colleagues, as I have extended my own loyalty and kindness to others. I have celebrated their marriages, childbirths, tenure, promotions, book publications, and art openings. They are like cousins, father and mother surrogates and siblings, a big, available "family," with all its attendant bickering, but enough affection left on the part of many. Some have watched me grow from a twenty-nine-year-old rebel to a middle-aged, mellowed but still fighting woman. How does one say good-bye beyond the lovely retirement party? How does one prepare for the little deaths upon leaving: a high-stress world of work and its preoccupied people that will go on without you, that will, even with a women's center named for you, largely forget you with the passage of time?

Time, now, however, to pack it in and pack it all up, I tell myself: the book collection lining the shelves, the photos and the framed awards on the walls, the desk paraphernalia, the files full of a career lifetime of research and writing and teaching and grading, and, finally, the engraved-in-brass title on the door that tells it all.

The semester has ended, and my colleagues have fled to distant shores. My back office sits in a silent corridor with only the sound of shredding paper filling the air: all the evidence of so many hours and years of arduous effort passing in front of my eyes before ending up in the waste bin or a sealed box for storage, perhaps never to be opened again. I decide to save some remnants of the effort—students' thank-you notes, a few good proposals, some reprints of my work, a course outline or two, and, of course, the handwritten note from the president confiding to me that I'd once been on a short list for dean.

I really want to toss everything out and be done with this material history, but what if in the future I cast doubt on, or become too senile to remember, all the work I have done—where will the proof be then? Suddenly, proof becomes everything: I pack up more and more cartons, more than I know what to do with. They line the long hallway, oversized cartons, medium-sized and little ones, all in a row, a cortege in the burial rite of a thirty-two-year career.

The "Early Morning" of Retirement

In the first weeks of retirement, I would wake up in early morning with a habituated response to get moving so as not to be late for my nine o'clock class or meeting across the river. I was a big bargainer when it came to time, never having enough of it, shaping and reshaping its use as if play dough in my hands. But I slowly came to realize that those obligations were a thing of the past, that I fully owned the next hour or two of the beginning of the day. I would turn over then and languorously sleep into those hours, hoarding them as if recompense for all the "stolen" hours in the name of work.

I would marvel repeatedly in those first weeks of freedom at this exceedingly strange "space" I found myself in; it was a space without imperatives, virgin space, like no other space I had ever inhabited. It was not as if I were in a state of suspended animation "doing nothing"—an impossible feat that some retirees joke about being high on their agendas—it was just that everything I did do, or had plans to do, was of my own making and in my own time. I became engulfed in a feeling of airiness and roominess. There was no prior experience to liken it to, certainly not that illusory state of innocence called childhood with all its developmental cycles to confront. No, this one was different, like being in a state of grace, on holy ground, earned ground, walking toward death for sure, but for now, in a seemingly inviolate place wholly one's own.

When friends and relatives called to inquire how life was going, I waxed ecstatic about my newfound freedom. I had been seen as somewhat of a workaholic in my circles and ardent about feminist education, even as I was known for burning the candle at both ends: enjoying entertaining, travel, romance, and the cultural riches of New York City. My friends worried about how I would adjust to a leisurely, less driven life. Fine, I was doing just fine, I quickly reassured them.

But after a short time a different mood crept in, and this "hallowed" ground began giving way under my feet. Cut loose from an identity that had been carefully crafted and hard won, I became shaky as I suddenly questioned who I was now. Would I ever do anything of real importance again, anything as compelling as what I had already done? I went to a Manhattan party just around that time, and the host introduced me to another guest in the past (im)perfect, as a "usetabe," as in "She used to be a chair of women's studies." And I found myself reinventing myself on the spot so as not to be brushed aside as yesterday's news.

You may be wondering, didn't she have a plan before retiring, like renting a house in Key West for the winter, or traveling around the world, or working on a book? Well, yes, of course I had some notions of what I would do: volunteer work, more extensive travel, studying a new language, and some writing, though I had no idea what I would write. With so many memoirs of second-wave feminists glutting the market, I did not think another one was needed. Perhaps it would be the poetry I had abandoned a long time ago.

But none of these plans seemed to assuage a gnawing feeling that I had lost my mooring, and that important parts of my identity were starting to disappear. Moving from working to not working was a startling experience. Did CEOs really just give it all up for the golf course, I wondered, or were they consulting and still pulling strings behind the scenes of the organization? Were easy transitions reserved only for those who disliked the work they were doing? I was haunted by a retirement image of a former neighbor of mine who for many years had owned a celebrated art bookshop in the neighborhood. After he sold the shop, he stood at the doorway of our apartment house talking to the doorman for hours each day, pipe in hand, seemingly lost. About a year later, he suffered a stroke, lingered in a nursing home, and then died.

I started calling younger former colleagues for reports on women's studies and campus gossip, but with each call I made, I felt diminished by the details of their professional projects and the ongoing life at the university. Although their days were frenzied, as mine had been, they were full of dynamism and purpose. I saw the young Barbara in them, and I envied the years between their ages and mine. I wanted to reclaim the playing field.

I found myself frantically making commitments to women's studies projects—a keynote address in November, a paper for a women's studies conference in June, and a volunteer assignment to plan an event celebrating feminist educators. These activities kept me professionally connected, a connection I needed as reassurance that all I had done in the past for women still counted, that I still counted.

Shaping an Identity: Work, Family, and Feminism

I hadn't come to a solid and pleasing work identity easily. My family had been work driven, mostly out of necessity, though I suspect partly out of temperament. Work was the interloper in our family affairs, seizing the hours some other families used for intimacy and play. My father and maternal grandmother, who helped raise me, were immigrant survivors, water buffaloes eking out a living. Dad's workday as a grocer began at six-thirty in the morning and ended at eleven o'clock at night, six days a week and a half day on Sunday. Motivated by large ambition and memories of lean times and loss, he lived among us, often not with us.

Mother was a doer as well. Always in motion, she swept by purposefully, heading to a not-distant finishing line of household chores and family maintenance. She must have awakened with maps in her head of the local neighbor-hood: the butcher shop and vegetable stand, the post office where she mailed salamis to her brothers in wartime, and the half block between where she lived and worked, unpaid, in my father's grocery store. Mother hated the ardu-ous work of being a shopkeeper, but when Dad sold his grocery and became a manufacturer of plastic bags after World War II, Mother's work life and out-look changed perceptibly. She was hired by my father and his two partners—with a salary—to be their secretary. It was a job she loved: the compliments for her competence, the closeness to my father, and the use of the skills in which she'd been trained.

Earning money, though modest in amount, pleased Mother too; it gave her back some of the financial independence she had enjoyed until age twenty-seven when she married my father. Money had become a source of tension between them: Dad was the banker and bank guard, tightly determining how much there would be for table money, allowances, and all other expenditures. Even as he made money, he could not part with it; his security was in the hav-ing of it. But once Mother's paycheck came in, we children got some "extras." When she died years later, all three children were left small inheritances that she had saved in her own separate bank account.

The fact remains, however, that she earned her self-esteem and small salary at great cost. She was a "superwoman" before the term had been coined. Run-ning a household and raising a young son and two daughters while working outside the home were her responsibilities, although her mother provided some help—always the women bonding in support. But there remained little if any time for leisure or languor or culture. The work ethic was soldered to our family's soul; not even a modicum of prosperity could loosen the "social metal" in which my parents had been unalterably cast.

My parents' work ethic was one of their legacies to me, for better and worse. I learned how hard and demanding work could be, and the differences in its difficulties and rewards depending on one's sex. I also observed the gratifica-tion my parents derived in later years when each was involved in appealing work. I noted, however, the personal sacrifices required for many people's suc-cesses, and that most outstanding work was not achieved by living a balanced life.

As I was growing up, I wrote for several school newspapers and set my sights on being a journalist. However, there were no models of women in nontradi-tional jobs in the forties and fifties, not in my primarily working-class neigh-borhood in Brooklyn. Mary Tyler Moore would not appear in our living rooms until a good deal later. Upon entering college, I chose to become a child psychologist until I fell in love in my junior year with a poor, about-to-be medical student. In a prefeminist gesture, I switched my major to education — a major most of my girlfriends had already embraced — in order to support Jules through medical school should we marry. We did not marry, and I ended up with a degree in education that I never really wanted.

This degree was a fated one, however: it eventually brought me into higher education, where I would do my feminist work. But before that would happen, I thrashed around in a career for nine years, never feeling entirely satisfied. Although I was a good teacher of young children and derived pleasure from it, and then a finely trained reading specialist with a graduate degree, I never felt my work could hold a candle in importance, or salary, to the work the men I dated in my twenties did. They were lawyers, doctors, and professionals of one sort or another — ambitious, self-important, and very aware of their needs. When I was twenty-four, I went out with an economist at the United Nations who worked in the water resources division studying the problems of African nations. I always accommodated his work hours, even if it meant meeting at nine o'clock on a work night after he'd completed his reports; I thought the needs of underdeveloped nations far exceeded my need for a good night's sleep. After all, I only had to deal with thirty children the next day, not whole populations.

The hierarchy of work and educated men's advantages in it, along with other obvious socializations, formed the framework for the dating patterns of most of my relationships. I believed that, as with the U.N. economist, I would have to defer to boyfriends' wishes, or a husband's should I marry, if I continued the work I was doing, because these up-and-coming young men I was seeing held the economic trump card. And although I recognized that the training of young minds, future leaders possibly, was extremely important work, little about society then, or now, affirmed this belief. I was *just* a schoolteacher, working at a job women mainly did and devalued because of it. There seemed not much hope of surviving with some degree of power and integrity any romantic relationship, to say nothing of the world at large.

Clearly I was ripe for feminism: I had been responding instinctively to many situations as though I had already been in consciousness-raising but without the reassurance the process offered. When I finally found my way into a CR group in the late sixties, there was no turning back. As we examined the profound relationship between the individual and the culture, between the personal and the political, between the private sphere and the public sphere, I began to understand how we had been defined and oppressed as women.

Later on, several years after I had been hired by Jersey City State College to train teachers and teach reading theory, I cofounded its women's center and women's studies program and went on to earn a Ph.D. in women's studies.

Any wish in my thirties to have children and a domestic life competed with my great desire to be part of the sixties and seventies zeitgeist in some profound way. I wanted to be a social change agent, out in the world. It was impossible, I believed, to have it all: the whole, winning human package. I did not think that the men I met were evolved enough for constructing an egalitarian family; nor was I for that matter. Living in any other kind just would not do.

There has never been a question in my mind about the value and importance of my work since I entered higher education, and, in particular, women's studies. The salary may have been small in comparison to those paid to other professionals, but the substance of what my women's studies colleagues and I did carried weight. We were pioneers changing the academic landscape: its canon of knowledge, the nature of teaching, and the structure of the university. I threw myself passionately into each day. The work became both mission and raison d'être. As the women's studies program grew, and as possibilities for many women increased, so did my self-esteem. After many years, I had finally established a work identity strong to the core.

A Time for Reckoning

But a commitment to women's studies and the larger movement can eat you up even as it feeds you. All social and political activists know this. Passions ensnare, like snakes coiling around the heart. Through much of my career, I lived a life half tended. My apartment, like Gloria Steinem's, had only been partially furnished; I seldom looked at my retirement plan, or got the exercise I needed, or did the writing I wanted to, the teacher and administrator in me more often winning the battle for time. Retirement, therefore, began to have its appeal; it was a chance to shift from work to the self, from responsibility to freedom, from a set structure to a fluid one. I could turn my attention to the neglected areas of my life where repair and reclamation were still possible.

But what about those unattended areas of my life that are no longer available to be had, missed boats, so to speak, creative acts left undone? How am I to reconcile the fact that I've blown my chances? Retirement, you see, is a time not only for rest, but also for reckoning: coming face-to-face with the life one has shaped, and without daily work to paper over its holes.

As I examine my life, it seems spare in some ways in comparison to those of my friends with intact marriages and children sprouting grandkids for them.

As their families expand with new descendants, mine contracts through deaths and desertions as relatives move to retirement homes in distant places. Brides and births and brisses are found in other people's homes; I live without inter-generational anchors or activities.

Although I often feel the pleasures of solitude in living alone, I admit to wrestling with solitude's underside, a loneliness that is never far away. In my younger days, I eschewed the culture of "coupledom," even as I was part of a couple, but a two-by-two march through life's vicissitudes seems eminently appealing today.

Taking stock of one's life has its dangers, of course: one can begin to feel sorry for oneself for the roads not taken. Myopia sets in when past choices are seen through a lens of present needs and values. The impact of gender discrimination and dysfunctional family life on my decisions of three decades ago are almost forgotten in the midst of a bout of regrets—so too the captivating promise of the sixties and seventies for a life of greater equality. I have to remind myself many times over that the life I lived often reflected the beliefs I espoused—and a few neuroses, no doubt—and that sometimes one pays dues for a consistency of principles.

So I take the holes in my life and fill them in ways that I can: through enjoying other people's children or being the "universal mother" of Sara Ruddick's "Maternal Thinking";[1] by tightening my friendships and making new ones across a span of ages; by growing the communities I inhabit and envisioning new ones for the future; and by still thinking, perhaps crazily, that I just might meet a man who can fall in love with an unrepentant feminist. To paraphrase Bette Davis's quote on old age: Retirement is not for sissies.

Volunteering: Gift and Trap

Two years before I retired, I became a volunteer for AARP on their New York-based, public access cable TV show, *Second-Half Strategies*. The program, which uses a magazine-type format, addresses the needs and concerns of an aging population. One of my friends is a volunteer director on the show, and while we were having lunch one lovely summer day she recruited me. I needed a change of venue, a new engagement, a preretirement exploration. I had flirted over the years with the dubious notion of doing something on TV, perhaps producing and hosting a show about women. I had appeared on TV occasionally, first on a media tour to promote a book I had co-authored in the early eighties, and then as a sometimes spokesperson for women's issues on Channel 9's *Straight Talk*.

The volunteer job I was offered on AARP's show was that of a technician, with the possibility of producing and doing on-camera work in the future. I was to train at Manhattan Neighborhood Network (MNN), our borough's public access TV station built by Ted Turner in return for part of the city's cable business. So in the midst of one of my most demanding stints in chairing women's studies, I attended night classes at MNN in how to use the camera, control board, and editing facilities and the up-to-date digital equipment. Training in a new field at this advanced age was heady. I was a neophyte and not unhappy for it.

In a short time, I began producing ten-to-twelve-minute segments and appearing on camera as an interviewer/moderator. I liked the dynamism of the studio and the glamour of the job; I liked the teamwork and putting together a creative product each month. I marveled at having access to all this airtime, and even though I produced some routine shows with issue-focused themes such as remodeling one's home for independent living, I was also selecting themes of my own. Part of each show features people who are making interesting contributions to society, even into their nineties. Here was a chance for me to highlight older women's needs and accomplishments.

But as the months went on, I began to resent the show's demands on my time and its stressful deadlines. It was interfering with a postwork calm I had started to enjoy. Once again, I was neglecting daily life and its imperatives. Why am I back in this workaholic mode, I asked myself, and without a salary to go with it? How many hours do I want to give before it feels too much like work or perhaps exploitation? After all, I volunteer for the largest lobbying group in the country, which also happens to be a big business.

I might not have brought up this "crass" subject of money and payment if I had still had most of the bundle I was counting on to see me through the next twenty years. But this isn't the case given the collapse of the stock market, not for me or many other 401(k)-ers. Lately, I've been thinking about what kind of part-time paid work I might do to supplement what I have lost if Wall Street does not recover. Some other retirees have confided to me that doing work and not getting paid does not interest them, even with a secure retirement plan. Volunteer work, though applauded for its good citizenship, just doesn't carry the same cachet in our society that paying jobs do, unless one is wealthy and sitting on a board—or volunteering on television.

So I need to rethink volunteerism, the nature of it and its place in my life, even as I acknowledge the importance of the work and the self-esteem it has afforded me. A good deal of built-in service has already been part of my history, the kind that falls to women to a larger extent than to men, such as tending family members and doing feminist activist work. But I am pleased right now to have volunteer TV work in my life, when I want it. I've limited the number of shows I produce to two or three a year, though I still do technical work on most programs. Perhaps as I "get my house in order"—update my will, stick to an exercise regimen, become more financially secure, and maybe even fall in love—I may recover a more balanced sense of service.

Every Day a Sunday

Speculating about my retirement, a friend said that every day must be like Sunday. "Well," I said, "every fourth day, maybe." But she had a point, and when I'm not driven by compulsions to produce, I can see a "day of rest" quality in postwork life. Sunday, at its best, had always been a time for indulging whatever pleasures one fancied. But Sundays were always followed by Mondays, those cold-shower days that reined us in and ostensibly gave definition and structure to our lives. Perhaps retirement is about modulating Mondays.

In my first months of freedom, I looked around for models who had preceded me into the liberated zone. How were they spending their time? I noted that some were traveling or taking classes or tending hobbies, others had rented vacation homes, or were "doing lunch" often, or seeing many movies. But all had Monday-type activities in their lives as well, for example part-time work, volunteering, writing postretirement professional papers, or giving service to aged or newborn family members. And I wondered whether these were activities freely chosen, or still dictated by guilt or selflessness or ego drives, leftover habits and assumptions we'd acquired as women and as workers. In retirement, even with pensions, don't we in truth take our worker selves with us, and often keep doing what we've always been doing, but in different guises? Or is it possible to deeply and dramatically shift into another mode and seize the Sunday spirit as daily fare?

I began searching for Sundays.

I wandered over to the nearby Barnes and Noble one morning, scanned its vast collection and settled on Zadie Smith's *White Teeth*.[2] I read uninterruptedly for hours, nestled in a large-backed chair. The next day, I repeated this routine, and then for many more mornings, with other books. I was becoming a Barnes and Noble junkie, getting my daily fix of fiction from its bookshelves, and now and then buying a novel to take home. The warehouse-sized store facing Union Square was always almost empty, with just about any seat to be had in its usually impenetrable café. Outside, workers rushed by, but I was deliciously ensconced in the luxury of literature's lap. These were definitely Sundays.

Inspired by all the reading I was doing, I decided to begin writing again. A call for essays for this book came just at the right moment. Once my proposal for the piece was accepted, I settled into the task. I awakened each morning with retirement themes in my head. Holed up in my bedroom, at my computer workstation, I screened calls and struggled with syntax. I was caught up in the obsessions and peregrinations of the writer's life.

As an academic living in a publish-or-perish world, I had other occasions to be similarly sequestered. I produced a book, papers, articles, essays, and that magnum opus, a late-stage doctoral dissertation, the writing of it wedged between full-time work and family responsibilities. I yearned then for the luxurious conditions under which I write now: free of obligations, voluntarily, and without a promotion riding on the outcome. I've had a love affair with writing on and off for years, with all the accompanying *Sturm und Drang* in getting thoughts on paper. One good page is a hard day's work. But when the ideas flow, and the language is leveraged, and it's all to my liking, there's nothing I would rather be doing. That is, if I can tolerate the seclusion it demands: the many solitary hours in a "room of one's own," with or without the 500 guineas, tending one's craft.[3] Admittedly, seclusion is seductive: it allows for contemplation, creation, and a return to the undistracted self. But seclusion takes as it gives, depriving one of a social life and its many comforts and pleasures.

So how will this writing conundrum play out for me in retirement? Now that demands for production are only of my own making, will I push myself hard to create? Or will I keep hanging out at Barnes and Noble feeding on the artistic nourishment of others? I think it will be a little bit of both: balancing the expressive urges with the receptive — giving out and taking in. Writing has been a need of mine since childhood, perhaps even a talent, and retirement is for discovering and honing one's natural abilities. So, yes, writing will be part of the retirement blueprint, but not as a steady diet, only when the impulse strikes, and, perhaps, never on Sunday.

Sundays were for sexuality, I discovered as a kid. My friend Arlene's parents would lock their bedroom door for the whole afternoon as we played in the rest of the apartment. For a ten-year-old girl just learning about the "facts of life," that locked door had Sundays sizzling with suggestion. Whatever

Arlene's parents were doing, I knew it was private and pleasurable, because they sure looked relaxed and happy when they emerged.

For this single woman who hasn't had a romantic relationship for a while, retiring freed up fantasies of sensuality: perhaps I could be the one with a lover behind the bedroom door, open or closed, on Sunday afternoons. I began to yearn for an intimate partner, a notion I'd put to bed in recent years when under the burden of work. But here I am free and in my sixties with the bloom of youth taking hold again. But, "ay, there's the rub" (as Shakespeare's Hamlet said): I may have aged myself out of the heterosexual "market"—one of those missed boats I alluded to earlier.

I began making a conscious effort to find a companion. I let my friends know that I would be interested in any of their available friends—who were few, if any, I can tell you. I even deigned to go once or twice to those awful singles socials. Here and there I furtively looked at the personals. What a telling experience that was! Men's checklists in searching for a partner do not seem to change in the aging process. Even as an attractive woman, I've experienced a few rejections from some dates when they have learned my age, or that dead giveaway, that I've retired. Men on the whole have always wanted younger women: as reproducers, trophy wives, or caretakers for their old age. But our youth-obsessed, celebrity-struck culture is really getting out of hand: seventy-year-old men are advertising in personal ads for women forty-five, if not younger. Cosmetic surgeons grow rich as women in particular, desperate in response to ageism, seek out face-lifts and tummy tucks to surgically remove a chronic chronology.

One need not be looking for love in retirement to become aware of the reality of aging. Without work to pay attention to, there's always the body. In spring, my ophthalmologist discovered in a routine exam that I had a slightly atrophied optic nerve. That sent me on two months of tests of all kinds, fortunately with negative results. But suddenly I began thinking: I sure don't want to give these years over to preoccupations with health just as I've released myself from preoccupations with work. That would be another tragic retirement irony.

Notice how I've shifted from romance to health and body image? Retirement is partly about not getting caught up in the standards of beauty and aging laid down by a distorted culture. It's about taking care of oneself and being grateful for still being here in the first place. It's about constructing a rich life, with or without a partner, and adopting some Zen principles when it comes to desire. And having a great set of friends—for Sundays and Mondays.

Embracing Retirement

I've come to conclude that one can rise from the career ashes, phoenix-like, to be born again in the freshness of youth to live through another cycle of years. I do believe this, now that I've discovered that while one may die in retirement, one does not die from it. My thrashing around in this postwork life, and all the denials of it, seems to be over. I have taken retirement to my bosom.

So I approach year two with the zest of an architect with a plethora of plans on the drawing board: I will complete (amen!) the furnishing of my apartment; produce a TV segment on aging women artists and their efforts to build an urban live-in community; refresh my Spanish-language skills at a school in Guatemala; and join a study group on globalization and the destruction of small economies. Somewhere in the future, I hope to assist women in some developing country to implement a small and important project to improve their lives. There seems to be an unsurprising continuity in retirement of the interests of my working years. And then there's always Barnes and Noble for reading, and my bedroom for penning a poem.

But all these plans can turn on a dime: one whim can have me heading elsewhere. Isn't that, after all, what retirement is about?

Notes

1. Sara Ruddick, "Maternal Thinking," in *Mothering: Essays in Feminist Theory*, ed. Joyce Trebilcot (Totowa, N.J.: Rowman and Allanheld, 1983), 213–230.
2. Zadie Smith, *White Teeth* (New York: Random House, 2000).
3. Virginia Woolf, *A Room of One's Own* (New York: Harcourt, 1929).

Creating a Self
in Context

CAROLE GANIM

The Dilemma of the Professional Woman

When I was in my thirties, in 1975, I taught at a small, rural college where the ruling matriarch was at least eighty-five. A gracious lady, fond of telling the students about her genteel past (in unspoken but apparent contrast to their lives), she took pride in associating with the women of the local high society. There was an annual tea to which the female faculty members were invited. Each society lady was introduced by her husband's name and title. We met Mrs. Robert Duchesne, Mrs. Dr. Leo Frash, Mrs. Joseph Goode, and so on. We were informed of each husband's position and importance in the community. With the impudence of the young, I asked one of the Mmes. if she had a first name of her own. I now regret my rudeness, but I remain annoyed by the actuality.

Although such a tea party would not occur today, at least in the world as I know it, the lees have not settled entirely. For some women in our transitional generation, identification with work has replaced our foremothers' identification with husbands and families as the hallmark of our lives. "Identity" for them depends on one's job, position, title, and importance to and within an institution or profession rather than on one's husband. Before our generation, professional women were a relatively rare phenomenon. Ours is the first generation to establish a large corps of women in the professions who are to be identified not vicariously, but by their own names, professional status, and personal interests. We say that women may now introduce themselves at tea parties. Now we are faced with a new problem: how do we become the first generation of women to put on our hats and gloves and leave the tea party with dignity?

Sometimes when I begin to look seriously at retirement, at which I am very new, I am terrified. Who am I, or who will I be, without my tags? How will I function in a world where no one knows how talented, important, smart, wise, knowledgeable I am? What if no one ever asks me about all the prestigious positions I have held? What if, because I am a small woman, people treat me as if I'm cute? How will I stand it? How will I subtly let them know of my past accomplishments and my successes and hide from them my mistakes and failures? Retirement is pretty frightening, although commonplace. But this is the first time I am going through it. So what am I going to do?

As I see it, I have three choices: I can unretire; I can become the "little woman"; I can choose to become a new self, a self in context.

If I choose to unretire, I can become that figure everyone tells tales about, the dean, the librarian, or the professor (or, in another world, the athlete, the entertainer) who will not leave. I can hang around so long that the college will buy me off, will send me on a year-long retirement cruise as they did one librarian in a state university, to keep me away long enough to sweep the floors and to change the carpeting and the locks. This is really not an option for me. I do not want to hang around forever. But I might hang around too long, thinking that I am invaluable and fearful of the vacuum that would be there if I weren't where I know how to be.

I know some women who have considered the second option and a few who have chosen it. These women reason that they have put in their time in the workplace, and now they can "really" be women. They can revert to the role their mothers played in the family and in society. For them, the prototype of the little woman is deeply ingrained and they are assuaging some demon when they accede to it. Some really will be happier, because they had never really wanted to be or thought they should be professionals. They have always wanted to wear the traditional garb. They deserve to do what they want, finally. I suspect, however, that there may be more women who go back to the little woman model out of fear of the unknown. Life for them is an either/or proposition; retirement means forsaking their former, professional life and becoming the little woman, playing, cooking, gardening, housekeeping, baby-sitting, and lunching—only. This option is somewhat more attractive to me than the first. As long as I did not have to do crafts or sew, I could handle it. I like to cook and I love to garden. I enjoy lunch and dinner and playing with the babies. I even sometimes like to go shopping. I can clean house very well, having been raised by Mathilda the Meticulous. I do not feel superior to this life; it's just that I cannot do it for a very long time.

But life is not either/or. (That is an absolute statement that is absolutely true.) The first and second options I have presented are really too extreme for me. The third option is the only viable one for me. I must choose to become a new self, a self in context.

This is a rather formidable task and I'm not sure I'm up to it. I have to create the context, discover who this new self is, how she is the same and how she is different from the self I have always assumed I am and the self I am in the process of becoming and the self I really want to be when I grow up. Then I must put the self and the context together. Luckily, I am not a mathematician, for I fear this is not a purely axiomatic enterprise.

The Opportunity to Choose

It seems to me that our generation is the first that has had real choices about our work lives. We middle-class women in our sixties had mothers who, for the most part, stayed home to rear families and care for house and husband. Some of them worked at jobs outside the home, but these jobs were ancillary. My mother and her contemporaries did not have careers. I do not speak of women who had to work to support their families, but of the mainstream middle-class U.S. family of my childhood and adolescence.

My mother was a very intelligent person who today would have an advanced degree and be an accomplished whatever-she-wanted-to-be. But she had no opportunity. She became instead a devoted and good wife, mother, caretaker. She read books and was an alert observer and analyst. I think she missed something in her life, but she did not question her role. As I grew up, I felt something of her unspoken discontent; I looked at her and her life and I knew early on that I would not be satisfied having coffee every morning with my friends and neighbors, cleaning the house, shopping, discussing ways to clean and cook better, managing the children. I never heard my mother or my aunts or their friends complain. They were fortunate members of their world. They had good marriages (or, at least, they accepted their marriages as permanent), good homes, few serious financial worries. Because they knew and accepted the context of their lives, they were content. When the changes came, they did not understand what the younger women wanted—except, I suspect, for my mother, who I think knew very well and knew she would have wanted the same thing. She was not, however, accustomed to articulating such interior musings. I grew into young adulthood with her role in life as my model and yet, although I had no language with which to describe it and no structure to choose in its place, I could not accept it.

In 1956, right after my graduation from a Catholic girls' high school in Cleveland, Ohio, I joined a community of sisters with whom I was to live for sixteen years. I still believe that one of the reasons I chose to enter the convent was to offset the inevitability of college, marriage, children, home. The convent was about the only alternative other than the then-unattractive possibility of spinsterhood available to me in my suburban, Catholic world of 1956. I was happy there and I believed I was following my predilection to serve God. My world then offered few choices.

A few years later, young women had other options. Whether for good or for bad, the world was turning upside down in those heady years of the sixties. I was still young enough to be affected by the change. My career as a college professor had just begun. I had an identity and suddenly I had choices. I chose to leave the convent and embarked on a life in which I took for granted my ability to create my life in a way that my mother had never known and many of my contemporaries would never know. Between then and now, my life has been full, good and bad, happy and disappointing. I have made choices, sometimes good ones, sometimes poor. As I ease discomfitly into retirement, I realize more and more that my past choices were made within the safety net of the academic world. Now my choices are more open, more freeing, more scary. I have to choose a way of retiring that will incorporate my past and create my future to my satisfaction, and not to my satisfaction alone, but to that also of those who are part of my world. I have such a multitude of choices that I become confused in the attempt to sort them out and proceed with them. The dilemma of plenitude is sometimes more perplexing than the dilemma of straitness.

It occurs to me that I and we had better do this right, that we as a generation have an obligation to our daughters and their daughters to create models that they might use and adapt in their time. There is no preexisting model for us; our mothers did not choose their retirement life; they had few changes in their daily lives as they aged. We, on the other hand, must create an economy of retirement, an ecology which will sustain us and our progeny as we grow old in an environment of challenge, peace, activity, productivity, freedom, and generosity.

Describing the Context

I feel like Anita Brookner's uncharacteristically active heroine, Fay, in *Brief Lives*, who told herself: "I should be training for old age, which takes a certain amount of training; better to start as I meant to go on."[1] There is no Modern Language Association style sheet to get me through this next stage. I have to figure it out myself. I have voices and images, and words, many words, but no itinerary. I have to make one. This is the hard part. As I write this essay, I am, in fact, figuring it out. So my plan is tentative and new, strange and unfamiliar, hesitant, thrilling. Creating the context for my self and understanding it, I know, are not finite tasks that will someday be completed. They are more like just-in-time product management; the parts will be there when I need them.

Right now I am in the transition phase of retirement. I retired in October 2000, a few months ago. Since then I moved from New Mexico back to Ohio; I substitute-taught for eight weeks at a local high school for my neighbor who gave birth to her second child about four days before I moved (there is a shortage of Latin teachers and I can do this); I visited my father in Florida, I unpacked and organized our new home; I did Christmas; and in January I began teaching part-time at our local community college. At the same time a very dear friend began her decline toward death and January and February became months of sorrow. Now it is April. I am in my second quarter of adjunct teaching. I am finally settling into an awareness of the reality of where I am, what I am doing, and what I will be doing.

Meanwhile, I applied for two jobs. Luckily, I did not get hired for either one of them, an editing job in the corporate world and a department chair position. My instant relief when I learned that I was not hired told me that I was acting out of fear or perhaps greed for a salary rather than desire. There are days, however, when I want to be at work, at a desk, away from home, in a classroom, interacting with colleagues in a familiar setting. There are other days when I settle into reading and writing and revel in the luxury. There are some days when I run from one seemingly mindless task to another. I still do not know what I want to do now. I will probably continue to apply for full-time positions that I think I might enjoy and that I know I could do well. I may choose to go in and out of retirement as the occasion demands and/or choice permits.

But here I am today, having more discretionary time than I have ever had in my life and still hurrying, still feeling pressure. I am thinking of the many needs out there that I could be meeting. There are jobs that need to be done. Why am I not doing them? Who am I to have the luxury of discretion, of choice?

I can see that I am due to repeat a decision-making process that I have gone through many times in my life. That process is this: I say to myself that people are poor, hungry, uneducated, and victimized. They need help. I can help them. Political corruption is rife; corporate excess is hurting the people and the economy. Health problems here and abroad are killing people. The environment is being destroyed. Those in control are abusing their power. Something has to be done. It is not enough to contribute to good works. I must get out into the street and make a difference. What, then, shall I do? I cannot do it all, or even support, be interested in, be knowledgeable about it all. So which do I do? How do I contribute? My profession and work are not enough. I must do more. But I am good at teaching. I believe that education can change the world. So I will stay where I am and continue to do what I do.

Now that I am nominally retired, I am asking the same questions. How can I do more and better? What good causes can I work for? I can volunteer at the homeless shelter, take in foster children, rehab homes, join picket lines, run for office, write political letters, go to meetings. I admire the people who do these things; I have always wished I had their fervor. But, as I know and as I have many times reaffirmed, my gift is teaching. More than any other truth, I believe that empowering the intellect and the spirit creates the real change. More than anything else, this is what I do best. Not many people can teach as well as I can. So I'll continue teaching, going the mundane way, trying to inspire in my students an appetite for learning and the belief that they can and should improve the world.

But I won't be comfortable.

What is this urgency in me that makes me continue to ask the same questions and to derive the same answers? Why is what I do never good enough for me? It's time to come to terms with these questions, which have plagued me all my life. But I know that I never will. Or perhaps never should. Their urgency has always lent the impetus to my passion in my work. Where does that go now? It will be there in the classes I teach. Will this be enough for me?

What else could I be doing? Here is a list (I've never actually made one until now):

tutoring children
working in a domestic violence shelter
editing
ushering for concerts and plays
volunteering in museums
working at a thrift store
teaching English in a corporation
working or volunteering in a library
doing freelance writing
teaching literacy or GED (general equivalency diploma) classes

And more options are presented by the many people who want me to join their cause, their interest group. In the last few months, I have been invited to take part in more committees and projects than there are months in the year. We live in an old, beautiful neighborhood in a city where most black people live on the west side and most white people live on the east side. My husband and I are white and deliberately chose a mixed neighborhood, one of the few in town. The people in our neighborhood are intentional about where we live and why. Needless to say, committees, meetings, projects, actions abound. The church we joined is in the same community and it, too, has an agenda. I sing in the choir and participate in both social and social justice activities. The community college where I am teaching has its own set of fascinating intellectual, artistic, and community activities—in particular, educational projects for the Appalachian community. I lived in eastern Kentucky for ten years and taught at two small colleges there. I know something about educating this population. I might easily fill all my days and nights with these very worthwhile and rewarding activities.

Meanwhile, I have many fears. Facing old age, no matter how sunny one's disposition, is at best terrifying. Sarah Durham in Doris Lessing's *Love, Again* said it well: "[T]he fate of us all, to get old, or even to grow older, is one so cruel that while we spend every energy in trying to avert or postpone it, we in fact seldom allow the realization to strike home sharp and cold: from being *this*—and she looked around at the young people—one becomes *this*, a husk without colour, above all, without the lustre, the shine."[2]

So what am I afraid of?

I am afraid of loss of ego and importance.

I am afraid that what I built my life on is really unimportant after all, that I have not helped and shaken into learning all those for whom I have taken credit.

I am afraid that my mask of modesty, declaring that I have chosen to teach in less-than-glamorous sites and with alternative populations, is really a cover for the absence of discipline and intellectual rigor.

I am afraid that I will slide into indolence and purposelessness.

I am afraid that I will no longer want to give to and work with the marginalized.

I am afraid that I will sit down to write and have nothing to say.

I am afraid that the long emptiness ahead of me will tempt me to become a full-time consumer and home beautifier.

I am afraid that the lusts of old age will become fearsome.

I am afraid that I will flirt with young men, and old men, and look the fool.

I am afraid that anxiety will overtake me because I will worry about not being busy all the time in a structured way and I will fill my time with useless pursuits.

I am worried that I will overdo, that I will become the eternal volunteer, or that I will be teaching everywhere every day to prove my worth.

I am afraid that I will get fat, ugly, and lazy.

I am afraid that my health will fail and that I will have to become dependent even in a small way.

I am afraid that I will lose my husband.

I am afraid that I do not have the slightest idea of how to manage my life without an external structure.

I am afraid that I have no real identity other than the one I have lived with for so long.

I am afraid that I will always feel guilty about something.

I am afraid of panic.

I am afraid that my children and grandchildren will not want to visit me or some day take care of me.

I am afraid that I will turn these children away when they try to help.

I am afraid that I will become cranky when I am no longer in control.

I am afraid of losing my friends.

I am afraid of becoming too well acquainted with hospitals and funeral homes.

I am afraid that I will never get over feeling rushed and pressured.

I am afraid that I will be making lists on my deathbed.

I sometimes feel like T. S. Eliot's J. Alfred Prufrock: will the eternal Footman snicker at me?

In short, I am in the place William Bridges calls the "neutral zone," the time in a transition process which is a "moratorium from the conventional activity of our everyday existence," where "in the apparently aimless activity of our time alone, we are doing important inner business."[3] In my religious vocabulary this is the desert, the place of aridity and aloneness where one fasts and prays and waits for the Spirit to end the dryness of thirst and discontent. It is a lonely and frustrating time, but we have been promised an ending, a fulfillment. It is a mythic journey, in which one must go to the underworld and return from the dead as a new person. It is the resurrection of the soul, described variously in belief systems and in literature, but always detailing the same process, the same experience. Would that I could be the mythic hero and emerge able to save the world, conquer all obstacles, slay the dragon.

Creating the Context

How can I put all of this together and create a self in context? How can I be a same self and a different self according to the various contexts of my life? How can I assemble them all into a giant lesson plan to satisfy my need for schoolmarm structure? I cannot, so I must first accede to the messiness of life and then fit into it as much order as I can. I know also that I cannot control the realities of the context, but that I can at least choose my responses to them. I must, then, let myself accept the vagaries and the disorder and go on to attempt a megacontext.

The contexts from which I will create a self in context are self, family, community, religious life, and profession. Although I suppose that self is the most important, in a sense it is the least important, since self can be defined completely only in relationship. Yet there must be an inner core, a self unassailable. Herself, myself. I am who I have always been, whether for good or ill. I really do not want to be other than Herself, notwithstanding my discontent with that self. As an introspective person, I have examined Herself. I know some of my strengths and weaknesses. I can be proud of some of my accomplishments and content in my successes and relationships, and I can agonize over past humiliations, failures, betrayals of duty and love. I have a strong inner conviction that in many ways I have become a crone; I have a modicum of wisdom garnered from living a reflected-upon life. I do have something to give to the next generation. My task now is to know myself better and not only to struggle against fossilization, but also to find new ways to grow and change.

But first, I must talk about death, the shadow of maturity. Carolyn Heilbrun says, "I believe that every time those of us in our last decades allow a memory to occur, we forget to look at what is in front of us, at the new ideas and pleasures we might, if firmly in the present, encounter and enjoy."[4] Heilbrun's rejection of memory is hard line, to me, but as one who does not habitually live in the past and in memory, I agree that staying there is enervating. I suspect that those stuck in memory are there because they fear death. Somehow they must reason that living in the past can forestall death, but we know this is not true. Each of us at one point or another must learn that death is no longer other. Our own mortality, for perhaps the first time, is an item to enter into our planner. Retirement is an acknowledgment that we are in the stages before the end. This is fearsome; it is better, perhaps, to live in one's past. The golf links in Florida are filled with old codgers reciting their tales of former prowess and power to one another as they totter into and out of their golf carts. These people are the subjects of sitcoms, yet there is a desperation there; they are those Constantine Cavafy calls "the confounded and contradictory / souls, that sit—comicotragical— / in their aged worn-out hides."[5] Dwelling in memory is not always a sign of dementia; sometimes it is a way to forget about the future, which to some is too empty and too mysterious to be faced. I am afraid of death also, but I do not think that living in the past is the way to handle it.

The imminent certainty of death does cast a shadow over one. For me, meditation, thought, conversation with friends, and literature succor me in unexpected ways as I face death. Laughing about our respective frailties and illnesses has become a popular sport with many of my friends. We find ourselves giggling as uncontrollably as we did as adolescents when we talk about sickness and death. When I recall driving old nuns to their doctors when I was young and swearing to myself that I would never go on as they did about my ailments, surgeries, and medications, we become convulsed with laughter because we have just finished having the same kind of discussion. I know, upon reflection, that the imminence of death colors the choices and activities of later life, just as surely as does frailty or illness. What I want to do is to not let it take over. I want to benefit from the shadow by appreciating light and color and beauty and sound and love more. I want my physical senses and my spiritual appetites to be whetted by the approach of death.

I do not believe that one retires only to do what one wants, which in many cases means to indulge in as many means of self-gratification as possible. Retirement for me implies the separation of industry and money. It implies that one no longer must work at certain jobs for financial reasons. It implies that one has choices not available earlier in life. It is a drawing back, a regrouping, a chance to look the field over and come back differently. So my self in context must account for financial changes which may mean less disposable income, but also less dependency on material goods.

Further, my retirement must give me a chance to succeed at my other goals: to reaffirm that I have significance in my world, to allow me to continue to be where I know how to be, and to enjoy a life full of choices. It should afford me the opportunity to address my fears and perhaps even dismiss many of them. I want to find in retirement a structure, but a bent structure. I want to maintain social interaction in formal and informal ways and feel in control of this aspect of life, not controlled by it.

Most importantly, my retirement must allow me to develop a sense of mission. For many complicated reasons, healthy and unhealthy, I cannot survive unless I have a goal, a mission. Like the much-maligned Hillary Rodham Clinton, I cannot bake cookies, although I am grateful that there are those who do. It is their mission; it is not mine. *Chacun à son goût.*

My retirement will not be static, but a developing perception of life and activity. I will try to accept the limitations of body and mind and the changes that will inevitably occur with time. I will try to remember John Henry Newman's dictum that "here below to live is to change and to be perfect is to have changed often."[6] Newman uses "perfect" in the sense of being done, completed. I am not done becoming myself; I am going to take what I have and try to modify myself into a wonderful old person. I most likely will not succeed unreservedly, but I believe that creating a self in context requires rather a great deal of effort at an unending process.

The second context, that of family, is a multiple complexity. I come from a large, close Lebanese family. We were reared with the notion that there are two categories of people in the universe: the Lebanese and the "Americans," or the others. I cannot help thinking that way still; I think it's genetic. The only thing that differs is my understanding of *Lebanese* and *other*. *Lebanese* now includes all those to whom I am bound in love and friendship; these are my family now. The group is immense. My family includes my husband, my children, my siblings, my in-laws, nieces and nephews, my parents, my cousins, aunts and uncles, and all the friends through the years who have shared my life as closely as family. It is a great joy as one grows older to count up, to be able to say that one has loved and shared, fought, and argued with so many people. It becomes also a burden as I cannot maintain these connections as I might wish. Then, sneakily, sickness and death intervene and I wonder if I can stand having such a large family. One is tempted to give up on family relationships and to become a recluse. It protects one against more hurt. I think this and meanwhile I am making new friends and getting involved in new lives. The wind is still moving the leaves of the trees and life is continuing. The inventory of life goes on. I will choose not to escape from the responsibilities of family life, but to honor them. I must also guard against allowing them to overwhelm me. My tendency is to take everything on; "they" tell me this is not good or necessary. I will learn restraint, but I will not learn refusal.

On a daily basis, I am wife to my husband. We enjoy having the house to ourselves and being relatively free of a daily schedule. We like staying up until we want to go to bed and sleeping until we awake naturally. We enjoy eating when and what we want and not worrying about either nourishment for the young or gourmet treats for the elderly. We delight in locking the door and go-ing where we wish and when without having to pack up children, trundle out a parent, or kennel a dog. The fact that our daily activities take place with some regularity and similarity is irrelevant. I sometimes look at my husband and wonder who he is, but most of the time I see him as someone very famil-iar. We are good friends and we are lovers.

On a weekly or biweekly basis, I am mother and grandmother to a few chil-dren and grandchildren. My husband and I moved back to Ohio from New Mexico because we did not like being so far from them, and we do not regret our decision. I delight in being with them, though I also like my own space and time. I want to see them in daily situations, not just on holiday or vacation trips. I want to watch the grandchildren grow and to be part of their lives. I am grateful for them, but I realize that I cannot be an old-fashioned, textbook grandma. I want my own life, too. I am sure they have no clue about this, as I did not when I was their age.

On a frequent, but irregular, basis, I am daughter, sister, sister-in-law, aunt, cousin, niece, friend, teacher, neighbor to the rest of my family. As a good communicator, I communicate with all of them, a task sometimes demanding but usually enjoyable. We have large, interesting, and boisterous gatherings of various family components. I know that someone in the family, and most likely many in the family, will always be around when I need them. This is a foundation of my retirement context. It is what a family should provide, one to the other. It is what my family provides for me and, I hope, I for them.

I am not sure that my greater family knows how much I love them because, although I can be gregarious, I am also somewhat reserved in expressing my affections. I do not want to become a bawling, sentimental old lady, but I think that now that I am at least nominally retired, I can drop the ironic mask so fashionable among academics.

My community context will become more dynamic in the near future. Our neighborhood has gracious old homes, flowers, trees, quiet, and especially, open space. I can hear birds call and smell lilacs as I write. Some call this neighborhood "deteriorating," meaning, for example, that black and white middle-class people live on the same streets and poor black people live nearby. A mobilization is taking place; the neighborhood is about to talk to the larger community about the meanings of community, poverty, equality, deterioration, rehabilitation, justice, and charity. I am already on a few com-mittees. I like being a part of this context; I will enjoy the ruckus. I have backed off from some concerns I used to be involved with because I have found that I do better in the smaller-scale world. (It is still important for me to keep up with political agenda by reading *The Nation, The National Catholic Reporter, The New Yorker,* and other publications, but those form an intellectual community context, not an action agenda.) It is alluring to think that this current neighborhood situation might lead me into other kinds of mischief. I want to stay open to the possibilities.

The religious context of my coming life is both comforting and troubling. Perhaps there is residual guilt; certainly there is continuing love for the ritual and need for the familiar theology and belief system, even as I question them. I cannot understand myself or my life apart from the questions of God, truth, love, goodness, justice. I have always been perplexed, perhaps obsessed, by questions about God. As a girl, I felt the call from God in a direct, physical experience, a light-filled message. We called it "vocation" and I know I had one, and have one. I know that the young can be delusional, or mystical, but as Mark Salzman explores well in *Lying Awake,* there is a certain artificial distinction between the physical and the spiritual which is more cognitively reassuring than true.[7] Karen Armstrong suggests in A *History of God* that "[h]uman beings cannot endure emptiness and desolation; they will fill the vacuum by creating a new focus of meaning."[8] She spells out the history of God as created by humans who need this meaning, but even she, in this rigorously historical, intellectual analysis, stops short of definition. I expect that in my retirement years questions about God will return to haunt me as forcefully as they first did at about the age of eleven and as they have continued to beleaguer me all through the other years of my life.

On a more mundane basis, my husband and I go regularly to church and participate in liturgical, social, and social justice activities. I love the liturgy and the music of the church; they are so much a part of me that I really cannot do without them. I love the kind of people who go to the kind of church we go to, not the factory express service, but the small, somewhat off-beat place where besotted intellectuals, otherwise disillusioned mainstream Catholics, or others who like High Church observances gather to create a community of seekers. I like this. I need this world. I am probably more to the Left and cynical side of church than most, but I still know that I must look at the questions of God and faith and human behavior in a light other than that of social science or sweet sentimentality. There are limits, however; I cannot fuss over a bishop or get excited about a pretty altar cloth.

My professional context is the most difficult. Although I am not attached to the academy as my only means of identity, I feel that in many ways I am not ready to retire, that I still have the energy and interest to be productive and viable in the classroom, I still have much to give to students. Their responses to me confirm this. I have also served in various administrative offices and, given the right situation, might find this attractive again. On the other hand, I have always wanted to write more and enjoy a more reflective, meditative life. This is my most ancient and deep-seated conflict: If I remain retired, I must be content with the identity of the adjunct professor and the elder-woman role. I will not be seen as important to the functioning and decision making of the institution. I will not be an esteemed professor. But I might be letting loose creativity and ideas that I have sacrificed to the job. I might be able to fulfill a longtime dream to enjoy the exhilaration of writing, which I have experienced too infrequently. This context is a work in progress. I am sure that I will never forsake this part of my life; the question remains as to how important a part it will be.

I have thus far taken several steps in my retirement process: I have examined my fears and desires as I face retirement. I have chosen what not to do and have decided to choose to be a self in context. I have described the contexts that are relevant to me. I see a self slowly emerging from these contexts. I can see now that this is a never-ending process. I do not have a finished product, nor will I ever have one.

The overarching context is the world in which I find myself and the world in which I choose to find myself. It is a world of self, family, church, community, work. It is not much different from the world I have always lived in; after all, one is always a self in context. But at this stage of my life, I can make more choices about how I relate to and behave in these contexts. I will be free of some constraints, for example the need to maintain a decent salary, the pressure to achieve success, the demands of time and schedule, the necessity of pleasing one's boss or colleagues. This is a most welcome form of freedom. There will also be the freedom of making more choices about how to spend my time and energy. I must consider, too, that even though I have been very healthy all of my life, I will face the decline of energy and, possibly, illness.

Since I am in the beginning phases of creating my self in context, I can only anticipate that I will make good decisions and will create a self that I can live with. I recognized myself in Marge Piercy's poem "If they come in the night" when she said she liked her life and hoped that at its end she would not have forgotten "to give what I held in my hands."[9] At this moment, I feel empowered by the realization of what I have done here. I have examined my life and looked at its next stage and made plans to participate actively in its evolution. The future is alluring and the possibilities for that future are multiple. I have always wanted to know all the answers, especially the answers to the big questions: Is there a God? What is the meaning of life? What is goodness? What is truth? Who are we? Why are we here? I know I will never have the satisfaction of getting answers, but I am still excited about the questions and I still want to find ways to look for answers. I have enthusiasm for what comes next and I can't wait to see what it is. I was once asked to write my own epitaph in a group exercise. I wrote: She kept looking.

Notes

1. Anita Brookner, *Brief Lives* (New York: Random House, 1990), 115.
2. Doris Lessing, *Love, Again* (New York: HarperCollins, 1996), 140–141.
3. William Bridges, *Transitions: Making Sense of Life's Changes* (New York: Addison-Wesley, 1980), 114.
4. Carolyn G. Heilbrun, *The Last Gift of Time: Life beyond Sixty* (New York: Dial Press, 1997), 124.
5. Constantine Cavafy, "The Souls of Old Men," in *The Complete Poems of Cavafy*, trans. Rae Dalven (New York: Harvest/HBJ, 1976), 11.
6. John Henry Newman, *An Essay on the Development of Christian Doctrine* (New York: Image, 1960), 63.
7. Mark Salzman, *Lying Awake* (New York: Knopf, 2000).
8. Karen Armstrong, *A History of God* (New York: Ballantine Books, 1993), 399.
9. Marge Piercy, "If they come in the night," in *Circles on the Water* (New York: Knopf, 1994), 223.

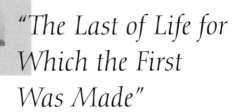

"The Last of Life for Which the First Was Made"

SUSAN G. RADNER

Grow old along with me!
The best is yet to be,
The last of life for which the first was made.
—ROBERT BROWNING, "Rabbi Ben Ezra"

Does anybody believe this?

I retired on February 1, 2000, at the age of sixty-one after more than thirty-six years of teaching English and women's studies at William Paterson University in Wayne, New Jersey, and a total of almost forty years of teaching in both high schools and colleges. After three bouts of breast cancer, the first when I was only thirty-seven, I always had assumed I would retire early (or would be forced to retire early). My husband, who had taught at a neighboring state university in New Jersey, retired in June 1999 and I wanted to keep him company. I wanted to sleep later in the morning, visit museums and galleries, see Wednesday matinees. But ultimately, these were not the reasons I retired when I did. I retired because I no longer felt a vital connection to my university or the larger women's movement. Even though no one was pushing me, it was time to get out of the way.

First a little background information. I got my first college teaching job as a substitute for a woman who had broken her leg the day before the semester was to start at Paterson State College (which later became William Paterson) in January 1963 when I was only twenty-four. A year and a half later I was offered a tenure-track position, and was tenured in 1967 at the age of twenty-nine. I had had minimal teaching experience in a Staten Island high school and only a couple of education classes during my last year at Smith College. But somehow I knew I could teach, and teach differently from the way I had been taught.

Back in the early 1960s, there were no models for the kind of instructor I thought I could be. Women who wanted to teach did so in the lower schools under the guidance of male administrators. This distribution of power was replicated in colleges. Women were found in education departments; there were few women in academic departments. At Paterson State College in the mid-1960s, power was in the hands of an education-school-oriented elite group of women and men. A woman president, a former army brat, ran the institution like a military elementary school. Her handpicked lieutenants spied on their colleagues and reported to her on the comings and goings of her faculty. It was not unknown for her to patrol the halls to see when classes were being dismissed. Of course, there was no union, only a faculty association whose meetings were attended by the dean and the college president. Colleagues referred to their students as "the children" and spoke about going to "the little girls' room." There was a dress code for both students and faculty; even in the depths of snowy winter, slacks were forbidden for women.

Paterson State College had recently dropped "Teachers" from its name and added secondary education to programs in elementary and early childhood education, but its mission was still exclusively teacher education. Several women in the English department that I joined taught language arts courses. Two bona fide English Ph.D.'s, women about fifteen years older than I, and about six men taught the English major courses. In 1964, when I started my tenure-track position, three women (one in language arts) and one man were hired with me. All of us had difficulty adjusting to the culture of this sleepy suburban college and its written and unwritten rules.

The women in my department did not feel any sense of solidarity among themselves. Though everybody in the department taught some first-year composition, the split between the language arts and the literature faculty held firm. However, friendships formed. The two older women, both specialists in Victorian literature (in those days hiring by specialty was not considered important), were friendly rivals. Both single and both raised in conservative religious environments (Roman Catholic and Dutch Reformed), they devoted themselves to their work. As full professors, they taught in a very traditional manner, lecturing, giving quizzes, taking attendance, addressing students as Mr. and Miss. Neither paid much attention to the new "junior" faculty. Neither tried to help us. If anything, they were suspicious of us, fearing that we would compete for the courses they liked to teach. I became friendly with a woman who had come into the department with me who was close to me in age, and together we gradually figured out what we needed to do to survive. We met our classes on time, kept regular office hours, went for lunch once a week in the faculty dining room, and smiled a lot and kept quiet.

On my own I learned the discipline of the classroom: how to set up a grade book, how to make up exams, how to plan lessons. With no one to show me the way, I learned mainly from my mistakes. I wrote lesson plans with key questions. I abandoned the composition textbook after I saw one student after another dropping off to sleep. I liked the tangents the classes went off on even when I couldn't figure out how they happened to occur. And I tried to make whatever I was teaching relevant to the lives of my working-class students.

The growing involvement of the United States in the Vietnam War greatly influenced university environments across the country, even that of suburban Wayne. While students organized a Young Americans for Freedom club in support of the war, faculty signed peace petitions and debated giving students A's to keep them out of the draft. Naturally, I found myself talking about the war in my classes and finding literature (Siegfried Sassoon, Wilfred Owen) to support the antiwar movement.

As I found myself discussing these political concerns, I became very aware of the precariousness of my situation as a member of a faculty totally dependent on the benevolence of our provincial, totalitarian administrators. Together with other faculty activists who had migrated to New Jersey, we formed a local of the American Federation of Teachers, American Federation of Labor and Congress of Industrial Organizations (AFL-CIO), rejecting the New Jersey Education Association because of its (at that time) antistrike policy. It was not easy to convince "professional" college teachers to ally themselves with trade unionists; however, capricious administrators who fired faculty because of personal antipathies (such as growing a beard) and who decided major structural changes in the summertime made our job easier. I was elected vice president of our local, a position I held for more than sixteen years. Locals at all the other state colleges were eventually organized and a structure was developed to give each local maximum autonomy yet also the power of bargaining collectively with the State of New Jersey. I became a delegate to the Council of State College Locals and the collective bargaining negotiations for a series of statewide contracts. I also handled negotiations and grievances at William

Paterson. Through my activities in the union I met a group of interesting, politically committed colleagues, very different from the president's lackeys who were in charge when I arrived. In addition to taking care of traditional union business (working conditions), we were able to convince faculty to participate in antiwar teach-ins and moratoria; to boycott grapes; to send busses to pro-choice demonstrations in Washington; and to protest tuition increases.

We were touched by the rising Black Power movement as well. Newark, which saw riots in 1967 in which whole areas of the city were burned down, is only twenty miles or so from William Paterson. The virtual absence of black students on a campus five miles from Paterson, New Jersey's second-largest city, was finally recognized by the administration as two (white male) English department colleagues set up a program to recruit and mentor twenty black students from Paterson high schools. Courses in African American literature were developed and staffed by white faculty (including myself) until black students held sit-ins and together with black faculty demanded a department of their own. The result was the Department of African, African American and Caribbean Studies and a full complement of major and general education courses. Finally, the fledgling women's movement, building on the antiwar and civil rights movements, began to influence my thinking and my teaching.

I first became aware of women's liberation by reading about it. By 1970, after the murders at Kent State University, life in my department had become unbearable. I was burnt out physically and intellectually by the struggles of the late 1960s. This was mirrored in my academic career as I gave up on my Ph.D. and my colleagues assigned me only first-year courses. I was generally shunned as someone tenure was protecting. Feeling a strong impulse to resign, I took an unpaid leave of absence and I read two important books: Kate Millett's *Sexual Politics* and Robin Morgan's anthology *Sisterhood Is Powerful*, both published that year. These books had an enormous influence on both my personal and my professional lives. I joined a consciousness-raising group in Montclair, New Jersey, where I live, and worked out a more equitable arrangement with my husband (Pat Mainardi's essay "The Politics of Housework" in Morgan's book was very convincing). And I totally reexamined both the literature I had been teaching and my approach to it. I developed what became the first women's studies course at William Paterson, "Women in Literature," which I based on syllabi collected from Know, Inc. My colleagues were forced to acknowledge that I was the only person qualified to teach this course, which quickly became enormously popular. When my older female colleagues saw my enrollments, they went above my head to our dean to demand sections of my course. After I heard about their actions, I divided "Women in Literature" in half and helped them develop a syllabus for their own English-major elective, "Nineteenth-Century Women's Voices." ("Images of Women in Modern Literature," the other half of my original course, was slotted as a general education elective.) I had secured my place within my department and earned the trust of two influential colleagues.

The women's movement taught me the importance of sisterhood—of working together with other women. For the next ten years or so, I tried to find feminist friends and colleagues campuswide with whom I could develop a women's studies program. This was made easier by my position in the faculty union. As I met more women outside my hothouse department, I encouraged them to develop feminist courses in their fields: philosophy, political science, health science, psychology. By the mid-1970s, William Paterson had a women's studies minor housed in the school of education—the only school with a female dean. From my point of view, an even more positive result was new friends and a strong support system.

The women's studies faculty was a very interesting, dynamic group of women. Activists as well as scholars, they felt similarly isolated within their departments and they valued feminist community. They had arrived at William Paterson during the big hiring period of the late 1960s and early 1970s, and were about ten years younger than I was. Since I had tenure, I became coordinator and public spokesperson for the program, taking whatever heat was generated. To make sure that their work in women's studies was recognized, I wrote letters of support for women up for reappointment or promotion. In annual reports that I typed myself (at that time women's studies had no secretarial support as well as no office), I listed every committee and every publication of every faculty member. I also worked very closely with students and became faculty advisor to the newly formed women's collective—a Student Government Association–funded club, which had founded a child-care center and a women's center on campus. In the activist 1970s, William Paterson's women's studies faculty and students were a very tight-knit group. The splits that affected other women's studies programs—lesbian and nongay, older and younger, liberal and radical—did not surface. We debated long among ourselves until we could reach a consensus. In the fifteen years I coordinated the program, I was never formally elected and we never took any votes. We all seemed to get along well.

I tried to make the English department a more congenial place as well. Using what influence I had, I lobbied for the hiring of "qualified" women. As more women joined the department, I tried to support them. I also tried to recruit them for women's studies. By the mid-1980s, women's studies had joined forces with the Department of African, African American and Caribbean Studies to sponsor a general education requirement in "racism and/or sexism in the U.S." This requirement (which still exists) could be met with the introductory course in each program or a new course, created and team-taught by faculty from the two programs. We set up the Race and Gender Project, consisting of faculty from both programs, to monitor our joint course. With more than nine thousand students needing to fill the requirement, staffing became an urgent problem. I was able to work out an arrangement with our provost that gave my new colleagues in the English department (and full-time faculty in departments across campus) recognition for the work they wanted to do in women's studies.

From the Race and Gender Project, which I directed for three years, came a collegewide effort spurred by a grant from the New Jersey Department of Higher Education to integrate scholarship about gender into existing courses. Faculty were released from one class to rethink their courses and rewrite their syllabi to include material on race, class, and gender. This effort would culminate in the New Jersey Project on curriculum transformation, which is now housed at William Paterson and is brilliantly directed by Paula Rothenberg, a founding member of our women's studies program.

In time, a few of the women's studies faculty became very good friends. We shared many interests within and outside of William Paterson, and the age differences among us didn't seem to get in our way. Throughout the Reagan years, we lobbied for support for women on campus. In department meetings, we were able to outthink as well as outvote our conservative male colleagues. Working with sympathetic women faculty across the campus and with the support of male colleagues in the union and the faculty senate, we wrote a university nondiscrimination policy, served on the newly created affirmative action advisory board, and lobbied for and wrote a sexual harassment policy. We even sponsored sensitivity training workshops in sexism for the entire faculty (for which we were not thanked).

I also began to see my new friends outside of campus. In addition to national women's studies conferences where we gave presentations from our program, we went to New York City theaters and museums and even took short vacations together. They supported me through my second mastectomy and my third breast tumor, which required seven weeks of radiation and six months of chemotherapy.

As I entered my fifties, I began to sense changes among both the faculty and the students. After years of being regarded as an organization of faculty agitators, the union had been integrated into the structure of the university, given an office, a secretary, even a fax machine. New officers with no union background (one was a Republican) did not want to take political positions because some faculty might not agree; they went along with administration plans to supervise tenured faculty and to conduct student evaluations in every class every semester; they handled few grievances. In both the women's studies and English departments, new, younger faculty had different priorities from mine. As the Women's Studies Program morphed into the Women's Studies Department and could hire its own faculty, internal schisms revealed themselves. Within the English Department, women who had not participated in our early struggles valued individual promotions and honors more than sisterhood. In their advancement of their careers, they used feminism to teach very traditional male-dominated works and male writers.

I found my relationship with my students changing as well. As I entered my fifties and then my sixties, I had to change my approach in the classroom and make political connections directly for them. Although most students seemed eager to learn about the feminist literature I was teaching in all my classes, they were very passive, in glaring contrast to the activist students of previous generations. While expecting me to do all of the work, they carried with them the stereotype of a women's studies professor. My student evaluations, through the years very positive, noted that I was not "angry" enough (though one student praised my "gentle manner"). Even the material I was teaching seemed no longer relevant. Young women did not respond to issues of sexism in advertising. They wanted to wear makeup and spike heels. They laughed when I told them about consciousness-raising sessions where we debated shaving our legs. They didn't understand how close we are to losing the right to abortion. (Many of my students did not vote in the 2000 presidential election.) They wanted to read "feminist" pornography and dismissed analyses of pornography as exploitation of women as boring. They told me that I reminded them of their mothers (or in the case of one student, her grandmother).

Not only had we all aged, but the political climate had radically changed without our noticing. The activism of the 1960s and 1970s, largely a response to the civil rights movement and the Vietnam War, had led to the women's movement. And many of the accomplishments from those years are permanent. Although women's salaries haven't reached parity with men's, gender equity has been written into law. Today laws exist forbidding sexual harassment (which feminists first named and defined) and discrimination because of gender or sexual orientation; affirmative action, though circumscribed, is still legal. Most women expect to work outside their homes for a good part of their lives and expect to be treated professionally when they do. They have access to birth control and (still) abortion; the concept of "choice" is widespread and co-opted. In the academic world, feminist courses and women's studies departments are permanent parts of the curriculum at colleges and universities across the country.

But the relationship between these accomplishments and the larger world in which we live has changed. In the early years of feminism, women worked for change for all women, and children, and men, as well as themselves. If not socialists, they accepted the premises of the New Deal and the Great Society. But as Jimmy Carter, with his cardigan sweaters and turned-down thermostats, gave way to Reagan/Bush, people turned inward. Yuppies and Buppies advanced their careers. With their lower taxes, they bought large cars and houses. Homeless people disappeared from the Port Authority Bus Terminal in Manhattan and were replaced by Mozart on the public address system.

These changes were reflected in the academic world as well. Individual career paths replaced concern for those without power—students, support staff, junior faculty. Feminism became an adornment rather than a life-motivating force. Smartly dressed young women fought for the goodies—courses, promotions—while at the same time mouthing feminist ideas by now cliché. It took me a while to comprehend what was happening at William Paterson; I only knew that I didn't feel comfortable any more. In a sign that my life had come full circle, I again found myself isolated in committee meetings and group discussions. I just didn't see things the way that others did. Thus in ways big and small, I came to feel that I had outlived my usefulness.

At the same time, my husband, Sanford Radner (who is six-and-a-half years older than I am), had finally decided to retire from the Montclair State University English Department. He had been talking about retiring for a long time and had finally had enough. After he wrote his official letter (the big step), I realized that he meant to go through with it. Some unattractive pictures formed in my head: going off to work and leaving him to enjoy the day without me; coming home exhausted and finding him refreshed and eager to talk; spending weekends reading student themes while he was taking long walks in the park or riding the bus into New York City. I began to see that if I retired I would have a companion to do all the things that we liked to do together—go to New York City theaters, operas, galleries, and museums; play bridge and tennis; walk in the park; see a lot of movies; drive up to the Berkshires in Massachusetts; go to Florida in the winter for a couple of weeks.

The summer that my husband retired we bought a small garden apartment on beautiful Lake Onota in unfashionable Pittsfield, Massachusetts. We had been going up to the area for parts of forty summers together. Now we would be able to live there for weeks or months at a time. I spent my last semester at William Paterson and my first six months of retirement driving back and forth (170 miles one way) to fix up our apartment and make it ours. This entailed finding contractors to do some major plumbing, counter work, and replace drafty windows, then carpeting and furnishing. Looking back, I see that I was planning our retirement for a year or so before I acknowledged it as a real possibility. I had used my last sabbatical leave from William Paterson (1997–1998) to fix up our New Jersey home. We have been living in the same apartment in Montclair since 1966. It badly needed modernization but since we weren't home much of the time we had never considered having work done. During our sabbaticals we had our kitchen and bathrooms renovated and the whole apartment painted, putting up with living with cartons, dust, and carpentry tools for many months. We were creating a nest for ourselves.

After I wrote my retirement letter, I told everybody I didn't want a party. It was the end of the fall semester, almost Christmas, and people were busy with exams and shopping. I just wanted to clean out my office (the woman who was moving in had already cased it and made decisions about what she would place where) and slip away. I was not granted my wish. In fact, I (a person who hates parties because I invariably end up alone in a corner) was given four retirement parties. Both my classes surprised me with parties (complete with cards, flowers, cookies, and drinks) on our last day. After a lot of pressure, I agreed to an informal afternoon party hosted by the English department on the condition that there would be no speeches. And a good friend and fellow Virginia Woolf fan threw a lavish *To the Lighthouse* dinner party for sixteen carefully chosen friends, complete with lighthouse decorations and the famous *boeuf en daube*. I was overwhelmed by these signs of appreciation and affection; yet I continue to think that I acted none too soon.

I have to recognize that William Paterson is a much better place now than it was when I joined the faculty those many years ago. It is no longer an almost-all-white, lower-middle-class teachers college. Students and faculty from many different backgrounds enjoy our beautifully landscaped campus and a wide variety of courses. There is a permanent diversity requirement as part of the general education program of the first two years. The Women's Studies Department, now a major, is thriving. The literature courses in the English Department, though still very traditional in structure, include the study of gender and feminist literary criticism. Young, enthusiastic instructors communicate their love of their subjects without me.

And I have become a housewife, after fighting it all my life. Fortunately, I have a good pension, some social security, and the same health benefits I had while working, which will continue until I become eligible for Medicare at sixty-five. (I could not have retired early without them.) If I want, I can sleep late (8:30 A.M!). For the first time in forty years, I read the *New York Times* without tearing out articles for my classes. I read novels without planning how I would teach them. I still have not discarded most of my files—those notes, clippings, and old lesson plans for the different courses I liked to teach. They are shoved into old, shabby book bags under my desk, where the dust is collecting around them. (I may be a housewife, but I'm not a good one.) We go into New York at least once a week, taking advantage of senior citizen bus fares and movie prices. We go up to Pittsfield when the weather is nice, and I have enjoyed seeing the seasons change in the Berkshires. We bought a little rowboat and have been able to explore our lake. My days seem very full, and I wonder how I ever had time to prepare for and teach four classes each semester.

But I can't totally tear myself away from William Paterson. I still get telephone calls asking for my advice. I try to go up to swim in the pool once a week and I occasionally meet old friends for lunch. I have learned that I have to take the initiative in seeking out my friends since I can't rely on running into them on campus. And it can feel lonely at home, when days go by and the only voices I hear are those of telemarketers.

As a tribute to me, my husband endowed a full-tuition scholarship in my name at William Paterson. I had wanted to do this for some time. Since we had no children of our own to send to college, we are in the happy position of enabling a total stranger to complete her education. Our scholarship was given out for the first time in 2001. The only restriction we had set was that it go to a student in the humanities. The first recipient chosen by the university is a young woman from the Caribbean who is majoring in English with a certification in elementary education. At a scholarship brunch, we were able to meet and talk with her. Setting up this scholarship is the most fulfilling experience I have had in my life.

After my retirement I had a few second thoughts. I signed up to teach a course I loved, "Law and Literature," with a colleague who is a lawyer. The course went well. We and the students were happy. But I know now that that part of my life is over. I resented every student paper I had to read, even though many of them were very good. I resented having to be in New Jersey every Wednesday, when I could have been in the Berkshires, or playing bridge, or at a matinee. Although I am a little disappointed that the English Department has eliminated "Law and Literature" from the curriculum, I wish my former colleagues well. Others will come along to continue the struggle.

Browning was right in one sense: life after sixty is a continuation and a sum of what went before. We may not consciously plan for retirement (I certainly didn't), but we will be the people our working, thinking, political, emotional lives prepared us to become. Does this mean that "the best is yet to be"? Aging also means coming to terms with loss and the fear of being alone. I hope I have developed the resources for what lies ahead.

Coda: Three months after I completed the final revisions of this essay, and totally unexpectedly, Sanford Radner died peacefully in his sleep. He was sixty-nine. We had been married for forty-one years. I have had the support of wonderful friends as I cope with financial details in which I previously had no interest and a silent, cavernous apartment. So "the last of life for which the first was made" has begun in earnest. I still can only hope that I am up to the challenge.

Afterthoughts

Phillipa Kafka

Two weeks after my retirement in January 1999, a former colleague asked me how I was enjoying retirement, which struck me as akin to asking someone just beginning her honeymoon how she is enjoying married life. Now, however, after more than two years of retirement, I can respond to my friend's question without hurling colorful Yiddish curses at him or at any of the other poor souls who innocently aroused my wrath by asking the same question.

At first, because my lifestyle was scarcely indistinguishable from my activities on summer breaks or sabbatical leaves, it did not really hit me that I had retired. I was still socializing with the same circle of friends, completing my third and fourth books of feminist literary criticism for simultaneous publication in 2000, and was contributing editor to a collection of essays and memoirs that has just been published. I was writing book reviews, judging manuscripts for scholarly journals, and had just begun to serve on the editorial board of a feminist journal. I was also engaged in the process of selling off my husband's and my home restoration business in New Jersey. In February 2000, we sold our last project there, and in a huge moving truck containing all our worldly possessions and with a trailer attached to our car, we drove to Boulder City, Nevada, where we immediately began work on our next project.

Born into poverty in 1933 in the midst of the Great Depression, I had few toys, but that never bothered me; my world was my toy. I used to love to gaze down after dark at the brightly lit shops lining both sides of the cobblestoned road far beneath the high steel pillars of the El that rounded a curve above the window of our tiny tenement flat on Fox Street in the Bronx. In 1952, my mother moved to Tucson, Arizona, for her health. Instead of joining her, I decided to move nearer to my school, to support myself by working full-time during the day, and take classes during my lunch hours and at night until I graduated. For over forty-eight years thereafter, I would not experience having a home, being at home, or being centered in my world and myself, which only my mother's presence had given me. Until I moved to Boulder City, my feeling of alienation, of homelessness, of displacement, of not quite belonging anywhere endured as a dull, steady ache within me, as if some part of myself had become disconnected from the rest.

From 1985 on, as the date for my retirement began to loom before me with ever-increasing reality, I engaged in a long search to find the one special place on earth where I would want to live. In or around 1995, my husband and I began to drive up to Las Vegas after visiting two of my children and other family members who were all living in Tucson. Just after passing Hoover Dam, an incredibly beautiful, otherworldly vision would suddenly appear before my eyes: a broad expanse of water set like a blue bowl in a mass of jagged lavender and pink and gray mountain peaks. I would always silently burst into tears at having to leave that sight, but in 1997 I finally admitted my feelings to my husband, who responded by turning off the road and driving to the nearest real estate office. This is how we came to move to the small town of Boulder City where I can now gaze down at Lake Mead from all the front windows of my own home whenever I wish.

Feelings of Displacement, Loss, Isolation, and Failure

Nevertheless I became despondent for a long time after coming here. I kept reliving my past career in cyclical whirlpools of regret and remorse that took the form of recurrent dreams. In one of them, I grew increasingly anxious, fearful that I would be too late for class, or, worse, that I would be unable to find my classroom, although I made many attempts to do so. Since I had never missed a class except for illness, this dream did not reflect reality. Rather, it reflected my sense of being displaced far out and away in space, of having lost the only meaningful work I had ever known because I had retired and moved away.

In a similar dream I was teaching a class while groups of students in front of me conversed animatedly with each other. No matter how many times I tried to get their attention, they continued to ignore me as if they could neither see nor hear me. This dream also reflected my dawning conviction that by retiring I had become insignificant, irrelevant, superfluous, and even invisible. Only as long as I had been a professor could I justify my existence as necessary and meaningful to society.

I also dreamt that I stood unnoticed and alone against a wall at a holiday party in a vast room at my university filled with hundreds of people who belonged there while I did not. To my amazement and despair, I did not recognize one soul in all that crowd, nor did anyone recognize me or notice my presence. The thought that I was an outsider there, a stranger, and invisible, overwhelmed me with grief. In reality, the wall that I leaned up against in my dream was the wall that I myself had created between my working world and myself when I retired and moved away.

In another dream I was standing in a corner of a vast, open space that was entirely strange to me. I approached one of the featureless female workers who sat absorbed in their work at long rows of desks and asked for directions to my dean's office. I was scheduled to attend a meeting there in a few minutes. All the other workers ignored me, but the one I spoke to noticed me and gave me detailed instructions on how to get to his office, even kindly pointing in the direction I should take. I obediently turned corners and walked down strange halls, but became increasingly apprehensive that I was moving ever farther away from my destination. No matter how I tried, I never succeeded in finding the door to the dean's office or arriving at our scheduled meeting.

Retirement, a Living Death

All these dreams reflected my most deep-seated anxieties about having retired and moved so far away. I felt that while I would never forget my friends and still wanted to associate with them, they had forgotten me. They were still involved in all the ongoing action, moving forward into the future and confronting continual changes and challenges of which I was no longer even remotely cognizant. Although still alive elsewhere I was now and would be forevermore out of the loop, in the dark about all that was going on past my time, just as though I were dead to that world. I was fixed forever in the past, the way someone is who has died and been forgotten.

Like the unremunerated labor of child rearing and housework, whatever work I performed in private, such as my "hobby" of restoring and upgrading homes, had never counted in my eyes because it did not have elite class status in our culture. Only being an academic had given my life meaning in terms of "work" out in the world. All my feelings of self-worth and importance that I had taken for granted for so many years suddenly evaporated after I retired from the university and moved away from the area. I had thus inadvertently brought upon myself a living death.

This feeling after retirement of being out of life while still living, of being swept away or shunted aside is perhaps the most commonly publicized experience in relation to male retirees. But grief over loss of the work world is not a gendered phenomenon limited to retired men only. A similar phenomenon, the empty nest syndrome, is attributed only to full-time homemakers when their children leave home and begin to live separate and independent lives. It is not attributed to fathers or mothers who work outside the home by choice.

Even if I had not been a full-time working mother who was also a single parent and my children's sole support, my career would still always have come first. I resented my three children's endlessly petty bickering among themselves, their repeated appeals to me to favor one or the other of them, their endless demands on me. Their shrill, tinny voices grated unbearably in my ears, especially when I was marking papers or reading texts for classroom preparation. I used to pray for them to grow up, for peace and quiet in which to pursue my adult interests uninterrupted. Yet to my surprise when the last of my three children left home I found myself suffering from empty nest syndrome: the silence in my home a dull vacuum devoid of life.

Today I miss my children's ebullient presence, the way they were when they were young, and in my dreams they are still young. When I see mothers with young children I feel pangs of envy immediately followed by the consoling thought that they little imagine that their little circle will not endure forever. My envy of young mothers also springs from the knowledge that I am not only retired from the workforce, but that I am now past all the duties, obligations—and pleasures—that I once experienced as a mother. It signifies to me that I am now superannuated as a mother. Having grown children living entirely separate lives of their own is a marker for me that I have reached old age. Friends and relatives repeatedly reassure me that grandchildren serve as a shield from the fear of no longer being needed in a parental capacity. But I have no grandchildren as yet to provide me with any such consolation.

Factors That Led to My Inappropriate Career Choice

My mother trained me according to her traditional Jewish shtetl values to become "a balabusta," a model in all things relating to the home, including caring for children and husband. But all I cared about was to go to school, to be in school, to spend the rest of my life in school. At ten, I decided to teach after I grew up so that I could remain in school forever. My favorite game was to pretend to administer tests to my friends in the lot near our tenements in the Bronx. I would dream that I had grown up and become a teacher. I stood on a wooden platform in a large open space and with outstretched arms passionately lectured to my students about literature. The sun's golden rays shone down from a bright blue sky onto their faces as they listened avidly and with delight to my every word, gazing up at me with adoration.

By the time I was eleven, I adamantly refused either to help my mother or to join my friends in their games after school. After I finished my homework I only wanted to be alone with my latest readings. Once a week, after school, I would take a large shopping bag to the library, fill it with as many books as I could on both my older brother's card and mine, and return them all the next week. By the time I was twelve, I had devoured all the works of Shakespeare, Dickens, and Twain, among many other authors, and had read Virginia Woolf's *Orlando*.

It was no wonder, then, that the idea eventually occurred to me to try to turn the habit that my family despised into a respected profession—to become a Ph.D., a doctor of philosophy, a professor of English literature. I believed that these titles would serve me as a magic talisman. I would finally win my family's approval, respect, and acknowledgment. I also believed that once I possessed academic titles I would automatically rise to elite, intellectual-class status in the world of my time. Unfortunately I had no guidance counselor to advise me as to the feasibility of attempting to realize such ambitions during the post–World War II period, when faculty who were female, from an ethnic minority, or of color were nowhere evident in academia.

I was blithely and ignorantly planning to join a WASP old boys' club, the world of white-male-only academia, during the McCarthy era when even just the sound of my voice and my gestures stereotyped me as pushy and aggressive. Having internalized my parents' speech inflections as well as those of the immigrant community of my early environment, I spoke (as I still do today) in a loud voice with a "lower-class," Polish-Jewish immigrant Bronx accent.

Once hired, from the beginning of my career to my retirement, the little I did manage to say during department and committee meetings offended and repelled my colleagues. Additionally, I was forever making angry, emotional, confrontational attempts to effectuate changes in their perspective and in the department's lackluster, outmoded curriculum by arguing for a more inclusive and multicultural perspective, which my colleagues viewed as a disgusting abomination. My constant gesturing while making my arguments also

struck my colleagues as crude, uncouth, and dumb. Even after an elderly
WASP male colleague expressed revulsion for my "exaggerated Jewish gestures," it never occurred to me (until I retired) that all women and men of
color, as well as ethnics with accents and gestures other than those considered
mainstream, are stereotyped as inherently lower class and lacking in intellectual ability.

On the other hand, I was judgmental and righteous toward my elitist, politically conservative colleagues and never mixed with them socially or participated in any of their interests. Except that we had a mutual interest in reading
literature, I was in every way entirely incompatible with my co-workers, who
spoke and acted in a dignified and professional manner. Somehow, throughout my entire career, it never occurred to me that what I did and said pressed
all their buttons. I provoked their anti-Semitism (in some cases, internalized),
their sexism, their profound opposition to feminism and multiculturalism. I
see now that I should never have chosen a career where gentility and "colle-
giality" are of paramount importance. For all these reasons I feel now that I
paid too high a price in emotional suffering and in impaired health by choosing and remaining in the wrong profession for nearly thirty years.

The product of wildly disparate parents who gave me wildly disparate messages, I never knew why I was always miserable if I failed and just as miserable
if I succeeded. In personality my father was crude, loud, blunt, spontaneous,
gregarious, sociable, and ever childlike. In character he was ambitious, optimistic, and scrupulously honest. He had come to the United States when very
young and believed intensely in the American dream. He taught me to live as
he did in keeping with that dream as he understood it. He fought all his life on
behalf of the little man, who only in this great country could pull himself up
by his own bootstraps and go from rags to riches through hard work and tenac-
ity in the face of all obstacles. Neither his father's incredulous mockery, nor
joblessness, nor poverty, nor the Great Depression, nor three dependents, nor
eight failures before he finally passed the exam at the age of forty-three could
prevent him from finally achieving his burning ambition to become a CPA.

My mother had come to the United States in a cattle boat after having suffered from anti-Semitism, as well as from malnutrition, in her native Poland,
and experienced hunger again during the Great Depression and many anti-
Semitic incidents throughout her life. She was entirely incompatible with her
husband in every way, except that she too was honest to a fault. Ashamed that
she was the scarcely literate daughter of an illiterate washerwoman, she appeared so gentle, tactful, and dignified in public that no one, including myself, ever guessed her secret. She trained me to always act like a lady and kept

demanding of my father that he act like a professional, but we both always disappointed her.

Whereas my father formed my character with a wealth of sayings like "*Arbeit macht das Leben süß*" (Work makes life sweet), my mother trained me to replicate her paranoia (justified by her experiences) and superstition. I must never under any circumstances stand out. I must never raise my head up above the crowd. I must never bring attention to myself or be noticed, or I would be immediately shot down. It was best, it was safest, to always hide out away from people, to stay obscure and be ignored, or the evil eye would get me.

Like my father, I earned all my degrees and titles only after overcoming monumental obstacles. I also ideologically expanded my father's belief in the American ideal of equality for all men to equality for all. Although originally trained like my colleagues as a traditional Ph.D. in English literature in 1964, I became a pioneer in the research and teaching of ethnic American literature in 1977.

When I discovered in the early 1990s that all "Landmarks of World Literature" courses at my university still offered the same readings I'd had in my own student days, and nothing else, it occurred to me that teaching this course would present me with a rare and wonderful opportunity. I could offer contemporary students a truly global world literature course for the first time: a course that would include as many examples of great literature by women writers as by male writers from around the world and throughout history. From then on, I became "the Queen of Landmarks," and when I retired, my "Landmarks" students surprised me at the end of the last class I ever taught with a sheet cake and a party. That honor means the most to me today, except for my title of professor emerita, of which—ever the unregenerate intellectual elitist—I am inordinately proud.

My mother's preoccupation in life, one that also became and remains mine, was to be "good"—a good girl, a good daughter, a good wife, a good mother. Actually my mother aimed (as I do) at being more than good. She wanted to become perfect (as she wanted me to become)—to always strive to think and do the right thing. Unfortunately, my mother was self-righteous and hypercritical in private. She judged everyone else's standards by her own and was forever harping on wrongs done to her. In her only daughter she had the perfect confidante for all her tales of woe. She was my heroine. Her view was ever my view. It was inconceivable to me to imagine that my mother could ever be wrong about anything.

During her many tales of woe, sometimes lasting for hours, I hung on my mother's every word. She always succeeded in keeping me in suspense, while simultaneously satisfying me intellectually with her deep analysis and penetrating insights, her intricately detailed critiques of the motives and conduct of all those who had done her wrong. As if she were a prosecuting attorney before God in God's court of justice, she would compile such formidable and convincing evidence against her oppressors that my heart would break for her and I would rage against her heartless enemies. Today I see how much my mother's perspective and her storytelling techniques have influenced my own critiques of the patriarchal oppressors of women.

My Perspective Shifts

I awoke one morning in the spring of 1998 feeling burned out. Rather than subject my students to what I had observed some of my older colleagues doing after they had "lost it"—teaching only for their paycheck and to have some place to hang out every day, I determined to retire as soon as possible. In my case, not only had I suddenly lost my life-long passion for teaching, I no longer wanted to be anywhere near an institution even resembling a university for as long as I lived.

But it wasn't until I moved to Nevada that I realized I had left behind everything that had made up my former life. When I first realized that for me retirement was death in life, I hit bottom until, as I have described above, I began my voyage into my own stormy depths of self. My depression came to an end only after I confronted, identified, and came to terms with my specious motives for choosing my career and for all the suffering I had endured in that career as a consequence of my disparate personality traits and unpopular political perspective. Then one morning I found my depression dissolved in the light of a new day in my life. For the first time, instead of mourning that I had cut myself off from the only world that had meant anything to me and in which I had meant anything, I felt fortunate to be exactly where I was, doing exactly what I wanted to do.

Yet whenever I thought of myself as retired, as a retiree, as in retirement, it still meant to me the step prior to death: the loss of functioning in the world, the loss of service to the world, being out of it. Then I thought of a way to do an end run around these dreaded words. I would conceptualize myself, instead, as never having retired at all. I could rationalize away the unbearable by asking myself how I would have described leaving academia if I had done so in my thirties, forties, or fifties—as going into retirement, or as making a career change?

This perspective change resulted in a remarkable shift in my whole attitude toward my past life, my present, and my future. For the first time I admitted to myself that I had quit a high-status job that I had tired of; that I did not have the courage to tell my colleagues why I really wanted out at the height of my career; that I had consciously manipulated an ageist stereotype—that one is ready for retirement at a certain age—to conceal the truth from them.

But by describing my career change as retirement I had lost my precious prestige and equally precious friendships that I had enjoyed in my workplace. And unless I defined what I had done as retirement, I could not justify picking up and leaving and beginning a new life only because I wanted to go somewhere else and do something else. Yet I could not bear to think of myself as selfish and self-indulgent, as consumerist, as using my advanced age as an excuse to serve my own needs and desires and not society. This perplexing question then arose for me: How could I justify my existence if I called myself a retiree? What would get me up in the morning if I weren't working actively and publicly to improve my world?

Gradually I began to see that in restoring and upgrading homes I could justify myself as serving society. Through dirty and difficult physical labor I create beauty for buyers of our projects while improving neighborhoods in the community where I work. In my writing and publishing, as well, I can still justify myself as serving society, especially since I have recently been awarded a contract to write my fifth book of literary criticism. I see my publications as small pieces that connect and merge with many other diverse pieces in a global mosaic whose goal is to improve women's lives around the world.

I also can see now that my mother's and my damaged psyches were never only our own private tragedy, but that all such damaged psyches come at a tragic cost to society, as well. Even though conflict or legislation may bring gender, race, ethnic, class, religious, and other oppressions to an end, the aftereffects on the victims—like festering, lingering wounds that gradually turn to scars—continue on for generations to come.

Conclusion

Many retirees worked in obscurity all their lives primarily for their own individual or family's survival, or comfort, or financial security, or even wealth. In contrast, another group of retirees—women like myself—worked in more visible professions and earned high status titles before we retired. Members of the second-wave feminist movement like myself attempted to gain equality for ourselves as well as for all women by struggling to enter into and change diverse institutions of our culture that were dominated by sexist and racist white males. Those of us who somehow managed to keep our jobs struggled long and hard against all the patriarchal odds to finally achieve the titles and status that our society identified as normatively male. Our goals were to transform the cultures' institutions from within as well as to make advances wherever we could toward access and equality for all women, and not to become docile tokens in the old boys' network while it carried on as usual. In higher education we were also class elitist and conceptualized ourselves as having "higher" aims in life than the "lower" classes.

However, as we now begin to retire from our hard-won and highly visible positions, we may find ourselves, as I did, experiencing great difficulty in emotionally adjusting to postretirement lives. My age cohort may engage in painstaking inquiries lasting for long periods of time as to the causes of our past mistakes and failures, as well as our past successes. Meanwhile, our generation's successors are also meditating on our past limitations and our past accomplishments. Some of them engage in this process in order to define and fix us in stone in the past and already perceive us (as we ourselves may do) in the past tense—not only as retired, but also as having passed away.

On the other hand, there are those of us who think of ourselves not only as still living, but also as still fluid, as changeable, and just as capable for as long as we are alive of improvement and growth as our juniors in time perceive themselves to be. It is possible, as I have shown in these afterthoughts about my own life and career, to emerge on the other side of the past into a vital present and to look forward to future accomplishments, just as younger generations do. With ceaseless, unsparing self-reflexivity, by endlessly challenging deep-level messages, training, codes, and stereotypes that we have all internalized, it is possible to continue to function now, today, and to work productively in whatever forms that takes for each of us to serve and improve our world.

A *Mennonite Retirement: From Work Projects to Play Projects*

LAURA H. WEAVER

For me, retirement at age seventy did not signify a dislocation, a cessation of the activities that determined my identity for forty-four years. Instead, it has, by now—two and one-half years later—rejuvenated me by creating a new relationship between work and play. In my childhood and youth, certain experiences catapulted me into involvement with issues of ethnic minorities and feminism. In adulthood, as I focused on them in my teaching and publications, they became my work. In retirement my past commitment to work has been replaced by a commitment to play—first, noncerebral forms, like socializing, and then cerebral forms as I have begun writing again. Now those twin topics, ethnic minorities and feminism, have become the subject matter of my play projects.

The catapulting occurred in a rural conservative Mennonite family in Pennsylvania during the 1930s and 1940s. The first movement, into ethnic minority issues, was predictable: as conservative Mennonite children in a public school, we were always the Other. We differed from our classmates in clothing, entertainment, and our political/religious stance of pacifism. When other girls had curled, cut hair and wore skirts and blouses and white socks and shoes, I had long, braided hair and wore plain dresses with sewn-in belts and no collars and long brown or black stockings and shoes. When others listened to the radio, went to movies, or danced, I dared not; instead, I read books and sang at school and in church. Beyond those external differences existed our profoundly different world view: the Mennonite emphasis on pacifism meant that our uncles registered as conscientious objectors; that we respected our Anabaptist ancestors who, persecuted by both Protestants and Catholics, died for their belief in nonviolence and in adult baptism; and that we ourselves were taught not to fight back but to return good for evil. This minority upbringing produced healthy nonconformists. We grew up knowing that we were different from other people in the dominant society.

My movement into feminism was more surprising. Supported by scriptural authority, conservative branches of the Mennonite Church taught women to submit to men, and married women usually worked at home while their husbands worked outside the home. However, because my father left us early in my childhood—but without a divorce since that option was denied to conservative Mennonites—and returned only periodically throughout my childhood and teenage years, and never (except for the first few years) provided financial support for our family even when he was at home, I grew up in a household in which women always worked outside the home and earned their own money. From our births my sister, Dorcas, and I saw models of independent women: two elementary school teachers who boarded in our home, providing income for our family, until I was eight years old; Aunt Sarah, a single woman who did domestic work in Allentown and Philadelphia; and my mother, who, when I was a small child, sewed for others, sold garden produce, and did some of the farm labor that my father had been hired to do on a tenant farm but neglected during his departures from our family. Later, my mother, from the time she was thirty-three until she retired at the age of seventy-seven, did domestic work (cleaning, washing, and ironing) outside the home.

As working-class people, our family was an anomaly in a rural conservative Mennonite community; if my father had been present consistently and had supported us financially, he eventually would have acquired his father's farm, placing us, of course, in a higher socioeconomic class. Our lower social position within the local Mennonite church and community created for our family, already members of the Mennonite minority in the dominant society, another outsider identity. For example, the other church members owned houses and cars. Our family rented a house and, living in a rural area without Sunday bus transportation, had to be driven to church by other church members. However, the stigma of our lower social position was offset by several factors. In our public high school, Dorcas and I achieved academic success; we were inducted into the National Honor Society, and I graduated first in my class. I also participated in certain extracurricular activities permitted by the church: I was editor of the school newspaper and business manager of the yearbook. In the public school my sister and I were identified not as the children of a man who left his family but as children who created their own identity as excellent students. Perhaps even more importantly, our social position, forcing my mother to work outside the home, gave my sister and me the opportunity to see a woman produce the family's income and handle all financial matters. We learned that we could overcome our apparent economic/social dysfunction within the conservative Mennonite community and become successful in school and the workplace.

Not only did I see my mother always work outside the home, I myself have done so for pay ever since I was twelve years old. The strong Mennonite work ethic sought to develop disciplined work habits, particularly in helping other community members, and other twelve-year-olds also worked at home and sometimes for relatives, but our precarious financial situation intensified the need to work outside the home. In the homes of other families I cleaned, washed dishes, washed and ironed clothing, worked in the yard and garden during summers (and even during the school year in grades 8–10). During the last two years of high school I was a part-time secretary and a bookkeeper. After high school graduation I worked for two years in a law office, again as a secretary and bookkeeper, so that I could go to college. Upon entering college I waitressed, cleaned, and did secretarial work during the school year, semester breaks, and summer vacations.

In adulthood my ethnic minority status continued but in a different form. I gradually stopped following conservative Mennonite Church rules: I removed my plain clothes, cut my hair, and began wearing jewelry and makeup. Ignoring the entertainment prohibitions, I attended theater events and watched popular movies. However, I maintained my connection with liberal branches of the Mennonite Church. I still identify with and support the Mennonite position on peace and justice; I still see the world from the angle of a minority person, a member of a group that originated as a radical element in the Protestant Reformation, or Rebellion, and experienced persecution. I immediately feel a kinship with people who grew up as I did, whether we are now conservative, liberal, or agnostic, whether practicing or nonpracticing Mennonites.

Also, financial independence continued to characterize my life. I always worked for my own education and my own living; after receiving a B.A., I taught high school for two years, got an M.A., taught in small colleges for eight years, obtained a Ph.D., and then taught in colleges and universities again. My assumption of financial responsibility persisted during an eight-year marriage to an artist during my forties and fifties. Consequently, except for the first few years of my life, I have not lived on the income earned by a man. As a child I lived on the income earned by my mother and me, and as an adult, on the income I earned.

No doubt as a result of my background, those two main interests, in ethnic minorities and feminism, became my focus in my academic career, the teaching and publications that constituted my primary work for forty-four years. Although my Ph.D. is in twentieth-century British literature and I taught a variety of courses in literature, composition, and world cultures, whenever possible I chose minority and women's studies material as the content of my classes and my publications. Actually, in many of my presentations and articles my two main foci have been fused, for example in a large project I began more than five years ago: a study of letters written by my mother. The letters document her social isolation and economic deprivation but also her consistent allegiance to the Mennonite Church, her courage and resourcefulness in finding jobs to support her family, and her encouragement of my assertiveness.

Those interests dominated my years of conscientious work—years in which, for two main reasons, retirement seemed remote and undesirable. First, as a child and a young person I had never heard much discussion about it. I had assumed that people work as long as possible—both physically and mentally. For example, I saw my mother do cleaning in a doctor's office until she was seventy-seven years old. Second, I could not imagine life outside of an academic setting. As a child I loved school; I wished that we'd have school on Saturdays and during summers. As a teenager and an adult I continued to thrive in academia—as a high school, college, and graduate student and as a teacher. In later years, however, several features of academia gradually became less attractive and induced me to look forward to retirement. Although I continued to enjoy interacting with my university colleagues and teaching composition, giving papers at conferences, and publishing articles, I began to resent the heavy teaching loads and to find the grading of papers onerous. I suffered exhaustion from earlier departmental politics (although the situation eventually improved), my attempts to arouse students' interest in the required "World Cultures" course, and the need to manipulate course content and classroom procedures and the record of my teaching and publications to ensure consistently positive student and administrative evaluations.

Consequently, at the age of sixty-two or sixty-three I began consulting with the human resources director at the University of Evansville (Indiana), where I worked, and checking my TIAA and CREF (Teachers Insurance and Annuity Association and College Retirement Equities Fund) accounts to determine when I could retire safely. Because of financial problems created by my ex-husband's debts, I knew that I could not retire at the age of sixty-five, but eventually I found that—after nineteen years at the university—I could retire at the age of sixty-seven.

Since I knew that I would keep on living in Evansville and continue contact with colleagues, the procedures involved in preparing for and accomplishing retirement were pain free: writing a letter of intent to the department chair, filling out TIAA and CREF forms, packing my files and books and moving them to my home, and returning my office key. I envisioned retirement as retention of the positive features of academia but release from drudgery, from the oppressive features of the system.

That exhilaration was sustained in each of my retirement parties. There were two university ones. One was a reception after I gave my last Andiron lecture (in an interdisciplinary lecture series at the university), "Three Voices in a Mennonite Woman's Record of Her Failed Marriage: The Letters (1960s) and Reminiscences (1990s) of Margaret A. Weaver." That reception represented an ending but not loss; the project, a collection of my mother's letters, is continuing. The other official function consisted of the traditional university-wide tree planting and reception for all persons retiring in a given year. That event, and specifically a tribute to me by my department chair, Dr. Michael Carson, produced closure. I felt satisfaction; I forgot the drudgery and, instead, remembered the joy of teaching. On that occasion Dr. Carson said:

> Dr. Laura Weaver came here to teach writing, and she has done so for nearly twenty years to hundreds and hundreds of students. I learned about Laura early on when one of our finest students, Kim Horvath, told me that because of Dr. Weaver's class she wanted to become a writer, to write for the truth. And she has done so. I could well understand the connection Laura made with a young student, for Laura is one of a certain breed that I most admire, a writing teacher, one who has the gift and the love of teaching others to write well. . . . Anyone who has had such a teacher in his life knows what a change it can make, the blessing of being taught by someone who is willing to do the hard and loving work of reading and rereading endless work, often putting more into it than the student himself. So, for all the students who came under Laura's care over the years, I say thank you and say that we wish you grace and light in your own good writings in the future. The Mennonite gift of plain writing is a virtue that the world has much need of.

I especially appreciated Dr. Carson's references to Mennonites and to my own future writing because I knew that sometime I would do more writing about my Mennonite past, which is always present.

After the official celebrations, two other parties were given by friends of mine: one by Dr. Shirley Schwarz, an art history professor, for my university and community friends and one by Dr. Beth Stone, a psychologist, for my friends at Patchwork Central, not a sewing group but an inner-city service organization with which I am associated. At both parties we drank toasts to the completion of a long teaching career and to my liberation to a new period of more flexibility in activities.

As the planned celebrations ended, I soon made an invigorating discovery: retirement gave me the time and, more importantly, the permission to play. The importance of this permission must be seen in the context not so much of the economic necessity that initially propelled me into hard work but rather the work ethic of my conservative Mennonite family and community. Work was the dominant value for all age groups, regardless of socioeconomic class. To be called a hard worker was the highest compliment; even a child might be called "a good little worker." Because of the value placed on work, children wished, even before they received work assignments, to help adults do chores. According to my mother, at the age of four I voluntarily helped to wash and dry the smaller dishes and set the table. At five I dusted chairs and swept the floor. By the time I was seven years old my family and community assumed that play would not dominate my time; I was assigned chores, such as washing large dishes (including the kettles used in canning), washing up the floor, helping with laundry (including ironing), mowing and trimming grass, preparing produce for canning and freezing—peeling peaches, shelling and stringing peas, straining tomato juice and apple sauce. We played, of course, but only after the work was completed. We were taught, "First we work, and then we play." Even when we visited other people, especially relatives, we asked, "What can I do to help [work]?" That training continued during my teenage and young adult years.

Subordination of play to work still dominates the value system held by conservative Mennonites, including my mother, my sister, and my nieces and nephews. They think in terms of a need to have something to show for one's time and especially something done for others. Even now my ninety-year-old mother says, "We aren't here to play but to help others." If I were living near my relatives, I would be expected to share their work—planting and gathering produce, freezing the surplus, mending. Although I admire this work ethic, I don't think it should be imposed upon anyone. Gradually, probably from my developing acculturation, I began to see the desire to help others, especially in domestic work, as an obsessive compulsion, a fetish. Especially in a rural conservative culture, women experience a double oppression: submission to not only male authority but also other families' work schedules. Consequently, now I resist accepting an obligation to help others, whether relatives or not, specifically in domestic work. Occasionally, I do volunteer to help others in activities that I enjoy, for example proofreading or editing friends' essays or reports, writing recommendation letters, gathering material for a local newsletter, and affixing mailing labels on brochures. However, those activities are fun. I feel no need to accumulate a list of volunteer accomplishments to validate my existence.

Rebelling against my background, I now believe in guilt-free play—multifaceted play. I have more time to do what I have always done for entertainment: meet friends for lunch, dinner, or a drink; go to plays, concerts, museums. But new activities have also developed. At various times during the day I can go to Penny Lane, a new coffeehouse, to listen to music, attend poetry readings, or just talk with people. Or I can go to hear musicians playing on the walkway in downtown Evansville on Fridays at noon. I especially enjoy going to hear a group of young friends play acoustic rock at places like Lamasco's Bar from nine-thirty to eleven-thirty on a Thursday night, something I couldn't do when I was teaching. I've learned to like not only acoustic rock but also other kinds of music, for example bluegrass. Some of these activities, like listening to bands in bars, are especially fun because, perceived as frivolous and even immoral, they were taboo in my upbringing. Breaking an earlier rule is exhilarating even for a seventy-year-old.

When I engage in these activities, whether old or new, I enjoy the ability to move, even on a given day, from one group to another among the people I've learned to know during my twenty-two years in Evansville: former university colleagues, Patchwork Central friends, and community friends, including liberal Mennonites. One of the groups I enjoy connecting with is young liberal Mennonites who, although taught the basic principles that I was, have not been burdened with rules concerning clothing and entertainment. With a few young friends I went to Mennofolk, a music festival in Bluffton, Ohio, in July 2000, and in July 2001 I went to another Mennofolk in Nashville, Tennessee, where I introduced bands during two sessions.

But socializing is not my only form of play. Some activities are more cerebral. Now I have more time to read what I want to, without its being related to a class or a writing project—to read the way I did as a child, when I developed the love of reading that led me to pursue degrees in English. Recently I read Kim Barnes's *Hungry for the World* and Margaret Atwood's *The Handmaid's Tale*. Sometimes I join other people in a book discussion, for example of Barbara Kingsolver's novel *The Poisonwood Bible*. Equally cerebral is my auditing of classes—from women's studies to chemistry—at the University of Evansville. Being a participant/student again gives me pleasure. All of these activities—from bars to books—are accessible to me now because of my flexible schedule.

In my first one and one-half years of retirement those noncerebral and cerebral activities constituted my play. They continue to be important, but, in addition, my workforce ethnic minority and gender projects have become important again—now transformed into play. I have found a way to play with the issues that dominated my childhood/teen experiences and my paid academic work. One of my major projects, the collection of my mother's letters, is continuing because it is enjoyable—not because it will be submitted to a university administrator for my annual evaluation.

But new types of projects have emerged, especially several collaborations with visual artists. My first postretirement project, a joint one with artist Matt Busby, culminated in a presentation and an exhibit, "Divided Together: Visual and Written Explorations of the Self," first at Patchwork Central and then at the University of Evansville. Now another collaboration with an artist has developed. In February 2002 I shared in a joint presentation with painter/printmaker Abner Hershberger, a Goshen College retired art professor, whose exhibit, "Heritage Works," was held at the University of Evansville. Both Hershberger and I discussed our use of our Mennonite background, he in his recent art (after a career devoted to abstract art) and I in my writing. As a serendipitous spin-off from those associations with artists, I tried something else new: writing an article about the work of Nel Bannier, a University of Evansville art teacher from the Netherlands, and submitting it to *Ceramics Monthly*. This attempt, not at all in my field of expertise, involved risk—but a risk that I could afford to take. Fortunately, the article has now been published, but if it had not been, I would not have been penalized. Just as retirement provides me the opportunity for guilt-free noncerebral play, this freedom to pursue new avenues of creativity assures me guilt-free cerebral play. I have retired from paid work on ethnic minorities and gender but not from those interests initially inspired by economic necessity. The catapult that created my work interests has now generated my play projects.

My turning work into play during retirement may stem from my academic training or my conservative Mennonite background or both. As a feminist I believe that a woman's usefulness is not determined necessarily by childbearing and the nurturing of husband and children, work which ceases or lessens in intensity over time, allowing time for play in retirement, but by other activities which can continue in retirement. And as a conservative Mennonite I was taught not to complain about work but to enjoy it. By playing with my earlier work projects, I may be acting as a good Mennonite and as an independent woman. I'm playing, but I'm working; I'm working, but I'm playing.

Rewriting the Books: Onward in Retirement

DIANE L. FOWLKES

Before I retired, I actually reached a point of getting paid for work in women's studies, a field I consider to be synonymous with the women's movement. Worn down from bureaucratic politics and the stress of living in increasingly congested Atlanta, however, I retired as soon as I was financially able, because I was no longer willing to take the daily (or so it seemed) misogyny of my workplace. While I am retired from paid work, I do not feel retired from the women's movement, although the focus of my commitment has turned homeward as I try to make a feminist analysis of my confrontation with caregiving for a sick husband. In this sense, my retirement is not what I want it to be. I stay involved in women's studies because it is this kind of thinking that will enable me to navigate this difficult passage. In this sense, my retirement is all that I want it to be: more time to read and write and to socialize intimately with good friends so that I can keep on learning and changing.

Why I Worked for Pay and Why I Stopped

When, at the age of fifty-eight years and eight months, I retired as professor emerita of political science and founding director of the Women's Studies Institute at Georgia State University on July 1,1998, I had been working for pay since the age of sixteen—forty-two years. As I approached an age and income level that made retirement possible in the particular pension plan of which I am a part, I studied the rules that specify what each and every year and month of working count for in dollar terms. I calculated that with twenty-eight years in the system altogether as secretary, faculty member, and administrator, I would have enough to live on if I retired sixteen months short of age sixty, even with the penalty for retiring early.

My Social Security earnings record—starting small and finishing large—serves as a symbolic roadmap of my journey, and no doubt that of others, through over four decades of major change–social, economic, political, cultural—in the United States and in the world. My work history reveals a pattern of upward mobility nourished by my own desires and supported by others who helped me get around barriers. As I am also aware that my journey as a white heterosexual woman may differ in significant ways from those of girls and women of color, lesbians, and those of lower and higher economic class, I will weave understandings of such differences into my story.

Looking back briefly, I can recount five periods in my paid work life that correspond to my own passage through certain life cycles as the world was also changing. The first period was one of part-time jobs during high school and college in my hometown, Memphis, Tennessee. I was fortunate to have the help of my high school biology teacher, Dorothy Greene, in securing a scholarship to attend Southwestern-at-Memphis, a small, coed, Presbyterian liberal arts college. Unlike most of my classmates, I had to work to pay for the rest of my college education. That was a sign of my family's upper-working-class/lower-middle-class status and their attitude toward anything I wanted to do: if you want it, you'll have to pay for it yourself.

But these jobs were interesting. During high school I worked in a laboratory at the University of Tennessee Medical School for Dr. Esther L. McCandless, one of the first women to go into nuclear medical research. During college I worked as a sales clerk at a downtown jewelry store and as a phonograph record librarian at the CBS-affiliated radio and television station located in the basement of the Hotel Peabody. When I graduated from college in 1961, there was still racial segregation in the workplace and in public accommodations as well as in schools and colleges, so management in all these workplaces was white and predominantly male, co-workers were white and female, while janitorial services were done by black men and women. In contrast to my options of low-paid teacher, nurse, secretary, or store clerk in a white institution, a black girl's or woman's options would have been mostly in lower-paid domestic service or farm work or in a service, educational, or business establishment in the black community.

The second period of my work life was devoted to full-time secretarial jobs, usually in academic settings. I had earned the B.A. degree with a major in French language and literature but did not want to take the education courses needed to get a teaching certificate. Also not wanting to be a nurse, my only other perceived option besides store clerking was to be a secretary. I worked first to earn my own living, then to support a first husband in law school, and finally, having left him to go with another man to Atlanta, to earn a living while returning to graduate school. I worked at Georgia State University while studying there for the M.A. degree in political science.

Though the 1960s became a time of vigorous racial, antiwar, and sexual challenges to the patriarchal social order, what Adrienne Rich has called "compulsory heterosexuality" remained the unspoken norm.[1] Setting up with my new partner, a political science professor fourteen years older than I, meant breaking up both our marriages; he also had young children. While there was stigma attached to taking up with a married man, I later learned that this stigma was a less punishing part of a homophobic dimension of the social order. I might have been considered straying or sinful but never unnatural or perverted. I was free to pursue work without questions about my sexuality, as long as I remained discreet; but my lover and I were both fired from my collegiate alma mater for indiscretion. Even heterosexual liberation had its limits.

The third period of my work life was short, sweet, and quite different from the first two: I received a fellowship to study full-time for a Ph.D. degree in political science at Emory University in Atlanta. This was the culmination of a desire to complete my higher education after having received encouragement for such an endeavor both from reading Betty Friedan's *The Feminine Mystique* and in discussion with my partner.[2] By 1971 there was some openness to white women's studying political science, then a masculine-typed social science.

The fourth period of my paid work life was a consequence of my third: returning to Georgia State University to take a faculty position in the political science department. This was the only other time I faced a direct question about sexuality in relation to earning my living, and my response had significant personal political ramifications. In the obligatory interview with the university president, he asked me, "Are you single, and do you live alone?" He should not have asked, and I should not have had to answer. The university system also required candidates for faculty positions to answer a security questionnaire, which could be verified by follow-up investigations. The early 1970s, at least in the South, were still years of extreme sensitivity to communist infiltration, and I was asked to swear that I had never tried to overthrow the U.S. government. I was more concerned that investigators would find out that I was cohabiting with my partner, since I had answered "yes" to the question about living alone. Since both my partner and I were now divorced, out of fear I insisted that we either marry or establish separate residences. We decided to declare ourselves married under the common law, not wanting to submit to Georgia's statutory marriage. As soon as I reported that I was married, I found that the university system added my husband's last name to my name in my personnel records. I protested, to no avail, and had to spend money and time in court getting a decree that my legal name is Diane Lowe Fowlkes. This is in fact my first married name, since I did not want to return to my father's last name when I divorced. Heterosexuality and patriarchy have connecting roots, which I challenged only in part.

In the political science department I worked my way with difficulty but doggedly up the ranks to professor. The difficulties I encountered were in large part due not only to sexism but also to my ongoing commitment to integrate black studies, women's studies, and American Indian studies into my U.S. government courses and to my increasing involvement in the women's movement. I wanted to help create the new subfield of women and politics and beyond that women's studies. But there were not many in my department or in high places who supported my way of doing political science, even though I did the required research, publication, and conference participation. A few key people helped me gain eventual tenure and promotions.

This university was no different from other institutions of higher learning in being white-male-dominated, though as a public, urban university its constituency was similar to that of my own childhood, white working-to-lower-middle class, but beginning to desegregate racially. A number of younger white women were hired as I was in the early 1970s. Among these were several who joined together to start a women's studies group, which finally became the Women's Studies Institute following twenty long years of academic political struggle.

I consider women's studies to be an interdisciplinary field, a center for critiquing all the disciplines and professions and for envisioning more inclusive and less hierarchical ways of living in the cosmos (including everyday life on Earth). This admittedly grand vision stems from a recognition I had one day while on research leave in the fall of 1975. On a short trip to London to seek materials on women's movements in Europe, I had bought and immediately read Sheila Rowbotham's *Hidden From History: 300 Years of Women's Oppression and the Fight Against It.*[3] That book changed the way I walked into bookstores for the rest of my trip and the rest of my life. From it came my recognition that virtually every book in every other section of every bookstore was not inclusive of women's lives and perspectives and would have to be rewritten. Working to establish women's studies in my institution and making women's studies and the institution as inclusive as possible became a commitment that grew for me as a still-junior faculty member. I finally realized that I had not come this far on my own, although my parents had inculcated in me a strong strain of individualism. I would need to be part of a larger movement if I were to have any say in rewriting all those books.

The fifth and final period of my work life was the sweetest but also the bitterest. The sweetness was that I became director of the Women's Studies Institute, which continues to operate as a full-blown academic unit offering graduate and undergraduate degrees. I always considered women's studies to be the academic arm of the women's movement, and the civil rights and women's movements to be the basis of my own desire and ability to be an activist scholar. As women's studies itself became more self-critical and struggled to become more inclusive, it came to represent the academic arms of lesbian and civil rights movements as well.

My kinship with the civil rights movement went back to my years growing up and working in Memphis. I had cut my political teeth as that movement emerged while I was still in college and as it grew in intensity as I took my first secretarial job at my alma mater and then married the first time. During this period I began to diverge more and more from my parents; they turned right and I turned left. They joined the John Birch Society after the defeat of Barry Goldwater in the 1964 presidential election whereas I was protesting the shooting of civil rights activist James Meredith, or, later, standing in W. C. Handy Park on Beale Street with black men and women in peaceful demonstration against the war in Vietnam. When I left my first husband to move to Atlanta with my lover, still working as a secretary and beginning my graduate studies in political science, the women's movement became for me another branch of the struggle for justice. Without these movements and having been able to enact my beliefs through paid work, I would not be where I am today. While building a basis for retirement was the furthest thing from my mind, especially while working as a low-paid secretary but even as I began my career as a faculty member, I learned from other women during the fight to ratify the Equal Rights Amendment that it was important to do as much as possible to prepare financially for the years after I no longer drew a paycheck. Without our movements and the changes they wrought, my Social Security earnings record would resemble a gentle incline rather than an upward spiral, because the only kinds of jobs open to white women would have remained low-income ones. The content of my work might have continued to be interesting, but I would not have had the status to help create a program within academia intended to transform education and society.

But why would I retire early, having finally reached the pinnacle of my desires? I retired early because, worn down and embittered, I had lost my long-standing optimism that women's studies could make a difference at Georgia State. When the Women's Studies Institute emerged from long years of institutional politics, I thought we had accomplished the ultimate, only to find that while we had gained administrative validation, getting necessary budget nourishment to grow was another battle, despite their commitments on paper. In order to fight on, we forged links to other women's studies programs and to local feminists, grassroots organizations, and state legislators. In response to a local activist representing herself and others, the Women's Studies Institute, with cooperation from the Special Collections Department of the library, established the Georgia Women's Movement Project, which includes library archives of personal and organizational papers, oral histories, institute fellowships, and visiting distinguished lecturers. I have given my papers, endowed a fellowship, and still serve on the advisory committee for the project. This is the project over which I ultimately clashed with the university before retiring.

The final blow came in the university's new focus on development. After I fought to get the institute recognized as a legitimate player in the university's first major capital campaign and we established the Georgia Women's Movement Project, our lead donors were insulted by the vice president for development (and did not make their gifts for three more years). In turn I felt insulted. My dean told me not to take it personally, but I felt the administration was treating both my life and women's studies with disrespect. The working environment by then felt so toxic to me that I decided to leave it. I knew others in or associated with the institute could and would carry on our battle. Having personally reached a point of no longer being able to work in the university setting, I knew it was time for me to take my ideas and connections with other feminists into retirement and continue my life's work of rewriting the books.

How Rewriting the Books Will Help Me Live in Retirement

I headed into retirement with the idea that I was going on a long sabbatical, funded by my university retirement plan in the near term, by Social Security beginning at age sixty-two, and by my supplemental retirement account beginning at age sixty-five. I had planned with my husband to build a dream house on St. George Island, Florida, where we had been vacationing for over twenty years; and we were able to accomplish that before I retired. We made that home our primary residence.

We also bought a small condo in Ocala, in the heart of thoroughbred horse country in Florida, because we had three mares and a stallion in partnership, boarding on a farm there. I have to backtrack to explain how our romance with horses provided a way to get away from academic pressures. From the late 1980s on, we had gotten involved in a small way in the business of breeding, selling, and racing thoroughbred horses, as we both had loved horses since early childhood. Prior to retirement, my interest in horses gave me a way to get far from Georgia State; I traveled to racetracks from upstate New York and the Jersey Shore to Kentucky and Florida, becoming a small-businesswoman in the process. One of the most thrilling moments was on Kentucky Derby Day in 1991, when our group had a two-year-old colt in a small-stakes race before the big race. Never Wavering won! But even before the races began for the day, I was able to walk on the track at Churchill Downs, from the stables on the back side to our seats in the clubhouse, looking up at the Twin Spires and thinking that here was a childhood dream that I had thought would never be realized.

When I left Georgia State and we left Atlanta, I was more than ready to change gears. My husband continued a research project while I took charge of our moving and establishing residence because I felt more adept at it—still the administrator. But mainly I reveled in the freedom to establish my own schedule, reading and writing without pressure from deadlines. Finally living in a house that could accommodate visitors, I invited good friends from England, also recently retired, for a two-month visit over Thanksgiving, Christmas, and the New Year: he to practice his dream of making furniture by crafting cypress bookcases for our new house, and she to write a commissioned piece. In addition to one another's company and reports on work in progress, we enjoyed good food and wine and beautiful scenery. We saw bald eagles and great horned owls and ospreys regularly. We took up the mantra of others living on the island: "another day in paradise." We all did something to preserve the fragile environment of the area by answering a call from local activists to join in founding the Apalachicola Bay and River Keeper. This was like the ultimate sabbatical I had longed for. After our friends left, I continued to savor the afterglow of our idyll.

But suddenly that dream ended. First, in a routine health check at a local grocery store in the spring of 1999, I learned that my blood pressure was dangerously high. I was shocked that this could happen to me when I no longer lived in the pressure cooker of Georgia State. I had been taking low doses of hormone replacement therapy (HRT) for five years, ostensibly to prevent heart disease in menopause, but in reading back through my women's health books I found that hypertension is a possible side effect. I decided to stop HRT, but now another doctor was prescribing medications to control blood pressure. I also had to confront the idea that my vitality might be lessening.

Then, that fall, my husband descended quite rapidly into a severe anxiety disorder and depression as his blood pressure medication, Serapes, failed. It contained reserpine, a dangerous depressant, but his doctors over the years kept him on it. As his depression progressed, he went through a stage of feeling inordinate guilt and seeking forgiveness. That included telling me that he had been unfaithful to me with several other women and asking me to forgive him. In the distant past he had seemed to be flirtatious with other women. Of course, he had been unfaithful to his first wife and family, as I had been unfaithful to my then husband. But on a trip to the Kentucky Derby in 1994, in the same period that I was becoming director of the newly established Women's Studies Institute, I had discovered, while searching his briefcase for a horse-related item, a recent letter from a Boston woman he had met while on sabbatical in England thirteen years earlier. Back then, I had discovered a postcard to him from this woman suggesting some kind of relationship more than an academic friendship. I had complained, been told by him that he would stop corresponding with her, and had believed him; so when I found the letter I was more than shocked and dismayed. I felt betrayed and bereft of my soul mate. I had finally decided to stay in the marriage rather than expend more energy than I had on dissolving the relationship, which by then felt mainly economic. We had gradually arrived at a working companionship by the time I retired.

But now I was so distressed by his condition that I said I forgave him. Little did I realize then that I was going to be his full-time caregiver for an indeterminate number of years. I sought the help of a friend to drive him the 225 miles to Ocala so that he could be nearer all the needed medical facilities for as long as necessary. His depression has lifted somewhat because of medications and hospitalization, but his anxiety disorder continues and he has also developed symptoms of Alzheimer's and Parkinson's diseases. I am now learning that Medicare and Medigap insurance really work, at least for his acute-care medical needs; but I am also learning what constant attention to caregiving entails for me. I have had to give up living in two places, to sell both the island house and the city condo, and to buy a house in Ocala that is proving to be amenable to both our needs. Whereas he had declined to the point that I was going to use his long-term care insurance to support his living in a nursing home, the change of physical environment to a new one-story house has made it possible for him to regain sufficient control of his functions for me to take care of his basic needs at home.

Long ago I chose not to bear children (and feel privileged and fortunate not to have done so). Ironically I now have a "child." Except that this childlike person will not be able to grow up. When my husband is not resting, he asks what he should be doing—in effect asking me to live his life for him while I am also trying to live my own life. He watches the clock, acutely conscious that time is slipping away. And the questions go on, day after day, with no capacity for a learning curve: when are we going to eat, what are we going to eat, are we going to have dessert? Along with time, food is his most basic interest, and I feel that I am being asked to provide it on demand. Occasionally he throws in a wry comment or initiates a small conversation, and he has regained some ability to help with a few chores. I have learned to set a boundary between, on the one hand, taking care of his physical needs for food and cleanliness and, on the other, securing time and space for my own needs. I remind myself that I am learning some of the things that can go wrong in the human brain and that this could happen to me. I also remind both of us that I will not survive to care for him if I do not care for myself.

For myself, in addition to trying to keep up with the outpouring of women's studies scholarship, I have taken on a project of self-education in philosophy with the help of a feminist philosopher friend. Learning philosophy will take the rest of my life and feeds my writing projects. Currently I am working in the area of epistemology on a philosophy of identity politics: why it is important for a writer/speaker to acknowledge and connect various aspects of her identity to her subject matter. I send what I am writing to my Atlanta writers' group as well as to a few other friends, all of whom read and respond to it. And I reciprocate for them. Reading and writing with my friends is keeping me alive.

One of my ongoing personal-political issues revolves around how caregiving has restricted the freedom that I along with others have struggled to achieve. Now, yet again, the feminist critique of society is borne out as I read the long-term care insurance policy and the Medicare acute-care-focused rules and try to find satisfactory help from home health and other senior services: there is a pervasive underlying assumption that women's work is caring for others but not for ourselves. I have been most heartened by the response of many who express as much concern for me as for my husband when I tell them how sick he is. I am still learning how to receive help when it means that I might have to change some of my own routines. Yet I am appalled that so many care providers are low-paid women with their own families to support. Somehow I have to find a way to connect to organized others who have already been addressing these issues. In the meantime, I need to reconstruct what modicum of freedom I can.

Another issue is the contradictory nature of my enactment of feminism in relation to my husband. Raw feeling makes me ask how I let myself get caught in a subservient position of caregiver to someone I now wish I had left when I discovered one of his betrayals. Recognition of the complexity of human relationships leads me to reflect that I exercised my choice then, too loath to give up certain economic advantages of a two-person household and too proud to admit to friends that our relationship was not what it appeared. Was I still saddled, after all the years of involvement in the women's movement, with that good girl image, by which I think white middle-class heterosexual women, especially, are judged in order to be kept in place? Compassion is a form of love that I would do well to learn how to practice—for others and for myself.

As a feminist, how do I make sense of all this? Can I? If others and I thought we needed women's studies to help us survive in academia, not to mention transforming it and society, then now I need women's studies to help me understand how to get through this stage of my life. As often happens, I have found a book that seems relevant to my dilemma: Eva Feder Kittay's *Love's Labor: Essays on Women, Equality, and Dependency*. She claims that theories of democratic equality have failed to take into account "the fact of human dependency [of infants, small children, and sick elders] and the role of women in tending to dependent persons." In fact, she could be listening in to my inner conversation about freedom when she says, "The encounter with dependency is, I believe, rarely welcome to those fed on an ideological diet of freedom, self-sufficiency, *and* equality."[4] Studying this book is my next homework assignment.

My grand vision, as my life, has segued into a more limited place for myself and a more limited idea of what I can do. But writing this essay has made me realize that I am still in women's movement, following my vision of rewriting all those books.

Acknowledgments

I gratefully acknowledge the encouragement of Eloise A. Buker to write about caregiving in retirement and the constructive criticism of earlier drafts of this essay by M. Charlene Ball, Linda A. Bell, Valerie Fennell, Susan Ryley

Hoyle, Elizabeth W. Knowlton, Gayle Lloyd, Karen J. Maschke, and Elizabeth A. Ware.

Notes

1. Adrienne Rich, "Compulsory Heterosexuality and Lesbian Existence," *Signs: Journal of Women in Culture and Society* 5, no. 4 (summer 1980): 631–660.

2. Betty Friedan, *The Feminine Mystique* (New York: W. W. Norton, 1963).

3. Sheila Rowbotham, *Hidden From History: 300 Years of Women's Oppression and the Fight against It* (London: Pluto Press, 1974).

4. Eva Feder Kittay, *Love's Labor: Essays on Women, Equality and Dependency* (New York: Routledge, 1999), 4–5.

Doc Finds Happiness in Arts Community

DORIS GOLDBERG

Retiring from my work as a physician in the New York City Health Department has felt freeing, like taking off a suit of clothing that constrained, chafed, no longer fit me right. Being able to live in a small town that is supportive of artists and applying myself to painting and printmaking has felt to me like putting on a looser garment that allows freer movement and lets some of my feelings show—a much better fit for me in my sixties.

There is still the physician in me, however, and I have not discarded some of the concerns and skeptical thinking I acquired during my training and work years. Retirement from a professional role necessitates small shifts in attitude. An important shift comes from not having to respond to demands for decision making and adhering to a schedule. For example, when a friend comes to me with a medical/health problem, I am more aware of the need for consultation and opinions about a full range of options and more removed from the pseudo-urgency of following through on the first opinion.

Entering Medicine

A medical education in the mid 1950s challenged my notions of how to learn as well as what I wanted to learn. My schooling had started in a secular, progressive Jewish day school in Queens, New York, with happy summers spent at the Ethical Culture School Camp in Cooperstown, New York. When my family moved upstate to Albany, I attended a middle school and then a high school attached to a teacher training college. The intellectual and feminist attitudes that were nurtured by my mother were scorned in this environment. My identification with my father's democratic/liberal politics was considered communist, and Jewish observance and interests were seen as strange. I entered puberty at age ten and was interested in boys, but I felt unpopular and peculiar. In high school I felt more alien and isolated.

I went to a Seven Sisters college on scholarships, and although I continued to feel marginal to the mainstream, many of my intellectual and expressive abilities were strengthened, and I made some lasting friendships. Supportive recommendations from my college, rather than any shining academic achievement, helped me get into medical school at age twenty. My choice to go to medical school was prompted by my mother having a nervous breakdown when I was in my sophomore year in college. Her illness and hospitalization greatly troubled me; somehow I thought that I could gain greater understanding, control, and be more useful in the world at large by becoming a doctor. I also thought it would be desirable for me to relate to people from an occupational vantage point of authority and information. I was interested in making art, too, and at certain times I hoped I could combine my interests by becoming a medical illustrator, but it became evident that this would not satisfy my interest in either field. I remember going for medical school interviews and being asked: "What would you do if your child was about to have a fifth birthday party and you were called by a patient who needed you?" and "Why does a pretty girl like you want to do this?" The implication of these remarks was clearly that there was inherent conflict for a female between wanting a family and becoming a doctor. No wonder there were only four women in my medical class of ninety when I entered Boston University School of Medicine in 1953.

The expectation of medical students in those days was that a certain percentage of the class would be flunked out before the preclinical years were finished. There was great anxiety about passing exams and a lack of clarity about the context of our learning. I did not have experience working in the field of medicine to guide me, and I rebelled at learning only to pass exams. So I tried to combat the anxiety of being flunked out with the bravado of organizing the information into some kind of functional context rather than rote memorization. This seemed to work for me because after two years I was able to transfer to a medical school in New York City where my husband-to-be was a settlement house social worker and camp director.

New York University Medical School had a larger class (approximately 110 students) with 10 female students, most of whom were married. The clinical training took place mainly at Bellevue Hospital. The atmosphere was competitive, fast paced, and academic, with an enormous class gap between physicians and patients. There were many kinds of institutional rules imposed on medical decision making. There would be debates in midwinter, for example, about how many alcoholic men could be admitted from the emergency room for warmth and shelter if they did not have severe pneumonia. Such dilemmas upset me and made absorbing as much medical information as I could seem less important than creating a more equitable social system. Thus, I entered a rotating internship ill prepared for being a fully active young doctor. My naïveté was taken advantage of, and I was placed in situations where I would learn and be humiliated at the same time. For example, I was sent to the home of an orthodox Jewish family to ask for an autopsy consent when it was against their religious practice; on another occasion I was ordered to remove a huge amount of fluid from a patient's abdomen when a more moderate amount would have been a more conservative approach, both for the patient and myself.

Training

When I finished my internship and became a licensed physician, I was still uncertain of what I wanted to do in medicine and how it would fit with the life that my husband and I wanted. A friend told me of an ambulatory care fellowship in pediatrics at New York Hospital that combined pediatric care with advising parents about the developmental and social concerns of raising children, a program that Dr. Benjamin Spock and other child advocates had been involved with. The fellowship helped me find a clinical role that was intellectually stimulating and also provided gratifying interaction with children and parents and colleagues who shared mutual interests.

Then, unexpectedly, at age twenty-eight, I experienced a confluence of losses that stunned and devastated me. I developed toxemia early in my first pregnancy and was hospitalized for several months; the baby was born prematurely and died in the first two days of life. Four months later, my parents were in an auto accident in which my mother was killed and my father left paralyzed. Eight months after this, my husband was killed in a different auto accident caused by a moment's distraction from the road. At the time of his death I again had toxemia, with my second pregnancy, and delivered my daughter a few weeks later. She weighed one and a half pounds and after three and a half months in a preemie unit was discharged home.

I found myself overeducated but without great employment opportunities in which I could earn a living for my infant daughter and myself. I decided to finish my pediatric residency training because after this specialty training I could have better choices of work. My emotional state as well as my identification with children and parents caused me to feel at odds from some of my training experiences at that time. I remember being dismayed and angry during my rotation on the Sloan Kettering Pediatric Service. Not only did children suffer the treatments for leukemia but young families would incur huge debts to have their child treated at a prestigious institution—for a disease that in those days had no cure. A pediatrician whom I greatly admired for her clinical acumen and warm manner also dismayed me when she returned from having her baby in the standard two-week vacation time allocated for staff rather than asking for any special consideration that would set her apart from the male physicians. I distanced myself from much that I was participating in.

Working

My emotional and work life greatly improved in subsequent years. I remarried after several years of widowhood and gave birth to another daughter under much happier circumstances. I did clinical work in ambulatory pediatrics that was both hospital and community based. In the 1960s I followed a friend/colleague into the New York City Health Department. The assignment she gave me was to complete a developmental screening test that could identify young children and their parents who were having serious problems so that they might get some help prior to school entry. This was the right challenge and opportunity for me. I decided to continue to work in the Health Department. For over ten years I served as medical director of the large network of child health stations that offered free, prevention-oriented health care to preschool children in the five boroughs. I took pride in providing a free service to the public and was convinced that the quality and comprehensiveness of the service were good by the standards of the time.

However, the department became increasingly politicized. Its structure was considered passé, and the wisdom of providing service without imposing a fee was seriously questioned. I went on to do other things in the department that I found rewarding, including getting a degree in public health from Columbia University and training doctors in public health and preventive medicine in a joint residency training program run by the department and the university. I enjoyed working in the departmental network of colleagues. However, after over twenty years of being in a political bureaucracy, I became fatigued by the endless forms that needed to be filled out and the constraints of political and fiscal expediency that had to be satisfied. At age sixty-two, I happily took an early retirement plan that was offered.

Retirement

Retirement has allowed me to shift my activities, expand my thinking and social relationships, and rely on myself to organize my time. It has also meant changing where I live to a small community from the bustling and anonymous Big Apple. When I took a watercolor class in Woodstock, New York, one summer in the 1990s, I learned about Woodstock's history as an arts and crafts town as well as its current art school and artists' association. I was struck by the beauty of the natural surroundings, as well as the feeling of openness and tolerance in the town. I bought a house in the village and when I retired in 1995 I became a full-time transplant from Manhattan.

Retirement gave me the time to pursue my interests in making art without the necessity of earning a living from it. Painting and printmaking had been pleasures in my childhood years, and I had seriously considered going to art school rather than medical school. For several years prior to my retirement I had taken painting classes at the Art Students League as well as classes in Chinese brushwork.

After attending classes at the Woodstock School of Art and becoming an active member of the Woodstock Artists' Association, I am looking forward to mounting a solo show at the association's gallery. So far, I have exhibited in many of the juried shows there, which change every five or six weeks throughout the year. I also share interests with other artists in the community and will soon be investing in a monotype print press with a local artist and friend.

For someone from New York City, it is particularly sweet to walk down the street and meet and greet people rather than trying to avoid eye contact. There is a friendliness that prevails. When I had a bout of bronchitis last winter, a new acquaintance phoned early one morning to announce that she made very good Chinese matzo ball soup and would I like some? Before I knew it, my doorbell was ringing! I know of the opinions held by other Woodstockers on matters affecting the town, since the local newspaper has a generous letters-to-the-editor policy. There are many communal events taking place as well as cultural and recreational events that I find stimulating and informative. There are weekends when it is difficult to choose between attractive offerings: a chamber music concert vs. a play reading vs. a lecture by a visiting journalist at a local college.

My medical interests have led me to participate in a grassroots group called the Mid-Hudson Options Project that educates and advocates for breast cancer patients. The mission of the project is to present the full range of effective treatment options to patients, not only the mainstream medical therapies. Although proof of effectiveness is still a matter of scientific rigor for me, I feel open to reviewing the evidence of non-Western healing practices (such as herbal remedies and acupuncture) and believe in the importance of supporting patients to become active in making medical decisions in their own best interest.

My medical perspective has also been influenced by the serious mental problems of close loved ones. My mother had chronic depression and then Alzheimer's dementia at the time of her death. My second husband also struggled with depression. My older daughter has been trying to achieve independence with severe dyslexia and bipolar illness. Their experiences have taught me the importance of persistence, clarity, and hopefulness in adjusting to life with chronic and debilitating difficulties.

Retirement has been a very good period of my life. I am grateful for my health and energy and the many circles in my community that welcome me to join them. I am grateful that I can bring things of value from my past into my present life. Reflection has given me a clearer sense of myself and this is a process that continues.

Does an Activist Ever Retire?

CAROLYN GOODMAN
(INTERVIEWED BY
ROSALYN BAXANDALL)

*C*arolyn Goodman, eighty-six, is a psychologist and lifelong social activist. She is the director of the Andrew Goodman Foundation, which was founded to carry on the hopes and dreams of one of her sons, who was murdered while working for civil rights in Mississippi in 1964. This interview took place in March and October 2001.

RB: Why don't we start with your telling us about the work you did before you officially retired?

CG: Officially retired? What's that? I don't think there's a day I've ever officially retired. I left my last job about five years ago. I worked at Bronx Psychiatric Center, as a psychologist, where I started an interesting program back in the sixties. It was for mothers who had either been hospitalized or who had been outpatients at a state psychiatric center, and who had children who were five years of age or younger. The program was called PACE, which stood for Parent and Child Education. The idea was to prevent the children of these women from being hospitalized by helping the women, who were abused and neglected themselves. The idea was to help them understand child development and how important it was to provide their children with care, love, and tolerance. It turned out to be a program that won awards and was replicated all over the world, as far away as Australia. It was a very unusual program and it was only there because the head of the psychiatric center was a marvelous man, a community psychiatrist who welcomed this kind of a program. I remember having visitors from other psychiatric centers who said, "How come you have children and adults in the same program? That's unheard of." Well, it was really nontraditional in every sense of the word. It was a wonderful experience.

RB: How long were you in this job?

CG: The program operated for about twenty years and, interestingly enough, I still see some of the women and have made some really wonderful friendships. One woman in particular calls me often. Not too long ago, I was arrested because I was picketing in front of the New York City police headquarters, and this woman who was in the program and one of the most difficult mothers called me up. We're friends, but she never called me anything except Dr. Goodman. She said, "I was so worried when I heard that you were arrested." I said, "It was because I absolutely refused to move." This was during the Amadou Dialo case, the man who was shot forty-one times by the New York police and we were picketing. Susan Sarandon, the movie actress, was there, and we didn't move when we were told to, so we were taken in the paddy wagon and we were booked and fingerprinted. It was a farce; we were never tried and the case was dropped. But she was worried about me because she heard that I was arrested. She was one of the most difficult women in this program that I ran. I'll give you an example of what I am talking about. She had three little girls, she was a very intelligent woman, she was incredibly disturbed because she herself had been abused and neglected, and she had no tolerance for the children, whatsoever. It wasn't that she didn't understand how to handle them, but she, herself, was upset and she would be very abusive. We were talking one day and she was looking away from me. She had absolutely no use for me, whatsoever. She thought I had no idea what pain was, what it was to suffer, and she thought I was just kind of a rich bitch who was doing this work as kind of a charity or some such thing. And then she noticed a little book that I had on a bookcase in my room. It was a memorial book for my son, Andrew Goodman. And then she turned back and looked at me for the first time, looked at me in the eye and said, "Andrew Goodman, was he a relative of yours?" And I said, "Yes, he was my son." Well, she broke down and cried and got up out of her chair and hugged me. It was an epiphany! From that moment on, we really became friends. There was just a total change in her life and she was able to be responsive. That was the kind of thing that would happen with many of the women. I approached them not as patients, they were never called patients, they were mothers, and that's what they were called. It was a wonderful experience.

RB: What was your educational background?

CG: I waited to return to school until my kids were in their teens and were pretty much able to manage themselves. I started part-time while they were at school. They didn't object in the least. I started my psychology master's in 1959, but I was interrupted a few times. In 1964, when my son Andy went to Mississippi, I just dropped everything and for a while I just couldn't even think about studying. We didn't know immediately that he had been killed. We thought that he was in jail, because nobody knew where these boys were until an informer of the FBI was paid and then he told them. My husband, Bobby Goodman, and I did everything to try to find out where they were and a way of reaching them. We actually got quite a few phone calls at that time from people who were trying to get us to leave bail money at such and such a place to bail them out. They'd say, "We know you're very rich and have lots of jewelry." Many horrid things happened. I was so frozen as far as those kinds of calls because I was willing to do anything to get the boys free. Of course, it's all history now and we now know that they were murdered immediately. So at that time my studies had been dropped, as there was nothing that I could concentrate on except that.

RB: But you were able to return to school at some point.

CG: Well, I went back because the head of the department at Columbia University was a wonderful man. He said to me that even though terrible things impact your life and remain with you, you must not let that change your whole life. He urged me to go on with my studies. So, I took his word that this was going to be important. My wonderful husband supported me at the time, so I did go back to college after Andy was found. I tell people that the whole thing took me twenty years. I began in '59 and then stopped for a while at the time of Andy's death. Then I went back and then there was this whole period of student upheaval in '68 at Columbia. I was part of that. I didn't want to go through the lines when the kids were out there picketing and so I was there with them! I was not a kid then but I was very much supportive of what was happening at the time. So I stayed away from classes too. When that was all over I went back. I didn't get my doctorate until the late 1970s.

RB: What was your major at Columbia?

CG: I studied psychology which is no accident in terms of my early life. I just wanted to know more about human relations and how I could help other people who are having troubles. My sensitivity to them is one thing, but it's important to have some academic knowledge and the study of psychology will provide that.

I got my master's degree in psychology and was able to do some work in the field. I didn't particularly want a Ph.D., but a wonderful professor said, "Look, you're going to want more than this; you're going to want to work with people in a way that a master's degree will not allow you to work with them. You better go to school and get your doctorate." Psychology is a different field than social work. In psychology, they are very restricted and kind of snobbish; you have to have a doctorate degree in order to introduce a new kind of idea or program. After I got my doctorate, I wrote the proposal for the PACE job.

RB: When did you leave the PACE job and why?

CG: Well, everything has to end. I did some other work in a developmental center in the Bronx, and then I went on to do some other kinds of work. It was a period of time when I was just sort of gathering my thoughts and didn't know exactly what I was going to do or what path I was going to take.

Retiring wasn't that hard. I thought about it for a while and prepared myself by trying to work for some causes. I tried a few things. Working, for example, for the Fortune Society with ex-offenders, trying to do some counseling, where my training in psychology came in very handy. My retirement was also connected to the death of my second husband, Joe. This just added to all the other losses I had. Andy and then Bobby Goodman and Joe; it was just a lot, too much. Joe's death was sudden. We had been out walking on a beautiful Sunday afternoon in May, we had come back and he was just resting, and he said he had terrible pain. I called an ambulance and they came over and tried to resuscitate him. I didn't know he was as bad as he was. They put him in the ambulance and took him to the hospital, and he was dead when they got there. It was just incredibly sudden, like that—an hour later. All the deaths, every single solitary one of them, my father, my mother, my son, and my husbands—all I could do was just lie on my bed and think of all that loss. What is there to live for?

About that time I realized I needed some kind of help. I've always been a self-help kind of person. I had always worked on that basis at the hospital with a lot of the clients. Well, it didn't work at that point. It was just too much for me. So I met a wonderful man who doesn't call himself a therapist; he calls himself part of a support network. I still see him now and then. He was just marvelous; he was absolutely the person I needed. I realized at that time that it was important for me to get into something, and he helped me see that there was another route that I could take. That's when I really started working with young people.

I decided that I wanted to do something with young people and get into some work that was a little bit more political. So, I managed to meet some young people who were filmmakers—now I'm not a filmmaker, but you don't have to be one to make a film. I got a young producer who had never made a film before and an assistant producer, a cameraman, and a soundman, and all the people that you have to get together. I became the executive producer, which meant that I raised the money and got the people to do the work, and we made a film. It was called *Hidden Heroes: Youth Activism Today*. The film took about five years to make because we had to stop while I raised the money for it. We went all over the country making it. The film is only a twenty-five-minute documentary, but it's rather a powerful one about young people who are doing some remarkable things, such as organizing for quality education in a small town in Mississippi or young people who are doing peer counseling or who are working for ecology, AIDS education, or condoms in the high schools. We filmed young people all over the country and it was very expensive. I always felt in whatever work that I've done, I don't want to ask people, especially young people, to do things for nothing. Although I felt that they were novices, I felt that they should be paid, so I raised the money through the Andrew Goodman Foundation, which was founded a couple of years after Andy was murdered by the Klan in 1964.

The film shows that even though people don't see a movement today, like the one in the sixties that Andy was part of, there still is a lot going on. It shows that the media makes it out that all kids are violent and consumer hungry, but there are others who are changing the world in a positive way. So, the film is now available and it's being sold to schools and colleges, synagogues, churches, community centers and given away, where people cannot afford to buy it. Anyone can get *Hidden Heroes* by contacting the Goodman Foundation at 161 West 86th Street, New York, NY 10024. I have been going all over the country, showing the film and talking about it. The film has won several awards and has been shown at festivals.

RB: What do you say when you show the film?

CG: It varies with the group. For example, if it's a young group that I show the film to, I don't like to do a lot of talking. I like to ask them if they have questions about what I've shown them. It is so interesting to know that even people in their thirties and forties who might be the organizers don't know who Paul Robeson is. That sometimes shatters me. Here's a man who represented so much in this country, an actor, a singer, a scholar, and a lawyer. I knew him, but you don't have to know someone personally to know the name and to know what his achievements were. People say, " Paul Robeson? No, I never heard of him." I feel in many ways that what I'm doing is educational— even missionary—because the young people I speak with, speak with their parents or somebody else. They don't know some of the giants of our time who changed what happened in the world overnight. These heroes opened doors for others to enter.

RB: I know you continue to be very involved with social activism. Maybe you could describe a typical week in your life?

CG: I don't know if there is a typical week, it varies so. Tomorrow, for example, I'm going to the Brooklyn Academy of Music. The education department is doing a project on prejudice. They're going to be showing a Sidney Poitier film that was made about thirty-five years ago, *In the Heat of the Night*, and the film that I made. They'll bring in a whole bunch of young people from public schools in Brooklyn. They will see the two films and then there will be discussion. I'll be doing that tomorrow and in the weeks to come I'll be speaking up in Boston, using the film as a stepping-stone. I'll be speaking in the Southampton [N.Y.] schools and in the Parish Art Museum in Southampton. I'll be speaking up in Provincetown [on] Cape Cod at a film festival, so there's very little time in between the talks.

When the summer comes, I will take a little bit of respite. I'll go out in the direction of the Hamptons, where I hope to find some quiet time and write a book. People have been asking me to do this for a long time, and I think I'm going to do it if I can just stop some of the other activities. The world that I've lived in has had a big impact on the path that I've taken in my life, and I've had some impact on the world that I've lived in. I've had some time to think about it, and my life has been stormy and a lot has happened.

RB: Give us some idea of what you mean by "a lot has happened."

CG: I've had a lot of losses; I've had a lot of wonderful things happen. I've lost two husbands and I've lost a son. After my sons' father died, I was married for twenty years to a wonderful man. I've lost other important people in my life, including my parents, but one expects that. One of the things that you don't expect to happen is the loss of a child. The wound of Andy's death is always with me. It's a wound that has a scar tissue, but it's always there. There's this wonderful picture of Andy in the living room. It's not a morbid thing; it's not draped with all kinds of flags, or what have you. It's just a wonderful photograph of my son and grandson and there's my granddaughter, and it's, well . . . he's my child. Andy's life and his death were ennobling. It's not the kind of thing that I go around mourning.

This morning I got a call from the Washington correspondent for the *Toronto Globe and Mail* because there is going to be a new trial down in Mississippi. This reporter said, "Look, you've lived through a whole, long era and I don't expect you to remember me," but I did. He was from the Jewish community, and there were certain things that he would remember about the Holocaust, which others who were down in Mississippi wouldn't remember. The man who is doing the story when it comes to trial, Michael Moore, doesn't know about the background of the Jewish boys and so forth. So, he wanted to get my view on things. I said I felt that the important issue was that justice be done after so many years. The men who killed the three boys were jailed for a slap on the wrist and for violation of civil rights. The killers should be tried for murder. Justice will not have been done until that trial comes up. So, now there is going to be a trial. I don't know when it's going to come up, but I know that it is not going to be easy, especially if I'm called down there. Now what the outcome will be, I don't know and who can predict, but at least they should be tried. I'm not a masochist; I won't go if I'm not called. I don't want to be there and have to live through it if I don't have to. I live through it anyhow. But if I have to go, I will, and it'll be like opening a wound. If need be, my son will come with me. But that's how it is and how life is. I guess the analogy is like the stock market; life has its ups and it has its downs. Maybe a better analogy is that it's like the sea when you're on a boat: it goes up and it goes down. I've been on a lot of boats.

RB: Let's go back to some other examples of your activities—how about a typical day?

CG: I get up very early, and I might clean up my house because kids are coming here. I don't have a lot of help because I don't like to have a lot of people around, cleaning up and doing things. These are the ordinary, mundane things that I do.

I'm involved with an education project called Curriculum Arts Project that brings artists to public schools. Artists come in with music or drama or we take kids to museums. We had a meeting in my apartment last week and some of the kids had never been to a museum and they talked about what their feelings were when they saw some wonderful paintings. It was so exciting and wonderful for them; these were Hispanic and Italian kids. They went home and told their parents about it. I'm very involved with this Curriculum Arts Project. I have this large apartment and people say what do you need it for? I need it because I have meetings here. I have young people coming here. For example, we had a group of kids all gather here to go to a school in Brooklyn where they were doing a history project.

I have so many things going. I am very involved with Symphony Space, which is quite a wonderful place. It's a community-based arts center here on the Upper West Side, and it's a place where people come for many different kinds of experiences. It's not like going to Lincoln Center, although that has its place; I'm not knocking it. I've been involved with Symphony Space since its inception, which was back in the seventies. When I moved into the neighborhood about thirty years ago it was this broken-down movie house. Then these two men bought it for very little and renovated it for practically nothing. One day, I was walking up the street and I saw a prominent violinist walking up Broadway. In those days, you didn't see anybody like that walking up Broadway. I decided to follow him. He walked into this old movie house. I'm wondering, What's going on here? I followed him in and I saw the place full of people. It said "Wall-to-Wall Bach" on the marquee. It was a fantastic program, twelve hours of Bach, top rate! I sat there all day, walked out, got a sandwich, and came back and stayed for twelve hours . . . great performances. I called up the next day and asked what was happening there, and they explained to me that it was now taken over and called Symphony Space. I said that I would love to support it in any way I could, maybe raise money for it.

I was never a professional fundraiser, but I have raised millions of dollars by just calling people and saying, "This is a great thing, and I have a foundation if you want to give to it or give to this nonprofit organization, et cetera." I said, "What do you need?" They told me that the sound wasn't so good and that they needed acoustic panels. I said, "Well, how much will that be?" The general manager and the artistic director came here to the house and said, "If you can raise $15,000 for these panels, we'll call them the Andrew Goodman acoustic panels." I said, "Great!" I raised the $15,000, they asked if I wanted to be on the board, and that's how I got involved and have been involved ever since.

Yesterday I went over to Hunter College for the Jim Aronson Awards. He was a journalist who started a progressive paper called *The Guardian*. I'm a good friend of his widow, who's a great woman. Then I came home, saturated because it was so rainy out, and had time to get a bite. I left to go see *Judgment at Nuremburg*. I got home at about 10:00 P.M., and then finished up the work that I didn't do earlier in the day, because I was in and out all day. I got to bed around midnight, watched the news, and that's my day yesterday.

I'm going all the time, trying to think about all these different involvements. Later I have to prepare for tomorrow at the Brooklyn Academy of Music. Tonight I'm going to go out with a friend of mine to see this film, *Enemy at the Gate*, that is, I understand, not such a great version of *Saving Private Ryan*. So, I do get time for recreation, but it's a long day.

RB: The activism of your retirement has really been a continuation of the activism that you've been engaged in your whole life. Now you do it full-time. What keeps you at it?

CG: Let's see if I can put it this way: When I actually did retire from my professional life, and after Andy and after both my husbands died, I was lying in bed one morning and I was feeling depressed and I thought, "What's the use? I've had all these losses and I'm retired from my work and all the things that were me and all the people that I loved are gone—you know, what's the use? Does it make sense?" And I thought about something that hadn't occurred to me for a long time. When I was about nine years old, I went to camp. I had been brought up in Long Island and I used to swim in the ocean. I was a pretty good swimmer, but I couldn't swim long distances; I was never able to do that. So, I went to a camp that had an enclosed swimming area for kids called a crib. If you wanted to go out into the lake, onto the dock, or jump off the diving board, you had to pass a "red cap" test. The counselors would get in a rowboat, and you'd have to swim out to a point and back, and then you would wear a red cap and be allowed out of the swimming crib. So, I was in camp for about a week when I said I'd like to take the red cap test. The counselor said, "Are you sure? You've only been here for a week." Being a big shot, I said I wanted to take it. So I swam out to the point and did fine, but on the way back I started to huff and puff, because I never could swim long distances. So, they said, "Come on, get in the boat and try again next week." I kept swimming. They said, "Come on; you're huffing and puffing, you'd better get in." I kept thinking to myself, "Carolyn, it's not going to get any easier next week, keep going." And I kept huffing and puffing, and I said to myself, "Now Carol, put one arm over the other, don't stop because if you do, it's going to be just as hard next week." The counselor was in one ear saying, "Get in the boat, get in the boat." I kept saying to myself, "Place one arm over the other, keep going." I finally made it to the end, and I passed the test. So, when I was lying in bed that morning, that thought came to me. I thought, "Look, are you going to let this get you down? You've got those nine grandchildren, you've really got a life, you've got to find it. Put one arm over the other and keep going." That's what I did. I got some help from this wonderful therapist, and I made it. But it was a tough struggle. I really felt as if I was sinking, but through sheer force of will and with some support I made it.

RB: And you have good friends who have been supportive?

CG: Yes. I had dinner the other night with a marvelous woman who is going to be ninety-three years old; she is totally fantastic! She married this wonderful man and became very progressive. She went to Spain; she climbed the Pyrenees to get to France, to get away from Franco. She is ninety-three and she still works; she's a social worker. That is quite marvelous. She lives in Vermont, practices in Boston, and has this beautiful apartment on Eighth Street and Fifth Avenue [in New York City]. We met the other night to go to a nearby restaurant. She walks with a stick and she said, "Let me hold on to you, Carolyn." I'm a little wobbly myself, but I said, "Okay, I hope I can make it." When I think about her I somehow feel stronger. After all, she's seven years older than I am and somewhat disabled. I think it's a matter of will. I wake up in the morning with a pain here and an ache there and I don't know if I'll make it, but I say to myself: "Now get out of bed and get started." You start moving around, take a hot shower, and you feel better. And that's how it goes.

RB: Do you think that commitment to social activism organizes your life?

CG: I do think that commitment is very important. I have a son who's very protective of me. I don't usually tell him if I'm not feeling great, but he knows. He says, "So what are your plans?" When I tell him he says, "Now, do you have to do it?" I say, "David, I said I was going to do it, and I am going to do it because they expect me to do what I said I would." The other night I went to a remake of *Oklahoma!* and there's one song in it called "I'm Just a Girl Who Can't Say No," and David said, "You know, you can say no sometimes." I said, "Well sometimes I do say no, but other times it's important for me to be there. I'm the one who represents something to this group, so they want me to be there."

RB: You still feel your commitments are to civil rights and working people and trying to make the world a better place, even though it's been a long struggle?

CG: I think that my view is broader. It's more human rights. I first felt responsive to that when I was very young. My parents were very interesting people, not politically involved as such. My mother was a radical without a cause. She was most nontraditional; she did everything differently. If you were supposed to have long hair, she'd cut her hair. If you were supposed to be straitlaced, she'd go without a bra and wear short skirts. She didn't set limits for us either, so we were all over the place. It was difficult because kids need limits, and I needed to learn that, both for my children and myself. I think that's one of the reasons I became a psychologist. My father wasn't political. He was a lawyer, a quiet man, and his head was somewhere up in the clouds. He was the first lawyer in New York City to hire a black man for an associate. All of this I was aware of, but there was no proselytizing in my home. No one said you should be aware of how laborers are slaving and how they are underpaid, et cetera. In addition to his being a nice, kind person, he also loved gardening. We lived out in the suburbs and he had a gardener do the heavy work for him. I used to watch the gardener, an Italian, a very nice man. I used to talk to him about his family and everything, and I asked him how much my father paid him, and I decided that he was underpaid. I said to him, "Frank, you should ask my father for more money." He said, "I don't want to lose my job, and I manage to get along." I said, "Look, my father has these grapes, if you're making wine—and this is during Prohibition—he likes the wine, and you're taking care of the garden, ask him for a dollar an hour more." I said, "I'll ask him for you," and so I did! I told him that Frank has four kids and he works hard. So my father said, "Well, all right, I'll give him a dollar more." I told Frank, "See how easy that was? Now, you go next door and tell the neighbors that my father is paying you a dollar more." So he went and asked and he got a dollar from all the neighbors because he worked the whole area. It made a difference!

When I met my husband Bobby, his mother was a socialist, so he was already radical. When we were at Cornell University, there were the dairy farmers, and I got in with the bunch that was organizing them. And then, of course, the whole thing began with the antifascist movement. So, it went. I just sort of fell into the whole movement, and it just seemed right. The antifascist movement was also a humanist movement. Sure, you had to be radical; you went down to Union Square, you saw cops and the people up on soapboxes, and I was very involved in all these organizations. I think half the time I wasn't sure what it was all about.

Bobby was an intellectual. He got me involved in a lot of things and he encouraged me, of course. He had tuberculosis and had to rest in a sanitarium in the mountains, and he asked his father, who was a true blue American and a wonderful man, to get the three volumes of *Das Kapital* and all of Lenin's works. His father got it for him. Bobby was his first child and he loved him very dearly, the sun rose and set on Bobby. So, Bobby read three volumes of Marx and all of Lenin and that's what he would pass on to me. His father had one brother who was really nuts. A sweet guy, but crazy. He visited Bobby in the sanitarium and he saw all these books there, and he said, "You shouldn't be reading these books; don't you know that this guy is a Communist?" Then he pulled out of his pocket a little American flag and he waved it over the books! (Laughs) So, that was how I learned a lot of what I learned. During that whole period I became actively involved in the antifascist movement. Bobby died quite young; he was fifty-five. I guess it was hypertension. And then I [got] married three years later to Joe. I remember saying at the time, "I'll never marry again." But Joe was a darling guy.

Bobby was the president of Pacifica Foundation when he died, and so they asked me to be the chair of the local board and I said I would. I thought it was doing some wonderful things. So I became chair, and I became very involved. I didn't want to be just a figurehead. The vice president of the foundation was sort of a weak person; he would say: "Oh, Carolyn, why don't you take that job, you could do it better than I." I said okay, and then the president of the foundation decided to retire, so I became the president of the foundation.

There are always things coming up unexpectedly; I never know from time to time. I do try to put things in some kind of priority. I don't say yes to everything, I assure you, because I'm constantly being asked to do things because of my history and I suppose people feel, well, at the age of eighty-six, how much longer is she going to be around? (Laughs) I do have a history of being involved over quite a few years and I've seen and lived through a lot of things.

RB: Any words of wisdom for parting?

CG: Jean Jacques Rousseau, who was frequently asked to speak at events, said that he always thought of the right thing to say as he was leaving, as he was walking out the door. The literal translation from the French was "on the steps down." I probably will think of many other things "on the steps down."

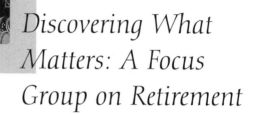

Discovering What Matters: A Focus Group on Retirement

GEORGIE GATCH, MARILYN
KATZ, ELIZABETH SAUNDERS,
AND PHYLLIS SCHWARTZ

How Did We Begin?

One blustery winter afternoon in New York City, four women sit down to talk about retirement, an experience we share, but a word we want to redefine. Among us, we have been retired from one to six years. We are curious about what we can learn by swapping our stories and have agreed to meet a few times, using the group process women have traditionally invoked to understand themselves and their lives. With each comment, we expect to tease out the similarities and differences among us and stimulate one another to closer and more nuanced reflection. We will invite two other recently retired women, Libby Moroff and Lila Croen, to a later session, and ask them to respond to the issues and concerns we have discovered together. We have asked Marilyn, who writes professionally, to write an essay based on our discussions. We believe our observations will prove helpful not only to ourselves, but also to other women who are retiring or considering retirement.

Uncomfortable with the word *retirement*, we agree it belongs to another era, when it was associated with being sent out to pasture, with being no longer useful to society. "I prefer to think we are evolving," Marilyn begins, "moving to a new definition of ourselves." Now sixty-eight, she left her position as dean of studies and student life at Sarah Lawrence College almost three years ago, in 1998. Marilyn is settling into a sofa in Georgie's study in a loft building in Manhattan. Georgie laughs, but she is somewhat distracted, because she has just gotten off the telephone after having had a complex conversation with one of her friends. "We get drawn into their lives so much more now that we have more time," she says. Georgie, sixty-five, retired as dean of student life at Barnard College less than a year ago, in 2000.

Elizabeth, sixty-seven, leans forward to listen attentively before commenting. She retired in 1998 from the Pierce Leahy Corporation where she had been director of sales and marketing for the Imaging and Micrographic Division. The last to arrive, Phyllis, seventy-four, has come to the session directly from her volunteer job at the Whitney Museum. She worked in public relations for a number of nonprofits and retired in 1995 from her last full-time position, as executive director of New York Women in Film and Television.

Who Are We?

Born in the late 1920s and early 1930s, we consider ourselves members of what Georgie calls the "bridge" generation of women, a bridge between our mothers, who did not work full-time outside the home, and our daughters, who consciously prepared themselves for careers. We each worked full-time for at least thirty years, trying to find work that had meaning and would make a difference in society. Both Phyllis and Georgie interrupted their studies and took their first jobs to help their husbands through graduate school, completing their own college educations while raising families. Marilyn attended graduate school and began teaching when her children were young. After Elizabeth finished college she worked with her husband in the theater, with their foundering audiovisual company, and in the corporate world. Following her divorce she became the sole support of her four children and realized she needed a job in the business sector to provide the highest possible income and the greatest flexibility. The other three women, as well as our guests, Libby and Lila, eventually developed careers in the nonprofit sector, in educational, political, and arts organizations.

Unlike many young women today, we of the "bridge" generation married and had children before we began our careers. We put our families first and felt guilty whenever we thought we might be neglecting them. Because we still had primary responsibility for our homes and our children, we were always working at two full-time jobs.

In the sixties and seventies, we all became involved in civil rights, women's rights, and antiwar activism, as both volunteers and professionals, and when we gained positions of responsibility, we were disturbed to find not only few women represented, but few, if any, people of color. Deeply influenced by both the civil rights and women's movements and by our own moral imperatives, we worked hard to hire a more diverse group of employees and to mentor women younger than ourselves. Elizabeth is proud she made certain her company provided women with equal pay and equal treatment, as well as flexible hours to accommodate child-rearing demands and other family related obligations. "I accomplished this within a highly patriarchal and conservative organization," she remarks. Both Marilyn and Georgie feel responsible for hiring more people of color, particularly African Americans, and for helping to educate their colleagues about the importance of developing diverse teams of administrators at their institutions. Phyllis takes satisfaction that she not only mentored young women in her work at the Neuberger Museum and at Lehman College, but was able to galvanize women to network within the film industry, an industry dominated by men. We would like to believe, as Elizabeth puts it, "our working lives showed younger women that there is opportunity for advancement and recognition."

Why Retire and When?

As we begin to confide in one another, we discover that dissatisfaction with our jobs happened to coincide with our reaching retirement age. We speak of changes in our workplaces that brought a feeling of exploitation or loss of control. In Elizabeth's case, retrenchment at her company occurred when she became eligible to retire and enabled her to negotiate a good severance package. "Once my children were launched into relative financial independence, I found my motivation for remaining in the business world dropping considerably." One of our guests, Libby, sixty-five, was active in Democratic politics for thirty years, first as a volunteer and then as a paid employee, and eventually became a deputy for the Manhattan borough president before retiring in 1997. She explains, "I had plans to retire, but I don't know if I would have gone through with it if I hadn't been so dissatisfied," she says. "I was committed to women, an activist. But when I began working for money, the work became an end in itself." Our other guest, Lila, seventy-one, who retired in 1997 as director of institutional research and evaluation for the Albert Einstein College of Medicine, puts it best when she remarks, "Although I continued to enjoy my job, I felt an intellectual fatigue, and I'd find myself thinking, 'we tried that ten years ago.'"

Perhaps, Marilyn speculates, fatigue itself made us exaggerate what we saw as change in our organizations so we could leave. "During my last semester," she explains, "I found myself complaining about the college exactly the way senior students do to make it possible for them to graduate." Georgie, Marilyn, Elizabeth, and Lila had remained with the same organization for more than fifteen years. Georgie comments that this is typical of many women in our generation, who, instead of changing jobs for advancement as young women do today, continue in a familiar setting, having to accommodate personnel changes beyond their control, and doing work that becomes repetitious and/or frustrating. "It leads to burnout," Phyllis says. "Had we been younger," Marilyn adds, "we might have changed our working conditions or found other jobs."

How Well Did We Do in Our Careers?

As we begin this new phase in our lives, we find ourselves looking back to assess our careers. Did we make a difference? And, did this become more important to us than our paycheck? "Women sometimes put morality, loyalty, and teamwork before advancement," Georgie comments, recognizing that there were points in her career when she deferred to organizational needs rather than satisfy her own. Phyllis regrets not having persisted long enough in one area to become as successful as she would have liked. "But then, I'm a restless person," she explains. Marilyn is sorry she allowed her professional work to become so absorbing she wasn't able to complete her Ph.D. dissertation in literature. Elizabeth speaks of her frustration at having to work at a career that generated the most money and not having had the luxury to work full-time for the causes that mattered to her.

Yet on balance, we are astonished at how much we accomplished, particularly since we did not really plan ahead for our careers or receive professional training when we were younger. Rather, like many women in our bridge generation, we managed to hone our skills as we went along, accepting positions and then identifying problems in our organizations, and developing expertise as we worked to solve them. "In my early jobs I learned the tools of communication—sharpening my writing skills, for example—that I was able to use later in my career in public relations helping nonprofits," explains Phyllis. Elizabeth comments, "I never dreamed I would be able to earn as much as I ultimately did or succeed in business as I did. Nor did I ever think I'd want to, since I fancied myself a woman of the theater where of course one worked for love, not money."

What Did We Lose When We Left Our Jobs?

As we begin to shape a new life, we must first examine what we lost in this transition. Our group identified particular losses: income, identity, structure, challenge, appreciation, and community. As our discussions continued, we found ourselves articulating these losses more clearly because we were reexperiencing them each day.

Living on a fixed income from social security, a pension, and perhaps investments can be stressful. While none of us has had to alter the way we live, we are all more aware than ever of our expenses and must budget and plan more carefully. "The nasty part is financial," Elizabeth comments. "I can't afford to live in New York City, yet I need the stimulation, so I commute as much as possible."

Most immediate and most expected is the loss of identity. Losing a title and a business card can be symbolic of a loss of self-worth, but we believe the problem is exacerbated by aging. Not only are older people invisible in our society, but older women are particularly invisible, since women are often valued for their appearance and for their roles as mothers of growing children. "Our careers gave us visibility regardless of gender and age," Marilyn says. Phyllis and Georgie agree that this loss of identity is sometimes accompanied by guilt and shame for becoming self-involved, for no longer being a productive member of society. "This is a particular issue for women, who often define success as making a difference rather than making a lot of money," Georgie says.

We sometimes miss the structure provided by full-time work, a schedule determined by external demands. We admit being troubled by the ease with which we can fill our days with seemingly insignificant errands we used to accomplish before and after our full-time jobs. "I'm afraid of caring more and more about less and less," Marilyn says. But Elizabeth suggests that "we have to find a new way of evaluating time."

We also miss the challenges of the workplace, what Phyllis calls "having a stage" to act on outside of our family, a place where we can stretch and exercise our abilities. "I miss the daily challenges and problem solving of my office," Georgie says. Elizabeth and Marilyn agree they found excitement in confronting difficulties in their work. "I miss the improvisational nature of the work, the sense of sometimes performing on a high wire," Marilyn says.

Phyllis wonders whether we may also miss the approval we received, the recognition when we'd done a good job. She shows us an article from the

New York Times, in which a costume designer considering retirement, Theoni V. Aldredge, comments, "at least they [the actors] bother to say, 'I love it, thank you.' That keeps you going. Especially women. We eat it up."[1] We speculate about whether women need appreciation more than men, and if this is so, whether it is because they often receive less prestige and pay.

Finally, we feel the loss of our community of colleagues. We no longer belong to a working community, which in many cases was a diverse team of individuals, unlike our social group, which is generally composed of others more like ourselves. "I miss getting different perspectives, speaking daily to others, who, while joining me in a single effort, are of different ages and backgrounds," Marilyn says. Georgie notes that she has not returned to her office since she left, but Libby tells us she does not see this as a problem because she stays in touch with the individuals she cares about. We speculate that the loss of community may be felt more by women retirees because we often develop more personal relationships with our younger colleagues than men do. Georgie says, "When I retired, some of my colleagues felt I was abandoning them." They may have shared personal problems they would never have discussed with a male supervisor. "Sometimes this could be exasperating," she adds, "but I do miss the opportunity I had to nurture my young colleagues and build a strong team." "When I first retired," Phyllis admits, "I was terribly lonely."

Why Do We Seem to Worry More, Not Less?

We all agree that full-time work was often the way we escaped from our inner conflicts, from family problems, concerns about our spouses or partners and our children. "Without the distraction of work, I find myself feeling responsible for my grown children's problems, and I'm more available to help," Georgie says. With more unscheduled time, we can become increasingly introspective. We also pay more attention to health issues we might have minimized or ignored when we were busy working at demanding jobs. As we age, these health issues, our own and our peers', become more significant and give us cause for worry. Lila has found she has had to spend a substantial amount of time since she retired four years ago dealing with illness and deaths in her immediate family. Marilyn says, "I have time to worry about everything from the existential (aging, death, and what is the meaning of all this?) to the trivial (why are my closets so messy?)."

What Are the Pleasures? What Are the Possibilities?

We are learning to allow ourselves the many personal, intellectual, and cultural pleasures we missed, or were too tired to enjoy, while we were working at full-time jobs. During our careers, we absorbed the value society places on work. When we retired we found we had to recognize that, as Phyllis puts it, "what you do is not all you are."

We have time to savor small experiences, to take in new experiences, to read more and with better concentration, learn a new skill that always interested us. We can afford to fail, to make mistakes, to develop dormant talents, to explore intellectual and cultural areas, to travel more frequently. Libby, who has embraced retirement with joy, says, "I don't miss work. I am intellectually interested, focused, and intense. I take courses. I'm learning French, reading with greater concentration. I feel healthier and more intellectually stimulated." Lila adds, "I like being a dilettante, going to art shows, traveling, and taking courses, having the freedom to do what I want to do when I want to do it."

We are more available to our husbands or partners. Lila speaks eloquently of enjoying this central relationship. "I find this a very satisfying time of my life. I spend more time with my husband. The relationship becomes more critical when we know our good time is limited." Both Georgie's husband and Phyllis's husband are retired. Marilyn is a widow, but her significant other is also retired. Georgie and Phyllis had been worried they would find their spouses too present, too available. "Before my husband retired, I was anxious. I felt I would be in danger of losing my personal space. I was afraid of too much scrutiny," Phyllis says, adding, "I was uncomfortable with the thought that my husband would be in the room when my women friends called." They have had to, as she puts it, "renegotiate" the relationship. Georgie smiles and comments, "The first time my husband asked me, 'what's for lunch?' I was taken aback. I usually don't worry about lunch. He has to have lunch." Nevertheless, they have all been delighted to discover that, in general, the men are busy, independent, and actively pursuing their own interests, Georgie's husband doing research in his field of religious history, Phyllis's doing philanthropy and taking courses in music and history, and Marilyn's companion working as an editor for a trail conference and writing poetry. Elizabeth's partner, who has not reached retirement age, is still working full-time as a social worker. "Her income helps make my retirement possible," she remarks. In sum, whatever issues we have, they have not been aggravated by our companions' availability, but rather are our own concerns. We find our-selves happy that we have more time to spend with our partners.

We can also see our children more often and can watch our grandchildren grow, particularly if they live nearby. For example, Libby spends every Tues-day with her two young grandchildren and Marilyn is able to invite her grand-daughters, who live in Connecticut, to visit with her in New York City during their school vacations. And while we are all cautious about encroaching on our children's lives, we are glad we are more able to participate in them. We are also able to help our family and friends in times of need and illness, which occur more often as we age.

We see our friends more frequently, meeting them for cultural and intellec-tual activities in the city. Last year, Phyllis and Marilyn enjoyed planning a dinner together to ensure a large group of friends would attend a concert by a young cellist they knew. They also had time to organize a couples' book group that has been very successful.

We can take better care of ourselves physically, exercise regularly, and feel and look better. We are no longer exhausted by trying to satisfy the demands of work and of home. "This spring I was asked by my college to help in the dean's office for two or three weeks because they were short handed. I'd forgotten how wiped out I used to feel all the time. That tired feeling had become so much a part of my existence, I'd thought it was normal," Marilyn says.

Some of us feel we are cultivating aspects of ourselves that we had abandoned when we were younger and that had become subsumed in work. "I feel I have gotten my original self back," Elizabeth says. Marilyn agrees. However, we real-ize that if we do follow some earlier dream of our youth, to be involved in the theater as Elizabeth is, or write fiction as Marilyn is doing, we have to accept the limitations of having started so late. "I have to remind myself again and again that I write fiction because I love it, and accept the fact that I may be the author of three unpublished novels and many more unpublished short stories," Marilyn says. Elizabeth remarks, "I will never become the theatrical producer I had hoped to be." She adds, "We are not twenty-two, and may not be willing to work as hard as we did then." We are learning to do what we love for the joy of doing it, rather than for achievement. These values, traditionally women's values and con-trary to the values of the marketplace, are what we all treasure in retirement.

Can We Ease the Transition by Doing Part-time Paid Work?

For financial or psychological reasons, retired women may choose to do part-time work for a paycheck. Marilyn and Phyllis have done paid work since retirement, and Georgie says she would consider it if she could utilize her experience and expertise. Marilyn works the equivalent of a day a week at the college she served as dean of studies and student life, but in a different capacity, as a consultant for the fund-raising effort. She finds this a way of both increasing her cash flow and easing the psychological separation from her working life. However, it involves being willing to accept the limitations of the part-time position, being distanced from decision making, underutilized, or pressured by supervisors. "It has taken a while for me to accept the fact that I no longer have authority, am less involved in and less knowledgeable about daily events," Marilyn says, "but I will continue as long as I can still make a contribution to an institution in which I believe." She uses the commitment as a way to structure her week. For a while after she retired, Phyllis formed a consulting group for nonprofits with two other women who were over sixty, but getting paid employment was difficult since most prospective employers were far younger and seemed skeptical of their expertise. Later, she took a part-time paid position as director of special projects for a documentary film company that was completing a historical film. She found the experience "extremely stressful" and was relieved when the film was finished. "I retired to avoid such stress," she adds.

While the experiences of two women are hardly sufficient to draw conclusions, retired women should examine carefully their objectives in seeking part-time paid work, because it generally offers less control and fewer rewards than full-time employment.

How Do We Find Socially Useful and Meaningful Activity by Volunteering?

This became a key issue in our conversations, since, while we enjoy our private lives enormously, retirement also gives us time to devote ourselves to the causes and organizations in which we believe. "I don't have a sanguine personality. I'm restless. I look back and say I have a lot to offer and have learned so much, and now where am I going to take all this," Phyllis says. As Libby points out, computers are changing the way things are done, making it possible to be involved without having to go to an office. Nevertheless she adds, "It is sometimes hard for us to respect work we are not paid for, because getting a paycheck was an important achievement for us." Like the word *retirement*, the word *volunteer* may need reexamination. "At one time I did pro bono consulting," says Phyllis, "but we called ourselves 'pro bono professionals.' The word *volunteer* is more off-putting."

Once past the psychological barrier, finding volunteer opportunities can be more difficult than we realized. "When we offer our services, we face more obstacles than we expected given our expertise in management, problem solving, or writing," says Phyllis. Nonprofits are not always welcoming to retired professionals. First, most nonprofits do not have an organizational structure to support highly skilled volunteers. Elizabeth notes that the coordinator of volunteers is generally the youngest, least experienced member of the organization. Second, retired professionals may threaten the paid staff. "When I was the executive director of a nonprofit, I had to defer to board members. Now that I am chairperson of the board of a nonprofit, I worry about not offending the paid staffers," Phyllis says, noting the irony. Since we are used to being in charge, "it is difficult when we identify larger problems, but are not in the position to correct them," as Georgie comments; she spent her first months of retirement working for a political campaign. "I thought I would have some position of strength, but I ended up working for two young women, twenty-five or thirty, who were very cautious about giving me responsibility." She felt that as a volunteer she could say nothing.

Sometimes, what we are asked to do by a nonprofit is not what we want to do. "'Can you do data processing?' I've been asked," says Phyllis. "My answer may be 'yes,' but I may not want to do this at this stage of my life." Having held a number of volunteer jobs in the six years since she retired, Phyllis says, "I've learned to laugh when I complete a project and my staff supervisor decides it should be redone and differently."

Another problem, Marilyn notes, is that many organizations are only interested in our services if we can give or raise money. Serving on boards of nonprofit organizations often requires having more financial resources than most retired women have. As a current board chairperson of a nonprofit, Phyllis suggests women hoping to participate at the board level seek a small enough organization or one that is just beginning to expand.

In sum, at different stages of retirement and in different ways, each of us is considering whether and how we can continue our commitment to social change. We believe the issue of retired women professionals seeking meaningful volunteer work is going to become more of a societal concern as more and more of us retire from responsible positions. One way we believe our generation of retirees can be helpful is by organizing groups of highly skilled professional women as consultants or mentors who can offer their services for specific projects. We must be creative to sell an idea or an event to an organization, and forceful and ingenious to create our own opportunities as volunteers. We can choose a cause, assess how well it is served in our community, and then approach it with all the problem-solving skills we developed in our careers. Instead of going through channels and contacting the coordinator of volunteers, we recommend approaching the head of the project or the department you wish to serve. Phyllis, who has had the most experience as a volunteer, frames this in an interesting way: "We have to consider ourselves self-employed, freelancers. While freelancers have to seek work and structure their own time, they also have the freedom to refuse work they are not comfortable doing."

How Have We Responded Individually?

Because retirement is a process rather than an event, we are developing our own answers and reassessing them periodically. "I have had to become more self-reflective, to reinvent myself sometimes every few months," Phyllis says. Marilyn adds that she continues to seek the right balance between personal involvement and social commitment. A schedule of activities for one year may not work the next. A volunteer job may turn out to be less satisfying than expected or take too much time. A personal or family crisis or a travel opportunity may interfere with the best laid plans. While the issues we explored are common to all, each of us has responded somewhat differently.

Phyllis, who has been retired the longest, is now chairing the board of SAVI, the Mount Sinai Sexual Assault and Violence Intervention Program. She also works one day a week doing special research projects in the Whitney Museum library. Phyllis had been frustrated after receiving no response to her applications for other museum volunteer work. One day, in the ladies' room of the Whitney, she began a conversation with a woman wearing a museum staff ID tag, learned she was the librarian, and asked her whether she needed any research assistance. She has been working there ever since.

Elizabeth is working for The Women's Project and Productions (WPP), an off-Broadway theater that produces plays written and directed by women. "It combines my love for the theater with my commitment to creating greater opportunities for women," she says. After several months as an intern, she was offered a full-time job in development, but quickly realized that after the autonomy and freedom she had had in her business career, she didn't want to do full-time office work of any kind at any level. She now volunteers her time at WPP according to the particular needs that arise at the theater.

Marilyn, who for the past three years worked part-time as a consultant for Sarah Lawrence, spends much of her time writing fiction. But she finds retirement has also prompted her to write about what she learned during her years as a professional: "I now have the time to write articles about issues in higher education, and about the college experience for students and their parents. I seem to need a long-term project to keep me focused and happy." She suggests retirement may give some women the opportunity to put into writing the knowledge they accumulated during their careers.

Georgie, who retired less than a year ago and worked for Hillary Clinton's campaign for New York senator, is seeking ways to become involved in politics, particularly in the area of reproductive rights. She is also interested in creating an organization to provide resources for retired professional women so they can continue to make a significant contribution to society.

After a long career in politics, Libby finds herself pulling away from social commitments: "I was worried I would feel useless because I wasn't contributing. And now I worry that I don't care. I still speak to friends who do care, but I feel they don't need my advice." Like Georgie, Libby did agree to do some work for the Hillary Clinton campaign, but is primarily enjoying the freedom of her retirement, spending time with her grandchildren, reading voraciously, and doing coursework in French.

Lila also pursues many interests, and is helping to organize a walkathon to raise money for research on autism. She developed a survey for nonresident taxpayers in Wellfleet, Massachusetts, and is in the process of analyzing and summarizing results of the survey. "I like the fact that much of this can be done at my convenience and involves a relatively short-term commitment, although I would be willing to do more for autism research, given the opportunity."

How Can We Form New Communities?

Perhaps our most significant realization was that, as retired women, we need to create new communities for ourselves outside our social circles, by seeking groups sharing a common interest or cause. Some of our most positive experiences since retirement have occurred in such groups. Marilyn corroborates this, saying, "My experience of retirement was enhanced when I joined a group of women writers who meet weekly to discuss one another's work. They range in age from twenty-five to seventy and are far more diverse in background than my group of social friends." Elizabeth has found such a group at the Women's Project, where like-minded women are offering opportunities to women directors and playwrights. Phyllis enjoys the young women on her board at SAVI. "They are terrific young people and they keep me active and engaged," she says. Georgie hopes that after this initial year, when she was busy with the political campaign and then spent a good deal of time enjoying being with her husband and other family members and traveling, she will find a group devoted to the political and social causes that matter to her.

It may take some trial and error, but, as Marilyn, Elizabeth, and Phyllis learned, it is possible to find or create a group of people of varied ages and backgrounds, who meet regularly to pursue a common interest or cause. Such communities help us continue to evolve as individuals, as well as make a contribution to our society.

How Did the Group Process Work in Writing This Essay?

Georgie, who designed and organized the discussion group, reflects back on the experience: "I am amazed at the ease and forthrightness of putting the group together and completing a task that was well defined and had a specific time frame. Each of the four women brought an expertise that was taken seriously by everyone. This was especially true in trusting Marilyn to do the writing. Our respect for her as a writer allowed us the freedom to concentrate on the content." In our professional lives, we have written reports and articles with others and know well how contentious it can become when a committee of individuals struggles over organization and phrasing, only to produce a compromise that satisfies no one. In this case, Marilyn took extensive notes at each session, organized our far-ranging comments into categories, and then presented a summary we could read before each subsequent session. After our final meeting, she wrote the essay, and we found we needed to make only a few changes. The experience was a model of egalitarianism, rather than a struggle for control. "While writing the essay was very time consuming, it was also exciting," Marilyn comments. "The writing process deepened what I was learning from the group process."

Phyllis, our veteran retiree, says she welcomed the chance to reflect back on her early reactions to retirement and measure how far she has come in shaping and reshaping her life. She too was struck by the way in which the individuals in the group supported one another in defining this life-changing time. "Of all the women's groups with which I've been involved, this was the most cooperative," she comments. Elizabeth adds, "Perhaps we lucked out, finding that we were not there to prove anything to ourselves or anyone and were truly interested in having an honest discussion of the subject as we had [been] and were presently experiencing it. I continue to mull over our conversations and am amazed at how ongoing and challenging the process is. A full-time job not only provides a framework for the rest of one's life, but also an excuse for what one could not or did not accomplish. Instead of the more concrete obstacles encountered in work or child rearing, the obstacles are now more likely to come from within and are far more elusive. Our discussions helped put many of those issues out on the table to be dealt with openly and honestly."

We recommend strongly that women who are considering retirement or have recently retired meet together as we did, to identify common issues, share experiences, and find creative ways to nurture both themselves and the society in which they live. We discovered, as women always have, that the process itself can be as valuable as the conclusions reached.

Note

1. Robin Pogrebin, "Backstage Pins and Needles," *New York Times,* 16 March 2001, E1.

Still in Circulation: A Librarian Retires

ESTHER RATNER

I didn't really start working until I was thirty-nine years old. My husband and I were married in September of 1952, when I was nineteen. He was in the Navy at the time (it was during the Korean War) and I had a year of college to finish, so I lived with my parents until the following June, when I graduated and joined him in Norfolk, Virginia. His ship was being refitted at the Portsmouth Navy Yard, and I got a job teaching first grade. It was fun, but we knew it was temporary. When his four-year enlistment was over, we would be returning to New York. When he was discharged, I was nine months pregnant, and for the next twelve years I stayed home in suburban Long Island and tried to be a perfect wife and mother. It seemed to be the thing to do at the time, but those years were not an unqualified success. Baking and cooking classes led to Weight Watchers, a move to end the Vietnam War by bringing a strongly worded resolution to the National Parent-Teacher Association convention ended at the county level, and when I ran a friend's campaign for Congress, he was resoundingly defeated. I did make some good friends and I did enjoy much of the time I spent with my children, but I moved, restlessly, from one cause or project to another.

After my father died, in 1966, my mother wanted to come and live with us, and I agreed, despite dire predictions from everyone who knew us both, because it would give me a chance to go to graduate school without feeling guilty about leaving my children to fend for themselves after school. In my social set, at that time, a mother worked if her income was needed to support the family or if she had some talent or accomplishment. We were managing on my husband's income, and although college tuition costs loomed in the future, we were never good at planning ahead. If I had any talent or accomplishment, no one had noticed. My mother wanted to keep house and make dinner every night, which was how she defined herself, and I needed to do something else. I had suffered from what were described as neurotic symptoms, such as tachycardia, panic attacks, and unexplained allergic reactions, ever since my children were born, but now, I began to experience more disabling problems. I developed globus hystericus, now in more feminine-friendly times known as globus sensation, which is a lump in the throat or a choking feeling, and claustrophobia. I could only sit in aisle seats in a theater or concert hall, and it was less expensive not to risk not finding one. I finally started therapy and began to understand that my symptoms were evidence of my feeling overwhelmed and smothered, but they did not go away. My husband and my mother began to fight almost daily, usually at dinnertime. Neither of them would give an inch. I would get into bed right after dinner, but my husband slept there also and my mother would back in several times a night to deliver the folded laundry or complain about the kids or deliver messages that had come hours earlier. I tried to mediate between the hostile camps, but both sides thought I was disloyal. I actually thought that if they both got angry at me they could make an alliance against their common enemy, but that didn't work. I looked for an escape.

I decided to go to library school and was accepted, provisionally, into the program at Columbia University, after some negotiation. When I called and asked for an application, I was asked if I had two years of a modern foreign language on the college level. I said no and was told very curtly that I didn't have the necessary requirements for entrance. Bang, the person hung up on me. I was so angry at her that I immediately called back and in answer to the same question from the same person, said yes. I would at least have the satisfaction of getting an application or provoking an argument. I was asked for my name and address and in a few days received the application and a catalog. I read the catalog carefully and discovered a footnote that said requirements could be waived if the candidate was otherwise qualified. Transcript in hand, I met with the dean's secretary, who discovered that I wasn't eligible because I had majored in elementary education, but she was impressed with the scores from my recently taken Graduate Record Examinations and suggested a way for me to gain admission to the program. I agreed to take two additional liberal arts undergraduate courses in the summer session at Hofstra University, one of which would be German IV. I hadn't taken I through III, at the college level, but had studied German in high school and had won third place in the New York citywide annual Goethe contest in my senior year. It was a family joke that there had been only two other contestants, but the prize was a beautiful Georg Jensen silver pin. I figured if I worked really hard, I could pass the course.

I was the only person in the class who was over twenty years old, wasn't repeating German IV, sat in the first row, and did the homework. The instructor had to remind me that in college it was called "assignments," not "homework." He asked me what I was doing in his class and offered me as much extra help as I needed to pass. I also took a course in modern Russian history, which was fascinating, and by emulating the coal miner Alexei Stakhanov, and trying harder than everyone else, I passed both courses with A's and was admitted to the library school in September.

I loved going to graduate school. I had to drive to the nearest Long Island Rail Road station, take the train to the city, and then take the subway up to Columbia. On good days, the trip took an hour and twenty minutes, but that didn't deter me since I enjoyed doing research and writing papers as well as having sherry and biscuits in the faculty lounge on Friday afternoons, and I took as long as possible to get my degree. I started when I was thirty-six, and left three years later. There were more women my age in classes than the college appreciated. They called us "young matrons" and often warned us that our advanced age made us unemployable. One adjunct advised me to lie about my age on job applications.

Those were also the years of the Vietnam-era student demonstrations. I was so grateful to be at Columbia that I wasn't supportive of the demonstrators, although many of their grievances were justified. In the three years I was there, I never took a midterm or a final. Something always galvanized the campus just before exams. It was exciting and fun, and, at times, positively insane. We had an instructor who worried that the library could be totally disrupted if the cards in the catalog trays were dumped on the floor. He was sure that this held a high place on the agenda of Students for a Democratic Society and proposed that whenever a disturbance broke out, the library school students should run down and form a human chain around the catalog. He even suggested that we sign up for specific sections, but wiser heads prevailed.

I graduated with honors and, after a few temporary positions, found a job as a high school librarian in Roslyn, Long Island. I worked there for twenty years, and I loved my job. It had all of the rewarding aspects of teaching, working with children, interacting with talented colleagues, and learning new things, without having to prepare daily lesson plans, grade papers and report cards, and deal with parents who were disappointed in those grades. My supervisors thought I was doing a good job, and I began to believe I had some ability. The first time I had to speak at a faculty meeting my head started to swim, but within a few months, all of my neurotic symptoms had abated, if not completely disappeared. I served on committees, organized cultural arts programs, and evaluated other school libraries for the Middle States Association. As I flew to a conference in Rochester, New York, I realized that it was the first time I was traveling anywhere alone, unaccompanied by parent, husband, or children.

It was the beginning of the computers-in-the-classroom era, and I was encouraged to take courses and to develop my skills as an electronic researcher. After a colleague retired, I became the senior librarian. I was not a department chair, but I was in charge of a more than adequate budget and had five people to supervise. I had to deal with all sorts of problems, but I learned how to do it without exploding in anger or crying. I was praised by my supervisors, liked by most of my students, and acted as advisor to the junior class and two or three clubs and other extracurricular activities. The library was centrally located, and we encouraged teachers, staff, and students to stop by during the day. I would help colleagues with their own children's homework, and we fought to house a computer lab in a corner of the library. I volunteered to supervise student teachers from a nearby library school, and always had one or two in tow, although I was taken aback when one of them said that my greatest asset was my self-confidence, not my teaching ability. In retrospect, I think she was right. Those years were the longest time I had gone in my adult life without being in therapy or on medication.

My husband and I began to plan our retirement in 1987, when I was fifty-four years old and he was fifty-eight. We thought we would work for another eight years at least. He had worked for more than thirty years for the Grumman Corporation, which made planes for the Navy and was Long Island's largest employer. In 1987, we sold our house on the South Shore of Long Island, where we had lived for more than twenty years, and rented a house on the North Shore, which was much closer to both of our jobs. We bought a cottage in New York's Hudson Valley, which needed extensive remodeling, but we liked doing that and with both of us working, and our children out on their own, we had the money to redo the house, travel, and generally enjoy our lives.

All of this changed when my husband was forced to retire one month after we bought the cottage. Although the company had been laying off employees, my husband assumed he was secure and was totally surprised by his dismissal.

At first, he scrambled around, looking for another slot in the same company, but none of the people he had come to know in his long career could help him. In fact, people he had helped went out of their way to avoid him. He was angry and resentful. The emotional devastation was so great we didn't even think of what his job loss would mean to our finances. Since he was sixty years old the week he was fired, he was eligible for a pension. He also thought that with his considerable computer skills, he would quickly find another, comparable job. However, the pension was much smaller than we had thought it would be, and it took him four months to find a job at less than half his former salary. He had to take the Long Island Rail Road into New York City, then the subway to his office. His second day on the job, his pocket was picked on the subway platform. The person my husband reported to was difficult to work with, and it took months for him to make a place for himself within the company, but eventually his abilities were recognized and, with a lot of economizing, our lives settled down again.

After two years, the company was sold and my husband was again out of a job. This time, because of the additional skills he had acquired and the more commercially viable job description he now had, we thought another job would be easier to find. It was not. In addition to the disappointment, we began to realize that we couldn't continue living as we had been. We couldn't meet all our expenses on my salary alone. We were eating into our savings. One of our kids moved home and helped with expenses, but it was clear we couldn't continue as we were. Even if we sold the country house, we couldn't live on Long Island on my salary and his pension. He was now sixty-two and could start collecting social security. Since I had been teaching for twenty years, I would be eligible for a pension if I retired, even though I wasn't quite sixty years old. There seemed to be nothing else to do. Against my better judgment, I agreed to retire and move up to our cottage in Woodstock, where we could live on our pension income alone. I was very angry. I wasn't ready to leave my job, my colleagues, my friends, and the life I had made for myself. I went back into therapy, and again I understood the reasons for my depression, but it wasn't much help. To placate me, my husband and I agreed that if I hated living upstate, we could always make other plans. The last six months at work were excruciating. I fought with everyone, was unreasonably strict with students, and sulked. There were the usual retirement parties and speeches, but they did little to make me feel better. The school district offered me a part-time job as a consultant, which would have been in addition to my pension, but it wouldn't have been enough for us to live on where we were. I began to break out in hives again, once so severely that I was hospitalized for seven days. My children had always picked fights with me just before they left for camp or school, and now I understood why. It is easier to leave feeling angry and righteously indignant.

My husband loved our new life. We lived at the end of two dirt roads. The house was heated by a woodstove and he discovered log splitting. All I remember from that first fall is the sound of an axe striking wood. When the first snow fell, the sound changed to that of a shovel scraping the walk and driveway. I convinced myself I couldn't drive in icy conditions and spent most of the time at home. I was angry, depressed, and convinced that I had made a supreme sacrifice, which was unappreciated by the ecstatic woodsman I lived with. He got rid of his frustrations by physical labor. I sat, stewed, and got fatter and fatter. In the spring, I went back into therapy, found an exercise class, and started driving again. At a party that Fourth of July, I met someone who had gone to the library school at Columbia and was now writing textbooks. She told me that publishing companies were looking for fact checkers. In the past, they had had their own staffs of librarians to verify texts, but for reasons of economy, they were now outsourcing the work. My acquaintance gave me the names and addresses of people to contact. My husband created a brochure for me on our computer, and I sent out copies with a cover letter to about six companies. I received two responses and was eventually asked to submit a proposal for a small job. I had no idea how much money the work was worth and asked for less than half of what I was eventually paid. The editor I worked for took a chance on me because of the recommendation of the writer I had met and also offered me what was the going rate. I will always be grateful to both of them for their kindness and generosity.

I now have contracts to do entire books. It took time, experimentation, and a growing confidence to figure out how best to run my business. Initially I hired people to work for me and then realized I spent as much time going over their work as it would take me to do it all myself. I am too compulsive to trust anyone else, no matter how good a job they do. I also do research for writers and have worked on three books with a local author. None of them has made a best-seller list so far, but we have hopes for the next one. I also do medical research for a physician in New York who testifies in malpractice suits. He happens to be my brother and we work well together. When I began my business, eight years ago, I did most of my work in libraries. I would travel to the New Paltz campus of the State University of New York (SUNY), which is about twenty-five miles from our house. Now, I can do most of my work on my computer. My husband works with me. He was scornful of my efforts in the beginning, complaining that the twenty-eight dollars I paid for a DBA

(Doing Business As) certificate was a waste of money. He was sure that nothing would come of it. He did help with the computer set-up and kept things in good repair, but he was not encouraging until I began to make money. Then his attitude changed. I promoted him from employee to partner and had business cards printed up with his name on them, and we have worked together ever since.

Since I was at the college library at SUNY/New Paltz so often, I joined their group Friends of the Library, which entitled me to circulation privileges. I came to know the library director and was asked to join the steering board of the Friends. The library, named for Sojourner Truth, a slave who was born in the Hudson Valley and later gained her freedom, is excellent. It has tremendous resources and a wonderful staff. I feel very much at home. Library stacks may not be everyone's favorite place to be, but I thrive there. The college also offers all sorts of lectures, concerts, performances, receptions, and exhibits, which we regularly attend. I am flattered that students ask me for help, although I always restrain myself and refer them to the librarians.

In the last few years, however, more and more of the sources I need are available on line, and we can do more of the work at home. We have two computers, side by side, networked together, with printers, a scanner, and other high-tech equipment. The work is intense at times. Publishers deal with deadlines and on occasion we work a seven-day week, but we are well paid and I love doing it. Life is good again. I feel appreciated, if not by praise articulated, by contracts to do additional work. The now-seventy-three-year-old woodsman can stop splitting and shoveling to prove something and is invaluable as my computer expert and co-worker. In our slow seasons, he has built two additions onto our cottage, which now qualifies as a house. We have a professional life and a fulfilling social life. We have some discretionary income and an enhanced sense of security. I have come to appreciate living in the house at the ends of two dirt roads, especially for the beauty and serenity of the surroundings and the wildlife there (I should admit that while I adore the wild turkeys and tolerate the deer destroying too much of what I plant, I am ambivalent about bears). The town of Woodstock is only seven miles away and, if we crave company, we can find it there. We belong to a book group, a religious congregation, and are Friends of as many libraries as we can find.

What does this all add up to? What advice can I offer people who find themselves retired before they are ready? Take chances, have confidence in yourself, and, above all, present an agreeable face to the world. Keep up with the changing nature of your profession and don't be afraid of learning something new. If you have something to offer, a special skill or talent, or enjoy something, tell people about it. Go places where people who may need your services congregate. Find a community institution such as a library or school or hospital. They all need volunteers. If it doesn't work out, move on to something else. Appreciate good and generous people. There aren't enough of them out there, but they exist. Try to behave in kind.

Things haven't been always wonderful for my husband and me in retirement. We've been through life-threatening surgeries, emergency trips to the nearest hospital, which is ten miles away, and the Y2K worries, when we stocked up on bottled water. We have learned to live with no electrical power for six days after a storm, when the bottled water came in handy. We've learned to cherish good friends and neighbors, which we are fortunate to have. We have learned to appreciate the local volunteer firefighters and the Emergency Rescue Squad. We have learned to tolerate, from as great a distance as we can arrange, the toxic types, who exist here as well. We truly consider ourselves fortunate to have each other, to celebrate the good things in our lives, especially our children, and to have enough room to escape to different parts of the house when we feel the need.

Harvesting the Threads
of Commitment

LANIE MELAMED

Yesterday I started to lose my hair, another step on the cancer journey that initiated my retirement from teaching and set me on yet another path toward enlightenment. At sixty-five, I was diagnosed with breast cancer. I was teaching full time at Concordia University, in Montreal, Canada, caring for my husband, who was entering the final stages of Alzheimer's disease, and facing surgery soon to be followed by radiation. Something had to go. Since eliminating the two illnesses was impossible, I chose to leave the hallowed halls. The decision would have been more difficult had changes not been occurring at the university, significantly affecting my enthusiasm for teaching.

It was 1993, a time of drastic reductions in government spending resulting in escalating budget deficits in education, health care, and social services. Twenty-four years earlier, at the start of my teaching career, classes of twenty to thirty students were the norm. Teaching was considered a skilled and reputable profession. In the early nineties, class sizes escalated, faculty ranks and student-centered programs were downsized, and computers were marking student papers. Excellence in teaching became a fading objective as universities hungered for research monies to replenish disappearing funds. Soon after I retired, my colleagues were facing class sizes of 65 to 140 students. This was anathema to my views of effective teaching and learning, requiring performance-style lecturing with little opportunity for small-group work and interactive class discussion. Upon reflection, I realized that years of activism had shaped my teaching interests and concerns. One of my greatest pleasures was to help students become critical thinkers and to move them to become actively engaged in shaping their lives. With mixed feelings I closed the door on full-time paid work.

Fears about what to do with the rest of my life did not become an immediate issue. I was dealing with my own health problems, reduced energy due to radiation treatments, and full-time caregiving for my husband. Being homebound during the following year gave me the opportunity to attack layers of papers in twenty overloaded file drawers. (I am an obsessive collector of too many things!) This was a useful undertaking. It afforded me space for contemplation, to mourn the loss of past moments in time, and to reassess my current interests. The last course I developed was "Leisure and the Environment," a topic about which I was becoming increasingly concerned. I barely noted at the time that files on cancer and the environment assumed a place of prominence in my reorganizing efforts.

Naming the Threads

My intellectual interests over the years have been eclectic. I have been blessed with curiosity genes, a fair amount of intelligence, and hands that revel in activity. An only child of Russian-Dutch parentage, I attended Antioch College, a model liberal arts college in Ohio, founded by the Quaker Horace Mann in the mid-1820s. Each day while crossing the campus I passed a plaque that read: "Be ashamed to die until you have won some victory for humanity." Did those words shape my future or do I remember them because I was already en route?

I worked at the Highlander Folk School, a training center for social change activists in the deep South, for my college work-study placement. Moving from middle-class, urban New York City to the poverty-stricken, racist, rural South was a life-transforming experience. So was the inspiration I gained from working with Myles Horton, a bootstrap theologian and popular educator. Rosa Parks, the woman who refused to move to the back of the bus, was trained in nonviolent action at the school; Martin Luther King and Paolo Freire contributed to strategy and policy-making conferences.

Postcollege (and after a year abroad), I married a folk-singing city planner and raised three children in an intentional, multiracial, Quaker-inspired community in Central Philadelphia. One of the community's goals was to illustrate that blacks and whites could live together in harmony. (The civil rights movement would soon explode.) Community projects included a cooperative nursery school, a choir, a baby-sitting co-op, recorder groups, a food co-op, and social events that brought people together. Involvement in this rich social experiment proved to be an excellent training ground for learning group and community development skills. My mind was stretched rather than enervated while tending to the more mundane chores of child rearing. Many of the young mothers were active in Women's Strike for Peace and the League of Women Voters. As part of a national test for strontium 90, many of us collected our children's baby teeth to measure fallout from the nuclear tests that were being conducted at the time. Letter writing and attendance at antiwar demonstrations were part of our family activity during the Vietnam War—the quest for peace was high on our daily agenda. As a folk dance enthusiast (addicted by the age of eight at summer camp), I started a folk dance group that thrived as a multiracial community event in Philadelphia and Montreal for over a period of twenty years. When the children were in school full time I began to yearn for more intellectual substance. I combined a program in folklore (a lifetime interest) with a program in human relations at the University of Pennsylvania to earn a master's degree in arts and sciences.

At the height of the Vietnam War my husband and I decided to move to Canada. The fact that 68 percent of the federal taxes we were paying went to support the U.S. war budget became an increasingly difficult pill to swallow. We also anticipated that one day our sons would be called to fight in a war we would consider unjust. Canada beckoned, as a country that had a universal health care system, was not afraid of the word *socialist*, and represented to us a more humanitarian and less violent society. Our transfer to a French-speaking city was eased since my husband had studied at the Sorbonne (we met in Paris) and spoke French like a native. Montreal, Canada's most cosmopolitan city, became our new home.

With a master's degree it was easy for me to find work. The School of Social Work at McGill University hired me to teach a course in activity methods in group work practice. The course drew on my years as a camp counselor, recreation leader, and consultant. Later I taught courses in social work, folklore, and folk music and "Understanding Small Group Behavior" in a local community college. When the feminist movement and women's studies were established in Canada I became director of programs for women in the college's newly formed Continuing Education Department. When budgetary restrictions began to erode the community nature of the job a new challenge presented itself. Should I consider entering a Ph.D. program at the age of fifty?

An advanced degree in adult education would enable one to teach adults in a wide variety of fields. This was a population I had come to respect as older women began reentering school in large numbers to augment their skills and contribute to the family income. I sought a program that would value adult life experience, had a progressive faculty, and that attracted community change activists. I found it in the Department of Adult Education at the University of Toronto. The director, Roby Kidd, was a world-acclaimed leader in the field, had been a friend of Myles Horton's, and encouraged students to pursue qualitative research methodology. My first term paper was an analysis of what and how I learned thirty-four years previously at Highlander as an Antioch intern. (Copious notes from that time had already been relabeled in my files.) I loved being a student again, and learned more than I thought possible for a woman in her fifties. To quote Gail Sheehy, these were clearly my "nifty fifties."[1]

I hoped to find a thesis topic that would contribute to understanding the world, that might help to change it for the better, and that would provide joyful moments in the process. Colleagues prodded me to explore playfulness as a necessary balance to work and learning, insisting that I had something unique to express on the subject. Years of valuing play in my own life, with my children and as a recreation leader, turned into a theory of older women's playfulness and how it enhanced their learning and development.[2] During this time I was greatly supported by my close friendship with the authors of the book *Women's Ways of Knowing*.[3] When I needed permission to "color outside the lines," the study group initiated by the authors provided fertile discussion. I was then able to influence the thinking of my thesis advisors, who themselves were learning more about qualitative research methodology. It was an exhilarating time for the development of my mind and my sense of self.

After graduating, I explored several venues for my new skills. While waiting for an academic opening, I worked for three years as a peace educator, organizing local teachers into a peace education network. (The world was once again in a major state of crisis with the escalation of the cold war and the proliferation of nuclear weapons.) A series of contracts with the National Film Board resulted in my preparing study guides to accompany their films on media literacy, environmental concerns, and social justice. I traveled across Canada giving workshops and showing films at national and international adult education and teacher conferences. An invitation by the director of the Leisure Studies Program at Concordia University gave me the chance to teach a university course based on my thesis findings. This connection grew into a full-time teaching contract and structured my life until the time of my retirement.

Retired at Sixty-five

So now I am "retired," my files are in order, my husband has been placed in a long-term-care facility, and my cancer treatments are over! I will be cancer free for the next five years. What to do with all this accumulated wisdom and Goddess-gifted energy? Almost immediately, I was invited to join the board of Breast Cancer Action Montreal (BCAM), the group of women who were most there for me as I searched for data and options on cancer treatment. (I was hoping for choices that were less noxious than the traditional "slash, burn, and poison.") My fate was sealed at the first board meeting. The subject was how to spend a ninety-five-thousand-dollar grant from Health Canada. The aim was to educate women to become aware of breast cancer issues, to become advocates for government policy change, and to reach out to diverse ethnic communities whose information about the disease was less than adequate. By the meeting's end, I was hired as the project's principal trainer. Project Advocacy lasted for one year—six months to train fourteen women in leadership skills and another half year to bring these new skills to local community groups. I was in my element—teaching and learning again.

My association with BCAM continues to be the principal cerebral work of my retirement years, filling about 50 percent of my available time. The work is fully engaging. I am learning constantly and feel effective in my ability to influence public opinion. After ten years the organization has realized that prevention (stopping cancer before it starts) is *the* key policy issue. An article I wrote entitled "Why Spend So Much Treating Cancer, So Little Preventing It?" explains the organization's point of view.[4] Because of increasing citizen concern and media attention, a study circle was initiated (based on the best in the adult education tradition) so interested people could learn more about the relationship between cancer and the environment. The group has been meeting for three years and engages me in reading, writing, and conducting research in this area. My files are filled with information about pesticides, toxins, hormones, radiation, genetically modified foods, organic farming, global warming, and biodiversity. We are living in a world collapsing on the reckless edge of sustainability.

The Raging Grannies

Another major commitment of my retirement time and energy is to an organization of grandmotherly women who use satire and other forms of humor to draw attention to social issues on a national and international scale. The Raging Grannies are familiar to most Canadians, having appeared on national TV and radio and on the front pages of the country's newspapers. The Grannies organized to attract media attention and to spread politically incorrect ideas. The movement consists mainly of women who had previously been involved in peace, antinuclear, and disarmament issues. Many were members of the Voice of Women (Voix des Femmes) and the Women's International League for Peace and Freedom.

The Grannies made national headlines in 1989 when eight women hitched a ride on a Greenpeace sailboat to protest nuclear testing and the presence of U.S. ships carrying nuclear warheads in the Strait of Georgia in British Columbia. At the start of the Gulf War they appeared at army recruiting stations volunteering to serve in lieu of young men who needed to stay home with their families. From then on, nothing was too outlandish or off limits to activate Granny action.

Aware that long briefs and reports to Parliament rarely receive media attention, the Grannies use song, comedy, and street theater to get their message across. They dress in old-lady costumes adorned with peace symbols and banners, and are bedecked with crazy hats and pink running shoes. Tambourines and kazoos are their chosen instruments. They sing at peace and environment rallies, at academic and popular conferences, and submit "briefs" in song at legislative hearings where they create comedic interlude in officious boardroom settings. They also sing in schools, at women's events, and wherever the public congregates, invited or not. Music, as we all know, is a powerful way to energize people and to create feelings of solidarity. Since their words are set to familiar melodies the songs are easy to hum along with. Audiences are frequently encouraged to join in on the chorus.

The Raging Grannies are politically informed and nonpartisan and support nonviolence and peaceful alternatives as a way of solving social problems. United in a loosely organized federation, there are about fifty groups today in the major cities across Canada, Greece, and parts of the United States. A yearly "unconvention" is held for the exchange of songs, dialogue, and political action. "Blown away" by a Granny performance in Calgary, Ralph Nader declared the Grannies to be one of Canada's most effective exports. While the message is deadly serious, the approach is anything but. Not to be confused with high style entertainers, the Grannies use theatrics to attract attention and to raise political awareness among the uncommitted. The first year the Grannies organized in Montreal, a newspaper analysis noted that they were mentioned over sixty times in various media.

The Grannies might best be described as activist popular educators. The members educate themselves about current issues, read and exchange information, attend conferences, and are active in a variety of peace, social justice, and environmental causes. They compose and rework old and new songs for the purpose of encouraging listeners to examine issues and to become involved in social action. One song, for example, constantly repeats the postal code of Parliament and reminds people that the postage (in Canada) is free. Flyers are frequently distributed, as in the case of the annual anti–war toys campaign each Christmas season. Press releases announce the group's appearances at noteworthy events. Several Grannies could be seen on the front lines in Seattle and Quebec City recently, protesting the Multilateral Agreement on Investment and North American Free Trade Agreement.

Because their productive days are considered to be numbered, older women are more able to step outside the mainstream, to be outrageous and to commit everyday acts of rebellion.[5] More acutely aware of their strengths and shortcomings, they tend to be less worried about status, fashion, or being obediently submissive. In the words of one Vancouver Granny, "We've been taught to be nice and caring and to mind our own business—but rage is an energy for transforming things." This gives Grannies and all older women enormous power.

It is said that almost 70 percent of volunteer workers for peace, social justice, and the environment are women. Women tend to be caregivers, collaborators, and nurturers of hearth and home. Adept at cleaning up after themselves, they are propelled by the urgency of cleaning up the environmental pollution they are leaving for their children and grandchildren. Yet the objects of their concern extend far beyond their immediate families to the health of the earth and those who depend on it for sustenance. Seven generations are barely enough, as the native saying goes, for the duration of this caring. The accumulating nuclear and other toxic wastes will be with us for tens of thousands of years despite our efforts to temporarily pawn them off on the hungry and the unsuspecting poor. How long, one must ask, will future generations be able to withstand the health hazards caused by the wastefulness and greed of the rich industrial countries?

Is This Retirement?

At seventy-three, once again I ask myself, am I retired? Retired from what? I take delight in knowing that this period of my life is the final gift of time, to be used authentically and with good intent. Unquestionably, I have a relative freedom to choose my activities, to decide what to tackle each day, whether to battle snow and ice to attend a meeting or to curl up with a good book (hook a rug, string beads, piece a quilt). I can be a spokesperson for unpopular causes without compromise and can withstand and even invite criticism in order to remain open to what is unexpected and unknown. My chosen work is with honest, dedicated people who offer friendship and know-how in collaborative exchange.

I do not miss university life except for the occasional camaraderie among colleagues and the fullness of working with eager students. A new bout with cancer has required that I face issues of life and death more mindfully. Paradoxically, it has catapulted me into more intense study into the causes and treatment of cancer. In effect, most of the causes are known. What is needed is the political will to stem the tide of carcinogenic emissions in the air, soil, and water, which for centuries have nourished life in all its forms. That will require major structural changes in the ways governments and corporations envision and carry out their mandates. To replace profit making as the economically driven bottom line with concern for democratic rights and the health of the planet will necessitate a revolution (one hopes a quiet one) and human activity the likes of which we have recently witnessed in Quebec City and San Diego. This is clearly not a job for one or a few, but for citizens working together in common cause. These words of anthropologist Margaret Mead (1901–1978) are a reminder that it is up to each and every one of us: "Never doubt that a small group of thoughtful, committed citizens can change the world. Indeed, it is the only thing that ever has." (Given the events of September 11, 2001, in New York and Washington, D.C., and the escalation of terrorism worldwide, two months later I am now questioning this statement—one that I have believed in for so long: Is a culture of peace still conceivable as those with power talk of and prepare for war, retribution, and revenge?)

It has been illuminating to look back and observe how the threads of my early life wove in and out to create the cloth of the final tapestry. By these threads my retirement narrative has been given shape and is propelled onward.

Notes

1. Gail Sheehy, "The Nifty Fifties," in *Passages: Predictable Passages of Adult Life* (New York: E. P. Dutton, 1974).

2. Lanie Melamed, "Play and Playfulness in Women's Learning and Development" (Ph.D. diss., Department of Adult Education, Ontario Institute for Studies in Education, University of Toronto, 1985).

3. Mary Belenky, Blythe Clinchy, Nancy Goldberger, and Jill Tarule, *Women's Ways of Knowing: The Development of Self, Voice, and Mind* (New York: Basic Books, 1986).

4. Lanie Melamed, "Why Spend So Much Treating Cancer, So Little Preventing It?" *The Monitor* 5, no. 10 (Canadian Centre for Policy Alternatives, April 1999).

5. With apologies to Gloria Steinem, who titled one of her books *Outrageous Acts and Everyday Rebellions* (New York: Holt, Rinehart and Winston, 1983).

Retirement without Regrets

DOROTHY KAPSTEIN HAMMER

Think of being confronted at a cocktail party with that prosaic query "And what do you do?" For many recent retirees that question can be disturbing and the need for a quick, appropriate answer is often discombobulating. Those three little words "I am retired" rarely fall trippingly off the tongue unless retirement is your dream realized.

My own retirement came suddenly with my second husband's terminal illness. I had worked throughout our eight years together but chose to be with him during his last days. As an individual contractor, I had never considered retiring as an option and had made no formal provisions for retirement outside of a small TIAA-CREF (Teachers Insurance and Annuity Association College Retirement Equities Fund) pension and personal savings. I always believed there would be time for a new work project later. But it was apparent after my second husband's death in 1994 that I would have to recycle and redesign my life. I don't mean your cosmetic-counter, fashion-advisor makeover, although that can be a good idea too. In my case it meant taking stock of my past and utilizing those experiences to keep my life as rich and mobile as possible. Blessed with good health and high energy although I was already seventy, my girlhood fantasies, which had been a factor in determining my entire work life, were still at play, albeit with realistic limitations that these later years bring.

When I was small, I dreamed of travel and adventure; my dreams were fueled by the tankers and freighters that delivered cargoes of oil to the giant containers of the Standard Oil Company in view of our home on a bay in Bayonne, New Jersey. My appetite was clearly whetted when I compared the faces of the sailors to those in my book *Children of Many Lands.* This little book and the foreign sailors on their tankers piqued my imagination and led me into a life of wanderlust. Luckily, I have realized many of those childhood dreams through six or seven work and personal reincarnations demanded by various changes in my life. Sometimes I feel like the cat with nine lives—which means I might get two more if my luck holds out.

As a child of the depression years, I experienced at first hand the reversals of fortune that befell and nearly destroyed my family, and it was at that unhappy time that I determined to have a meaningful career. My father wisely counseled me to be independent as a woman and to be aware of life's precipitous changes. It was unusual advice in the forties, when most women were being advised to make a good match, as the saying went.

To enter the field of fashion was my prime goal. It was a field in which there were, in the forties and fifties, enough women of ambition and success, who never doubted their own ability or that of other women, to emulate. Estée Lauder, Pauline Trigere, Dorothy Shaver, Claire McCardell, Hattie Carnegie, and Helena Rubenstein were just a few examples of the leaders who created a golden time for career-minded women in the fashion and beauty industries. I don't think any of them ever gave a thought to retiring.

I had chosen my career path long before graduation from the New York University School of Retailing by working numerous odd jobs—in Lord and Taylor's College Shop, modeling at department store fashion shows on Saturdays, being a gofer at the Museum of Non-Objective Painting and the Metropolitan Opera. After graduating in 1944, a much-coveted job as a reporter with the *Tobe Report* was offered to me; I later became an editor there. This was the first of the international fashion advisory services. A monthly publication, it was the bible for department store executives, buyers, manufacturers, and advertising agencies. It had real cachet throughout the fashion world for its on-target predictions and interpretations of fashion trends. Tobe Coller Davis, the brilliant director of the report, was a mentor to all who worked for her. Many who began under her tutelage went on to become fashion authorities in journalism, in advertising, and in textile and fashion design, as well as department store executives.

Opportunity knocked again as a result of a search call to one of my *Tobe* friends from the executive fashion director of *Seventeen* magazine, which was then enjoying the reputation of the magazine with largest circulation in the world. They needed an editor immediately and, as I was always ready for a new challenge, I applied for the position, was hired on the spot as sportswear editor, and was soon promoted to senior editor. Besides planning all the fashion pages with my fifteen assistants each month, I supervised much of the photography at various foreign as well as domestic locales, arranged and presented fashion shows, and worked with manufacturers and advertising executives. The multifaceted requirements of the job were demanding, challenging, and exciting; I loved every minute of the seven or eight years I spent there in the late sixties.

This happy period in my career ended when my husband, who had become successful in his own international work, declared that he needed an executive wife in Europe, where he headquartered. Wanting to preserve the marriage, I left the job I loved in order to abet him in his work in Paris. A crumbling marriage was the result, and I returned to New York jobless and footloose but with a new resolve to be completely in charge of my own decisions in the future.

At this point my life truly changed. I was forty-seven years old, my sons were grown and off in their own directions, and I was motivated to prove I could do it all on my own. I had been professionally successful at a time when most of my contemporaries were staying at home to raise their families. A demanding husband, a widowed mother, growing children, an active social life, big winter and summer households, and a high-voltage career to boot were my imperatives. Superwoman, Mistress, Mom, Cook, Housekeeper, and Bottle Washer rolled into one was the expectation. Those of us who tried to live up to this package didn't know enough to say "Enough!"

The women's movement spearheaded by *Ms.* magazine and Gloria Steinem, Betty Friedan, and Germaine Greer, among others, accompanied by the peace, gay rights, and civil rights movements, those mind-blowing occurrences of the sixties and seventies, became a whole new support system for me and my contemporaries, helping us to rev up our courage to become independent of conventional pressures. The early seventies were take-charge time for me. I was undeterred by the lack of a regular paycheck and uncertain assignments, loving the challenge of new, sometimes risky projects seeking native crafts in remote, exotic places. I decided that becoming self-employed rather than being locked into a full-time job suited my newly emancipated spirit. I am certain that after all the years of pleasing other people, the entrepreneurial choice was right for me. I also believe it gives one a longer shelf life if one can afford and is willing to forgo the perks of a regular job: companionship with your peers, a steady income, and retirement benefits, an irresistible troika for most. Going it alone is not for the fainthearted.

I soon became restless without my family and without steady work and was ready to test the adventurous life by exploring the remote areas of the world I'd always dreamed of. With my background in design and journalism, I applied for and received grant money to go to Africa (an intriguing but completely unknown-to-me place) with the purpose of studying and collecting textiles and crafts whose decorative forms were relatively new as sources of design inspiration in the United States. My first trip, in the fall of 1971, was financed by the DuPont Corporation and was followed by many more, including to South America, under their auspices. Their intent was for me to collect endangered textiles from cultures around the world that would be housed and preserved in a textile library they were planning to build at their headquarters in Wilmington, Delaware. Simultaneously, the Museum of African Art in Washington hired me as a consultant to collect handcrafts for them in Africa.

For this exciting, high-energy work I needed a partner with very specialized know-how. Luckily, I found an associate who had lived in Africa, and we formed Bamboula Associates to deal in African crafts. As we were far ahead of the curve in introducing the beautiful textiles and crafts then rarely seen outside of Africa, we were invited to do shows for department stores, art galleries, charities, and organizations interested in promoting "things African." We were each traveling back and forth alone three or four times a year, to more countries each time, to meet an ever-increasing demand for these handcrafts. Eventually my partner and I had a falling-out, and I decided it was time to spread my wings in other directions.

Early in the 1980s I joined a group of craftspeople on an invitation-only trip sponsored by Japan Society to meet many of the Living National Treasures of Japan. This group of artisans worked in every field from cake making, textile design, and pottery to making lacquerware, umbrellas, and combs, and were accorded the highest honors and reverence for their outstanding skills. We had the opportunity to work and visit with each of them. Inspired not only by the visual beauty of Japan but also by the earnestness of the wonderful craftspeople we were fortunate enough to have met, I came back to create Shibui Blues, a clothing and home-furnishings concept considered highly innovative at the time. As my knowledge of business was negligible, the downturn in the economy in the early eighties forced me to close up shop after only three highly creative years.

Almost immediately I was called to Washington. The Museum of African Art was being absorbed into the Smithsonian Institution, and they needed a crafts expert to develop original products for their gift shop, both in the United States and in Africa. Given my previous association with the organization, it was a perfect fit as well as perfect timing.

My entrepreneurial, freelance life was working for me as I lived modestly and had invested the money from the sale of my large apartment and summer place. I even had time for a new relationship that was developing twenty years after my divorce. This led to a most happy but, due to my husband's death, too-short marriage. I continued to freelance for the Smithsonian during most of our years together but as we both loved to travel, I was spending more and more time adventuring and less and less working. Whatever commitments I had were being taken over by a younger staff that I had trained to scour the African markets while I continued to develop new products for the museum locally. My priority was to travel to wonderful, remote places with my husband while we were still adventurous and able.

His year-long illness and subsequent death left me with a lot of new thinking time. Going back to a job was out of the question. I had no great desire to start a new business and while I had never regarded my age as a factor, thinking not only of my priorities but of my realistic options required some appropriate resolve.

An eighty-four-year-old acquaintance who had been a highly successful real estate agent said to me, "Why did I ever give up working? I miss the calls, the people, the excitement of making a deal." She seemed to be laboring under a pressure that many retirees face, asking, "What do I do with my life now?" The longer, healthier life some of us are fortunate to be living does not seem to have the answers to: How do I make it work for myself? How do I stay awake, active, engaged? How do I not become invisible and stay in sync with the times? Where do I find my rewards in these retirement years?

These were the hard questions I had to ask of myself. I have always had a lazy streak but I could not imagine drifting into my last years in a vegetative state, which could have happened if I hadn't pulled myself together. When my work life ended, I realized I had to approach my retirement years like a new vocation. As I am the ultimate list maker, I started new lists of everything and anything. Nothing was insignificant. My lists included my finances, trips I wanted to take, friends I liked to be with (and those I didn't), magazines and papers to be dumped, things that made me happy, and projects that were worthwhile. The lists covered the highs and lows of my work life as well as of my personal life. I had included my successes, failures, passions, interests, and hobbies and when the yellow pad was filled I had arrived at what gave me the most pleasure at that point in my life and what I found stultifying and boring.

I realized that I was, after all, living on the shorter end of life's stick and therefore my choices were no longer infinite.

I concluded that with the continued blessing of good health and a sense of humor, I could continue to do really wonderful things I loved to do, things that would satisfy, nourish, and engage me. My old life had been informed by splendid peaks and plateaus, by risk taking in my chosen careers and travels, and although I did not currently have the option to repeat most of that, I could write about it for my children and grandchildren with the pleasure of reliving the high points. This became my number-one priority soon after my husband died and I started taking courses in memoir writing, which have given me the discipline to write three or four hours a day, two or three days a week. This has happily structured much of my time, along with activities such as working out in a gym class, tending my garden, volunteering with an AARP (American Association of Retired Persons) program producing videos for public-access TV, keeping up with old friends, making new ones, and lending a hand to those in need of help. Cooking and entertaining now and then is still fun as is taking advantage of all the priceless treasures—museums, concerts, parks, theaters, lectures, and courses that New York City has to offer. Friends and family (two sons and their mates and two granddaughters and more to come) are scattered in faraway places and the opportunity of seeing them either here or there always heads my list. Travel continues to be high on my agenda. And if my energy holds up for the rugged travel I so enjoy I might soon head off to one of the three B's I haven't yet covered: Bhutan, Botswana, and Burma.

Any remorse? Yes, there are always some do-overs in our heads and hearts, but at this stage I try to replace them with what is doable and gives me pleasure. I celebrate what I have done and seen, what I can still do, and what I look forward to doing. So what is this thing called "retirement"? It can be a joy or a bugaboo, depending on how you view it. I believe I've retired to more free time to do the things that I love without stress and although I am clearly slowing down, I've tailored myself a work-and-play ethic that is rich and rewarding. It truly makes for a retirement without regrets.

Carpe Diem/Follow Your Passion

IDA HENDERSON

I had a very varied work life between the ages of eight and fifty-six. When I was eight years old I started doing shopping for the elderly people in our Brooklyn apartment complex. I had a regular group of customers who always needed my services. In high school I worked Thursday evenings and all day Saturday at Woolworth's five-and-dime. (Alas, those stores have disappeared from New York City.) During the summers I worked full-time at various factory jobs because when I appeared for an office job and they saw my black face, the job was "just filled"!

By the time I entered Brooklyn College, in 1951, the racial prejudice was starting to slowly ease. I worked for one year as a full-time file clerk at the Metropolitan Life Insurance Company, and I attended college in the evenings. When I started going to college during the day, I found employment as an office assistant after classes. When I received my bachelor's from Brooklyn College, in 1955, I thought I would pursue a career as a social worker. To that end I started working at the Department of Welfare with the intention of saving money to go to social work school. However, after working for two years I decided to seek a more hopeful career.

I started working as an elementary school teacher in the fall of 1958. I started teaching sixth graders but went down a grade every year or two until I finally ended up teaching first grade. I did this to find out why I was getting students with such poor academic and social skills. I found out some of the answers, but that's a subject for another article. My other Board of Education position was as a paraprofessional trainer in a pilot study program called Teacher Mom. This program was the precursor to something that is now a part of special education. The program was essentially a tutorial program for students who were identified by their classroom teachers as in need of academic, social, and psychological help. Each student was given a "mom" or a "pop" to work with on a regular basis. I provided the curriculum and other support needed by both the student and the paraprofessional. Because there were no true guidelines, I was free to try all of the creative tools that my staff and I could brainstorm in order to respond to the kinds of issues the children came up with in the course of our work together. I also worked for three years as a reading counselor in a program that was a support system for teachers in the area of reading and provided a reading resource room where teachers could get both assistance and materials.

For the last ten years prior to my retirement, I worked as an assistant examiner at the New York City Board of Examiners. The Board of Examiners was the licensing agency for the principals, assistant principals, psychologists, social workers, and teachers who worked in the New York City school system. (The agency was abolished three years after I retired.) The Board of Examiners oversaw both the written and the oral examinations required for working in the school system. I worked on the examinations for teachers of special education. I loved my job because I got to work with all of the personnel in the city schools. I even got to travel to Puerto Rico in search of bilingual elementary school teachers. My job required working evenings and Saturdays when large written or oral examinations were taking place.

The fall of 1988 was a very challenging time for me. Three years earlier my mother, who was diabetic, had been diagnosed with bladder cancer. When it became clear to us that she was not going to recover from her illness, my three siblings and I secured the services of home hospice care. I was the primary coordinator of her affairs and health care. My duties involved being at her home in Brooklyn at least once a day, which meant a subway ride to and from Manhattan, where I lived. Hospice did not provide a live-in nurse, so I had to secure one. I continued all of my professional duties while living with the *Sturm und Drang* of my mother's illness. She made her transition in October of 1988. I was left feeling physically, mentally, psychologically, and spiritually exhausted. (I tended to somatize all of my mother's physical and psychological pain.) I felt I needed to relax, take stock of my life, and get on with it.

After much rumination and prayer for Divine Guidance, I decided that I would retire. Since I had been working since I was eight and had thirty-one years at the Board of Education, I felt no guilt about retiring at the age of fifty-six. However, my friends and colleagues admonished me about talking retirement. They advised, "Why not take an extended vacation? You have been under a lot of strain. It's never a good idea to make a major life decision while you are still mourning. What about your pension?" I listened to their "advice," and I consulted a financial planner. However, I have always believed in seizing the moment and following both Divine Guidance and my passion.

And so, after much internal debate and more prayers for Divine Guidance, I decided to go to the Kripalu Center for Yoga and Health in Lenox, Massachusetts, in order to recuperate and to help myself get on with my life by taking training to become a yoga teacher. (I had been to Kripalu over the years for various programs.) My one reservation was that I would in all likelihood be the only black person there. But I knew that, in a sense, this concern was not a major one, since I have always connected with people on a much deeper level than skin color or ethnic background. In February of 1989 I retired from the Board of Education and headed for Kripalu.

The bus ride from New York City to Kripalu takes about four and a half hours and is always for me one long meditation. I have traveled this route through each change of our seasons. Each time I travel I think I am in the perfect season to watch the trees and neat little houses that dot the New England landscape. That February morning was a little different. It was snowing and the landscape looked like a holiday greeting card. Every aspect of the landscape seemed much brighter and even cheerier. I started to wonder, "What's different about all of this beauty?" It finally hit me that the difference was internal. I wasn't going for a brief vacation; this was the first phase of my retirement.

When I arrived at Kripalu, I thought to myself, "And now the adventure begins." I had requested a private room that looked out on a beautiful lake surrounded by the Berkshire Hills. What a treat! On the evening of my arrival my yoga teacher training officially began. The yoga instructors devised a very entertaining way for the participants to connect with one another. They started some very unusual music and told us to dance in anyway we wished, using all of the space in the room. Suddenly the music stopped and they told us to get together with the four other people nearest to us. They then announced that each group of five would be a "family" for the next three weeks. We spent the rest of the evening with our family, sharing our stories. We were a very diverse group ethnically, socially, in age, and in other ways, and yet we clicked immediately. My family and I shared many experiences during those three weeks and three of us continued our friendship well beyond our Kripalu experience. I spent six weeks there enjoying long walks, sometimes with a member of my family and sometimes alone in deep walking meditation. As the days passed, besides learning my new skill, I enjoyed wonderful massages, reading, good conversation, meditating, and eating very nutritious food. Each day I felt another layer of fatigue and mourning melt away. I felt I had indeed found a most nourishing way to launch my retirement years.

When I returned home to New York I felt completely refreshed and ready to hang out while I waited for the universe to reveal the next phase of my retirement. I didn't quite get to hang out, however. On the day I returned to New York I went for a manicure in my neighborhood. I was wearing a Kripalu T-shirt, and, as I was about to leave the shop, a woman getting a manicure commented on my shirt and asked if I gave private yoga lessons. Thus began the next phase of my retirement.

I started giving private yoga lessons to that woman (she remains a good friend today), as well as to others, all by word-of-mouth recommendations. I also began teaching a group lesson in the apartment complex where she lived. I had great fun teaching at the New York Kripalu Center and the Kripalu Center in Lenox. During one of my sessions at the Lenox Kripalu Center, I met another African American yoga teacher; we began discussing the fact that there were no people of color at Kripalu and what we might be able to do to remedy this lack. After several meetings together with another African American yoga teacher, we put together a diversity training program which the staff at Kripalu (after many meetings and much discussion) agreed to allow us to present. I am happy to say that our first presentation to the staff went well, and we now have a diversity program at Kripalu; in addition, there is now an African American on the board of directors. I consider this inclusion of people of color a great accomplishment—plus, one of the yoga teachers I mentioned above is now one of my buddies.

I retired from teaching yoga in 2000. I had a bad fall which caused damage to my left knee. I felt I didn't want to continue yoga if I couldn't demonstrate all of the yoga postures. Two of my private clients refused to let me go; I gradually weaned them. I secured another yoga teacher for them. Since teaching yoga was a great source of enjoyment for me, I went through another period of mourning. However, I continue to do my own personal, modified yoga.

My many volunteer jobs have been another source of fulfillment. I volunteered at a Brooklyn nursing home for a year. I worked with three women. One of my clients was a real challenge. She was bedridden, unable to speak, and could only move her eyes and hands. I read to her and devised an exercise program. I brought in some music and, using her bed table as our dance floor, we did finger dancing. I told her to visualize her body and legs moving as we danced to the music. Her eyes lit up and we both had a great deal of fun. Her nurse told me she had never seen my client's face so alive! I also volunteered as a greeter and office assistant for the now-defunct classical music radio station WNCN. I even went on a trip to London with their listeners' club. I was also a volunteer Big Apple Greeter for the City of New York. I led neighborhood walking tours for French- and Spanish-speaking visitors. I resigned after over nine and a half years of enjoyable service in 2001 because I was overextended.

I started docent work at Carnegie Hall in 1992 and it remains one of my great passions. I find great pleasure in sharing the history of this legendary concert hall and telling musical tidbits about the many performers and performances that have taken place here. However, once again I have found myself the only person of color. I encouraged many of my friends to consider becoming a docent. Finally, after five years of thinking about it, one of them has begun the training, and she loves it. And recently another African American has become a docent, so now we are three.

Traveling has always been an important part of my life. When I started traveling, in 1956, I didn't consider traveling in the United States because of all of the racial discrimination. I traveled to Mexico, Africa, Europe, South America, and the West Indies. When I retired, in 1989, I decided it was time to see some of the United States. I started traveling with Elderhostel. Once again I have been the only person of color. Despite that, I have made some wonderful friends on Elderhostel trips, and we have enjoyed visiting each other's cities. I would recommend Elderhostel travel to anyone who enjoys a structured vacation.

Some of my other passions include choral singing and playing my flute (which I started learning to play after retiring) in a chamber music group. In the cultural smorgasbord of New York City, as a retiree I am free to enjoy a great deal of theater, concerts, museums, and dining out and in with friends. Another of my longstanding fun activities since retirement has been attending a monthly French speaking group I co-founded with a friend. This group has become an important part of my community. We have been there for each other through life's various challenges.

One of the most nourishing additions to my community was the birth of my grandnephew in 1994. My niece and nephew generously shared him with me every month for four years. He and I had our once-a-month private time. One of our favorite haunts was a place called Rain or Shine, an indoor play space that had a sandbox, an art room, many toys, a fully equipped playhouse, musical instruments, and a theater stage with props. We participated in all of the activities one could enjoy there for over two and a half years. I was heartbroken when his parents left New York City in 1998 for employment in North

Carolina. We still see each other, though the monthly private time became too expensive to continue; however, I have never missed his birthday.

In search of community I had joined a group called Womanshare (although I'm no longer a member) and two reading groups, and attended church, first at Unity Center of New York City and now at Marble Collegiate Church. Also, I attended many meetings on co-housing in the city but decided that was not a viable option for me. I made this decision before September 11, 2001.

The September 11 attacks were a traumatic time for all of us, but we in New York City were particularly affected. For many days we New Yorkers were quiet and walked about as though we were zombies. The honking horns and loud talking were almost entirely gone. I was weepy, depressed, numb, and angry all at the same time. I found the small-group grief counseling service at Marble Collegiate Church helpful. I gradually began to feel better, but there is a part of me that is still grieving for my wounded city.

Life for me now, after September 11, is about assessing what is truly important. I have not visited the grave site that was once the World Trade Center. I do not know if I ever will. I do know that despite my love for New York City, I'm no longer at ease in my hometown. I also know that according to some statistics, the city ranks third in the nation in racially segregated housing. I have been lucky to have lived in my housing of choice, through the kindness of strangers. (I have never been able to find an apartment without the assistance of white people.)

It will be hard for me to leave my luxury building in search of a new community. I will start to look where I can be close to my family in North Carolina. It's a place to start while I am still in good health and have many options. My friends are all shaking their heads in disbelief about my starting to talk relocation. They're saying, "You're the quintessential Manhattanite. You take advantage of everything positive in New York City; how can you even think of leaving?" However, I have learned that the universe "talks" to me when it's ready, and I'm open and ready. In the meantime, I continue to pray for guidance and take one day at a time.

My advice to anyone thinking about retirement is to listen to others and then sit with your own inner voice and wait for guidance. You will know when it's your time to retire. To those already retired, I say, "It's a big world, follow your passion and seize every moment. Come on in, the water's fine. Can't swim? Don't worry; there's always someone willing to coach you." In conclusion, I have to say I have been truly blessed with good health, a loving family, and an abundance of sincere and caring friends.

I am always ready to seize the day and follow my passion!

Three

NEVER RETIRE

Retirement—The Final Question Mark?

CAROL BURDICK

For weeks, my natural sloth has been fortified by a strong reluctance to discover my real feelings on this subject. I have been unable to confront the computer screen in any guise except interacting with E-mail and/or waging inscrutable scrabble tournaments with Maven. Even now, making a last-ditch effort, my whole body resists: I am perched uneasily on the edge of the chair, my teeth are clenched, my stomach tensed—while my mind scurries like a demented mouse trying to avoid whatever might turn out to be honest and/or painful. It's almost ten-thirty in the morning and I'm not dressed, I haven't done my stretching exercises, the yard needs mowing, the bed isn't made, I still have to call for opera reservations at the Chautauqua Institution, a friend is coming for lunch—and on top of these calls to duty, images from last night's roadside encounter with a fawn, a spotted infant so young that messages from its brain weren't reaching its legs, keep obtruding between me and the keyboard, seeking words of their own.

Once again I have managed to postpone any real engagement with the subject. Have to get lunch.

Two days later:

This is it. Retirement, in my mind, equals death.

All of the other passages we undertake during the course of a lifetime lead to something new, something, if not always inviting, at least challenging. Infancy stumbles into childhood, childhood leaps into adolescence, adolescence improves into adulthood, adulthood flows into maturity. The only change forthcoming after retirement is dying. As a nonbeliever, I see death as extinction, oblivion. Life is all.

So what if I am afraid to die? Does this not-uncommon fear really have something to do with my not wanting (or daring) to retire, or is it a mere whale of an excuse, a way of sidestepping the decision? These are just a couple of the questions rising to the surface of my consciousness while I perform the daily routines of my Edenic life here at the pond house—feeding birds and the dog, disposing of a few weeds, writing letters, telephoning friends, sorting through the chaos of long-neglected closets and cupboards.

One of the first ideas to surface with any validity is how much I should emphasize that my antipathy to retirement is idiosyncratic and situational. Death-phobe or not, I probably would not be so vehement in my rejection if one (or all!) of the following life scenarios were available: if I lived with a partner whose vitality sparked mine as we searched for exciting varieties of new experiences, from hiking in Nepal to helping out in Haiti; if I had enough ego strength to believe that whatever works emerged from my hours at the computer would make some kind of dent in the publishing world; if I was lucky enough to have ten or twelve nearby grandchildren with whose lives I could become involved (rather than the four who, though tremendously lovable, are growing up thousands of miles away); if I could maneuver a reduction in various travel/motion phobias; or if I had fewer of the deteriorating aches and pains and stiffnesses that overtake aging bodies. A working bladder would be good, too.

These nonviable options remind me that I've not revealed enough of what has led up to my current situation for readers to feel either empathy or revulsion. Or to feel anything at all, for that matter.

Quickly, then. Born: 1928. Married: 1949. Divorced: 1970. (We produced three very satisfactory children who chose—or lucked into—fine partners.) Pleasantly single (but somewhat sadly celibate) since my forties. In May 1999, aged almost seventy-one and feeling a bit tired and anxious about being so old and still taking up office space, I enjoyed a full-scale, upbeat retirement from teaching writing and 200-level literature courses at a small university in New York State. One of many women in the 1950s whose jobs paid for their husbands' degrees, I lacked a Ph.D. at the time of the divorce; later, while the children were in school, I needed to work. Later on, this lack barred me from full-time teaching status, a mixed blessing since, although I carried a lighter burden of papers and preparation, I also had to scramble some to make up for earning only half of an assistant professor's salary. Social security kicking in at sixty-five, in addition to inheriting my parents' home, helped me build my present—and nearly perfect—abode. (Note: Though many of us feel discussing money is crass, in terms of talking retirement it is essential. My fortunate twenty-four thousand a year is more the result of luck than planning—and in the world beyond Allegany County, New York, that sum would probably not seem quite so satisfactory!)

If I had orchestrated the retirement ceremonies myself, they couldn't have been more exciting. I had the gall to deliver a swan song lecture at the university, in which I combined criticizing some current administrative policies with giving the audience a glimpse of some outstanding student writing. The literary magazine editors asked me to give a poetry reading and the colleague who introduced me said exactly what I would have liked him to say; another colleague wrote an encomium, which stressed my basic teaching philosophy (from e. e. cummings's "I'd rather learn from one bird how to sing than teach 10,000 stars how not to dance"). I was honored, with other retirees, at a trustee dinner, and later that week awarded an honorary degree from the alumni association. It was just great.

The most appropriate response to all of this hoopla would have been to die—or, at least, to join the Peace Corps. A librarian friend of mine did just that (the Peace Corps, that is) when she retired, and her life has been full to the brim with new friends and fresh experiences ever since. But I, emulating Emily Dickinson and her established preference for her own backyard universe, stayed at home. As certainly has been evident in the preceding lines, although my small house in the country is a wonderful space and I finally had time to write, retirement didn't work out as planned.

What went wrong? Mostly, I think, the fact that the daily discipline of writing never kicked in and my immediate habitat became, I quickly learned, somewhat confining. Not quite enough space. And I had never learned to sit still.

Fortunately, by the time decompression set in, I was involved in a summer's teaching, including an Elderhostel writing course and a graduate course in children's literature. That fall I drove all around New England feeling smug as could be about this new freedom from schedules and papers. The next spring I taught a joyous seven-week poetry workshop. In the fall of the following year, the chair of the English division at Alfred University, from which I'd just retired, offered me a four-credit "Comp 101" course; there had been an overrun of fifteen students, most of them first-year artists. I'd always wanted to see what could be done with fewer than twenty-five students in a basic writing course—how could I refuse? And since I'd already signed on for a half semester environmental literature course, there I was, on half time again, except with adjunct pay (less than a fourth of what I had earned before). Then came Poetry Workshop in the spring again and now, in the upcoming fall, another six credits has been made available. I can use the extra paycheck since my TIAA-CREF (Teachers Insurance and Annuity Association College Retirement Equities Fund) annuity has sagged noticeably.

Starting to talk about money makes me uneasy and this piece is becoming exceedingly dull; perhaps I've said enough to show that when it comes right down to it (and much to a few of my colleagues' discomfiture), I have not really retired. When paranoia murmurs from some crevice of my brain, I seem to hear a few low voices: "She's too old for this! Why doesn't she leave?" In defense of any murmurers, I should remind myself that they are right—not only is sixty-five the proper, the conventional age to remove one's self from the classroom, many professors today are opting for sixty-two.

Partly because the state, in its profound wisdom, has made it impossible for a mere master's degree holder to teach graduate education courses any longer, something I'd done for many years in summer schools, on this sunny June day I look forward to fall.

There's the crux, isn't it? I look forward to it.

My life draws its breath from interaction with people. Family members, though essential and dear, are far away, friends do make daily life involved and interesting, but for the past thirty-odd years it has been students who have given me the strokes that soothe my leonine ego, who have ignited my spirit, and whose demands have filled my schedule. I have become a student-addict.

If writing that self-description doesn't give pause, it should. As one perceptive draft-reader has suggested, the word *addiction* suggests no choice. Have I really no choice? Will the withdrawal symptoms be fatal, as I seem to feel? How and why have I become so dependent on student contact?

Even living in a small village in a remote part of the state, it would be easy enough to fill my time by volunteering to shelve books at the local library, or to run for the school board, or to be a literacy tutor, or to help out at the kennels of the Society for the Prevention of Cruelty to Animals, or, or, or. It's all necessary and important work—and thank heavens there are others to do it. For me it would be just that, filling time. With the sands draining so rapidly through the glass, I want to spend as many of my allotted hours as possible in a classroom or my cluttered office. Both are cherished spaces where my insights about life and literature are listened to with not-always-cynical respect, where

I am challenged by youthful approaches to the business of living, where I exercise some power and achieve a sense of importance (although I am often cornered by a student's superior logic and once again reminded that age doesn't imply answers). We also, my students and I, laugh a lot—though not always at the same things. They irritate and exasperate me, they enlighten and amuse me, and they keep reminding me that the earth is, as Frost said, the right place for love.

Although I am far from overwhelmed by affectionate letters and tokens of esteem, a number of students have become part of my life. A few from whom I haven't heard since they graduated years ago surprise me by turning up on E-mail or in person. A few days ago I received a graduation invitation from a fine university with a little note penned inside. At the risk of aggrandizement, I quote it here:

> CB,
>
> I hope you can remember who this is! I just want you to know that you have been the most influential teacher I have ever had. Thank you for giving me the guidance I needed to strive for only the best,
>
> > *Sincerely,*
> > *Naomi ___*

While working on a paper for the first Rachel Carson conference a few weeks ago, I had an E-mail from a student who wrote:

> Bet you don't remember me, CB, but I was in your "Place in the Universe" class and liked it the best of any course I took in college—which is saying something since I was a ceramic engineer—and yes, I do remember the place I had to write about twice a week for seven weeks!
>
> > *Kevin____*

And though I do not, indeed, remember Kevin, my next few hours were filled with the pleasure of knowing that course had been good for him—and I added his note to my paper about teaching environmental literature. As for Naomi, I had only offered her a bit of encouragement, really, and sent a few follow-up notes when she left school after having an abortion, deeply troubled in spirit.

So there's the heart of the matter, really. Sometimes I do have a positive effect on the young lives with which I come into contact—and it makes me feel good. Other people get to feel good by taking drugs or drinking alcohol. It is called addiction.

Entering into the addiction are the occasions I can only call "magical moments," which occur quite unexpectedly and quite rarely, in the classroom. These are times when the students listen to and support each other, when laughter is shared rather than directed at someone, when they are as moved as I am by a passage from Annie Dillard or Loren Eiseley and I am not the only one in the room with tears in my eyes. There are also the private moments, when, reading something written in a journal or an essay or a poem fills me with wonder at the writer's perception and prose.

I do not believe, however, and I will never believe, that my motives with regard to my relationships with students are other than selfish. My ego craves the feedback. Also, I can hardly count the number of students I have damaged in some way: students who needed higher grades than I gave, students who never realized the literature spread before them had sustenance if really ingested, students whose distrust of authority made them itchy and unresponsive, students who needed extra attention whom I ignored. There is always the dark side of the good teacher coin.

Writing about this makes me sad, and I have said enough about it, anyway.

Sometimes I worry about taking up office space and budget dollars that could be used by some younger person. (That may be a variant on the overall guilt trip many women of my generation and background have been traveling with and on all of our lives. As a feminist, I should be able to dismiss the question. But it's there—and another subject entirely.) While it's a subdued concern, it's real. I will keep in touch with the division head to be sure a full-time person is not not being hired just because they have this eager elderly adjunct panting for a couple of courses!

Okay. After finally finding some words to express my feelings about retirement, I am beginning to realize that I am not going to retire—at least not completely. I'll watch the evaluations, formal and informal, with close attention (a short-term memory riddled with "senior moments" plus a long-term lack of organizational ability can certainly result in some confusion; so far no one has complained). If I do turn into a white-haired dracula draining youthful vitality from my captive audience, I hope I will be removed, even if screaming and kicking, from the classroom.

I've often tempted fate by saying I hoped to live long enough not to be afraid to die. That may not happen. What matters more to me right now is to continue teaching as long as I can climb the stairs, locate the correct classroom, and decipher student handwritings and personalities.

From this moment on, all the idea of retirement is going to mean to me is that I must reconcile myself to being paid a lot less to do exactly what I have been doing happily for the past few decades—argue with and learn from and care for and be nourished by the young people who show up in my classroom.

And there I thought I had wrapped up this excursion into the depths of self. But on the back of one of my recycled pages coming through the printer just now came a quotation I'd saved weeks ago from Charles Baxter's *The Feast of Love*. He says, talking about single people, "the workings of nature are mysterious, but they do account for a certain amount of despair among single persons, the *irrelevance* you sometimes feel."

Add to the word *single* the word *old* and mix with the word *retirement* and the force of his statement is doubled. Of course that's it. I fear retirement because I will become irrelevant. The easiest way for me to remain relevant is to stay with students. It's as simple as that.

Guess I'll postpone worrying about death a while longer . . .

Progressions

MERLE GELINE RUBINE

On paper, it appears that I am retired. At the age of sixty-four, I left my job after twenty-five years, and I am collecting my pension and social security. I fit the statistical profile of a retired person, but I reject that phrase, which, to my ears, makes it sound as if I am being put out to pasture. One retires for the night; the Navy retires battleships; economists talk about retiring debt. Yes, I am at official retirement age. Yes, I have left the corporate world. However, I do not consider myself retired. I am a year and a half into a new career that, I hope, will keep me busy, intellectually stimulated, and salaried for a long time. I think we should retire the word *retire*.

I began to think about this subject when I realized I was no longer in love with my job. I was a television news producer who had a low opinion of TV and rarely watched it. I felt that the scope of my life had shrunk to the size of a walnut. My mood was alternately irritation, impatience, or boredom. It is embarrassing to admit the length of time and the amount of money I spent shopping. Sometimes for kicks I played the old scold, but the effect was neither funny nor attractive. The truth was that my battery was dead, and I didn't have jumper cables.

The signs of burnout are familiar, but figuring out what to do about it is not easy. There was the option of retirement, but I was not ready to stop working—didn't even consider it. I do not see myself spending my older years sitting with a book by the fire. Financial realities were also part of the reason. I knew I would not be happy making do on a fixed income of pension, social security, and a portion of a modest 401(k) plan. Clearly, something new was in order. I would have to reactivate the cells that still had juice and reinvent myself professionally.

Starting over in my sixties was a little like starting from scratch at the age of twenty-two, when I left suburban Milwaukee and came to New York City with two hundred dollars, a few favorite LPs, a bachelor's degree in English, and a determination to work in television news. I had been glued to the set during the Army-McCarthy hearings, and I wanted to join Edward R. Murrow and all the other journalists at CBS News who were bringing Truth to the People. As it happened I never met Edward R. Murrow, but my first job in broadcasting was at CBS News. I was the personal courier for an executive producer who did not trust messenger services. If memory serves, there were only two women working in editorial positions in the newsroom at the time.

New York was great. My roommate and I lived in Greenwich Village—I'd seen *My Sister Eileen,* and so of course I had to live in the Village. The hip thing to be, I thought, was bohemian, so I tried to break out of my middle-class background by wearing black tights with high heels and cultivating weird people. At the end of a doomed love affair, my roommate opted out of the New York life and joined the Peace Corps. I stayed behind; I had had a promotion by then and was not looking for change.

When I married, my male colleagues assumed I would soon go home pregnant and stay there. They had it wrong. I went back to work three months after the birth of each of my two sons, even as people whispered behind my back that I was a lousy mother for doing so. Eventually, I was accepted as a woman who was serious about a career and spent years at both CBS and NBC. I produced everything from ninety-second local news spots to two-hour network documentaries. The job took me to summits, Olympics, conventions, and war zones. I met world leaders, celebrities, overachievers, underachievers, heroes, and villains. Most of the time I had so much fun I would have worked for free.

But over time the business changed, as did my feelings for it. Late in 1992, I went to the Balkans to do a story about the war in Bosnia. My crew and I went to refugee camps in Croatia where Bosnians who had survived the most harrowing experiences—betrayal, torture, gang rape, and murder—painfully and tearfully told their stories. I looked at broken people huddled together in the refugee camps in freezing weather and felt helpless. Would putting their stories on television make a difference? Maybe it would be more edifying if I crossed over from observer to participant. It was a fleeting thought.

A few years later I attended a story meeting to discuss another story about the Bosnian war, which would be pegged to the war crimes trials in The Hague. One of the executives commented that many of the victims who were going to be interviewed in the story had unpronounceable names. There seemed to be some unease about the assignment, and in fact it was risky. Foreign stories are expensive, and when they are about a complicated, grisly war in a far-off place called the Balkans they are hard to promote in prime time. The story might be worthy, but would it be worth it in ratings?

The correspondent assured everyone that the production team had lined up great, heart-wrenching material, and they would watch out about the names. With a final reminder to keep an eye on the budget, and an offhand remark about moving the audience to tears, the meeting was over. It was over for me, too. News has to sell. To sell it must be slick, and you have to keep it simple. I didn't want to be a part of it anymore. It was time for me to move in a new direction.

However, before I could decide on a new direction, I had to figure out where I could fit in and what I had to offer. I took a personal inventory and found that I had:

excellent health
no dependents
management skills
intellectual curiosity
wanderlust
a sense of humor
a youthful spirit
an apartment that could generate income

I found I did not have:

strong computer skills
a second or third language
a master's degree
status as a media superstar or a top executive

I had to confess I was worried about:

living outside the loop once I left the network
being old and poor, forced by necessity to downsize my lifestyle
becoming bitter

I knew what I hoped to achieve by moving on to something new:

to reconnect with the world and make new commitments
to find a sense of purpose and usefulness

When I added up the pluses and minuses, I realized that what I lacked was less important than what I had:

the intellectual and emotional energy to take on a huge new challenge
the ability to organize and manage groups and anticipate and resolve problems
the experience necessary to travel and live away from home for long periods
the possibility of income if I chose to leave New York and rent out my apartment

I concluded that I could do whatever I wanted. The only question was, what did I want to do? It's a heady question. First careers require some degree of pragmatism and compromise. Presumably, there will be children to raise and educate. Second careers can be, should be, a gift to oneself . . . within reason. I love ballet, for example, and even take ballet classes, but I did not see myself taking curtain calls for my *Swan Lake*.

I made a list of the things I most enjoy:

researching and reporting stories
poking around in antiques stores and flea markets
traveling, making new friends
going to the ballet and theater

I made a list of occupations that related to my favorite activities:

writer/reporter, specializing in issues of aging
antiques dealer
Peace Corps volunteer
character actress in television commercials

I explored my choices and eliminated everything but the Peace Corps. Remember, I had thought about joining the Peace Corps in the sixties, when one of my New York roommates signed up. The time was not right then, but now, perhaps, it was. Dealing in antiques requires deep pockets or a benefactor with deep pockets. I had neither. Writing about gerontology required, in my view, going back to school. Honestly, I did not want to do that. I found acting schools willing to take my money, and at my age I knew I would not have to worry about the casting couch. On the other hand, did I really want to find my fifteen minutes of fame asking, "Where's the beef?" That was the still-famous line spoken in a fast-food commercial years ago by an octogenarian actress. She had been a manicurist and beauty parlor owner; the commercial made her a star.

I was nervous when I went to the Peace Corps office in New York for my assessment interview. The Peace Corps has many programs—rural health, water and sanitation, agriculture, education, small business development—but there was not a program requiring a background in television. It was humbling. At the end of the interview the recruiter said she thought I would be an "amazing" volunteer. I wished that I could be as certain as she was, but I nonetheless started organizing myself for a future in a third-world village.

The first thing I did was let my hair, long-since gray but religiously processed brown, go natural. This was crossing a threshold. No more faking. If I was going to live without running water and telephones (a television producer without a telephone!), I could give up my colorist.

I was assigned to Ivory Coast, now named Côte d'Ivoire, a French-speaking country in West Africa. I boned up on my high-school French, put my furniture in storage, and kissed my family and friends good-bye.

On May 11, 2000, I landed in Abidjan, the capital of Côte d'Ivoire, with fifty-four other trainees, most of whom were under thirty. Three of us, all women, were over fifty. We were taken to a small town about forty-five minutes east of Abidjan, where we would prepare ourselves for service. We had language, technical training, and cultural sensitivity classes five and a half days a week, from eight in the morning until five in the evening.

Each trainee lived with a host family. I was assigned to stay with Lucy, a schoolteacher who was a single mother, her two daughters, a niece, and a maidservant. We lived together in a three-bedroom house. Lucy and I had our own rooms, while the girls shared. There was running water (cold only), electricity, television, a refrigerator, and a telephone, but no stove. We cooked over a charcoal fire behind the house. It took a while to boil water for morning coffee; otherwise the inconvenience did not matter much.

Life in Africa for single women is difficult, but Lucy is fiercely independent—actually a feminist at heart—and we bonded like sisters. There were many more similarities than differences between us. I am a widow, she is divorced, and we are both heads of our households. We each have clotheshorse tendencies. She liked my oversized T-shirts; I liked her oversized African print dresses, called *boubous*. Our kids were giving us angst. Her daughters—unenthusiastic students; my sons—taking a while to find their way. We laughed at each other's jokes and groused about the lack of good men. I will never forget the time she stayed up until midnight helping me write a speech in French about African religion for the next day's cross-cultural class. Then she got up early to help me put the speech on note cards. As the friendship deepened, matters of first world/third world, African/American, black/white dissolved and disappeared. Lucy and I are friends for life.

After twelve weeks of preservice training, we became full-fledged Peace Corps volunteers. We were sworn in, raised-right-hand and all, and dispatched to villages throughout Côte d'Ivoire, where we would live for two years. I was sent to Massala, a very traditional Muslim village in central western Côte d'Ivoire. Bluntly stated it is a backwater, but more interesting than most villages of its kind because of the mayor. The mayor is six-foot-four, French educated, and charismatic. He lived in France for fourteen years and had a wife and a daughter, but gave everything up to come home and help his country. One of the things he brought with him when he returned was a well-developed flair for promotion. He managed to have Massala profiled on television as an example of a village on the move. I had seen one of the reports and been impressed. There were pictures of a new hotel, a new water tower, and a new cultural center. The village appeared to have a rustic charm.

What a surprise when I got to Massala and found that there was no running water. No paved roads. No telephones. No newspapers. The hotel, the cultural center, and the water tower were not finished, and there was not a construction crew in sight. Moreover, there were neither sanitation facilities nor garbage pickup.

This community of about twenty-two hundred survives mainly by subsistence farming, and the people are very poor. Woman's work keeps the community alive. Women have the children, nurse the babies, cook the meals, fetch the water, gather the wood, wash the clothes, heal the sick, care for the elderly, and work in the fields. What don't they do? They don't debate the pros and cons of retirement. Village women in Africa never retire. They don't stop until they drop. Women are considered as old if they live to fifty; of the entire population, 2.22 percent are sixty-five and over.

Massala *is* charming in its own kind of way. I live in a four-room cement duplex, surrounded by huge mango trees, and cooled by north-south breezes. It is at the edge of the village, and at first I felt isolated. Now I appreciate the peace and quiet around me.

I did not like finding out that the toilet I was supposed to use was an outdoor latrine, which was shared with the neighbors. The coup de grâce was that the latrine hole was full. Remember the old adage about the squeaky wheel? I let the Peace Corps and the mayor know that the toilet facility, or lack or it, was a deal breaker. I got an indoor pour-flush latrine.

My new community welcomed me warmly. I was the new *La Blanche*, the new *Toubabou*, the new white person in their midst. Many had had good working relationships with the volunteer who had preceded me and were eager to continue working with the Peace Corps. There were others who asked me for presents. I found this perplexing. I would have had to be Santa Claus to meet the demand. The first months were difficult. My French was too limited for me to have a real conversation, and at that, almost no women speak French, so I was finding myself unable to communicate with the female half of the population. The local language is Worodougou, and I was having trouble learning it as well. When I wrote my friends at home, I worried that age was eroding my mental capacities.

I was sent to Massala to help the mayor to develop environmental protection programs, but it soon became clear that there was not money in the village till to plant trees or hire garbage collectors. If I wanted to accomplish something during my two years in Massala, I would have to improvise an alternative agenda. That was easy—it was just like working in television: you don't collapse if a story falls apart, you find a different one. I decided to concentrate on health and education projects.

Monique, the midwife at the maternity center, was interested when I suggested that we start a baby-weighing program. We invited all the women to a meeting to explain what we wanted to do. Actually, we called three meetings because no one came to the first two. About fifteen women showed up on the third try. We met at eight-thirty at night in a courtyard lit by a bright neon light that was a magnet for flying insects. Monique and I took our seats in front of the group, under the neon light. It took enormous self-control to sit there and not squirm while the bugs dive-bombed me. I was nervous. Monique was not optimistic that the women would be interested. She had tried setting up a similar program before, and it had failed.

I had prepared a short speech in French—in truth I had slaved over it, trying to find exactly the right phrases to express my commitment to working with everyone in the village and explain the importance of tracking infant weight. Someone was on hand to repeat my remarks in the local language. Talk about lost in translation! All of my words were summarized in a few short sentences, and I could see that no one was impressed. Then a woman asked me what I would give the mothers who brought their babies to be weighed. Money? Free medicine? Oh, I could see this was a tough crowd. I had neither money nor medicine to give, nor would I have given it if I had had it. The road to sustainable development is not paved with freebies. Monique took over. She read the women the riot act about the importance of baby weighing, infant nutrition, vaccinations—everything. She struck a responsive chord; the women voted to begin the program. Walking home, Monique asked me how I liked the way she had saved the situation. I said I liked it very much because, indeed, she had.

A few months later two of the primary-school teachers asked me to help them set up a literacy program. I thought this was a very important thing to do. The majority of the people in the village are illiterate, but literacy is a sine qua non if people aspire to climbing out of poverty. Again, we called a meeting, and the mayor came to show support and about twenty people expressed interest. After that it was uphill. People were slow to commit. The teachers seemed to hold me responsible for the lack of progress, but I was already blaming myself, and I felt terrible. This went on for months. Finally, after more meetings, a disastrous visit from state education officials, and a rained-out opening night, we had a core group of seventy-five students.

Working in the literacy program has been one of the most inspiring experiences of my life. Many of the students did not know how to hold a pencil when they started class. They could not draw a straight line or a circle on paper. Little by little they learned how to form and recognize letters, and combine those letters into words—sometimes very important words. One of the students, a carpenter, told me how grateful he was that finally he could sign a receipt with his name instead of an X.

The success stories are nice, but I learn more from the inevitable problems. As the novelty of something new happening in the village has worn off, students, particularly the women and girls, have dropped out of night school. There are many reasons: exhaustion after working all day in the fields; family demands; illness; the mourning period—there is a lot of death in African villages; the village culture itself, in which education is considered a good thing, but an "extra."

Our core group has decreased to about twenty, and we are in the process of restructuring the program to make it easier for people to attend regularly. As far as my old ideas about success and failure are concerned—I am letting them go. Social development isn't a numbers game. I will take progress one person at a time. My carpenter friend is learning to read and write, but more important, he is sending his children to school.

In the time I have been in Massala I feel that I have made a difference in the lives of others, but the experience has made a difference in me as well. I went to Africa a control freak. Control-freak-ism may be a job requirement in television, but it guarantees disaster in the village. For example, I don't worry about bugs. Can't. They far outnumber the human population. I take cold-water bucket baths without complaint. If the small grocery runs out of bread and eggs, I eat rice and sauce. If there isn't transport out of the village in the morning, I travel in the afternoon. Often it's too hot to do anything but just sit in front of a fan. Villagers always say, "*Ça va aller*" (it's going to be okay). In the old days I would have wanted to know exactly why someone thought a bad situation would turn out all right. Now I too say, "*Ça va aller*," and the weird thing is, it usually is.

Of course, there have been hurdles. There is a lot of down time in the Peace Corps. If you cannot stand your own company, you probably won't make it through the two years' tour. It is hard to be the subject of stereotyping or generalizations. People assume that as an American, I am rich, and that everything in America is cheaper and better. They are still asking me for presents: food, medicine, furniture for the house, money. Sometimes it is hard to be different. Although the previous volunteer was also Caucasian, my white-ness scares babies. Often I am the first white person they have ever seen, and the sight of me makes them cry.

On the more personal side I don't have ballet classes or a gym to go to; I can barely do a *plié*, my feet are stiff; my muscle tone is history. Maybe it would have happened anyway. Time and gravity answer to no one.

Overall, however, I would say my adjustment has been relatively painless. This has not been the case for everyone. Twenty-one of the original fifty-five in my group quit the Peace Corps before the end of their service, including one of the over-fifty sisters.

There is a saying in the Peace Corps that volunteers in Asia come home spiritual; volunteers in Central America come home political; volunteers in Eastern Europe come home cynical and depressed; and volunteers in Africa come home smiling and happy. It is true. I can't explain it, but joining the Peace Corps in Africa was overwhelmingly the best decision I have ever made for myself. It never occurs to me to play the old scold. What's more I am being paid—we get about two hundred dollars a month as a living allowance, full health coverage and two hundred and twenty-five dollars are put aside for readjustment costs after service. People who do not know the Peace Corps well may be a little confused about the term *volunteer*. We work seven days a week, and we work hard. There are expectations and there even is competition among the volunteers.

When I left NBC, I was scared. I had grown accustomed to the perks and privileges of a high-status profession. There was the possibility that I would not find my way outside of the corporate world and I would have little to look forward to but getting old and feeling irrelevant. But my Peace Corps experience is giving me all that I had hoped to find: challenge, a sense of purpose, a sense of accomplishment, a great adventure, and a path to follow. Peace Corps is boot camp where I am preparing for a second career, working to alleviate poverty and backwardness in the developing world.

So I haven't retired. I am progressing, moving on, starting over.

Social Insecurity:
A Cautionary Tale

CAROL K. OYSTER

I am a fifty-two-year-old professor at a Midwestern university. I have been teaching for over twenty years. From that information you would think that, like so many of my peers, I would be eagerly anticipating retirement or about to retire. Nothing could be further from the truth. Through a combination of conditioning, choices, and circumstances I am not sure I'll ever have sufficient financial resources to retire.

Money was a taboo subject in my family as I was growing up. I never had any idea how much money my father made (my mother did not work outside the home). I recall being asked about family income in my first year in college and being embarrassed not to have a clue. I knew that my father did well—though not rich, we had enough to have a pool in the backyard of our Southern California home, and I was never forced to differentiate between wanting something and needing it. If I was invited to a social occasion and decided I "needed" a new outfit, a shopping excursion was planned.

My education about financial matters was essentially nonexistent. I never bought my own clothes until I left home after college, and my parents financed my entire undergraduate education. My allowance from the ages of seven to twenty was contingent upon the performance of household chores. I never liked housework so I received an allowance twice in those years. In high school, when I needed money, I got a job outside the home where I was able to make enough money for entertainment—my only expense. Needless to say, I never learned to manage money.

If it sounds like I had a very traditional upbringing in terms of sex roles, that's only partially true. My parents' attitudes toward sex roles were paradoxical. My mother earned a bachelor of science in chemistry in 1942—an unusual achievement for a woman at that time. During World War II, after her marriage, she was the only woman employed in a government research laboratory. After the war, however, she retired to the home and stayed out of the workforce for the next thirty years. She made it very clear that she believed that mothers should not work, but that women should work for a time between marriage and motherhood.

The message was clear. Success and security were based in marriage. I was encouraged to make good grades in school for a very specific reason. I was coached to seem smart, but not too smart, because men don't marry women smarter than themselves. Good grades in high school meant acceptance into a good college where I was expected to earn both a bachelor's degree and my "MRS." And the pickings were better for a financially successful husband at a better school.

Clearly I was being groomed for the role of the upper-middle-class housewife—the house with the picket fence, 2.5 children, and a dog named Spot. Financial education was irrelevant to that goal. But golf lessons, attendance at a cotillion (to learn etiquette and ballroom dancing), art lessons, orthodontics, and dermatology were important. My husband would support me for the rest of my life. Earning a living or planning for retirement were to be his business, not mine.

Well, the best-laid plans . . . I married for the first time at twenty-nine, much to the relief of my parents. Marriage almost made up for the fact that I had chosen to enter a doctoral program. Between college and my marriage I held a series of what I viewed as temporary jobs in which I never invested much interest. There were no provisions made for retirement savings. They were stopgap measures on the way to "happily ever after." The marriage lasted three years—just about the amount of time it took to complete graduate school.

Although I now expected to use my education as the basis of a career, I was still on the lookout for Prince Charming. But I was beginning to suspect that I should be considering some sort of supplement to the Social Security checks I assumed would finance my retirement years (just in case). So in my first job on a college faculty I took full advantage of a generous retirement program to begin saving. Better late than never.

One year later my daughter was born (the very best thing that's ever happened to me—and probably the most expensive). Still single and without any additional income or support, I realized that I should seek work in a part of the country where my income could support a reasonable lifestyle for us both. I cashed in my entire retirement savings account (taking a major tax hit) to finance my first house. I started over on saving for retirement (I was now forty).

My relentless (and now somewhat desperate) search for Prince Charming seemed to pay off when I remarried at forty-five. My prince had a trust fund so I thought that retirement was no longer a matter of concern. Again the marriage lasted three years.

A prenuptial agreement is only as effective in protecting assets as the intentions of the two parties to honor (or fail to honor) the spirit of the agreement. Let me just say that I came out of the marriage in considerable financial debt. I had made major expenditures while married from my own resources assuming that eventually things would even out. With the costs associated with a series of health problems that were not covered by my health insurance, I went even further into debt.

So here I am, fifty-two years old. I'm beginning to see the light in terms of climbing out of debt, but that has taken every penny of every paycheck. There has been no extra money to save or invest. And in three years my daughter will begin college. I will be solely responsible for her college expenses at the undergraduate level, unless she qualifies for scholarships. While she is a straight-A student, I suspect that since my income on paper is fairly substantial (otherwise we'd have gone under completely), she may be eliminated from consideration for any scholarships that have a financial needs requirement. She's talking medical school, and I'm talking student loans for that portion of her education. And that traditional conditioning still haunts me to the extent that I expect to pay for her wedding if and when she chooses to marry. So when I read articles about people my age finally being free of child-associated expenses and having lots of discretionary income to invest or play with, I don't know whether to laugh or cry.

I don't look forward eagerly to retirement because I don't know whether I'll have enough money to live—literally. My daughter says she'll take care of me, but I'm so determined not to be a burden that I'd rather become a bag lady and live out of dumpsters. I don't expect at this point to receive much, if anything, from Social Security although I've paid in for thirty years. I don't know whether the system will have crashed by the time I can even consider retirement. I have paid into my state retirement system for twelve years and expect to for at least another decade—but I don't know what that will mean in terms of income.

I realize that at this point you may be shaking your head in disbelief that I could have made so many "bad" decisions over my life. After all, I came of age during the second wave of feminism. I was liberated enough to seek higher education, to enter a career not traditionally considered acceptable for women, and to become an unwed mother. But somehow I never was able to escape all of the traditional conditioning about my proper role. Despite myths to the contrary, women are still considered failures when their marriages end. After each divorce a number of well-meaning friends and acquaintances told me that if I had just been a better housekeeper or maybe less successful at my work I could have kept the marriages together. I'll never know. But while I'm not happy about my financial woes, I'm not sorry about the choices I've made. They were the best I could do at the time and I wouldn't be who I am or have the wonderful daughter I have had I made other choices. I like us both a lot. And I've had a wonderfully eventful life.

So what words of wisdom can I impart to help others to keep from ending up financially where I am now? I can encourage all women to learn about money from as early an age as possible. Take courses. Learn to handle money young. When you take your first career job, start packing away as much as you can. One day you're twenty, then you blink and you're fifty-two. Living on a shoestring is charming when you're young; it's exhausting and scary when you're older.

Retirement: From Rags to Rags

CAROL A. SCOTT

Coming from a poor, African American family with nine children, *retirement* was not a word I ever heard growing up in the hills of Pennsylvania. My father was a coal miner with a seventh-grade education and my mother, a high-school graduate from a small town in Alabama, was a housewife. Child rearing, washing, ironing, cooking, working in the fields, nursing, tutoring, being a playmate, and being a seamstress are jobs I watched my mother do tirelessly and without complaint, for all of her children and her husband, until she died of breast cancer at the young age of fifty-one.

My mother was born in 1911. Her parents were sharecroppers. She used to tell us stories about picking cotton from the time she came in from school to the time she went to bed, her hands swollen and bruised. However, my grandparents valued education and thought if she became a secretary she would be a success. She married my father at age twenty-five, an old maid in 1936. African American women of the 1930s could work at little else than domestic or factory jobs. There were no choices for my mother after marrying and having eleven children. If my mother ever thought of retirement in terms of money, she could never have collected a penny since all of her labor was unpaid. As for millions of other women, since she worked in the home, no pension would have been forthcoming. What my mother did, however, had value. She instilled in all nine of us a caring, creative, nurturing, and supportive character and taught us to be sensitive to the needs of others. It was my mother, not my father, who gave us this foundation. I learned from her the importance of developing my own identity. It was watching her live with only the love of rearing children that caused me to want a more liberating life, one that I had some control over. Because she died so young, I have often pondered the impact children, marriage, and motherhood have on women's economic, emotional, and physical health. I always think of her as having worked numerous jobs and been paid for none.

Though never without food, there was very little of anything in the way of material goods in our home. To make ends meet my father worked a second job picking up garbage and cardboard boxes. Making ends meet meant having enough money for food, shelter, and minimal clothing. Although he worked two jobs, he was paid for one and lived on a small pension after he was forced to "retire" due to failing health from silicosis. However, his role in the family was that of breadwinner while my mother's was primary caretaker/caregiver, placing an unequal burden on my mother. The burden was unequal because when my father came home at night his job was done, and he did not work on the weekends. My mother, however, never stopped being responsible for the mental, physical, and psychological health of nine children. Keeping a clean house, preparing the most nutritious and balanced meals with surplus food, and continuously nursing sick children did not come with sick leave or vacation days. While my father was off fishing, hunting, or playing cards on the weekends, my mother continued to labor. She worked with her head, her heart, and her hands. I wonder to this day if she ever really created anything for herself. Did she ever dare to dream, to escape, if only momentarily, to a place all her own where she held dominion over something or someone? I doubt it.

She was never able to build any kind of security because her work was not valued. She often said to me, "Don't ever depend on anyone for your existence. Make sure you never become a burden to your children." She meant a financial burden. That is why she encouraged all of us to further our educations, especially the girls. My five brothers served in the military; two went on to become postal workers, one became an auto mechanic, one an IRS executive, and one, after returning from Vietnam, chose to go underground and remain there—where we do not know. My three sisters became a teacher, a librarian, and an accountant, and I am an administrator.

My older sister, Joyce, was the first person in our family to attend college. She received a scholarship to what is now Clarion University of Pennsylvania and became the family's role model, graduating with a degree in library science. I paid attention. Though I didn't do well on the SATs or enroll in the college-bound curriculum in high school, I was accepted to Clarion in 1962, graduated in 1967, and entered the workforce as a caseworker. I later became a teacher of the mentally challenged at Schenley High School in Pittsburgh, Pennsylvania.

I married, in 1967, at the age of twenty-three and though I knew money was being taken out of my check for retirement, it never occurred to me that that was the beginning of building security for old age. I was also paying into Social Security and was aware that the program would assist me in my old age and that health care was somehow involved. When my husband took a job in Massachusetts, we decided to take the money from my retirement plan since we needed it for the move and expenses in Massachusetts. There, I continued to pay into Social Security during my years as a dormitory counselor at Boston University. While working, I completed a master's in education at the university. The job as a dormitory counselor paid little; most of the compensation was in the form of rent and utilities. While I worked in the dormitory for low wages, my husband was working as an assistant dean, making a respectable salary and building a retirement account. This was the sacrifice I made to save money for the purchase of a house and to be at home with my son, Robert, born in 1971, who was a toddler at the time. In 1977, my daughter, Cinda, was born.

In most families, members often need support and that usually means financial support. So, when sisters and brothers asked me for help, I gave it as I knew they would give to me if they could. However, at age forty, I began to pay more attention to my retirement account since I had by now worked both in the Boston public schools and the community college system. It never occurred to me to put more money away for retirement, but I became very aware of my retirement finances when I was divorced in 1989. That was when I began to be concerned about my old age. I needed to earn more money and completed my doctorate in higher education administration at the University of Massachusetts, Amherst.

The divorce was very costly. The only assets were the house and its contents. There were no savings since most of our income went to send two children to prep school. The house sold for less than its worth because it was too expensive to maintain and my husband and I had separate residences at that point. I received half of the value of the house and a little more than half of its contents. Both retirement funds were split in half. At the time of the divorce, my ex was not employed. He had lost three well-paying jobs during the course of the marriage. When he moved, because he had found a job, I assumed responsibility for both children. My son was seventeen and my daughter was twelve when we divorced. My ex-husband refused to pay for any of my son's college expenses, and when my daughter went to college he paid 15 percent of the tuition. The college gave her a scholarship for 15 percent of the tuition, and I paid the balance of 70 percent of the tuition plus spending money and the costs of her computer, books, supplies, travel, and miscellaneous other expenses.

In the spring of 1992, I took a position as a campus dean at a community college in upstate New York, where I worked until 1999. The college offered employees the opportunity to match its contribution to their TIAA-CREF (Teachers Insurance and Annuity Association College Retirement Equities Fund) accounts. I matched at the highest level because I knew I would need that money to help send my daughter through Middlebury College, where the tuition was about thirty-five thousand dollars a year. I was right; the money I put in I took out to help with tuition. I paid half the expenses in cash and borrowed the other half using Parent Plus loans. I will pay on those loans for the next ten years.

Because I assumed about 90 percent of the total costs of my children's postsecondary education, I was unable to save more. As a parent of African American children, it was crucial to me to give them a fine education and to lessen their financial burden upon graduating from college. Since I had graduated college in debt, I wanted my children to have the best possible start in life. Expenses to educate my two children totaled in excess of two hundred thousand dollars.

I am extremely fortunate to have a great circle of friends, many of color. They, too, have had many of the same experiences with divorce and ex-husbands that I did. When we sit around and talk about our experiences, we often speak of what we like to call "deprivation syndrome." We define deprivation syndrome as the need for, in our case, African Americans to feel important, included, equal, whatever the nomenclature, by showing white America that we have the same cars, houses, time shares, and clothes many of them do. We fall into the trap of supporting a lifestyle that makes us a slave to our possessions. What is important to understand is that whites have had privileges for years and many can have not only the cars, houses, time shares, and clothes, but the bank accounts, annuities, stocks, and the early, comfortable retirement.

When, as an African American, you feel you have been assigned a position of inferiority you sometimes overcompensate. This may cause you to spend money foolishly and therefore grow old without adequate resources and have to work long after you are physically or emotionally able. This reminds me of one of my favorite authors, Erich Fromm, who states that many people feel that because they have nothing, they are nothing.[1] Are those who spend a life scrubbing floors, working in sweatshops, and raising children *nothing*? On the contrary, they were and are extraordinary.

I often ask myself who takes care of the children, especially black children? Usually, it is mothers and other female family caregivers. They take responsibility for children's education, physical and emotional health, and career development, and for providing some sense of security for a child. Child rearing and domestic responsibilities traditionally left to women also impact retirement, especially if one is divorced and the noncustodial parent remarries, starts a second family and contributes little to the first family economically or emotionally.

At age forty-five I thought I could retire at age sixty. I am now almost fifty-eight and will have to continue to work until age sixty-six or sixty-eight. Why? Because of my lack of education regarding retirement, because of divorce laws, because women are often left to care for and educate children alone after divorce, because being black and female can be an extra burden, and because, like most mothers, I wanted more for my children.

Because of the choices I made, I must continue to work. After leaving upstate New York in 1999, I took the position of executive vice president of the Urban League of Greater Cleveland, a nonprofit organization whose mission is to help improve the lives of citizens in economically and socially marginal neighborhoods. I continue to assist my daughter, who is enrolled in a research project that will prepare her to enter a Ph.D. program in marine biology. My son, recently married, is a licensed pilot and is currently serving his country as a naval officer working in naval intelligence. They are two exceptional young people who would make any parent proud. I am honored to be their mother.

I have had to use retirement funds for financial emergencies because I was unable to save money since child rearing and education expenses exhausted my paycheck. Did I give my children enriching experiences and expose them to as much as I possibly could educationally and culturally? *Yes*. Would I do it again? *Yes*. Will I be able to retire when I originally planned? *No*. Will I educate my daughter about my personal experience with retirement, employment, and education? *Yes*. She is already very much aware of what is necessary to build the right kind of financial portfolio to ensure she does not become a retiree with few benefits, or someone who cannot retire until she's eighty.

The quality of one's retirement is directly tied to choices one usually makes early in life. It is important that a woman pick the right partner, one with similar values and financial interests and who will share in the responsibility of child rearing, including their education; she should marry a man and not a male; she should plan for a lifestyle she can support, which includes deciding when and how many children to have. And, more than anything, she should feel so comfortable with her ideas about retirement that she decides when she can retire and what is required to support that decision.

Though I will be unable to retire for another eight to ten years, I do hope to retire by age sixty-eight. If, as my mother used to say, "the good Lord's willing and the creek don't rise," I plan to spend those years helping to educate young women, wherever I meet them, to be conscious of their investment in work and family and to ensure they are adequately compensated for that work. That may require investing time and energy in changing public policy regarding what women are paid for rearing and nurturing children, a job which our society professes to value and honor.

If retirement at age sixty were possible I would do so without reservation. I began my journey into the world of work at age thirteen. I remember my father taking all of us to a neighbor's farm to help plant acres of trees, for which the farmer paid him. I was not paid. I spent all of my summers while in college working in a summer camp. By the time I was twenty-two, I had worked five years.

Most of my professional life has been in service as a teacher, caseworker, and community college administrator. Working with disenfranchised, poorly educated, poor, dependent individuals and families whose social and economic deprivation creates feelings of isolation, hopelessness, and helplessness is both rewarding and challenging. Dismantling feelings of despair, anger, and sometimes rage is hard work. I have been working in these environments for over thirty-five years and though the work is critically important, I am ready to retire. I have some ideas about what I would like to do next.

I was fortunate to travel to foreign countries both in the course of my work at the college level and as a result of my interest in other cultures, and I have visited over thirty-five countries and forty-eight of the fifty states. Trips to Egypt, China, Mexico, Italy, Ireland, and the Czech Republic were favorites. While in Mexico about ten years ago, I became intrigued by the wood carvings called *alebriges* done by the villagers in Arrazola, San Martin, and La Union outside of the city of Oaxaca. I began to collect them and am now very interested in starting a small business. When I come home from a foreign country I always bring gifts for family and friends. Beautiful *galabias* and papyrus from Cairo; cloisonné and peasant art from Beijing; rugs and *alebriges* from Mexico; hand-carved music boxes from Sorrento; lace, linen, and sweaters from Dublin, and crystal and watercolors from Prague.

What I get the greatest joy from, besides giving the gifts, is sharing the stories behind the purchases—talking with the cab drivers, having dinner with a family in their hacienda, learning about the tools they use to create their products, meeting their children and grandchildren, hearing their hopes and aspirations for their families, and telling them of my country. I'm not just interested in selling a product, I'm interested in sharing cross-cultural understanding about the traditions, practices, mores, and folkways of people from around the world. We have a great deal to learn from their example, and they from ours.

I have thought it would be great to own a small bed-and-breakfast in Harlem, New York, with a gift shop full of products from my travels, a small café, a library that informs our intelligence (locals would be invited to speak on issues of interest and concern to the community), and a jazz-and-blues room. It would be my honor to hold educational forums twice a month for women on the topic of retirement, to be taught by friends and family who are lawyers, accountants, certified public accountants, IRS employees, and estate planners. Also, enlisting other retirees to give of their time and knowledge to tutor local students after school would be value added to strengthening families. Giving back to the community and investing in the community are my responsibilities as a member of the community.

For me, there could be nothing more enjoyable than making people comfortable in a well-appointed room with an Amish quilt and Turkish towels; inviting family and friends to listen to local artists looking for an opportunity to share their talent; reading books I consider great, such as Howard Zinn's *A People's History of the United States*, Maurizio Viroli's *Niccolo's Smile*, Cormac McCarthy's *Blood Meridian*, or Annette Gordon-Reed's *Thomas Jefferson and Sally Hemings: An American Controversy*;[2] drinking a good cup of tea or a glass of Egly-Ouriet and tapping my feet to the wonderful sounds of Frank Sinatra, Wynton Marsalis, and my all-time favorite, Etta James singing "Almost Persuaded."

I look forward expectantly to retirement in eight or ten years (or at least to semi-retirement) and, as always, to learning, teaching, and sharing.

Notes

1. Erich Fromm, *To Have or To Be* (New York: Continuum Publishing, 1997).

2. Annette Gordon-Reed, *Thomas Jefferson and Sally Hemings: An American Controversy* (Charlottesville: University Press of Virginia, 1997); Cormac McCarthy, *Blood Meridian* (New York: Vintage, 1992); Maurizio Viroli, *Niccolo's Smile: A Biography of Machiavelli* (New York: Farrar, Straus and Giroux, 1998); Howard Zinn, *A People's History of the United States* (New York: Harper Perennial, 1995).

Change of Life

MARY STUART

Trembling on the cusp of my next decade birthday—which happens to be the one that makes people think of words like *old, retirement, golden years, senior citizen*—I find myself smack in the middle of establishing a new career at an age when many of my peers are thinking about improving their golf games. And not just any career, but one for which parents admonish their children to have something to fall back on: I want to be a writer. I must be mad. At age fifty-nine, I fall into the category of the preretired—not quite at the official retirement age of sixty-five and still needing or wanting to work. It's a little late to be thinking about a fail-safe occupation.

"Don't jump around from company to company," counseled my parents when I got my first job. "Employers will think you're unstable. And be sure you know how to do something practical to fall back on." Considering I was only fourteen and working as a flunky-of-all-trades at a local department store, those words, viewed from the perspective of adulthood, now seem a bit silly. That was sage advice for their generation of Great Depression survivors, but I didn't understand that context when I was fourteen. Nevertheless, their words haunted me for the following decade because even then I had a sneaky suspicion that staying in one job for forty years wasn't going to work for me. My parents' words reverberated in my mind and made me uneasy about my natural proclivity for change.

I have a low boredom threshold. Not just for jobs, but for careers. I've been a secretary, a tour escort, a gofer, a middle manager in various businesses, an escrow officer, an entrepreneur, a teacher, a social worker, and a psychotherapist. And those were the steady jobs. Laced around them are some things I've tried and not liked or tried and failed to accomplish. Now I'm staring into the not-so-golden years of retirement and wondering what that means.

Retirement for my parents meant that after thirty or more years in one job you got the gold watch and then lived on your pension and social security. At least that's what they said when I was fourteen. It didn't turn out for them that way, and young as I was I noticed it wasn't turning out that way for many of their elders. At a very early age I came to the conclusion that my generation would be lucky to get back the social security money the government was theoretically socking away for us, and that retirement as such might be a dicey affair. I don't think I was too far off the mark. In fact, when my father died unexpectedly at the age of fifty-five, my mother found herself in difficult economic circumstances. Having worked only part-time while I was growing up, her skills were minimal for the job market as it was then. Although equipped with a formidable intellect, she had trouble as a woman in her mid-fifties finding work that either paid or was interesting enough, and she's had a rough time financially ever since. That had an impact on me throughout the following years. I worried I might end up with the same problem.

Graduating from college in 1962 at age twenty with a degree in psychology, I discovered that the world was not as liberated as I'd been led to believe. My background and upbringing, not to mention my personality, dictated that I could do anything, including brain surgery, if that was my choice. But as a fellow student observed, "Our degrees and twenty-five cents will buy us a cup of coffee anywhere in the U.S." I discovered my psychology degree was only good for low-paying unvalued jobs that had nothing to do with psychology, so I decided I needed an advanced degree. I went to law school.

Well, it seemed like a good idea at the time. The women's movement was gearing up, and though it didn't have a lot of steam just then, going to law school seemed like a proper feminist thing to do. I lasted for a year and a half, clerking with a law firm during the summer between my first and second years. In the midst of the "you can do anything" rhetoric I had heard during my formative years, a concomitant discourse about talent, innate desire, or a calling was absurdly absent. My choices became clinical and objective and lacked anything even vaguely associated to passion for the subject. This, as it turned out, was a fatal flaw because I discovered I didn't like lawyers and I didn't do well in law school. Not doing well was a blow to my ego. I didn't understand the link between excelling and wanting something badly enough to do well at it. Not only was passion for the subject matter missing; so was the talent. I felt like a failure and fell back into low-paying, low-self-esteem jobs for many years, always looking for ways to advance in whatever company I was working for. Climbing out of the lower-echelon rut in any given company proved to be a myth, at least for me. I never made it.

It wasn't until my late twenties that I fell into an occupation that was dominated by women and where opportunities seemed open for advancement. I have my first husband to thank for that. I had met him in the law school in Arizona where we were both students, he a year ahead of me. We married some years after he graduated and he became an attorney for a title insurance company that relocated us from his home state of Texas to Nevada. He knew how frustrated I was working as a paralegal, and he suggested I go into escrow, a business related to real estate and title insurance involved in the closing of the sale of homes and commercial enterprises. I'm grateful to the industry for pulling me out of the depths of my previous mind-numbing jobs, and I found the work challenging. But I must say that a field more conducive to the verbal and psychological abuse of employees by their bosses and clients was never invented. I've often wondered why women predominate in escrow positions, and believe it has to do both with the extremely nitpicky details of the work and the fact that it was, and perhaps still is, rife with abuse. Women put up with abuse far more than men do. You have to have some smarts to be an escrow officer, especially in California, where I worked and where the field is a separate industry. Because the job deals with people's money, often enormous amounts, feelings run high and the level of tension can be extreme, and usually is.

My husband and I moved from Nevada to California, and eventually divorced after living first in San Francisco and then San Diego. I had a job offer in the mecca of big bucks and large egos—Beverly Hills—and moved to Los Angeles. The tension in that job was so bad that by the time I got the gumption to start my own business as an escrow consultant I had had major surgery and was in deep therapy just to cope with the stress. I think it was the day that an angry wheeler-dealer type came into my office and shoved me across the room because his deal hadn't closed that the light dawned. The fact that his escrow couldn't be closed legally didn't deter the man's anger, and I had an epiphany. I wouldn't put up with that behavior in a relationship. Why was I putting up with it at work? Why did/do any of us? Another of my colleagues at my job level was led weeping out of her office and given an indefinite leave of absence so she could enjoy a nervous breakdown at her leisure.

I was very involved with the feminist movement during that time; I was a member of a local chapter of the National Organization for Women and on that chapter's speaker's bureau. I gave speeches to many all-male groups about the Equal Rights Amendment and why it was not only a good idea, it was necessary. I was good at it. Even initially hostile audiences seemed to like me. It's embarrassing to look back and see how long it took me to piece together that my chosen field was in direct opposition to my belief system about equality and the rights of women. In a moment of happy synchronicity I had the opportunity to hear Gloria Steinem speak at the University of California, La Jolla. I went on the spur of the moment and remain forever glad I did. She was fabulous—poised, gorgeous, smart, and a feminist. Her speech reinforced my own feminist underpinnings. I wanted to be her when I grew up.

It took a while after my epiphany to engineer a change, but in my late thirties (married to my second husband and living in Missouri) I went back to school for a master's degree in counseling psychology. I was working full-time, commuting two hours a day between St. Louis and the small town we lived in, and going to school nights. It was my last escrow job and it paid for the degree. For years I had been listening to fellow employees and their problems, and found that they naturally gravitated to me for "advice." I don't think this had anything to do with me being wise and wonderful. I simply had a willing ear, and people were hungry to be heard, especially in the corporate arena where the human side of workers is often not given a voice.

I became a psychotherapist and thought I would be a psychotherapist for the rest of my life. This was it—my final frontier, my last career change. I figured that even if I became physically infirm I could still manage to sit and listen to people's problems. I have always wanted to help people, and this career seemed a natural choice for me. I had the talent and the passion and I was committed to it.

Have you ever noticed that life has a strange way of working out, even if it's not how we envisioned it? Events conspired, and after seventeen years of marriage an unexpected and devastating divorce wrenched my head around and forced my vision toward a different vista. I acquired yet another point of view. I was experiencing an all-too-common crisis—an older woman being divorced. Two failed marriages are not good for the ego. Although my parents had not divorced, I found myself uncomfortably close to my mother's situation after my father died when she was my age—a woman in her early-to-mid-fifties, suddenly alone and without major resources. It was much like being caught in a wrestler's chokehold and about as pleasant. When I emerged on the other side of my drama, I discovered that I had undergone the ubiquitous sea change. My field had been transformed in a drastic way by the advent of managed health care. Many of my colleagues were abandoning their careers in favor of anything that produced an income not dictated by unfeeling bean counters at the insurance and managed-health-care corporations. On the personal front, my divorce caught me in the middle of closing down my private practice in order to spend more time with my husband. I had sensed our marriage slipping-sliding away and decided I would shift my established practice from St. Louis to the small town where we lived, an hour away. That was the precise moment when my then-husband informed me he wanted out of our marriage. So there I was, on my own with my "forever" career disappearing over the horizon like the ending of some B cowboy movie.

It was disconcerting to find myself at the age of fifty-four with no direction, no clear path, and no new ideas for the what-next questions that hovered at the edges of my consciousness like a nervous tic. I truly had not thought I would be alone at this stage of my life, unsettled and with no compass point to aim for. But these words are paltry attempts to describe my true feelings. Perhaps panic would be a better word. I was pretty well scared witless about my future. I floundered for a long while, wondering how I was going to handle my life. This included the all-important issue of money. I began working part-time at an outpatient alcohol and drug rehab clinic, and while I enjoyed the work I knew this was a career dead end for me. As anyone who has been through a midlife divorce well knows, it takes time to recover from the aftereffects. I felt like I was living in a blast zone, a once-familiar landscape decimated and leveled, not a living thing left. I was lucky I had some financial resources that allowed the time away from a demanding career to contemplate my navel (which on some days was all I could manage), but I knew the finances were finite and I couldn't go on like that forever.

I moved into St. Louis and one day I had lunch with a new friend, a woman writer around my age who had also survived a divorce. Over the next month, after many cups of coffee and a lot of laughter about our midlife predicaments, we discovered that both of us had tried to find books to help us through the divorce trauma. There are plenty of books on the subject of divorce, but we were looking for specific help—how to physically and emotionally get through the significant turmoil of a relationship coming apart—and neither of us had found that kind of printed help. We knew we were the ones to write that book. We did, and it was the single most enjoyable working experience of my life. Our book, *The Divorce Recovery Journal*, was a joy to write and a catharsis. We aimed the book at people like us who were looking for more than advice, who wanted practical, hands-on help. The result was an interactive book of insightful observations (our own and others') splashed with humor, useful advice on divorce and starting over, and space for readers to write their own thoughts and feelings.

My coauthor and I worked well together as writers and I began to realize that I'd been writing all my life but never gave it much credence. I started in high school, writing for the school newspaper. I've always kept journals. In my corporate incarnations I did a good deal of technical and instructional writing, all of which I enjoyed. How could I have forgotten this avocation? More to the point, how could I have forgotten the blissful experience of the act of writing? When I write, time disappears, the world disappears. I'm in an altered state of consciousness without using drugs. It's a high born of creation coupling with the deepest parts of myself. My next career was born. I would be a writer.

After the book was published, reality set in. I took a trip back to Arizona, where I had spent the majority of my childhood. While there I fell in love with the place again. It was winter, and I didn't have to shovel snow, which was a decided plus for a fifty-something woman with a bad back. The desert landscape has a mysterious beauty all its own, and I was smitten. Every day of that visit I looked at the brilliant, sun-filled, sapphire sky and at the rose and purple hues tinting the mountains at sunset and I felt the blissful, warm temperatures. My spirits lifted. I wrapped up my affairs in St. Louis, gritted my teeth for a cross-country move, and have been here for two years.

I had written a nonfiction book, but I harbored a long-held desire to write fiction. In my old state of mind, the one that dictated "you can do anything," I set about writing a novel. I've always been an avid reader, I know what I like, and I thought I had a good idea for a best-seller. I tangoed with visions of being on Oprah as I thought about writing this epic piece of prose that would be filled with the wisdom of my experience. Notice that I was thinking about it, not doing it. After some false starts I realized I was afraid, and I was afraid because I didn't have a clue what I was doing. It's an old joke that everyone thinks they have a novel in them, and I was no exception until I actually tried to write it. I began to wonder if I could bring it off.

The solution was my usual one—more school. Of all the things I've done in my life, going to school is one of my favorite activities. Learning has become a lifelong pleasure and has served me well over the years. I signed up for a writing course at a local community college. And that's where I discovered I didn't know anything about my next career. I don't know why I was surprised, but I was. I took writing for granted because it had always come easily to me. But the *craft* of creative writing was a brand new world. I discovered just how much unsung talent there is in that world, and I despaired. I had the innate desire and the passion for the craft, but I wasn't sure I had any talent.

But I kept at it. Passion is a fierce engine. I took more courses. I plan on taking even more. I don't know how this new career will turn out, but I've rediscovered something during the start-up process, and that's the youthful exuberance of looking ahead to the horizon and feeling there's no end to the possibilities. One wry addition to this discovery is the knowledge that while there's no end to the possibilities, there is an end to the time to accomplish them. It is time that is my most precious commodity now, and it is time that is my enemy.

I am retired from many jobs and careers, but it is difficult to retire from life. Life means doing, acting, contributing. The writer's life consists of a great deal of quiet time and solitude, and the doing-acting-contributing has no immediate gratification other than the act of writing itself, which, for me, is bliss. However, these days when people ask me what I "do," I'm hard pressed to answer "I write" because in our culture that occupation is so ephemeral it often defies description. The first question out of these same people's mouths is "are you published?" Happily, I can say yes, but that's really beside the point. Publication and being paid for it is making a living, which is important when it comes to paying the bills, but being published is the gravy, the cream, the chocolate of the writer's life. It's the *process* of writing that constitutes the real career. That's the doing-acting-contributing part. The rest is just business.

I have good friends who are urging me on from the sidelines on the days when I ask—out loud—am I crazy? They tell me I am courageous, that they envy me as I attempt to follow a dream, to do something that makes me happy. I listen, and I agree with them, but I have to fight the good fight daily as I spend my precious and hard-earned retirement funds, the funds that are the engine of this endeavor, and fight the fear of and the insecurity about what the future will be bring. This is especially true on those days when I sit down at my computer and mediocre garbage flows forth. Because now, you see, after many writing classes I know garbage when I see it and I know that crafting a piece both literary and interesting is no mean feat.

To assuage this fear, and being a practical soul (sometimes), I've turned to one of my previous endeavors to help pay the rent—teaching. I've taught in all my chosen fields over the years, and perhaps will do so again in creative writing. But for now, I'm considering teaching in my most recent career of psychology and counseling, and much to my surprise I'm excited at the prospect. I love to teach. I've always had a facility for recalling how I learned a task or a subject, which enables me to break it down for students so they can learn easily.

The excitement at the prospect of returning to a previous career interests me. I realize I've almost made a fatal mistake in changing my career path. The mistake for me is thinking that a career must be one thing, one job, one task. There are carhops at restaurants. I'm a jobhop at the Restaurant of Vocation. Change *is* my career. I am a multitasking, multilayered personality. I enjoy doing *lots* of things. The pressure of limited time I feel these days is that I have less lifetime to do the lots of things I still want to try. To limit myself at this point would be ridiculous.

I'm the sum of my parts. I don't think I'm the sole owner of this property. When people ask me what I "do," I stumble a bit because I'm everything I've ever done, and I still do much of what would be considered previous jobs or careers. I type. I travel. I counsel people (for free now). I have business interests. I teach. I write. I cannot fathom retiring from anything because it's all still with me. And in writing I've found a career that allows me to tell about my past experiences and encourages me to have new ones to add to the store of what can be written about. I have ideas about writing and reading-appreciation programs for children in my neighborhood at local community centers. I want to encourage budding writers and poets to pursue their interests and to appreciate what the arts can offer. I want to be a voice that advocates for passion along with the practical considerations of life.

The concept of retirement is a corporate-world invention to move out the old, the tired, and the plain burned out. I used to think it was a bad idea. It's generally known that many men, upon retirement, die shortly afterward (as yet there are no statistics for women). The reasons for this are complex, I'm sure, but I think they die of boredom and a lack of self-identity because their lives were so bound up in what they did, rather than who they were.

Out here in the valley of the sun, retirees are legion. I think it must be something in the air, or the sand of the desert, that is rejuvenating. I've felt it in my bones. Recently the senior citizens of Sun City made the news. It would seem that there are some naughty seniors in full revolt and acting out— sexually. Stories abound—they're having sex in public on park benches, in swimming pools, in spas, and in parking lots. Stern warnings from the local morality police haven't stopped these intrepid sexual adventurers. New lights installed in dark areas to prevent scandalous behavior have only created senior vandals, aging ninja warriors who take the lights out by whatever means available. So what's up with these seniors? And what, exactly, is the definition of *senior*? Ever since reading about these sexy seniors (in an editorial in the *Arizona Republic* coyly subtitled "Silver Haired Hanky Panky") I've been pondering aging and the definition of *senior citizen*. If you ask the ticket seller at the local movie house, I *am* a senior, and you can bet I take advantage of the price differential. Denny's Grand Slam Breakfast for seniors? I'm right there. Where *senior* is defined as sixty-five or older I lose out, but it's okay because I know those folks are the ones having sex as a consolation prize for being elderly, and it gives me something to look forward to. On the odd days when I'm having senior moments, it even makes me wish for more wrinkles.

I have a close friend who is eighty-two years old and has more energy than I have ever had or ever will have. At age seventy-one she took up painting and became an accomplished artist. She is currently involved in launching her own travel business, one of her previous jobs resurrected to serve her new art career. Now she organizes specialized educational trips and cruises for artists. She, too, is the sum of her parts, and I'm sure it's no accident we're friends. She is so busy we have trouble finding time to get together. I asked her about being her age and starting something so new and so taxing as a business venture. She said, "When you're my age, you have a choice. You can atrophy, or you can stay mentally flexible or at least as mentally flexible as age allows. I have no desire to atrophy. It's just too boring. My problem is finding enough time to do everything I want to do." When people talk about her "retirement," she just laughs and says she's busier now than she's ever been. She's an inspiration to me, and whenever I falter in my resolve to be a full-time writer, she's my biggest cheering section.

So. Will I ever retire? Hell, no. I want to be her when I grow up!

Never Retire

JOY DRYFOOS

As I am a white-haired female aged seventy-six, everyone I meet assumes that I am retired. The question is never "What do you do?" If there is a question, it is "What did you do?" And most often there is no question addressed to me, only to my eighty-three-year-old husband. As a matter of fact, neither of us is retired.

I recognize that my "case" has been different from most people's. I didn't even start what turned out to be my career until I was in my forties, and I didn't ever plan to become whatever it is that I have become. Things just happened. I should say, good things just happened. I have been extremely fortunate.

For just about two decades, I have been an independent researcher, writer, and youth advocate, working from my home in Hastings-on-Hudson, New York, with support from foundations, mainly the Carnegie Corporation. Before that, I was for many years the director of research and planning at the Alan Guttmacher Institute (AGI) in New York City. Along the way I was a visiting professor at several schools of public health, and have served (and still do) on myriad advisory committees, panels, and commissions. I have just completed my fifth major book and have written more than one hundred published articles and chapters.

One concept that has guided me throughout this long life is "follow your muse." Find something that you care about and just keep working to improve or change that condition, or create that masterpiece, or sell that item. My mission has been to improve the life chances for poor and minority people in this country. Like most people, I was strongly influenced in my orientation by my family. I grew up in a very solid, Jewish, liberal household in the thirties and forties in the protective environment afforded by Plainfield, New Jersey. I thought it was a boring place and I couldn't wait to leave. But over those years with a nearly perfect mother and very difficult and talented father, I picked up their strong sense of commitment to do what was right. The key word was *responsibility*. In the thirties, to them, what was right was left. My father was a cause person, supporting the Lincoln Brigade volunteers as they went off to war and helping to organize the first chapter of the National Association for the Advancement of Colored People in a quite segregated community. As their awareness of Hitler's atrocities began to increase, both my mother and father shifted all of their community work to Jewish causes and eventually to the formation of the state of Israel. And I became the chairperson of the Victory Corps in my high school.

The responsibility part of their lessons included early exposure to the labor force. Our family was hard hit by the depression. By the time I was twelve (in 1937), it was clear that I would have to finance any articles of clothing that would help me conform to my peer group (hand-knit sweaters, crew socks, hand-sewn loafers). Demand for babysitters was high but the pay was low. As soon as I turned fourteen, I was able to obtain working papers and started my career at Rosenbaum's Department Store, in the handkerchief department. Every Saturday and all holidays you could find me there. I had a great time and enjoyed working with the other "girls," who were grown women.

When our high school ran out of fuel because of the war, I went to work in my family's factory, which made children's dresses. My job was picking dresses for orders in the packing room. Another work experience involved taking care of a woman with a broken foot. Her major demand was for gin and tonic, and after she had had a few, she would share her negative feelings about Jews and, using a term common at the time, Negroes. When I told my father about this, he came over to her house, told her off in no uncertain terms, and that was the end of that job.

By the time I was ready to go to college, I knew that I enjoyed working and respected the workplace because it would provide an array of experiences and opportunities to relate to different kinds of people. So my selection of Antioch College was quite logical; I could work half of the time because of their cooperative program. The Antioch work program turned out to be the best part of college. I started there in the summer of 1943 at the age of seventeen. I soon discovered the Horace Mann monument in the middle of the campus, which displays the quote: "Be ashamed to die until you have won some victory for humanity." Along with my new friends, I vowed to follow that dictum.

By September, I was sent on my first field placement, to the Michael Reese Hospital in Chicago, as the assistant to the social worker for the emergency room (who was also the wife of Saul Bellow). The Baltimore City Recreation Commission came next, with an assignment to work in the Hampton Community Center as a youth worker. I lived at the Young Women's Christian Association and was a hostess at the Maritime Union United Service Organizations (USO) right across the street.

One adventure in Baltimore certainly belongs in my work history. It was the time of the final Franklin Roosevelt election, 1944. As a campaign worker on the streets, I had had the heady experience of touching his hand. Election day approached, and I was asked to be a poll watcher (although I was not old enough to vote). I checked with my boss at the community center, who told me "absolutely not"; as a city worker I could not engage in politics. She threatened to contact Antioch and get me fired if I failed to come to work on election day. You can probably figure out what happened. I didn't go to work and spent a glorious day as a poll watcher in Baltimore's inner city. When I turned up at work the next day, my boss told me that I was in real trouble, that she and I had been summoned by the director of recreation for a dressing down. We all met together at a restaurant in the evening, and the director greeted me warmly, saying, "You are a great kid. Enjoy your dinner." End of story.

Another job was in Ypsilanti, Michigan, with the Public Housing Authority, as an art instructor in a community center for bomber workers. I lived in a trailer and observed with interest the lives of the Appalachian workers dumped into this strange place to take part in the war effort. After that, I was sent to Pittsburgh to become the executive director of the Hill District People's Forum, a community organization sponsored by the Irene Kaufman Settlement. The hill district had been the home of Jewish immigrants and was beginning the transition that changed its color from white to black. This was a real job, organizing the people in this community to work together to try to maintain racial stability and address urgent neighborhood problems such as housing.

Now, interspersed with all these adventures around the country, I was also supposed to be going to college. I seemed to be majoring in sociology; it was a lot easier than science or philosophy. From reviewing those jobs, you would think I was preparing for a career in social work. But I gave very little thought to the future, and spent minimal effort on academic pursuits. I was actually majoring in "life." And little mention was made of graduate school at Antioch. Then in 1947, with only a few college credits outstanding, I had the chance to go to Europe (my grandfather had left me $500). I went with some Antiochians to the first World Youth Festival in Prague, in what was then Czechoslovakia, and after traveling around Italy and France went back to Prague for a fascinating year of politics and Slavic culture. I supported myself teaching English and returned home with most of the money still intact.

Now was the time I had to figure out what I was going to do with my life. What I most wanted to do was to find a husband. I had consciously managed to avoid marriage until the age of twenty-two but I could see the inevitability of it all. For a nice middle-class girl from Plainfield, New Jersey, unconventionality and adventures could not go on forever. What you had to do was to get a man, have children, and live in the suburbs.

In late 1948, I found a place to live in midtown New York City and employment at the United Jewish Appeal Junior Division. Having been exposed to the horrors of the Holocaust through visits to Auschwitz, Warsaw, and displaced-person camps, I was very conscious of the necessity to support the newly emerging state of Israel. My job involved organizing rich young Jews in the suburbs to have fund-raising parties in their fancy homes to support the cause. I would bring along Israeli heroes as inspirational speakers. I must admit that the kids were quite immune to my overbearing fund-raising techniques and I was not happy at that job, although I admired my co-workers and certainly the cause.

I was rescued from this situation and from my marital search by a chance meeting with a really attractive man who lived upstairs from me, George Dryfoos. We met in February 1949 and married in September. I had a few "cute" part-time jobs while waiting to get pregnant, managed to get Antioch to give me a bachelor's degree through the mail, and then produced a wonderful son, Paul. A year later, we moved to the suburbs, fulfilling my dreams of being a wife, mother, and suburbanite. We became community leaders. George was one of the first Democrats elected to the village board, and I was the youngest president ever of the local League of Women Voters.

But volunteer work turned out to be quite a hassle and when Paul was six, and no siblings had appeared, I began to look for some kind of work. Not only was I fed up with community work, but we needed the money. For a couple of years, I was a substitute in the local school and even considered seeking a graduate degree in education until I reviewed the course offerings. Then the school board hired me for two years as a community organizer to pass a school bond issue. After that, I began to be drawn to social research, building on some statistical skills and interests that I had acquired at Antioch. Three local friends and I set up a group called Research, Writing, and Editing Associates, offering ourselves as a team with those skills for freelance assignments. I edited a new edition of Leo Rosten's *Guide to the Religions of America*, an experience that heightened my interest in research.

During this period, I had started, on a rented calculator (this was pre computer) at my own kitchen table, trying to figure out how to use 1960 census data to plan social programs including family planning, public housing, and child care. One of the papers I wrote spelled out a methodology for estimating the number of low-income women in need of subsidized family planning. At this time, family planning advocates were just beginning to think about how to create a framework for a federal family planning program.

My paper found its way to the national Planned Parenthood's elite social research advisory committee (which included Ashley Montague) and that's how I first made the connection to the field of reproductive health care. Contacts with some of the members of the committee led to my decision to go to graduate school, possibly in the field of demographics. Columbia University in New York City was a logical choice but I couldn't park my car when I went to get a catalog. I could, however, get to Sarah Lawrence College in eight minutes. So, an easily acquired master's in urban sociology (they had no courses in demography) was the final step of my entry into real professional life. Before I had even finished, I was recruited by Fred Jaffe, the director of the Center for Family Planning Program Development, an outgrowth of the Planned Parenthood organization. From 1968 to 1981, I functioned as director of research and planning and then fellow, contributing to the evolution of this agency into the now much-respected AGI. My job was challenging. Working with a staff of fifteen to twenty assorted researchers and support people, I produced many local, state, and national studies and plans (including an annual five-year plan for the federal government). Data were compiled to prove the need for family planning (based on my earlier formula), to show the growing network of family planning providers, and particularly to document and pinpoint the needs among low-income families for access to birth control services. We were awarded huge government and foundation grants for our efforts. From this vantage point I had the unique opportunity to observe the growth of the family planning movement, along with the role of government and voluntary agencies. I also learned a lot about how to deal with organized opposition. The same methodology was applied to the need for and diffusion of abortion services after legalization in the early 1970s.

In the mid-1970s, we at AGI "discovered" the "epidemic of teenage pregnancy," broadly spreading the news that one million teenagers were becoming pregnant every year. It was in this context that I first began to explore the lives of American teenagers and the patterns of behavior that lead to negative outcomes. Over the next few years, I began to question whether the solution to the problem of teen pregnancy really belonged solely in the domain of reproductive health care, as we so strongly attested in AGI's publications. Perhaps other factors were equally important, such as social class and economic disadvantage, mental health status, and access to quality education. My parting with AGI in 1981 reflected this divergence from their path. For a final publication about teen pregnancy, I wrote a last chapter reflecting my questions about solutions. It was rejected in favor of one that was more consistent with the AGI mission. In any case, my departure was long overdue. I was tired of working with other people, those whom I had to supervise and those who had higher authority than I did.

Two weeks after I left, a casual acquaintance who worked for the population division of the Rockefeller Foundation confided in me, "We don't know what to do about teen pregnancy," and asked for my help. For the next two years, I tried to objectively address the question and reported back with what I hope was a strong case for the "life options hypothesis." Teen pregnancy would never go away unless disadvantaged and high-risk kids had access to the same opportunities as advantaged and low-risk kids. This meant access to a large and holistic package: better schools, attachments to caring adults, health and mental health services, and safe communities.

This work was widely circulated. The Carnegie Corporation approached me to advise them about "how to put the boys in the picture" of pregnancy prevention. The answer, in the form of a short book, was pretty much the same as for girls—increase life options. In the process of exploring adolescent pregnancy and prevention programs, my lens widened rapidly. Beginning in 1985, I began receiving support from Carnegie for what became a long-range youth-at-risk project, looking at the issues surrounding teen sex, drugs, violence, and educational failure. This funding continues even today and has helped me produce four more books and many articles and speeches. It has also allowed me to take an active role in the spawning of two more social movements: the development of school-based primary health clinics and the organization of the Coalition for Community Schools.

For the past decade, I have actively been trying to promote what I call "full-service community schools," new kinds of institutions that embody all I have learned about helping disadvantaged young people overcome barriers to learning. These schools are open all the time, run by a partnership between a school and one or more community agencies, offer health and mental health services on site, involve parents, and pay attention to individual and community needs.

Although I am now definitely "over the hill," why would I want to walk away from continuing to follow my muse? I continue to relate to hundreds of wonderful people all over the country who share this interest and who actually do the work. (I only write about it.) How can you retire from your beliefs? Yes, I could volunteer my services to one of these institutions. But I firmly believe in getting paid for work. Those checks coming in are excellent symbolic evidence that I am still very much alive and valued.

I cannot address the issue of my work history without telling you about my husband's history as well. I don't think that retirement is a women's problem. By the time people are my age, I see little difference in what happens to men versus what happens to women. That may be purely a function of my particular situation, in which I have been the one in the family with the straight course while George's history is more tortuous. He has not had a career in the classical sense, but he has had a life.

I think it is fair to say that he didn't have any particular muse to follow. He had to drop out of college after two years to support his mother, a widow with very few resources. He apparently didn't really mind because he wasn't very engaged as a student commuting from New Rochelle to Columbia University. He went to work for some family acquaintances in the X-ray business and eventually trained himself to be a technical salesman. That first work experience was interrupted for five years by World War II, during which his knowledge of X-ray equipment put him into a choice medical unit. He enjoyed the overseas experience, especially an extended stay in Oxford, England, and then, after D-Day, working his way to Belgium where he was acting mayor of an American-occupied town because he was fluent in French.

By the time we were married, he was back in the X-ray business and really hated it, especially dealing with the arrogance of doctors. After a couple of years, he just plain quit, with little idea what to do next. One of his friends was starting a home-improvement information business, so he hooked up with him for a while. Then, he had a brief encounter with an animated-cartoon production company. Finally, my family persuaded him to join our family business.

Did you ever hear of Chubbette dresses? My father invented them. At about ten or eleven, I grew so chubby I couldn't fit into the regular-size samples that he brought home from the family's factory, where he was the chief designer. So he created a whole new line. Lane Bryant was a big customer and in the early sixties the business was flourishing. George signed on and was given a sales region to supervise. He coped with the job for a number of years but certainly derived little real pleasure from it.

Finally, in the late sixties, through our connections to the anti–Vietnam War movement and the New Democrats, he met up with Paul Davidoff, an advocacy planner. Paul had recently started an organization called Suburban Action Institute and recruited George to be the manager. For the first time during his work years, George felt that he was doing something worthwhile, working with wonderful people for an important cause. The idea was to support affordable housing in suburbs through studies and litigation. The group eventually evolved into the Metropolitan Action Institute with a broadened goal of opposing exclusionary zoning, redlining, and other obstacles to fair housing opportunities. George's job entailed going after grants, keeping track of the staff, organizing meetings, and promoting publications. His salary was marginal, but by then I was making a handsome salary at AGI, and we had a small inheritance that liberated us from financial worries.

You can probably guess what happened. After the 1980 Reagan revolution, whatever funding had been around dried up. And unfortunately, Paul Davidoff died from cancer at an early age. The days of the institute were numbered. But that is not the end of the story.

As the paychecks were beginning to decrease, George got the idea of supplementing his income by becoming an actor. This is not as far-out as it sounds. His brother Bob (Dryden) had been a very successful radio actor for many years and George was well known as a raconteur with many accents at his command. He signed on with an agent and began to make commercials.

That was more than twenty years ago, and now at eighty-three he is still trying to become a big star. I mentioned at the beginning that people may ask George what he does, but not me. When it comes out what we each do, people are entranced with George's work ("Have I seen you on TV?") and his connection to mass media. On the other hand, despite my self-designated "guru" status, the same people are not terribly interested in what I do.

It is important that George has found something that continues to demand his attention. In thinking about work life, it is useful to have a muse right from the beginning, or at least a strong career interest to pursue. However, you can also find that muse later in life, or you can change directions as new opportunities occur to you. It helps not to take yourself too seriously, and to remain flexible and open to new ideas.

George's work history may sound depressing, especially the earlier years of unrewarding work. But it also important to add that throughout all those years George was often involved with family life, politics, and protest. Some lives are lived outside of the work experience, for men as well as for women.

In the early years of our marriage, George was the sole breadwinner. We had to struggle to make ends meet, especially since he had to help support his mother (who lived to be ninety-one). Somehow we managed to have a good time with very little money. After I entered the labor force, our income status changed dramatically. At AGI, I was paid very well, and every time I complained about being overworked, my salary was increased. After I quit, I wondered how we would make out. But George's early years in show biz were astoundingly lucrative, I had foundation grants, and we also began inheriting money from the previous generation. And then pensions and social security checks began to pour in.

So here we are, with our freelance careers, financially secure at last. Neither of us has to work. Yet, we are driven to not give up. George still very much wants to be a big star. And I must confess that I am still driven by the desire to be a "big expert"; I would love to be featured on *Oprah* and have my next book sell six hundred thousand copies. I would love to have one of my op-ed pieces published by the *New York Times*.

Can one every really retire from the hunger for recognition? I was recently invited to contribute all my papers, books, articles, and files to the Sophia Smith Collection at Smith College, to join Margaret Sanger and other women in becoming part of women's history. I am thrilled to think that future generations will be able to track the transition in my thinking about adolescent behavior and the functioning of schools, families, and communities. Not only will I never retire, my thoughts can be projected into the future. What a privilege.

I believe that the strong dose of social conscience that I got from my parents and had reinforced through my college years greatly shaped my life. The cornerstone of my long marriage is that my husband and I share the conviction that you have to make contributions to society. I am pleased that my son has inherited this belief and in his work and family life displays a heightened sense of social responsibility. I should also report that he has inherited his parents' proclivities to be freelance workers. We must have passed on to him the joys of working out of one's home without co-workers or bosses. (He is a consultant in the health-care-financing field and an active on-site father to young children.)

These feelings of commitment and social responsibility certainly stay with you. You don't leave them behind as you age. You don't retire from caring about what happens to other people.

I should add a caveat to this optimistic portrayal of life. Several weeks after I began to write this piece, I was literally struck down by a serious back problem that required surgery. For several months, I was in pain and unable to function very well. Worst of all, I could not sit at the computer and grind out my words, nor could I travel or go to meetings and give inspirational speeches. I still feel very vulnerable. I recognize that a time may come when my physical condition may force me to retire. And that would be a very different story. At least for now, I am back at my desk for short periods of time. The lesson here is that we don't really ever know what will happen, further evidence for doing as much as one can while one is able.

Selected Bibliography

Ackerman, Diane. *Deep Play*. New York: Random House, 1999.

Alexander, Jo, Berrow, Debbie, Domitrovich, Lisa, and Cheryl McLean, eds. *Women and Aging: An Anthology*. Corvallis, Ore.: Calyx, 1986.

Almvig, Chris. *The Invisible Minority: Aging and Lesbianism*. Utica, N.Y.: Institute of Gerontology, Utica College of Syracuse University, 1982.

American Association of Retired Persons. *A Woman's Guide to Pension Rights*. Washington, D.C.: American Association of Retired Persons, n.d.

——. *Your 401(k) Plan: Building toward Your Retirement Security*. Washington, D.C.: American Association of Retired Persons, n.d.

Atchley, R. *Social Forces and Aging*. Belmont, Calif.: Wadsworth Publishing [1977], 1990.

Barrow, Georgia. *Aging, the Individual, and Society*. New York: West Publishing, 1996.

Bridges, William. *Transitions: Making Sense of Life's Changes*. New York: Addison-Wesley, 1980.

Brody, Jane E. "Ways to Make Retirement Work for You." *New York Times*, 24 July 2001.

Brookner, Anita. *Brief Lives*. New York: Random House, 1990.

Brown, Colette V. *Women, Feminism, and Aging*. New York: Springer Publishing, 1998.

Butler, Robert N. *Aging and Mental Health: Psychosocial and Biomedical Approaches*. 5th ed. Newton, Mass.: Allyn and Bacon, 1998.

Calasanti, Toni M. "Bringing in Diversity: Toward an Inclusive Theory of Retirement." *Journal of Aging Studies* 7, no. 2 (summer 1993).

Calasanti, Toni M. "Gender and Life Satisfaction in Retirement? On Assessment of the Male Model." *Journal of Gerontology* 51, no. 1 (January 1996).

———. "Retirement: Golden Years for Whom?" In *Gender Mosaics*, ed. Dana Vannoy, 300–310. Los Angeles: Roxbury Publishing, 2001.

———. "Theorizing about Gender and Aging: Beginning with the Voices of Women." *The Gerontologist* 32, no. 2 (1991).

Cantor, Dorothy, with Andrea Thompson. *What Do You Want to Do When You Grow Up?: Starting the Next Chapter of Your Life*. New York: Little, Brown, 2001.

Carstensen, Laura L. "On the Brink of a Brand-New Old Age." *New York Times*, 2 January 2001.

Catchen, Harvey. "Generational Equity: Issues of Gender and Race." In *Women in the Later Years: Health, Social, and Cultural Perspectives*, ed. Lois Grau and Ida Susser. Binghamton, N.Y.: Harrington Park Press, 1989.

Chambre, Susan Maizel. *Good Deeds in Old Age: Volunteerism by the New Leisure Class*. Lexington, Mass.: Lexington Books, 1987.

Cort-Van Arsdale, Diana, and Phyllis Newman. *Transitions: A Woman's Guide to Successful Retirement*. New York: HarperCollins, 1991.

———. "Women's Transitions in Retirement: The Role of the Retirement Planner." In *Women in Mid-Life: Planning for Tomorrow*, ed. Christopher L. Hayes. Binghamton, N.Y.: Haworth Press, 1993.

Cox, Meg. "Zero Balance: Watch Out! Your Retirement Funds Are in More Trouble Than You Think; or, Why Most Women Can't Afford to Retire." *Ms.*, February/March 2001.

Dailey, Nancy. *When Baby Boom Women Retire*. Westport, Conn.: Praeger, 1998.

Dennis, Helen, ed. *Retirement Preparation: What Retirement Specialists Need to Know*. Lexington, Mass.: Lexington Books, 1984.

Doress, Paula Brown, Diana Laskin Siegal, and the Midlife and Older Women Book Project. *Ourselves Growing Older*. New York: Simon and Schuster, 1987.

Dowling, Colette. *Red Hot Mamas: Coming into Our Own at Fifty*. New York: Bantam Books, 1996.

DuPlessis, Rachel Blau, and Ann Snitow, ed. *The Feminist Memoir Project: Voices from Women's Liberation*. New York: Three Rivers Press, 1998.

Ekerdt, David J. "The Busy Ethic: Moral Continuity between Work and Retirement." *The Gerontologist* 26, no. 3 (1986): 239–244.

Erdner, Ruth Ann, and Rebecca F. Guy. "Career Identification and Women's Attitudes toward Retirement." *International Journal of Aging and Human Development* 30, no. 2 (1990): 129–139.

Erikson, Eric. *The Life Cycle Completed: A Review*. New York: W. W. Norton, 1982.

Freedman, Marc. *Prime Time: How Baby Boomers Will Revolutionize Retirement and Transform America*. New York: Public Affairs, 1999.

Friedan, Betty. *The Feminine Mystique*. New York: W. W. Norton, 1963.

——. *The Fountain of Age.* New York: Simon and Schuster, 1993.

Gornick, Vivian. "Alive in NY until the Last Minute." *The Nation,* 24 May 1999, 22–23.

Gould, Jane S. *Juggling: A Memoir of Work, Family, and Feminism.* New York: The Feminist Press at The City University of New York, 1997.

Gullette, Margaret Morganroth. *Declining to Decline: Cultural Combat and the Politics of the Midlife.* Charlottesville: University Press of Virginia, 1997.

Hayward, Mark D., William R. Grady, and Steven D. McLaughlin. "The Retirement Process among Older Women in the United States." *Research on Aging* 10, no. 3 (1988): 358–382.

Heilbrun, Carolyn G. *The Last Gift of Time: Life beyond Sixty.* New York: Dial Press, 1997.

The Hen Co-op. *Growing Old Disgracefully: New Ideas for Getting the Most Out of Life.* Freedom, Calif.: The Crossing Press, 1994.

Joulain, Michèle, Etienne Mullet, Christèle Lecomte, and Rebecca Prévost. "Perception of 'Appropriate' Age for Retirement among Young Adults, Middle-Aged Adults, and Elderly People." *International Journal of Aging and Human Development* 50, no. 1 (2000), 73–84.

Kehoe, Monika. "Lesbians over 60 Speak for Themselves." *Journal of Homosexuality* 16 (1988): 1–111.

——. "Lesbians over 65: A Triply Invisible Minority." *Journal of Homosexuality* 12 (1986): 139–152.

——. "A Portrait of the Older Lesbian." *Journal of Homosexuality* 12 (1986): 157–161.

Kimmel, Douglas C. "Adult Development and Aging: A Gay Perspective." *Journal of Social Issues* 34, no. 3 (1978): 113–130.

Lessing, Doris. *Ben in the World: The Sequel to "The Fifth Child."* New York: HarperCollins, 2000.

——. *The Golden Notebook.* New York: Simon and Schuster, 1962.

——. *Love, Again: A Novel.* New York: HarperCollins, 1996.

——. *Mara and Dann: An Adventure.* New York: HarperCollins, 1999.

Levinson, Daniel. *Seasons of a Man's Life.* New York: Knopf, 1978.

Martz, Sandra, ed. *Grow Old Along with Me: The Best Is Yet to Be.* Watsonville, Calif.: Papier-Mache Press, 1996.

——. *When I Am an Old Woman, I Shall Wear Purple.* Watsonville, Calif.: Papier-Mache Press, 1987.

MetLife Juggling Act Study. MetLife Mature Market Institute, 1999.

Minkler, Meredith, and Carroll L. Estes, eds. *Readings in the Political Economy of Aging.* Farmingdale, N.Y.: Baywood Publishing, 1984.

Myerhoff, Barbara G., and Andrei Simic, eds. *Life's Career—Aging: Cultural Variations on Growing Old.* Beverly Hills, Calif.: Sage Publications, 1978.

Onyx, Jenny, and Pam Benton. "Retirement: A Problematic Concept for Older Women." *Journal of Women and Aging* 8, no. 2 (1996).

OutWord: Newsletter of the Lesbian and Gay Aging Issues Network of the American Society on Aging.

Pearsall, Marilyn, ed. *The Other Within Us: Feminist Exploration of Women and Aging.* Boulder, Colo.: Westview Press, 1997.

Perkins, Kathleen. "Working Class Women and Retirement." *Journal of Gerontological Social Work* 20, nos. 3/4 (1993): 129–132.

Pogrebin, Letty Cottin. *Getting Over Getting Older: An Intimate Journey.* Boston: Little, Brown, 1996.

Price, Christine Ann. *Women and Retirement: The Unexplored Transition.* New York: Garland Publishing, 1998.

———. "Women and Retirement: Relinquishing Professional Identity." *Journal of Aging Studies* 14, no. 1 (2000): 81–110.

Quam, Jean K. "ER = Emerging Retirement Options for Older Lesbians and Gays." *The Networker* 1, no. 3 (fall 2000).

Quam, Jean K., and Gary S. Whitford. "Adaptation and Age-Related Expectations of Older Gay and Lesbian Adults." *The Gerontologist* 32, no. 3 (1987): 367–374.

Rayman, Paula, Kimberley Allshouse, and Jessie Allen. "Resiliency amidst Inequity: Older Women Workers in an Aging United States." In *Women on the Front Lines: Meeting the Challenge of an Aging America,* ed. Jessie Allen and Alan Pifer. Washington, D.C.: Urban Institute Press, 1993.

Richardson, Virginia E. "Women and Retirement." In *Fundamentals of Feminist Gerontology,* ed. J. Dianne Garner. Binghamton, N.Y.: Haworth Press, 1999.

Rosenthal, Evelyn R., ed. *Women, Aging, and Ageism.* Binghamton, N.Y.: Haworth Press, 1990.

Ruddick, Sara, and Pamela Daniels, eds. *Working It Out: 23 Women Writers, Artists, Scientists, and Scholars Talk about Their Lives and Work.* New York: Pantheon Books, 1977.

Rumpf, Andrea Taylor. "Support Networks and Life Satisfaction among Older Women: A Comparison of Lesbians and Heterosexual Women." *The Discourse of Sociological Practice* 1, no. 2 (winter 1999).

Sarton, May. *After the Stroke: A Journal.* New York: W. W. Norton, 1988.

———. *As We Are Now.* New York: W. W. Norton, 1973.

———. *At Eighty-Two: A Journal.* New York: W. W. Norton, 1996.

———. *At Seventy: A Journal.* New York: W. W. Norton, 1984.

———. *Collected Poems: 1930–1993.* New York: W. W. Norton, 1993.

———. *Coming into Eighty: New Poems.* New York: W. W. Norton, 1994.

———. *Faithful Are the Wounds.* New York: W. W. Norton, 1955.

———. *House by the Sea: A Journal.* New York: W. W. Norton, 1977.

———. *Journal of a Solitude.* New York: W. W. Norton, 1992.

———. *The Magnificent Spinster*. New York: W. W. Norton, 1985.

———. *Plant Dreaming Deep*. New York: W. W. Norton, 1968.

———. *A Reckoning*. New York: W. W. Norton, 1978.

———. "Toward Another Dimension . . ." In *The Other Within Us: Feminist Explorations of Women and Aging*, ed. Marilyn Pearsall. Boulder, Colo.: Westview Press, 1997.

———. *A World of Light: Portraits and Celebrations*. New York: W. W. Norton, 1976.

Shavishinsky, Joel S. *Breaking the Watch: The Meanings of Retirement in America*. Ithaca, N.Y.: Cornell University Press, 2000.

Shaw, Lois B., and Rachel Shaw. "From Midlife to Retirement: The Middle-Aged Woman Worker." In *Working Women: Past, Present, Future*, ed. Karen Shallcross Koziara, Michael H. Moskow, and Lucretia Dewey Tanner. Washington, D.C.: Bureau of National Affairs, 1987.

Sheehy, Gail. *Passages: Predictable Passages of Adult Life*. New York: E. P. Dutton, 1974.

Slevin, Kathleen F., and C. Ray Wingrove. *From Stumbling Blocks to Stepping Stones: The Life Experiences of Fifty Professional African American Women*. New York: New York University Press, 1998.

Steinem, Gloria. *Moving Beyond Words*. New York: Simon and Schuster, 1994.

———. *Outrageous Acts and Everyday Rebellions*. New York: Holt, Rinehart and Winston, 1983.

Szinovacz, Maximiliane. *Women's Retirement: Policy Implications of Recent Research*. Beverly Hills, Calif.: Sage Publications, 1982.

Szinovacz, Maximiliane, David J. Ekerdt, and Barbara H. Vinick, eds., *Families and Retirement: Conceptual and Methodological Issues*. Newbury Park, Calif.: Sage Publications, 1992.

Tauber, Cynthia, and Jessie Allen, "Women in Our Aging Society: The Demographic Outlook." In *Women on the Front Lines: Meeting the Challenge of an Aging America*, ed. Jessie Allen and Alan Pifer. Washington, D.C.: Urban Institute Press 1993.

Thorne, Ruth Raymond. *Women and Aging: Celebrating Ourselves*. Binghamton, N.Y.: Haworth Press, 1992.

Villani, Patricia J., and Karen A. Roberto. "Retirement Decision-Making: Gender Issues and Policy Implications." *Journal of Women and Aging* 9, nos. 1–2 (1997): 151–163.

Walker, Margaret Urban, ed. *Mother Time: Women, Aging, and Ethics*. Lanham, Md.: Rowman and Littlefield Publishers, 1999. See, especially, Sara Ruddick, "Virtues and Age," 45–60; Margaret Urban Walker, "Getting Out of Line: Alternatives to Life as a Career," 97–111; and Hilde Lindemann Nelson, "Stories of My Old Age," 75–95.

Waxman, Barbara Frey. *From the Hearth to the Open Road: A Feminist Study of Aging in Contemporary Literature*. Westport, Conn.: Greenwood Press, 1990.

Weaver, Frances. *The Girls with the Grandmother Faces: A Celebration of Life's Potential for Those over 55*. New York: Hyperion, 1996.

Woodward, Kathleen, ed. *Figuring Age: Women, Bodies, Generations*. Bloomington: Indiana University Press, 1999.

Woolf, Linda. "Gay and Lesbian Aging." www.webster.edu/~woolflm/oldergay.html, 1998.

Wyatt-Brown, Anne M., and Janice Rosen, eds. *Aging and Gender in Literature: Studies in Creativity*. Charlottesville: University Press of Virginia, 1993.

Zanders, Judith, and Karen Waters. "Retirement Options for Gays and Lesbians." *In the Life*, May 1998.

About the Editors and Contributors

NAN BAUER-MAGLIN, former professor of English at Borough of Manhattan Community College, is the academic director of the CUNY Baccalaureate Program at The Graduate Center of The City University of New York. She has coedited *Women and Stepfamilies: Voices of Anger and Love* (1989) and *"Bad Girls" / "Good Girls": Women, Sex, and Power in the Nineties* (Rutgers University Press, 1996). Now that she is sixty, retirement is a real question for her. With her four children and four grandchildren spread out from Kansas to New Jersey, she plans to remain in New York City.

ALICE RADOSH received her doctorate in neuropsychology from The City University of New York. Her teaching and research have focused on women's reproductive health. She directed the New York City Mayor's Office of Adolescent Pregnancy Services and recently retired as a senior program officer at the Academy for Educational Development. She lives in Woodstock, New York, where she is a volunteer firefighter, studies the piano, works on local social issues, and tries to keep up with her reading groups and garden. She and her husband, Bart Meyers, have four grown children.

ELAYNE ARCHER was born in London in 1943 and raised in Toronto. She graduated from Radcliffe College in 1966, received her master's from Columbia in 1969, and has worked for over thirty years as an English teacher and writer/editor. She has two grown children and lives in Brooklyn, New York, with her husband, Cliff Rosenthal. She plans to retire in 2008 at the age of sixty-five.

JUANITA N. BAKER is an associate professor at Florida Institute of Technology, teaching ethics, program evaluation, sexual abuse seminars, and child behavior disorders and psychotherapy. She directs research for a sexual abuse treatment program that provides community service and gives doctoral students clinical experience. She is an advocate for libraries, education, women and children, the environment, and working for peace and change in the world.

TERRI M. BAKER, Ph.D., is a professor in the Department of English and serves on the Native American studies faculty at Northeastern State University in Tahlequah, Oklahoma, and lives with her husband and son on a ranch in the Illinois River valley. She is a citizen of the Choctaw Nation of Oklahoma as well as an American citizen.

During her teaching career, CAROL BURDICK worked with students in settings ranging from grade school to Elderhostel, touching on high school, college, and graduate classes along the way. She is tangentially responsible for four grandchildren, and completely responsible for words which have found their way into magazines, papers, and three books: *Destination Unknown, Stop Calling Me Mr. Darling!* and *Woman Alone.*

JEN CHRISTENSEN is a five-time Emmy-nominated investigative projects producer with WSOC-TV in Charlotte. She also freelances for several national magazines and newspapers and has co-authored a book chapter about Frances Perkins.

HOLLY CRENSHAW is an on-line producer with ajc.com, the Web site of the *Atlanta Journal-Constitution,* where she has also worked as a news researcher, reporter, and editor. She has also freelanced for several national magazines and Web sites.

Since 1991, NANCY DAILEY and KELLY O'BRIEN have operated Dailey & O'Brien, Inc., a consulting firm helping companies address the "people side" of technology implementation and organizational change. The publication of Dr. Dailey's award-winning book, *When Baby Boom Women Retire* (1998), persuaded them to turn their expertise toward helping financial firms build baby boomers' financial literacy. Dailey and O'Brien is nationally recognized for its pioneering work in helping the financial services industry use customer relationship management strategy to reach the women's consumer market.

TERRY DAVIS, born in 1940, was a rank-and-file labor organizer in a Chicago factory in the seventies, after which she worked as a field organizer and international representative for the United Electrical Workers union. Since retiring on 1 September 2000, she works part-time on death penalty mitigation in Illinois.

DONNA HILLEBOE DEMUTH, LCSW, retired in December 2000 after fifty-three years of service to families as a clinician, teacher, and consultant, including thirteen years as a full-time mother of four. She has published in nuclear age psychology and on the influence of professionals on divorce. She and her husband live in a homemade house in rural Maine.

At age seventy-six, JOY DRYFOOS continues her work as an independent researcher and writer focused on adolescent behavior and responsive community schools. She has been supported by the Carnegie Corporation of New York and other foundations for two decades, producing six major books and hundreds of articles. She lives in Hastings-on-Hudson, New York. Her husband of fifty-three years, George, died after her essay was completed.

DIANE L. FOWLKES retired in 1998 as a political scientist and women's studies activist scholar. She lives in Ocala, Florida, where she is president of Diable Stable and a member of a senior policy issues group at Central Florida Community College. She has published books and articles and most recently "A Writing Spider Tries Again: From Separatist to Coalitional Identity Politics," in *Identity Politics in the Women's Movement* edited by Barbara Ryan.

CAROLE GANIM has been teaching English and holding administrative positions since the sixties. She retired in 2000 from The College of Santa Fe, moved back to Ohio near many of her relatives, and hasn't stopped working since. She unretired in 2001 when she began teaching at Miami University.

Focus group organizer GEORGIE GATCH retired in 2000 as dean of student life at Barnard College. She works for organizations seeking to involve women in the political process, particularly in the struggle for reproductive rights. The group's writer MARILYN KATZ retired in 1998 as dean of studies and student life at Sarah Lawrence College, having previously taught disadvantaged students in the State University of New York system. She serves as a consultant for a school of education, helped edit a book of prison writing, and publishes on higher education and the teaching of writing. The sole support of her four children while they were growing up, businesswoman ELIZABETH SAUNDERS most recently worked in marketing for a software company, retiring in 1999. She participates in conservation groups, women's, lesbian, and gay rights organizations and in a theater producing plays written and directed by women. PHYLLIS SCHWARTZ worked for nonprofit organizations doing fundraising, public relations, marketing, and board development. She last served as executive director of New York Women in Film, retiring in 1994, and now chairs the board of the Mount Sinai Sexual Assault and Violence Intervention Program.

DORIS GOLDBERG is a physician who chose early retirement from the New York City Department of Health and the practice and administration of pediatrics and preventive medicine. Since her retirement in 1995, she has lived in Woodstock, New York, where she works at painting and printmaking and volunteers in community activities.

Retired in the mid-1990s, CAROLYN GOODMAN became involved in radical politics organizing migrant workers while a student at Cornell University in the 1930s. After graduating she joined the Joint Anti-Fascist Refugee Committee, which supported Spanish Republicans who fled or were exiled by General Francisco Franco. When her three sons were in school she obtained a master's and a doctorate in psychology. On 21 June 1964, her middle son, Andrew, age twenty, a civil rights volunteer in Mississippi, was murdered, along with Micky Schwerner and James Chaney. Instead of drifting into rage and self-pity, she found solace in fighting for social justice. ROSALYN BAXANDALL is a professor and chair of American studies at the State University of New York at Old Westbury. She is the author of *Words on Fire: The Life and Writing of Elizabeth Gurley Flynn* and numerous books and articles on reproductive rights, class, race, and gender as well as coauthor of *Picture Windows: How the Suburbs Happened*. Her thirty years as a feminist activist include participation in Red Stockings and WITCH (Women's International Terrorist Conspiracy from Hell). She served on the Mayor's Task Force on Day Care in New York City.

DOROTHY KAPSTEIN HAMMER graduated from New York University School of Retailing. She had two sons, Matthew and Ethan, with her first husband, John Kapstein. Her career path includes work at Tobe Associates, *Seventeen* magazine, and the Museum of African Art. She owned Bamboula Associates, trading in African textiles and crafts, and Shibui Blues, specializing in Japanese design. She married Arthur Hammer, who died in 1994, the year in which she began the process of retirement.

IDA HENDERSON was born in Brooklyn, New York, and currently resides in Manhattan. She was an educator for thirty-one years and a yoga instructor for twelve. She has been retired since 1989 and continues to be a lifelong learner. Her current pursuits include participation in two book clubs, an exciting Bible study group, a course in practical philosophy, and flute study.

A German native, SYLVIA HENNEBERG is an assistant professor of English at Morehead State University, where she teaches American literature and women's studies. She has published on such poets as Judy Grahn, Adrienne Rich, and Emily Dickinson and was awarded a Postdoctoral Research Leave Fellowship from the American Association of University Women to conduct research on women poets and aging.

DIANE HORWITZ, an activist in the civil rights, antiwar, and women's liberation movements in the 1960s and 1970s, was a community college teacher for thirty years, retiring in September 2000. Currently she teaches a course on education issues for teachers, works on Middle East peace and justice issues, and dabbles in old and new interests.

PHILLIPA KAFKA was a professor of English literature and director of the Women's Studies Program at Kean University in Union, New Jersey, until she retired on 1 January 1999. Currently she is working on her sixth book, a literary criticism of contemporary Indian women writers, forthcoming in 2003. She is also upgrading three properties in Nevada and California.

Professor of English at the University of California, Santa Barbara, SHIRLEY GEOK-LIN LIM has published anthologies, critical studies, collections of poetry, short stories, the novel *Joss and Gold* (2001), and an American Book Award memoir, *Among the White Moon Faces* (1996). She is the mother of a grown son.

LANIE MELAMED retired in 1993, at age sixty-five, after twenty-five years of university teaching. She currently works to create a healthier, nonviolent planet by influencing public opinion and policy makers. She has pieced quilts, taught folk dancing worldwide, presented workshops on adult play and playfulness, and collects folk art in various forms.

CAROL K. OYSTER is a professor of psychology at the University of Wisconsin–La Crosse, specializing in criminology. She is author or coauthor of three books (two texts), writes for the Web site womenhunters.com, and reviews books for *Foreword* magazine. She lives with her daughter and animals in the Midwest. In her spare time she knits, quilts, hunts, and target shoots.

CAROL FOX PRESCOTT grew up in New York City going to the theater and yearning to be on the stage. She graduated from The City College of New York in 1962 and entered the world of professional theater, where she fills the roles of actress, singer, director, and teacher. She often fantasizes about retirement.

SUSAN G. RADNER was married in June 1960, two weeks after graduating from Smith College, and did graduate work at Hunter College and New York University. She taught English and women's studies at William Paterson University in Wayne, New Jersey, for thirty-six years, retiring at sixty-one on 1 February 2000. She has published articles and reviews on women's language and literature.

ESTHER RATNER was born in New York City and attended New York City schools from kindergarten through P.S. 122, Hunter College High School, and Brooklyn College. She was a school librarian on Long Island for more than twenty years and retired in 1993 to live in upstate New York.

ELLEN CRONAN ROSE was chair of the women's studies department at the University of Nevada, Las Vegas. She chaired the search committee interviewing candidates for her replacement as department chair after her retirement in summer 2002.

BARBARA RUBIN, Ph.D., is professor emerita of women's studies at New Jersey City University. In the early seventies, she cofounded the university's Women's Center and Women's Studies Program, which she taught in until her retirement in 2000. She is coauthor of *Children and Sex: The Parents Speak* and her essays, articles, and poetry have appeared in academic journals and the popular press, including *Women's Studies Quarterly* and *Ms.*

MERLE GELINE RUBINE, mother of Bill and John, grandmother of Jacob Francis, was part of the first generation of women working in broadcasting to break out of the researcher pool and become a producer. She had a long, gratifying career at the networks; then, looking to move on, she turned in her corporate identity card and joined the Peace Corps, working as a volunteer in Côte d'Ivoire for two years. She currently works in West Africa.

CAROL A. SCOTT, Ed.D., is currently the executive vice president of the Urban League of Greater Cleveland, a social service agency whose mission is to advocate for those on the social and economic margins. She has been a college administrator, teacher, caseworker, and consultant during her professional career. She resides in Cleveland, Ohio.

MARY STUART, M.A., is a retired psychotherapist, but not a retired person. She has worked at many jobs, ranging from secretarial work to psychotherapy, and has coauthored a self-help book on recovering from divorce. She is currently working on a novel, the first in a mystery series, and applying for a grant to fund a writing program for at-risk students. She is an adjunct professor in behavioral science at Western International University.

BARBARA FREY WAXMAN grew up in New York City and has been a Tarheel since 1981. She is professor of English at the University of North Carolina–Wilmington. She has written two books on aging in literature and edited a collection of essays on multicultural literatures. She is married to S. Robert Waxman and has two children. Barbara is a fair tennis player and a better cook.

LAURA H. WEAVER, Ph.D., taught English at various schools, including the University of Evansville (in Indiana), from which she retired in 1999. She has focused on ethnicity and gender issues in her publications during both her teaching career and her retirement. Recently she has been collaborating with visual artists on several projects.

Cover artist GRACE HARTIGAN was born in 1922 in Newark, New Jersey, and lives in Baltimore, where she is the director of the Hoffberger Graduate School of Painting, Maryland Institute of Art. In the 1950s she was recognized as part of the abstract expressionist movement, often called the "New York school," and she is acknowledged as a stylistic precursor to pop art. She was the only woman selected for the Museum of Modern Art's pivotal exhibition "Twelve Americans" (1956) and for its influential "New American Paintings" (1958–59). Her work was recently featured in the Whitney Museum of American Art's exhibition "The American Century: Art & Culture, Part II: 1950–2000." Hartigan's works have been purchased by the Whitney Museum in New York, the Art Institute of Chicago, and the Corcoran Gallery and the Hirshhorn Museum in Washington, D.C., among many others; she has received numerous awards and honors; and several books on her life and work have been published.

Photo Credits

Nan Bauer-Maglin: Anthony Marino/Spitfire Films
Alice Radosh: Joan Mack
Terri M. Baker: Sean Kennedy—NSU
Donna Hilleboe DeMuth: Heidemarie J. Burke, Photographic Images
Carol Fox Prescott: Jerome Taub
Ellen Cronan Rose: Carole Bellmyre/Distinguished Publishing Co., Las Vegas, Nevada
Juanita N. Baker: Richard Baker
Jen Christensen: Holly Crenshaw
Holly Crenshaw: Jen Christiansen
Nancy Dailey and Kelly O'Brien: Tom Radcliff, Point of View Photography Studio
Terry Davis: Kelly Radinsky
Barbara Rubin: Wallace Sife
Phillipa Kafka: Olevi Koskinen
Laura H. Weaver: 60 Minute Photo, Evansville, Indiana
Carolyn Goodman and Rosalyn Baxandall: Ali Carzalho Santos
Georgie Gatch, Marilyn Katz, Elizabeth Saunders, and Phyllis Schwartz: Jimmy Katz
Esther Ratner: Dion Ogust
Lanie Melamed: Bob Belenky
Carol Burdick: Robin Caster
Merle Geline Rubine: James Stewart
Mary Stuart: Karol A. Koepp
Joy Dryfoos: Deborah Kates